W9-AZF-900

A GUIDE TO
GREEK TRADITIONS AND
CUSTOMS IN AMERICA

A *Guide to* Greek Traditions And Customs in America

Second Edition

Marilyn Rouvelas

Rev. Dr. George Papaioannou
Religious Editor

Illustrations by Olga Angelo Deoudes

Nea Attiki Press
Bethesda, Maryland

A Guide to Greek Traditions and Customs in America
© 1993 by Marilyn Rouvelas. All rights reserved.
ISBN 09638051-0-X

A Guide to Greek Traditions and Customs in America. Second edition.
© 2002 by Marilyn Rouvelas. All rights reserved.
ISBN 09638051-1-8

Published by Attica Press, Bethesda, Maryland, 1993.
Reprinted, 1994.
Published by Nea Attiki Press, Bethesda, Maryland, 1994.
Reprinted, 1995, 1996, 1998, 1999, 2001.
Second Edition published by Nea Attiki Press, 2002
Reprinted, 2003
Reprinted, 2006
P. O. Box 34008, Bethesda, Maryland, 20827
Nea Attiki Reg. U.S. Pat. Off.

Jacket design: Ernesto Santalla, Studio Santalla, Inc., Washington, DC.

Book design: Alicia A. Angelides

Printed in the United States of America by
Automated Graphic Systems, White Plains, Maryland

Rouvelas, Marilyn
    A guide to Greek traditions and customs in America / Marilyn Rouvelas; George
Papaioannou, religious editor; illustrations by Olga Angelo Deoudes. – 2nd ed.
Bethesda, Md.: Nea Attiki Press, © 2002
    xiv, 411 p. : ill. ; 26 cm.
    Includes bibliographical references (p. 387-392) and index
    ISBN 09638051-1-18

1. Greek Americans—Social life and customs.

E184.G7 R65 2002 Library of Congress Control Number: 2002101597

To my koumbára, *Pitsa Papadakes, whose loving example showed me the joy of Greek traditions and customs.*

To my husband, Emanuel — my true love since that first glass of retsína.

MAY THEIR MEMORY BE ETERNAL:

Mary Edmunds (1914-1996)
Mary Rouvelas (1921-1992)
Eleftherios Rouvelas (1915-2001)
Elias (Louie) Spyridis (1946-1993)

Presvytera Maria Papaioannou (1932-1993)
His Grace Bishop George of Komanon (1933-1999)

Contents

PART ONE: THE ENDURING TRADITIONS OF ORTHODOXY

PART TWO: CUSTOMS OF EVERYDAY LIFE

PART THREE: FEAST DAYS, FASTS, AND HOLIDAYS

PART FOUR: THE GLOBAL COMMUNITY

PREFACE

When I met my Greek-American husband-to-be in 1965, everything from the food he ate to the church services he attended seemed foreign to me. One of our first dates was at a small Greek nightclub in Seattle, pulsing with the exotic sound of *bouzoúki* music. We nibbled on unidentifiable tidbits and drank a strange wine called *retsína* (the only time it tasted good to me!). When we became engaged in 1966, I wanted a single book to grasp the basics of Greek-American living. Such a book did not exist. So my early years of marriage required considerable adjustment. I had been raised a Lutheran and was of French and English background. This new culture mystified me. Over time, however, I began to love many aspects of Greek-American life: the closeness of the family, the reverence in Orthodox worship, reading *The Iliad* by Homer, and relishing Easter bread and olive oil.

In 1993 I wrote this book with a specific audience and purpose in mind. It was primarily intended to welcome people of non-Greek ancestry to this fascinating heritage and help them appreciate Greek traditions and customs. However, people of Greek descent have also found the book useful. Many readers have said they now understand why their *yiayiás* (grandmothers) did certain things. For example, a specific Bible verse inspires the use of wheat in *kóllyva,* a traditional dish made for a memorial service after someone dies. The cracking of red eggs at Easter symbolizes the opening of Christ's tomb. With a new understanding of why things are done the way they are, individuals can see how the traditions and customs of their ancestors are relevant to their lives today.

Nine years later, I am elated to report that the above purpose of the book appears to have been met. Despite the disclaimer in the first edition that the book was a "snapshot of how customs and traditions are practiced in America in the late twentieth century," and "not a complete and comprehensive history" of them, the substance has proved remarkably accurate and universal. A few errors were inevitable, and these corrections are detailed in the "Appendix" along with further information about the second edition.

The book's popularity in the United States, Canada, Australia, and South Africa, has brought personal satisfaction to me: an ever-deepening faith in God grounded in Greek Orthodoxy, joy that the book profits have helped numerous charitable causes, the pleasure of meeting many wonderful people across the United States, membership on the Archdiocesan Council of the Greek Orthodox Archdiocese of America, and involvement with the Church's interfaith marriage project and the Center for Family Care at St. Basil's Academy.

Yet the original book provided a limited view of the world of the Orthodox and Greek heritages. Increasingly, I realized it would be helpful for readers to see Greek Americans in the wider contexts of the historic Orthodox church and the worldwide Greek Diaspora. This new information would help readers understand events in the news. Who are the Antiochian Orthodox? Why are the Russian Orthodox and Roman Catholics at odds in the former communist countries? What is the World Council of Hellenes? Thus, a second edition with two new chapters, "The Historic Orthodox Church" and "The Greek Diaspora," was needed.

With this broader view, I expanded the original purpose of the book. I have respectfully tried to increase the reader's understanding of Hellenism and Orthodoxy, making clear the universal, timeless qualities that make them relevant and accessible to all.

Hellenism, developed by the ancient Greeks, emphasized human scale and spirit with its belief that people could use reason to solve problems, articulate dilemmas, create beautiful objects, question, observe, and compromise. A classical drama such as *Orestes* by Euripides poses the problem of how to stop the cycle of revenge killings, a dilemma still plaguing humans all over the world today. The idea of democracy came from ancient Athens and is now the leading form of government around the world. These ideas and many more from Hellenism are the basis of Western civilization, because admirers of the Greeks (Philhellenes) such as the Romans, intellectuals of the Renaissance, and the founders of America recognized their universal value.

Orthodoxy, one of the oldest religions in the world, proclaims the timeless Christian message of love, forgiveness, kindness, and eternal life. Of special interest is the historic connection between Hellenism and Christianity. Christianity was formulated in the

Greek language and Greek thought. Greek, therefore, is the historic language of Christianity in the way that Hebrew is the historic language of Judaism and Sanskrit of Hinduism.

For those born into this heritage, may this book inspire you to deepen your commitment to your legacy. For individuals like myself who were not born into this heritage, but who have become interested through other pathways, I say, *welcome!* Orthodox Christianity embraces you with love and warmth. The Hellenic tradition invites you to share its universal heritage. Isocrates, a Greek orator in the fourth and fifth centuries BC, stated in *Panegyrikos (Encomium of Athens):* "The name 'Hellenes' suggests no longer a race, but a way of thinking, and . . . the title 'Hellenes' is applied rather to those who share our culture than those who share our blood."

In this spirit everyone is invited to celebrate these remarkable customs and traditions.

Marilyn Rouvelas, May, 2006

ACKNOWLEDGEMENTS

Thousands of individuals have preserved Greek traditions and customs through the centuries. To this day vigilant custodians continue to give generously of their expertise, time, and money in many ways, including the preparation of this book. Without their cooperation, the book could not have been written.

The expertise and support of my parish priest, Rev. Dr. George Papaioannou, and his Presvytera, Maria Papaioannou, of the Greek Orthodox Church of St. George, Bethesda, Maryland, were invaluable. How fortunate I was to have Father George, a noted author, as religious editor. Sadly, just before the first printing in 1993, his wife, Presvytera Maria, died of cancer. I will never forget her lying in bed looking through her recipes for the *vasilópita* cake recipe reprinted here. How passionately she cared about the traditions! In 1998 Father George was consecrated Bishop George of Komanon, but only a year later in 1999, he suddenly died while attending an event at our church. As a memorial to His Grace Bishop George of the Diocese of New Jersey, I have left the religious content of Parts One, Two, and Three of this second edition unchanged. His Grace always emphasized the compassion of the Greek Orthodox faith and the value of the Greek secular heritage. That spirit is preserved.

I am also grateful for the review of the religious content of "The Historic Orthodox Church" in Part Four of the second edition by Rev. Fr. Athanasios Demos (Chancellor of the Diocese of Boston), Rev. Fr. James T. Paris of the Greek Orthodox George of St. George, Bethesda, Maryland, and Rt. Rev. Archimandrite Damian, Abbot of Ascension Monastery, Resaca, Georgia. I have been blessed to receive the compassionate perspective of Rev. Fr. Charles Joanides, the leading expert on intermarriages at the Greek Orthodox Archdiocese of America.

The liveliest source for the original book was a group of women from St. George who spent countless evenings with me and my tape recorder, fondly recalling customs and traditions from various regions of Greece. My deepest thanks to Presvytera Maria Papaioannou (Mitilini), Presvytera Moscha Despotides (Sifnos), Rea Assimakopoulos (Constantinople), Sylvia Basdekas (Thessaloniki), Martha Gourdouros (Peloponnesus), Roula Hunter (Athens), Julia Inglesis (Constantinople), Maria Koutrouvelis (Peloponnesus), Mary Merrill (Peloponnesus), Helen Hadgis Pappas (Asia Minor/Sea of Marmara region), Mary Tsangaris (Dodecanese Island), and Georgia Volakis (Simi/Dodecanese Islands). For the second edition, the following women were added: Stavroula Economos (Bethlehem, Pennsylvania), Helen Papson Panarites (Toronto), and Diana Papadopoulos (Brooklyn).

The original project was blessed with a very talented book production team: Olga Angelo Deoudes (illustrator), Alicia A. Angelides (book designer), Jeanne Moody (editor and indexer), Helen Petropoulos (Greek editor), and Alice Padwe, Helen Panarites, and George Anthan (editors). Additional members of the production team for the second edition included Marilyn Dickey and Nancy Borza (editing), Ernesto Santalla (cover design), and Gloria Hwang (graphic design).

For review of specific subjects, I relied on Ann Bazzarone, Pam and Farrow Beacham, Evelyn Bilirakis, Tom Brady, Jenifer Calomiris, Trianthe Dakolias, Peter Demopoulos, John Gavrilis, Lambros Hatzilambrou, Mary Ann Jobe, Maria Kouroupas, Elaine Lailas, Kally Lulias, Francie Makris, John Markos, Lily Menou, Nitsa Morekas, Connie Mourtoupalas, Aphrodite Pallas, Rena and Harilaos Papapostolou, Janet Peachey, Jude Schmidt, Pauline Spyridis, Presvytera Nikki Stephanopoulos, Gina Stephens, Presvytera Sophronia Tomaras, Kathy Tompros, Eva Catafygiotou Topping, Peggy Tramountanas, Mary Kay Turner, Irene Vagelos, Eva Vatakis, Speros Vryonis, Jr., and Andrew Walsh.   New friends overseas who were most helpful with "The Greek Diaspora" chapter include, from Australia: Con Berbatis, Terri and Paul Boyatzis, and Rev. Fr. Miltiades Chryssavgis; from Canada: Mary and Lazaros Kalipolidis, Rev. Fr. Panagiotis Pavlakos, Danae and Stephen Triantis, Hilda Tzavaras, and Eugenia West; and from Cyprus: Salome Economides and Miltos Miltiadou.   The Theodore J. George Library of Annunciation Cathedral in Baltimore, graciously shared its valuable resources.

I am especially grateful for the excellent work done through the years relating to book orders, billing, banking, and accounting by: Rea Assimakopoulos, Julia Inglesis, Audrey Jalepes, Diana Papadopoulos, Joanne Simeon, and Terry Stayeas.

My husband, Emanuel, helped day and night and was a remarkable resource and booster. I thank God for him, our son, Eleftherios, and our daughter, Mary, all of whom gave constant encouragement and suggestions.   Since the book's first publication, we have welcomed new family members: our daughter-in-law, Rebecca Leung (my computer angel), our son-in-law, William Gould, and grandchildren, Zoe Rouvelas Gould, Eleni May Rouvelas, William Dunbar Gould VI, and Emanuel Eleftherios Rouvelas. My sincere gratitude to the Larry Rouvelas and Elias Spyridis families in Seattle and the Harry Papadakes family in Norristown, Pennsylvania, who embraced me from the beginning.   I also thank my mother, Mary Edmunds, for nurturing my faith.

Special Acknowledgment

All book-sale profits are donated to the Bishop George Greek Orthodox Cultural Center of St. George, Bethesda, Maryland, the Ladies Philoptochos Society of the Greek Orthodox Church of St. George, Bethesda, Maryland, and charitable causes chosen by the Philoptochos. With gratitude, the church acknowledges the generous support of Rev. Fr. Nicholas and Presvytera Moscha Despotides, the Falls Run Family Foundation, and the Ladies Philoptochos Society of St. George, Bethesda, Maryland, for making the production of this book possible.

Pronunciation Guide

The Greek words in this book have been transliterated to render pronunciation in standard modern Greek. In some cases, however, a word may be shown with the popular English spelling. These exceptions are included when the word is widely used and accepted such as "*Oxi.*" In such cases the correct pronunciation will be shown in parentheses: *Óxi* (pron. *óchi*).

Greek Capital Letter		Transliteration	Pronounced as
A	*Álpha*	*a*	a in father
B	*Víta*	*v*	v in vase
Γ	*Gámma*	*g* or *y*	g in got or y in yes
Δ	*Thélta*	*th*	th in the
E	*Épsilon*	*e*	e in ten
Z	*Zíta*	*z*	z in zip
H	*Íta*	*i*	i in police
Θ	*Thíta*	TH	th in thin
I	*Ióta*	i	i in police
K	*Káppa*	*k*	k in bike
Λ	*Lámvtha*	*l*	l in laugh
M	*Mi*	*m*	m in me
N	*Ni*	*n*	n in no
Ξ	*Ksi*	*ks* or *x*	ks in rocks or x in ax
O	*Ómikron*	*o*	o in row
Π	*Pi*	*p*	p in piece
P	*Ro*	*r*	r in roll
Σ	*Sígma*	*s*	s in same
T	*Taf*	*t*	t in talk*
Y	*Ípsilon*	*i* or *y*	i in police
Φ	*Fi*	*f* or *ph*	f in farm or ph in photo
X	*Hi*	*h* or *ch*	h in hit or German "ch"
Ψ	*Psi*	*ps*	ps in caps*
Ω	*Oméga*	*o*	o in row
Dipthong:			
OY	*Ómikron ípsilon*	*ou*	ou in coup

*When "t" or "p" are combined with "s" at the beginning of a Greek word, the "t" or "p" is pronounced, *not* left silent as in the English pronunciation of "psychology."

INTRODUCTION:
GREEK AMERICANS
PAST AND PRESENT

When a young Greek-American girl in elementary school told her classmate that her background was Greek, the classmate responded, "Oh, do you believe in Zeus?" For many, the perception of Greeks stops with the classical period — ancient gods, the birthplace of democracy, the Parthenon, and famous philosophers such as Plato and Socrates.

Non-Greeks may not be aware of the heritage that shaped Greek Americans after the classical period: the Roman occupation, Byzantine Empire, Orthodoxy, four hundred years of Ottoman occupation, three wars in the twentieth century, the struggles of immigrants to America, and the triumph of developing a Greek-American way of life. Greek Americans come from a rich past. But who are they today?

What are the distinguishing attitudes, habits, and beliefs they hold in common? That is, what ethos did the immigrants bring with them from Greece, how has the American experience shaped them and their descendants, and how have these immigrants impacted American culture and society?

Early Greek Immigrants

GREEK IMMIGRANTS IN AMERICA

Although individuals and small groups had come to America ear-lier, a Scotsman recruited the first large number of Greeks from Mani in southern Greece as indentured laborers with the promise of land. About four to five hundred immigrants arrived in 1768 and settled in a community named New Smyrna on the east coast of Florida. These immigrants endured great hardships, and many died. Eventually they left the area, were formally granted free-dom in 1777, and moved north to St. Augustine, Florida.[1] (Two memorials commemorate these brave immigrants. The New Smyrna Memorial has been erected at Riverfront Park in New Smyrna Beach, Florida. The St. Photios National Shrine in St. Augustine commemorates the house where they worshiped.) During the next one hundred years, individuals and other small groups continued to arrive. In 1864 Greek merchants under the direction of the local Greek consul formed a multiethnic parish named the Eastern Orthodox Church of the Holy Trinity in New Orleans.[2]

According to a leading Greek-American sociologist, Charles Moskos, by the end of the nineteenth century around fifteen thousand Greeks had immigrated to the United States. Between 1890 and 1917, the largest wave of Greek immigrants, 450,000 arrived in America.[3] They came primarily for economic reasons, initially settling mainly in large cities. Eventually, though, Greeks could be found in most cities and in every state. In the big cities, they held jobs in factories, restaurants, shoeshine parlors, candy shops, and produce stands. In New England, they were blue-collar workers at textile and shoe factories; and in the Midwest and West, many worked in mines and helped build railroads.[4] Smaller groups went south to Alabama, North Carolina, Georgia, and Florida.[5] The tremendous flow of immigrants slowed in 1924 when the Ameri-can government set quotas for the number of immigrants allowed to enter the country. The Immigration Act of 1965 ended ethnic quotas, and the second largest wave of Greek immigrants (160,000) arrived between 1966 and 1979. Some 810,000 Greek immigrants came to America between 1873 and 1989.[6]

TRANSPLANTING THE GREEK ETHOS

While many of the original immigrants were single young men who came to make money and then return to Greece, a substantial number stayed and brought women from Greece to start families. They began to recreate the society they had left. A Greek ethos (system of values) was transplanted to America, a way of life built on the dual foundations of the Greek Orthodox faith and Hellenism. (In the Greek language the word for "Greece" is "Hellas." Thus the Greeks call themselves "Hellenes," and Hellenism refers to the secular Greek culture.) These values were based on family, faith, ethnic pride, education, personal honor, and hard work. (See *Greek-American Values.*) Early immigrants fiercely nurtured these values by building Greek Orthodox churches as centers for religious, cultural, and social needs. In addition, they established secular organizations dedicated to regional, cultural, professional, and personal needs. Admirably, these efforts helped sustain the transplanted ethos of the first generation.

THE ETHOS IN A CHANGING MILIEU

Greek values exist in an ever-changing society, and Greek Americans deal with issues of identity and ethnicity in different ways. The practice of traditions and customs differs enormously from one family to another.

The issue of generational differences is discussed in a book by Alice Scourby, *The Greek Americans.* Historically, she says, the first generation of Greek Americans vigorously tried to preserve values from the motherland and worried about the influences of the larger American society. The second generation (those born in America but having at least one parent born in Greece) were more assimilated but often felt ambivalent about their Greekness. They felt a strong attraction to American society and often rejected certain aspects of Greek tradition. The third generation (those with two parents born in America) usually felt comfortable as Americans with their Greek heritage.[7] In the 1960s, the American society's attitude changed, encouraging pride in ethnic background, making it easier to be both Greek and American.

The "Greekness" of the Greek-American community is also changing. Fewer immigrants are coming from Greece. In addition the number of marriages between Greek Orthodox people and those outside the faith has increased. Between 1980 and 2004 interChristian marriages fluctuated between fifty-nine and sixty-seven percent.[8] How do these marriages affect the "Greekness" of these couples and their children? And what makes someone Greek? How far removed can one be from one's ancestors to still be considered Greek? Fifth generation? Tenth? Do people with Greek ancestors on both sides remain Greek if they do not follow customs from the homeland or speak the language? What if someone adheres to part of the ethos but does not practice Greek Orthodoxy? These questions illustrate the diversity and change within the Greek-American experience.

The United States Bureau of the Census adopted the policy of letting people define their ethnicity themselves. It asked each American to indicate his or her ancestry. In both the 1990 U.S. Census and the 2000 U.S. Census, just over one million people claimed Greek ancestors.[9] How has the Greek-American community maintained its identity?

PRESERVATION STRATEGIES

Strong institutions still exist today to preserve the Greek-American ethos and its dual foundations of Orthodoxy and Hellenism: the church, university academic programs, museums, and community organizations. But each institution faces the challenge of preservation and appealing to younger generations and non-Greeks.

The Greek Orthodox church has always played a major role in the movement to preserve Hellenism. The Christian religion was developed in the Greek language and influenced by classical Greek thought, entwining the two as far back as The New Testament. The church played varying roles in the Byzantine Empire, Ottoman Empire, and modern Greek state. Today in America the church sponsors Greek language schools, festivals with traditional food and crafts, camps, religious retreats, and partial use of the Greek language in the church services. However, the increase in the number of non-Greeks in parishes as a result of interfaith marriages and conversions creates questions about keeping the ethnic component such as the use of the Greek language and celebrating Greek Independence Day. Would the church grow more if the ethnic emphasis were dropped? Some would agree, but others believe Hellenism is universal and expandable. Alexander the Great remains a role model as someone who spread Hellenism beyond the boundaries of Greece. The Greek Orthodox hierarchy and community are making an effort to welcome others to Hellenism and Orthodoxy with their current interfaith effort. Yet in the tolerant, multicultural society of America, the married Greek partner, family, and community must respect the faith and culture of the non-Greek partner who may also be devoted to a different heritage.

On the secular front, Greek Americans employ different strategies to keep Hellenism alive, from the study of classics to concern for American foreign policy toward Greece. While the classics were once part of the core curriculum in higher education, the recent trend downplaying the classics and adding a more diverse curriculum has met resistance by alarmed Philhellenes (friends of Hellenes) and Greek Americans. They have begun donating money for classics chairs at universities, sponsoring lecture programs, building cultural centers and working with the Greek government and Greek nonprofit organizations to halt the erosion. Thanks to their efforts, plus the innate brilliance of the heritage, they have met some success, resulting in a modest revival. Such efforts need to be strengthened and expanded even further in Byzantine and modern Greek studies. Preservationists are also building Greek-American museums, collecting documents such as local Greek-American histories, and writing memoirs. Cultural groups present plays and art exhibits. Writer Steve Frangos refers to this increase in activity as a "New Preservation Movement."[10] Despite all these laudable efforts, many still lament that not enough is being done. They want the next generation to visit Greece periodically, read Homer, and attend church more often.

Another preservation strategy involves staying connected with fellow Hellenes in the worldwide Diaspora (Greek communities outside Greece). Increased awareness of a shared heritage via travel, the media, and the Internet generates a sense of excitement and connection to people all over the globe who have the same values, holidays, and love for the motherland. In 1995 the Greek government established the World Council of Hellenes Abroad to facilitate cooperation and camaraderie among the Diaspora communities. The results of this effort and global communication are too new to evaluate. Will they help spread Hellenism to their host countries, or will Diaspora Greeks erect walls to keep out non-Greeks who might dilute the ethos? (See *The Greek Diaspora.*)

Preservation strategies vary, as does the depth of involvement. After all, Hellenism and Greek Orthodoxy exist in a third context, the culture of contemporary America, which prizes choice. Most Greek Americans today think of themselves as Americans first and then choose their own depth of identification and involvement with their Greek heritage. Some Greek Americans immerse themselves solely in the church, focusing on Orthodoxy. Some Greek Americans may not be members of the Orthodox church and choose to devote themselves to Hellenic cultural activities such as language, higher education, museums, and political causes. But most enjoy participating in both religious and secular activities. In addition, they care deeply about being successful Americans who present themselves to the rest of society as model citizens in keeping with the unchanging ideals of the golden age of classical Greece and the tenets of Christianity. These diverse, individual approaches may ultimately provide the most effective overall preservation strategy.

Today's Greek American proudly embodies a rich historic identity that comfortably coexists with contemporary American civilization. Each individual can balance and integrate the Hellenic, Orthodox, and American cultures in keeping with a spirit of freethinking and choice.

---

1. Charles C. Moskos, *Greek Americans: Struggle and Success,* 2d. ed. (New Brunswick, N.J.: Transaction Publishers, 1989), 3-4.

2. John H. Erickson, *Orthodox Christians in America* (New York: Oxford University Press, 1999), 53.

3. Charles C. Moskos, *Greek Americans,* 156.

4. Ibid., 13.

5. Ibid., 25.

6. Ibid., 156.

7. Alice Scourby, *The Greek Americans* (Boston: Twayne Publishers, 1984), 73-74.

8. *Yearbook 2006* (New York: Greek Orthodox Archdiocese of America, 2006), 122.

9. U.S. Bureau of the Census, *1990 Detailed Ancestry Groups for States,* CPH-L-97, 1 (1.11 million). U.S. Bureau of the Census, QT-02 Profile of Selected Social Characteristics: 2000 (1.18 million).

10. Steve Frangos, "Grassroots Efforts to Preserve Hellenism," *The National Herald,* 17-18 January, 2004.

PART ONE

The Enduring Traditions of Orthodoxy

Holy Cross Chapel
Brookline, Massachusetts

✤ *The Church*

The Greek Orthodox church plays a major role in Greek-American life. Many traditions and customs have a religious basis, and most churches offer a broad range of secular activities such as dances, festivals, and cultural events. At the church's core remains a treasury of tradition: beliefs, history, art, architecture, language, music, and services. That tradition satisfies the deep religious needs of Orthodox believers. Others may find the church somewhat intimidating and inaccessible. Through understanding, however, a new appreciation and faith may develop.

ORTHODOX BELIEFS

ORIGIN

Orthodoxy remains virtually unchanged since its beginnings almost two thousand years ago. The church began with the descent of the Holy Spirit to Christ's twelve apostles fifty days after his Resurrection, filling them with the grace, will, and ability to carry on his message. Through the Holy Spirit, God's will continues to be revealed and interpreted for the church on earth. This continuity and stable tradition are essential characteristics of Orthodoxy, giving it an "air of antiquity [and] changelessness" as described by Timothy Ware in his classic work on the church, *The Orthodox Church*.[1]

Over time a vast "Holy Tradition" developed. Ware explains that Tradition "means the books of the Bible; it means the Creed; it means the decrees of the Ecumenical Councils and the writings of the Fathers; it means the Canons, the Service Books, the Holy Icons — in fact, the whole system of doctrine, Church government, worship, and art which Orthodoxy has articulated over the ages."[2] The literal interpretation of the word "Orthodoxy" reflects this long Tradition: *orthós* (correct) and *dóxa* (belief).

DOCTRINE (DOGMA)

Doctrine (dogma) is a belief revealed by God as contained in the Bible or formulated by the church. The faithful accept it as a final and unchangeable truth. These doctrines are strictly connected with the basic beliefs of the faith and as such cannot be altered or replaced by other teachings. For example, the belief that Jesus Christ is the incarnate Son of God was revealed by God to man at Christ's baptism. This is a doctrine. Changing this belief is to change basically the Christian religion. For a comprehensive explanation of Orthodox theology read *The Orthodox Way* by Kallistos Ware.[3]

The most important statement of the faith is the Nicaea/Constantinople (Nicene) Creed, recited by the parishioners during each Divine Liturgy.

The Nicene Creed

I believe in one God, the Father, the almighty, creator of heaven and earth, and of all things visible and invisible.

And in one Lord, Jesus Christ, the only begotten Son of God, begotten of the Father before all ages. Light of light, true God of true God, begotten, not created, of one essence with the Father, through whom all things were made.

For us and for our salvation, he came down from heaven and was incarnate by the Holy Spirit and the Virgin Mary and became man. He was crucified for us under Pontius Pilate, and he suffered and was buried. On the third day he rose according to the scriptures. He ascended into heaven and is seated at the right hand of the Father. He will come again in glory to judge the living and the dead. His kingdom will have no end.

And in the Holy Spirit, the Lord, the giver of life, who proceeds from the Father, who together with the Father and the Son is worshiped and glorified, who spoke through the prophets.

In one, holy, catholic, and apostolic church.
I acknowledge one baptism for the forgiveness of sins.
I expect the resurrection of the dead.
And the life of the age to come. Amen.

To Sýmvolon tis Písteos (To Pistévo)

Pistévo is éna THeón, Patéra, Pantokrátora, Piitín ouranoú ke yis, oratón te pánton ke aoráton.
Ke is éna Kírion Iisoún Christón ton Ión tou THeoú, ton monoyení, ton ek tou Patrós yenniTHénta pró pánton ton eónon. Fós ek fotós, THeón aliTHinón, ek THeoú aliTHinoú yenniTHénta, ou piiTHénta, omooúsion to Patrí, thi ou ta pánta eyéneto.

Ton thi imás tous anTHrópous ke thiá tin imetéran sotirían katelTHónta ek ton ouranón, ke sarkoTHénta, ek Pnévmatos Ayíou ke Marías tis ParTHénou ke enanTHropísanta. StavroTHénta te ipér imón epí Pontíou Pilátou ke paTHónta ke tafénta. Ke anastánta ti tríti iméra katá tas grafás. Ke anelTHónta is tous ouranoús ke kaTHezómenon ek thexión tou Patrós. Ke pálin erhómenon metá thóxis kríne zóntas ke nekroús, ou tis vasilías ouk éste télos.

Ke is to Pnévma to Áyion, to Kírion, to zoopión, to ek tou Patrós ekporevómenon, to sin Patrí ke Ió simpros-kinoúmenon ke sinthoxazómenon to lalísan thiá ton profitón.

Is mían, ayían, kaTHolikín ke apostolikín ekklisían.
Omologó en váptisma is áfesin amartión.
Prosthokó anástasin nekrón.
Ke zoín tou méllontos eónos. Amín.

CANON LAW

Canons are the rules concerning church sacramental, disciplinary, and administrative practices developed over the centuries by council decrees and individual church fathers. These rules deal with the earthly life of the church: fasting, marriage of priests, political administration, etc., and serve to discipline both the clergy and the people. The most widely used English translation containing approximately 1,000 canon laws is *The Rudder* by D. Cummings.[4]

Changing Canon Law

Unlike immutable dogma, canons can be changed by church councils, regional synods, and individual church fathers. Many of the existing canons are not applicable to contemporary situations and thus have become obsolete. The church realizes this, and for many years a pan-Orthodox group, representing different churches of Orthodoxy throughout the world under the leadership of the Ecumenical Patriarchate of Constantinople, has been working diligently to prepare a list of canons to change, add, and omit at a future meeting. (See *The Historic Orthodox Church*.) Since the Orthodox church has not been administratively unified for centuries, the last council of the entire church administration was the Seventh Ecumenical Council convened in 783.

Oikonomía

Oikonomía (pron. *ikonomía*) means the act of mercy concerning the canons in extraordinary cases. For example, a canon states that a man and woman who have the same godparent cannot marry because they are considered brother and sister spiritually. The church may use *oikonomía* as an act of mercy to allow the marriage. Only a bishop and a higher church authority may make such decisions.

THE ORTHODOX CONCEPT OF *THÉOSIS*

The purpose of Orthodoxy is to help and guide the individual to reach safely the destination of *théosis* (pron. *THéosis*), a complete identification with God. *Théosis* is derived from the basic teaching of the Bible as stated in Gen. 1:26: "Let us make man in our image, after our likeness..." Your personal challenge, therefore, throughout your life is to find and reveal the godlike image within you.

Achieving *Théosis*

The task, though difficult, is not impossible. Sin gets in the way, blurring God's perfect image. God, however, did not abandon man to struggle alone and combat sin, but sent his son, Jesus Christ, to serve as a model and lead one to that destination. God became man so that man could become God, as stated by St.

Athanasios in the fourth century. By emulating Christ's life, you can become like Christ and therefore like God. This is a difficult task and requires the grace of the Holy Spirit. It is within the established services of the church and in your relationship with others that *théosis* can be approached.

Théosis through Participation in the Sacramental Life of the Church

You should attend church regularly, participate in the sacraments, pray to God, and read the Bible. In the Divine Liturgy you can identify with your fellow Christians and participate in Holy Communion, sharing the Body and the Blood of Christ. Through the Divine Liturgy and other services, you are helped to live a life worthy of this high calling, your own *théosis*. Private prayer, reading the scriptures, the practice of giving to charity, the use of the sacrament of confession, and the guidance of a spiritual father help you reach your goal.

In addition, the church provides many opportunities to emulate Christ through services that reenact the major events in his life: the forty-day blessing, baptism, fasting, burial, the achievement of eternal life. Just as Christ was brought to church after forty days by his mother, so are you. Even the Divine Liturgy is a symbolic reenactment of Christ's life every time it is offered.

Théosis through Relations with Others

In addition to regular participation in the church, you should act towards others as Christ did: kind, tolerant, helpful, forgiving, and loving. Christ's love of humanity is one of his greatest qualities, and he is referred to in the Divine Liturgy as *philánthropos*, (lover of man). His example of Christian charity and love is a model for daily living.

ARCHITECTURE AND ART

Orthodox churches are noted for the beauty and elegance of their Byzantine architecture. The grandest prototype is the cathedral of St. Sophia erected in Constantinople in the sixth century. Here can be seen the classic Byzantine style dominated by two elements, the dome and the church proper shaped like a cross. This form influences the design of most Orthodox churches though each has its own distinct style ranging from the modern Church of the Annunciation designed by Frank Lloyd Wright in Milwaukee, Wisconsin, to the classic St. Sophia Cathedral in Washington, D.C., to a modest hut with a thatched roof in Kenya.

CLASSIC BYZANTINE ARCHITECTURE

The main features of classic Byzantine architecture on the outside include a square on ground level, a cross on the second, and a dome on the third.

Classic Byzantine Architecture

On the inside the basic features are an entry section called the narthex for the purpose of assembly, lighting candles, and revering icons; a nave where parishioners worship; and the sanctuary with the altar for clergy and assistants.

NARTHEX

The entry point of the church, the narthex, provides an area of preparation for worship with its candle stand and icons. After making a donation, each visitor lights a candle in honor of Christ and for individuals to be remembered. Icons of the Virgin Mary holding Christ and the saint or event for which the church was named are prominently displayed. The visitor makes the sign of the cross and kisses one or more icons before proceeding into the nave.

During the first centuries of Christianity the purpose of the narthex was to accommodate the catechumens, those who were not already baptized. When the second part of the liturgy was to begin, the catechumens were ordered by the deacon to leave the nave and go to the narthex. Today this practice is still followed in a service called the Liturgy of the Presanctified Gifts. In addition, the first part of the sacrament of baptism takes place in the narthex.

NAVE

The beautiful, often elaborate, Byzantine interior transports the worshiper to a level of spiritual exaltation. It strives to create heaven on earth so the faithful may worship together with God and the saints. The floor symbolizes earth and the dome symbolizes heaven where the worshipers are reminded that although they reside on earth, their final and certain destination is heaven.

Large full-length icons of Christ, Mary, and other saints immediately engage those entering the nave. The saints serve as examples to the ordinary faithful that they too can attain the destiny of heaven if they live according to the teachings of the church. Just as these saints have achieved *théosis*, so can the parishioner. Other icons may depict important events in the life of Christ.

The church icons are arranged in a standard pattern. The dome displays the icon of Christ as the Pantokrator (omnipotent God), holding the Gospel and blessing the congregation with his raised hand. Additional icons can be found in different parts of the church but most notably on a large screen called the *ikonostásion* (icon stand) that separates the nave from the altar area. The icons are arranged in prescribed tiers. All churches have a bottom tier that includes (as viewed from left to right): the Archangel Michael, the saint or event for which the church was named, the Virgin Mary, the Royal Gates with the four evangelists, Jesus Christ, St. John the Baptist, and the Archangel Gabriel. Icons relating to the twelve great feast days of Orthodoxy, the disciples, and the Last Supper may be included in additional tiers.

Church Interior

Icons of other saints and significant Biblical events may be added to the walls of the church in frescoes, mosaics, and moveable boards. They, too, contribute to the extended family of saints that worship with the congregation.

Two other prominent features of the nave are the pulpit and the bishop's chair. From the pulpit the primary teachings of the day are delivered to the parishioners through the reading of the Gospel and the delivery of the sermon. The elaborate bishop's chair is reserved for a visiting bishop or archbishop.

SANCTUARY

The sanctuary, separated from the nave by the *ikonostásion*, is always located on the east side of the church because Christ, the light of the world, will arise again in the east. The sanctuary has four main features: the altar, the table of oblation, the Platytera, and the crucifix.

It is here that the greatest mystery of the church — the changing of the bread and wine into the Body and Blood of Jesus Christ — takes place. The central element is the altar which represents his tomb. The other elements are complementary to the altar, such as the table of oblation placed to the left of the altar. The table normally stands in a concave area that represents Christ's manger. The icon is that of the Nativity. The oblation table is where the priest conducts the *proskomithí* during the *órthros* service, in which he prepares the bread and the wine to be used for Holy Communion (Eucharist).

Most of the Divine Liturgy is conducted around the altar, usually made of stone or marble in keeping with the practice of the early Christians who used the tombs of their deceased brethren for tables to perform the Eucharist. Relics of saints are even placed in each altar to replicate those early tables. One or more columns support the altar. The one column signifies the foundation of the world, Jesus Christ. Four columns signify the four evangelists: Matthew, Mark, Luke, and John. On the altar the changing of the bread and wine takes place, the church's most important mystery. On the top of the altar lie the Gospel book and the *artophórion*, a large four-sided box made of precious metal with a cross on top that contains the consecrated bread immersed in the Blood of Jesus. This is reserved for emergencies and for the offering following the sacrament of baptism. Behind the altar stands a large crucifix on which the body of Christ hangs, a reminder of his sacrifice for mankind.

The ceiling above the altar shows the Platytera ton Ouranon (wider than heaven), depicting the Virgin Mary with open arms and with the Christ Child on her lap. She is called Platytera because in her womb she held the omnipotent God. Her outstretched arms welcome and encompass the worshiper.

As a usual practice, only clergy and male laymen go beyond the *ikonostásion* and into the altar area. More recently the individual parish priest may make allowances, for instance when a female baby is brought for the forty-day blessing. (See *Birth of Children*)

*Byzantine
Cross*

*Greek
Cross*

CROSSES

The primary symbol of Christianity, the cross, appears throughout the church. Many styles are used, including crosses with equal sides, T shapes, and decorative variations. None is more Byzantine or Orthodox than the other, but art historians have applied the term "Greek" to the cross with equal sides and "Byzantine" to the one with a longer vertical.

The cross holds a special place in the life of the church and each individual Christian. Orthodox Christians have crosses in their homes and wear them around their necks, not as ornaments but as a symbols of protection and constant reminders of their identification with the sacrifice of the Lord.

BYZANTINE MUSIC

CHARACTERISTICS

Mystical, non-Western music distinguishes the Greek Orthodox church service. It wafts and echoes through the church expressing the soul's longing to communicate with God and the saints. Deceptively simple, it integrates theology, text, and music to express the purpose of the church service and transport the listener into another realm. Classic Byzantine music has a single-line melody with a parallel background tone. It is based on an eight-mode system with non-Western rhythm and notation. The single-line melody (plain chant) represents a direct prayer to God from the heart, through the mouth. Traditionalists maintain that only the human voice can adequately express the feelings to be communicated. The chanter (*psáltis*) interprets text, turning it into worship. Even individuals singing in groups should use one voice like the angelic choirs in heaven.

The eight modes are varying scales, expressing different moods. Unlike the West where an entire song is composed in one time (such as 4/4), Byzantine music is tonic, i.e., it follows the syllables and accents of prose text and thus has no consistent rhythm. The musical notation bears no resemblance to that of the West either. In the nineteenth century, reformers made substantial revisions, resulting in the neo-Byzantine music system in use today.

VARIATIONS

In the United States, radical changes were made in Byzantine music during the twentieth century with the blessing of the church hierarchy. Today a typical Divine Liturgy features three types of Byzantine-based music: single-melody chants by one *psáltis*, chants in free harmony by several *psáltes*, and full harmony works sung to organ accompaniment by a choir with men and (unlike Greece) women. The choral works may combine Western music style and the Byzantine chant. One of the most popular choral liturgies today was written in 1951 by Greek-American Frank Desby. Other Greek-American composers have also written liturgies, most of them more Westernized than Desby's. Close to the Byzantine tradition is the music of Anna Gallos. Even more Byzantine is the music of Harilaos Papapostolou, choir director of St. Sophia Cathedral in Washington, D.C. In most parishes, the priest, *psáltes*, and choir perform the music in the Orthodox service. The congregation rarely sings, except for those parishioners familiar enough with the liturgy to "sub-sing" in low voices to themselves.

Use of the organ in America is a radical departure from Byzantine tradition. Many early parishes acquired existing non-Orthodox churches with organs and began using them. Archbishop of North and South America Athenagoras (1931-1948) believed that a similar instrument had been used at St. Sophia Cathedral in Constantinople and approved its use.

HYMNS

A wealth of hymns contributes to the treasury of Orthodox tradition and elevates worshipers with their elegant poetic style. The *psáltes* and choir sing most hymns, but many may be followed in the four primary hymn books: *The Lenten Triodion, The Festal Menaion,* the *Pentecostarion,* and the *Parakletike (Octoechos).*[5] All may be purchased for personal use.

LANGUAGE

Today the majority of Greek Orthodox churches in the United States conduct services in Greek and English, alternating the two languages as the service progresses. Certain portions of the service such as the Gospel, Epistle, Nicene Creed, and Lord's Prayer may be repeated in both languages. This accommodation is relatively recent, coming into widespread practice during the 1960s.

The introduction of English into the Greek Orthodox services has been a divisive and difficult problem. Factions adamant about preserving the Greek language dominated for three-quarters of the twentieth century. They feared the loss of Greek identity and important religious traditions. During his tenure as Archbishop of North and South America, the Ecumenical Patriarch Athenagoras insisted that Greek always be used in the church services and the sermons.

A large wave of new immigrants to the United States after World War II increased the number of Greek-speaking church members, reinforcing the anti-English sentiment. In 1950 English was allowed in the Sunday schools, but official English usage stopped there. Meanwhile parishes themselves began introducing English into the services, and the practice became sufficiently widespread that in 1970 a new Archbishop, Iakovos, proposed the use of English where needed in the service and sermons. It was resisted by many groups and disapproved by the highest church authority, the Ecumenical Patriarch Athenagoras. After the furor subsided, however, the clergy did what best suited their individual parishes, resulting in the combination today of both English and Greek. Various English translations of the liturgy have been in use for years, but the prevailing English version is the liturgy prepared by the members of the faculty of Hellenic College/Holy Cross Greek Orthodox School of Theology.[6]

The Greek portion that appears in the Divine Liturgy books today alongside the English is written in koine (common — pronounced *kiní),* the Greek language of the Hellenistic and Roman periods. Koine was used in the composition of the Old and New Testaments, and is the ancestor of modern Greek today.

SERVICES

The Orthodox church holds many services, ranging from the daily morning matins (*órthros*) and evening vespers to the glorious Easter service at midnight. But the most important and most frequently attended service is the Divine Liturgy held throughout the world every Sunday and on special feast days. The same service conducted centuries ago at the center of Orthodoxy in Constantinople is conducted the same way today. Generation after generation appreciates and loves its beauty and consistency.

There are four liturgies in the Greek Orthodox church:
>St. John Chrysostom (most frequently used)
>St. Basil (ten times a year)
>St. James (on October 23)
>Liturgy of the Presanctified Gifts (Wednesday and Fridays of Great Lent and the first three days of Easter Holy Week)

PURPOSE OF THE DIVINE LITURGY

The primary purpose of the Divine Liturgy is the offering of the Eucharist in which bread and wine are transformed into the Body and Blood of Christ (the holy Gifts). The faithful unite with Christ and one another during the service. Christ instituted this tradition at the Last Supper to establish an ongoing communion between himself and his followers. It provides a way for them to constantly receive renewal and grace. The entire liturgy leads to that moment when the parishioners come to the front of the church to take the sacrament (see *Communion*).

ROLE OF THE PRIEST

Between the congregation and God stands the priest. He is human, one of the congregants, but vested with the authority to offer the sacrament. In this capacity the priest offers the liturgy and acts in the place of Christ who is the real celebrant of the Eucharist.

AN INTELLECTUAL AND EMOTIONAL EXPERIENCE

Intellectually, the service enables one to communicate with God: offering praise, asking mercy, and learning lessons of life conduct. Emotionally, the prayers of the service penetrate deeply into the soul of the worshiper, stimulating the fervent desire to elevate oneself to a higher level of existence, the unreachable, the sublime. The senses are stimulated by many elements. The beauty of the icons, vestments, and architecture have visual appeal. The incense, symbolically lifting prayers to God, stimulates the sense of smell. The bells on the censer and the hymns please the ear. The taste of the holy Gifts satisfies the palate. These sensual experiences transport the worshiper to the spiritual world and are part of the Orthodox way of teaching God's message and bringing the faithful into union with him.

INVOLVEMENT IN THE DIVINE LITURGY

Some parishioners complain about their passive role in the liturgy. The priest, chanter, and choir appear to do everything. Work and concentration are required on your part to make the service meaningful.

- Follow the text in the service book. The priest's petitions and prayers are also yours.
- Learn from the Gospel and the Epistle.
- Recite the Creed and the Lord's Prayer.
- Understand the symbolism in the service.
- Make the sign of the cross and kneel where appropriate (see "Church Etiquette" below).
- Take communion as often as possible.

DIVINE LITURGY OF ST. JOHN CHRYSOSTOM

The following guide summarizes the most frequently attended service, the Divine Liturgy of St. John Chrysostom.

In the first part, the "Liturgy of the Word," the priest guides the people in their prayers and supplications to God for a peaceful Christian life. They ask for mercy for the saints, civil and religious leaders, for good harvests, and help for those who suffer. People are asked to commit themselves to God and to be saved through the intercessions of the Virgin Mary. Then the Gospel bound in a large gold book is brought in during the Small Entrance, symbolizing Christ's coming to earth as a teacher. A reading from the Epistles of St. Paul or the Acts of the Apostles gives worshipers advice on how to conduct their lives according to Christ's life. The Gospel reading then relates a specific teaching from Christ's life. This may be followed by the sermon, ending the teachings for the day. For practical reasons, because not all of the worshipers are in church at this time, it has become customary in America for the sermons to be given at the conclusion of the entire liturgy.

The second part, the "Liturgy of the Faithful," prepares worshipers to receive communion. It is known as the Liturgy of the Faithful because it was intended for those who have been baptized. In an earlier time, the unbaptized were ordered to depart from the nave after the first part of the service. Today the faithful are implored to put away worldly cares, and God is asked to cleanse them, making them worthy to receive the holy Gifts. The Great Entrance then begins with the priest, preceded by altar boys, bringing the holy chalice with the wine and water and the holy paten holding the bread, into the nave of the church. The priest represents Christ carrying his cross on the way to Golgotha. He returns to the altar with the holy Gifts and begins a set of petitions that culminate with the recitation of the Creed, the twelve basic articles of the Christian faith. A singing dialogue begins among the priest and the people, represented by the choir and/or chanter, as they prepare for the consecration of the holy Gifts. The eucharistic prayer gives thanks for the gifts and offers them to God. The climax of the liturgy occurs when the bread and wine are consecrated. With the priest and congregation kneeling, the Holy Spirit transforms the elements into the Body and Blood of Christ. After the recitation of the Lord's Prayer (Pater Imon), comes the communion prayer asking for purification and forgiveness. The priest takes communion and then offers it to those who have prepared themselves by repenting and fasting. Closing prayers follow, and a piece of bread is distributed to everyone in the church as a blessing and an expression of love and fellowship.

THE LORD'S PRAYER

Our Father, who art in heaven, hallowed be thy name. Thy kingdom come. Thy will be done, on earth as it is in heaven. Give us this day our daily bread; and forgive us our trespasses, as we forgive those who trespass against us; and lead us not into temptation, but deliver us from evil.

Priest only: For thine is the kingdom and the power and the glory of the Father, and the Son, and the Holy Spirit, now and forever and to the ages of ages. Amen.

PÁTER IMÓN

Páter imón, o en tís ouranís, ayiasTHíto to ónomá sou, ElTHéto i vasilía sou. YeniTHíto to THélimá sou, os en ouranó ke épi tis yís. Ton árton imón ton epioúsion, thós imin símeron. Ke áfes imín ta ofilímata imón, ós ke imís afíemen tís ofilétes imón. Ke mí isenégis imás ís pirasmón, alla ríse imás apo tou poniroú.

Priest only: Óti soú estín, i vasilía ke i thínamis ke i thóxa tou Patrós ke tou Ioú ke tou Ayíou Pnévmatos, nín ke aí ke is tous eónas ton eónon. Amín.

CHURCH ETIQUETTE

PURPOSE

If you were not raised in the Orthodox church, you may vividly recall your first service. There was a bewildering number of "do's" and "don'ts": Enter only at certain times; stand and sit sporadically; parishioners making the sign of the cross; English and Greek interwoven. What is the logic of it all? The rules of conduct in the church are external gestures that help you express and foster your faith. Their repeated habit can provide a sense of stability. The following suggestions will help you understand and master church etiquette.

ATTIRE

Since you are meeting God at church, it is respectful to present yourself in a clean and neat manner. For church services, dresses and skirts are preferred for women and jackets for men. In American Greek Orthodox churches, head and shoulder coverings for women are no longer required, but modesty is strongly recommended. If you plan to take communion, do not wear lipstick.

ARRIVAL TIME

Orthodox church services begin on time, but few parishioners are ever there! Parishioners arrive throughout the service. This is a matter of individual choice, of course, but late church arrival is a bad habit — bad for you and for your fellow parishioners who are interrupted. The Divine Liturgy usually lasts about an hour and a half. Do your best to arrive on time or before the reading of the Epistle and Gospel.

ENTERING THE NARTHEX

When you enter the narthex, stop all talking. This is a time to prepare for worship. Bow your head, make the sign of the cross, and make an offering for a candle. Light the candle from another one at the candle stand. Venerate the icons by making the sign of the cross before kissing them. If there are two major figures in the same icon, such as the Virgin Mary holding Christ, kiss them both if you wish. Many parishioners say short prayers during these preparations.

CANDLES

The lighted candle is a constant symbol in the Orthodox church. It represents the light of Christ according to Jesus' own words, "I am the light of the world; he who follows me will not walk in darkness, but will have the light of life." John 8:12.

When you light a candle, say a brief prayer that your life will shine as Christ commanded in Matt. 5:16: "Let your light so shine before men, that they may see your good works and give glory to your Father who is in heaven." Light a candle to honor him and reaffirm that you are a follower in the faith. It is also common to light one for someone in need, to honor a saint, or to commemorate a deceased loved one.

SIGNING THE CROSS

Meaning

The cross is the most powerful symbol in Christianity for it was on the cross that Christ died. In a sign of mutual recognition, an early Christian could quickly make the sign of the cross for identification. Today it is used in a variety of situations: to show the believer's faith, to invoke God's presence, to begin and end a prayer, to protect against evil and to show thanksgiving. The cross can be made with a spoken or silent prayer.

How to Make the Sign

Hand position for signing the cross

The proper Orthodox cross is made by holding the thumb and first two fingers of the right hand together and resting the remaining two fingers on the palm.

The three fingers together represent the Father, Son, and Holy Spirit, and the remaining two fingers the dual nature of Christ as God and man. The fingers and thumb are placed first on the forehead, then the center of the chest, the right shoulder, then the left shoulder. (The right shoulder is touched first because Christ sits at the right hand of God.) The motion should be continuous and distinct, done either once or three times consecutively. At the end the hand is then opened and placed on the center of the chest. Always make your cross distinctly and with conviction. A poorly executed cross is disrespectful. Sometimes a parishioner will bow, make a cross and then touch the floor (repeating the sequence three times). This is known as a *metánia*. On occasion a devout parishioner may kneel, make a cross, and kiss the ground numerous times.

Young children are first taught to make their cross while saying and singing the "Ayios O Theos" (pron. *THeós* — Holy God).[7]

When to Make the Sign of the Cross

1. Whenever you feel the need
2. Before and after any prayers
3. When you enter and leave the narthex and nave
4. Before you kiss an icon, cross, or the Gospel book
5. When you pass the altar
6. When you hear any of the following phrases:
   - "The Father, and the Son, and the Holy Spirit"
   - *"Áyios O Theós, Áyios Ischirós, Áyios ATHánatos, eléison imas."* (Holy God, Holy Mighty, Holy Immortal, have mercy on us.)
   - "Theotokos," "Panayia," or "Virgin Mary"
   - The name of a saint
7. When the censer is moved in your direction
8. After the reading of the Epistle and the Gospel
9. Near the end of the Nicene Creed at the phrase "In one, holy catholic, and apostolic church"
10. After kneeling for the consecration during the Divine Liturgy

11. At the end of the Lord's Prayer while the priest says, "For Thine is the kingdom and the power and the glory forever. Amen."
12. Whenever the priest makes the sign of the cross.
13. Immediately before and after receiving communion
14. Before receiving *antídoron* (see below)

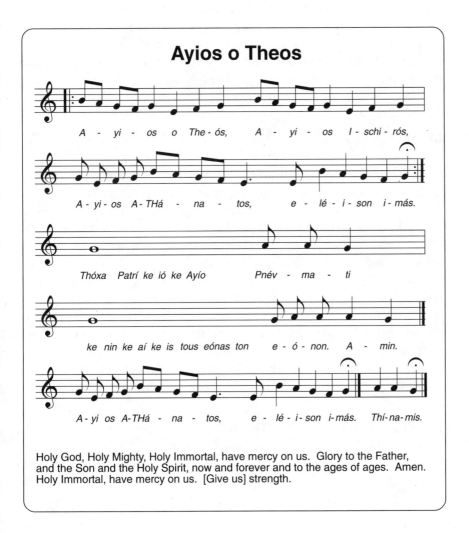

Ayios o Theos

Holy God, Holy Mighty, Holy Immortal, have mercy on us. Glory to the Father, and the Son and the Holy Spirit, now and forever and to the ages of ages. Amen. Holy Immortal, have mercy on us. [Give us] strength.

ENTERING THE NAVE

Make the sign of the cross when entering the main part of the church, the nave. If a service is not in progress, you should go to the front, make the sign of the cross and kiss the icon of Christ and then Mary in the *ikonostásion* and any other icons you wish. If a service is in progress, especially the Divine Liturgy, enter at the proper time (see "Etiquette for the Divine Liturgy"). If you are unsure, ask an usher if you may proceed. You may sit anywhere you wish, unless seats are reserved or a memorial service is scheduled. Normally the first several rows on the right-hand side of the church in front of the icon of Christ are reserved for the family and friends of a deceased person.

GENERAL DECORUM

General church decorum has changed through the years. The earliest churches in the United States were similar to those in Greece. There were no pews, and people were constantly moving around, in and out, frequently bowing and touching the floor while making their crosses. Except for the separation of men to the right side of the church and women to the left, there was an uninhibited quality to Orthodox worship. Occasionally this former style of worship is still seen in some American churches. For example, you may see a parishioner standing through most of the service with his or her body bent forward in a reverent bow, making the cross frequently, touching the ground, and singing the liturgy in a low voice. Today's American congregation, in contrast, is more reserved, perhaps because of the addition of pews.

ETIQUETTE FOR THE DIVINE LITURGY

1. Arrive on time or before the reading of the Epistle and the Holy Gospel.

2. Enter the narthex as described above, make your cross, light a candle, and kiss the icons.

3. Enter the nave any time except during the following:
   - Beginning of the service when the priest says: "Blessed is the Kingdom of the Father, Son, and Holy Spirit."
   - During the Small Entrance with the Gospel
   - During the reading of the Epistle and the Gospel

- During the Great Entrance with the chalice
- During the recitation of the Nicene Creed
- During the transformation of the bread and wine when parishioners are kneeling
- During the recitation of the Lord's Prayer

4. Make the sign of the cross at the appropriate places.

5. Stand during the Small Entrance, the reading of the Gospel, the Great Entrance, Nicene Creed, and the Lord's Prayer. For additional times follow the service book and watch for the priest's signal (a bell, light, or hand sign).

6. Kneel during the consecration of the Gifts (when the bread and the wine are being changed into the Body and Blood of Christ — except during the first forty days after Easter).

7. If you are taking communion, be prepared by fasting and confessing privately or by sacrament. Women should not wear lipstick. Go to the front of the church when the priest says, "With fear of God, faith and love, draw near." When you reach the priest, make the sign of the cross, tell him your baptismal name, hold the red cloth under your chin, and he will put a spoon containing the Gifts in your mouth. Hold the cloth for the next person. Make the sign of the cross again and take the bread offered by the altar boy.

8. At the end of the service, take the *antídoron*, a small piece of bread. Everyone, Orthodox and non-Orthodox, receives it as an expression of love and Christian fellowship. *Antídoron* (pron. *andíthoron*) is a compound word meaning "Instead of the gift." It is not consecrated but blessed at the altar. Go to the front of the church where the priest hands out the small pieces of bread. Make the sign of the cross while approaching the priest and kiss his hand as he gives it to you. Walk down the center aisle and as you leave the nave, turn and bow toward the altar, make the sign of the cross, and exit.

SUMMARY

The above description of Orthodox beliefs, church architecture and art, music, and worship provide practical information for a meaningful church experience. May you discover over time that the formality of the service facilitates a humble and grateful relationship with God. May you sense also, along with other faithful at worship, a comfort in belonging to the precious Body of Christ.

For a more detailed explanation of the development of beliefs of the Orthodox church, its political history, and evolution into various national churches, see *The Historic Orthodox Church*. This chapter explains how different churches evolved politically and geographically, but remained remarkably the same. For listings of Orthodox churches to visit in America and other parts of the world, see *The Historic Orthodox Church* — "Orthodox Internet Websites — Autocephalous Orthodox Churches and Orthodox Churches in the United States and Canada."

---

1. Timothy Ware, *The Orthodox Church*. 1963. New edition (London: Penguin Books, 1997), 195. The book covers the political history of the Orthodox church and explains its beliefs and traditions.

2. Ibid., 196.

3. Kallistos [Timothy] Ware, *The Orthodox Way* (1979; reprint, Crestwood, N.Y.: St. Vladimir's Seminary Press, 1986).

4. D. Cummings, *The Rudder* (Chicago: The Orthodox Christian Educational Society, 1957).

5. Hymns for nine great feast days have been translated in *The Festal Menaion,* trans. Mother Mary and Kallistos Ware (1969; South Cannan, Pa.: St. Tikhon's Seminary Press, 1990). Hymns for the ten weeks before Easter may be found in *The Lenten Triodion,* trans. Mother Mary and Kallistos Ware (1978; reprint, London: Faber and Faber, 1984). Hymns for Easter through the Sunday of All Saints are contained in the *Pentecostarion,* trans. Holy Transfiguration Monastery (Brookline, Mass.: Holy Transfiguration Monastery, 1990). Hymns for the cycle of matins, vespers, Eucharist and Saturday midnight services for the entire year except from the Triodion to the Sunday of All Saints comprise *The Parakletike* [*Octoechos* (Eight Tones)], trans. Mother Mary (Bussy-en-Othe, France: Orthodox Monastery of the Veil of Our Lady, nd).

6. Members of the Faculty of Hellenic College/Holy Cross Greek Orthodox School of Theology, trans. *The Divine Liturgy of Saint John Chrysostom* (Brookline, Mass.: Holy Cross Orthodox Press, 1985).

7. "Ayios o Theos" adapted from Nick and Connie Maragos, eds. *Sharing in Song: A Songbook for Greek Orthodox Gatherings* (Sherman Oakes, Calif.: The National Forum of Greek Orthodox Church Musicians, 1988), 3.

❧ *The Seven Sacraments*

The Orthodox believe that God should be present in all facets of life. Life is a continuous striving for perfection and sanctification. To help individuals reach that perfection, the church provides its members the sacraments *(mystírion)*, seven of its most important services. These seven sacraments are the jewels of Orthodox spirituality:

- Baptism
- Chrismation
- Confession
- Communion
- Marriage
- Holy Unction
- Holy Orders

The term "mystery" describes the miraculous way that the grace of God and the Holy Spirit come to worshipers through the sacraments, enabling them to perfect themselves in God's image *(théosis)*. In confession and communion, for example, God's healing forgiveness cleanses the individual of sins, and the Body and Blood of Christ replenish the sacred self. In marriage the grace of God's love nurtures the sacred union of husband and wife.

The sacraments are administered only by priests to the Orthodox who have been baptized in the church and who remain in good standing. Egregious violation of church policy, such as marrying outside the church, affects standing, and sacraments cannot be administered. To experience Greek Orthodox life fully, be an active participant in its sacramental offerings. Baptism, chrismation, confession, and communion are considered essential.

Infant Baptism

BAPTISM AND CHRISMATION

Baptisms bring great happiness to the Greek family. The special church service with the naked infant immersed in the baptismal font and anointed with holy oil is often followed by a joyful celebration of feasting and dancing. Family and friends celebrate the "rebirth" of the young child and the birth of the new relationship with the godparent.

THE SACRAMENT OF BAPTISM

The sacraments of baptism and chrismation were instituted by Christ himself when he commanded his apostles, "Go therefore and make disciples of all nations, baptizing them in the name of the Father and of the Son and of the Holy Spirit." (Matt. 28:19) For centuries these sacraments have initiated the individual into the Greek Orthodox church. Baptism cleanses the soul of the stain of original sin transmitted to the human race by Adam and Eve when they disobeyed God. Chrismation transmits the gifts of the Holy Spirit. Through these two sacraments, the individual takes the first steps toward *théosis* (becoming like God). Symbolically, Christ's baptism, death, and Resurrection, plus the gift of the Holy Spirit to the apostles at Pentecost, are reenacted.

Baptism begins in the church narthex where the unbaptized originally congregated. The godparent speaks on behalf of the child and forcefully rejects Satan, including blowing three times in the air and symbolically spitting three times on the floor.

Turning toward the altar, the godparent professes a belief in Christ and recites the Nicene Creed, a summary of the basic beliefs of the Greek Orthodox Christian. Then using the child's baptismal name, the priest asks God to make the candidate worthy of baptism by taking away old ways and filling the child with the Holy Spirit.

The priest, child, and godparent proceed to the front of the church to the large baptismal font that represents the divine womb in which the child receives a second birth as a child of God. The godparent promises to raise the child as a good Christian.

The priest blesses the water in the baptismal font, adding a small amount of olive oil that the godparent has brought to the church. The fruit of the olive tree has been a symbol of peace and reconciliation between God and humans since a dove brought an olive branch to Noah at the end of the great flood described in the Old Testament.

The child is undressed, symbolizing the removal of old sin. The priest makes the sign of the cross with oil on various parts of the infant, and the godparent rubs oil over the child's body. The oil serves as a silent prayer to God: "O, God, let there be peace always between this child and you." The priest immerses the child three times into the font, symbolizing the three days Christ spent in the tomb. He declares, "The servant of God [name] is baptized in the name of the Father, and of the Son, and of the Holy Spirit. Amen." This dramatic event is a reenactment of Christ's baptism, death, and Resurrection. Like Christ, the child is resurrected and reborn. The priest places the child in the open arms of the godparent, who holds a new white sheet as a symbol of the soul's purity.

THE SACRAMENT OF CHRISMATION

Immediately following the baptism, the priest administers a second sacrament, chrismation. Like the early apostles, the child receives the gift of the Holy Spirit during chrismation, a gift of grace from God to help the child lead a Christian life. The priest anoints the child with *miron*, a special oil blessed by the Ecumenical Patriarch, and says, "The seal of the gift of the Holy Spirit. Amen." Three locks are tonsured from the child's hair in the form of a cross. This gift to God shows gratitude and obedience.

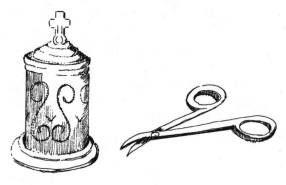

Oil of Chrismation and Scissors for Tonsuring

The priest blesses a piece of the child's new clothing, then puts it on the child with these words, "The servant of God [name] is clothed with the garment of incorruptibility." Relatives or friends then dress the child, and the priest puts a necklace with a cross on the child's neck, saying, "If any man would come after me, let him deny himself and take up his cross and follow me." Mark 8:34

After lighting the decorated baptismal candle, the priest, the god-parent holding the infant, and a few selected children walk around the font symbolizing a dance of joy for the new Christian who has been added to the church.

Following the dance and a reading of scriptures, the priest administers a third sacrament, communion, to the child. The child's parents approach the front of the church where the godparent hands the infant to them with these traditional words, "I present to you your son/daughter baptized and confirmed, dedicated to God." The parents kiss the hand of the godparent and receive their child.

PREPARING FOR THE CEREMONY

WHEN TO BAPTIZE

Baptize your baby as soon as possible after the forty-day blessing. (See *Birth of Children*) Baptism is essential for entering heaven and participating in other church sacraments. Since the fate of an unbaptized individual is unknown, parents who neglect to have their child baptized bear a heavy responsibility.

Baptisms are not permitted on the following holidays:

> December 25 through January 6, Easter Holy Week (dates vary), or on any of the Great Feast days of the Lord. Exceptions must be approved by the diocesan bishop.

CHOOSING THE GODPARENT

Significance

Give substantial time and thought to selecting the godparent. The godparent is responsible for the spiritual upbringing of your child and becomes a "member of the family." A lifelong relationship of love and friendship should develop between your two families. The relationship, sanctioned by God, is very special, and being a godparent is as close as one can come to being a family member. Many times parents select other family members as godparents.

Qualifications

The church requires that all godparents be baptized Orthodox Christians who are in good standing with their parish and in full sacramental communion. Check with your priest regarding a godparent's appropriate age. Although officially there is only one godparent, many priests allow a second person to assist. A godparent should set a good religious example and take an interest in the religious upbringing of the godchild.

Godparent of Firstborn Child

Traditionally, the *koumbáros* (male) and/or *koumbára* (female), the Orthodox witness(es) at the parents' wedding, will baptize the couple's first child. (See *Marriage*) Sometimes the *koumbáros* is much older than the parents, and it is in the child's best interest to have a younger godparent who will be available throughout the child's life. In such a situation, do not ignore the tradition, but be courteous and discuss the matter with the *koumbáros*.

Godparent for Additional Children

If the *koumbáros* is not going to baptize your baby or if this is your second child, it is customary to wait for someone to offer. Since being a godparent entails religious, emotional, and financial commitments, it is both a favor and a great honor. If you are concerned that no one will offer to be the godparent, subtle hinting may be necessary. In America's mobile society, however, parents may need to ask someone outright or consult their parish priest for suggestions.

If you receive more than one offer to baptize your child, select the most suitable person or use the method in the next paragraph.

Random Selection of Godparent

In rare instances a child's godparent is determined in the nave of the church. It may be impossible for the parents to choose among various offers of baptism. Or sometimes a child has been born after a *táma* to a saint. (See *Special Blessings, Prayers, and Appeals*) In those instances, the baby is placed on the church floor under the icon of Christ or the Virgin Mary during a Divine Liturgy, and the first person to pick up the child becomes the godparent. In Tinos, Greece, at the Church of the Evangelistria which is dedicated to the Virgin Mary, tourists who are not Christian Orthodox are warned not to lift any babies from the floor since non-Orthodox are not permitted to baptize.

Baptism of Male and Female Children

In Greece, godparents baptize only children of the same sex, because adults with the same godparents are not allowed to marry. In the eyes of the church, they are related. This rule, however, has been relaxed in the United States, and godparents can baptize both male and female children.

What to Call Each Other

Godparents and parents address each other as *"koumbáre"* (male), *"koumbára"* (female), or *"koumbári"* (plural). A godchild addresses a godfather as *"nouné"* and a godmother as *"nouná."* In America the masculine terms *"koumbáro"* and *"nounó"* are popularly used, but this is gramatically incorrect.

PREPARATIONS BY THE PARENTS

Celebration

The parents are responsible for the celebration after the baptismal ceremony. Celebrations for baptisms vary from small receptions of coffee and sweets to luncheons or dinners with dancing; budget and circumstances should prevail.

Selection of Assistants

Select two people to undress and dress the baby at the ceremony. It is customary to ask the baby's grandmothers to share this honor. If they are not available, ask other family members or close friends to assist. Also choose two or more children to walk with candles around the font at the prescribed time during the ceremony.

Bonboniéres

In some cases, furnish candy favors (see *"Bonboniéres"* below). Discuss this matter with the godparent.

Gift

Give the godparent a present to show your appreciation.

Optional Explanation

Provide guests with an explanation of the service. You may either reprint the explanation above or ask your priest for text.

PREPARATIONS BY THE GODPARENT

Name Selection

Select a name for your godchild that is acceptable to the church and the parents. Generally, names must be both Christian and Greek. In America, the name is selected before delivery, so the birth certificate can be issued at the hospital. In addition, naming can be done with the eighth-day prayer. (See *Birth of Children* and *Selecting a Name*)

The following custom in many villages and towns in Greece exemplifies the naming prerogative of the godparent. As the ceremony begins, all the village children huddle in the narthex, listening for the godparent to say the child's name after recitation of the Nicene Creed. After hearing the name, the children run as fast as they can to the parents' home where the mother waits to learn her baby's name. The mother gives the child who delivers the news a reward of money and/or food. The parents then go to the church to receive the newly baptized child from the godparent. A variation of this custom is still practiced in some American churches. The father or mother waits outside the church proper and hands a coin to the first child to announce the baby's name, or the godparent gives a silver coin to the first person who calls the baby by name.

Items Needed for the Baptism

Proof of Good Standing

Provide proof of your current good standing and membership in a Greek Orthodox church to the priest baptizing the baby. If married, provide proof of your marriage in the Orthodox church.

Items for the Priest

Bring the following to the priest in advance on the day of the ceremony:

2 white hand towels
1 white bath towel
1 white sheet
1 small bottle of olive oil
1 small bar of soap
3 or more white candles described below
1 set of new white clothing described below
1 gold cross and chain
(*Optional:* Inscribe cross with child's initials*)*

Baptismal Candles. The godparent provides one large decorated candle for the ceremony, which the godchild keeps. The other smaller white candles, decorated or undecorated, are carried by the children who circle the font during the ceremony.

Baptismal Candle

The traditional decoration for the godchild's candle is made by securing a large bow of ribbon or tulle with streamers on a large white candle and placing an artificial decoration such as a flower at the center of the bow (see *illustration*). The color blue remains popular for boys, and pink for girls. More elaborate decorations have evolved over the years and may be made at home or purchased at a Greek specialty store.

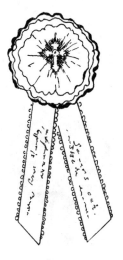

Martiriká

New White Clothing. The child is dressed in new white clothing during the ceremony to signify purification and new life from the rebirth of baptism. The outfit includes diaper, underwear, dress or suit, socks, shoes, two hats (one should be an absorbent liner) and possibly a coat, depending on the season. The clothing should cover the child as much as possible to absorb the holy oil from the ceremony. The godparent must carefully rub oil all over the baby's body during the ceremony. Some believe the superstition that any unoiled part will smell for the rest of the child's life!

Martiriká

Martiriká are the small lapel crosses distributed at the end of the baptismal ceremony and worn by the guests as proof of witnessing the baptism (see *illustration*). The traditional *martirikó* (singular) features a simple cross with a pin on the back and plain ribbon tied on the front. Over a period of time, more elaborate pins have become popular. The ribbon, traditionally blue or pink, surrounding a tiny cross, little metal icon, etc., is printed with the child's name, birth, and baptismal dates on one side, and the godparent's name on the other. These are commercially prepared and can be ordered through Greek specialty stores. The godparent or designated people distribute the *martiriká* at the front of the church, in the narthex, or at the reception.

Bonboniéres

Bonboniéres are the almond-candy favors given to each guest after the baptism. Since custom varies as to whether the parents or godparent should provide them, discuss this when making plans. Styles range from simple puffs of tulle tied with ribbon to elaborate containers to hold the candies. The most traditional are understated and easy to make. Place an odd number, usually five or seven, of candy-coated almonds (*kouféta*) in three layers of fine tulle cut in circles at least eleven inches in diameter. The edges can be scalloped for a softer look. Customarily white *kouféta* are used, but colored candies have become popular. Tie with a blue or pink ribbon and insert a small decorative item, such as an artificial flower at the bow (see *illustration)*. Ready-made *bonboniéres* can also be purchased from a Greek specialty store.

The favors can be handed out by selected assistants in the narthex as guests leave the church or distributed at the reception personally by whoever provides them. They may also be placed at the tables where the guests will be sitting. Use your imagination!

Some say *kouféta* are given in the hope that a sweet future awaits the child and the guests. Many people also believe that using an odd number is good luck and that seven *kouféta* represent the seven sacraments.

Gratuities

Thank the priest, chanter, and sexton for their assistance by giving them either money or a present after the ceremony. Check with other parishioners for specific recommendations. Such compensation is not a church regulation, but is an accepted gesture of thanks for services rendered.

Optional. Give a silver coin to the first person who says the godchild's name to you.

COMMON EXPRESSIONS

Common expressions for congratulating the family may be found in *As the Greeks Say.* If the baby cries during the ceremony, guests say, *"O thémonas févgi"* ("The devil is fleeing").

ONGOING RESPONSIBILITIES OF THE GODPARENT

The godparent's primary responsibility is to keep the godchild within the guidelines of the church and encourage him or her to live in the Orthodox way. Godparents must set a good example for it is said that children take on many of the characteristics of the people who anointed them with oil. It is common to remark that a godchild is like his or her godparent: *"Émiase tou nounú/tis nounás"* ("Took after his/her godfather/godmother").

IMMEDIATE RESPONSIBILITIES

- If convenient, give the baby the first bath after the baptism and wash the baptismal sheet, towel, and clothes. Because the wash water will contain holy oil, it should be poured some place outside where it will not be stepped on, such as the foot of a tree or a corner of the house. In the village of Sifnos, Greece, baptismal items are always washed in the sea. In Constantinople, the godparent puts a gold coin or jewelry in the baby's bathtub.

- Place all the baptismal articles in a box and give them to the godchild's family for safekeeping. Centuries ago the baptismal candle was brought to church for special occasions in the child's life such as his or her name day, wedding, and funeral. It was a reminder that the light of Christ was always in the person's life. An old custom on Mitilini was to save the baptismal sheet and use it as a shroud for burial.

- Take the child to church for communion after the baptism. The child should receive communion three times. However, if communion was given at the baptism, take the child only twice. Be sure to bring the baptismal candle, lighting it just before communion and carrying it and the child to the front for the sacrament.

LATER RESPONSIBILITIES

- Remember the child's name day, birthday, and special occasions such as Easter and Christmas. Give a decorated candle for the midnight Anastasi service if possible.

- Provide information to the godchild about the patron saint for whom he or she was named. Give the child an icon of the saint and encourage emulation as a role model.

- Attend church together if possible, especially on godparents' Sunday (variable date).

- Become the *koumbáros/a* at the godchild's wedding, circumstances permitting. (See *Marriage*)

SPECIAL SITUATIONS

ADULT BAPTISM AND CHRISMATION

Adults can be baptized in the Orthodox church after study and discussion guided by a priest. The priest approves baptism when he believes that true understanding has been reached by the individual. For those who have been baptized in another Christian faith such as a Roman Catholic or a Trinitarian Protestant denomination, only the chrismation service need be performed along with a shorter study and discussion session.

Women candidates should wear all white at the ceremony and men should wear a white shirt. Holy water will be either sprinkled or poured over the candidate's head, depending on the priest's preference. The godparent for the adult provides a cross and a candle.

EMERGENCY BAPTISM

In an emergency, such as severe illness or an accident, an infant can be baptized by any Orthodox person in several ways.

By Air

Lift the child into the air, making the sign of the cross with the child's body, saying, "The servant of God [name] is baptized in the name of the Father (lift straight up), and the Son, (lift to the right), and the Holy Spirit (lift to the left)."

By Water

Pour or sprinkle water on the individual while making the sign of the cross and saying, "The servant of God [name] is baptized in the name of the Father, and the Son, and the Holy Spirit."

Dance of Isaiah
Marriage Ceremony

MARRIAGE

Greek weddings sparkle. There is joy, laughter, loud *bouzoúki* music, mountains of food, and coiling lines of boisterous dancers. In the United States, most of the social customs surrounding the wedding festivities are American, with a few Greek customs here and there. However, the wedding ceremony itself remains pristinely Greek Orthodox, unchanged for centuries. It incorporates human joy with the joy of heaven when two people are united in holy matrimony.

The Sacrament of Marriage

Through the sacrament of marriage the Orthodox church joins a man and a woman in the sacred union of husband and wife. During the ceremony they commit themselves to one another and to raising a Christian family in a Christian home. God, in turn, bestows his love (agape) on them that they may live in harmony and peace for life. The service consists of beautiful hymns and prayers extolling marriage and emphasizing its responsibilities.

The service is conducted around a small table on which wedding crowns, the book of Gospels, two wedding rings, a cup of wine, and two white candles have been placed. These objects are used symbolically throughout the service.

THE BETROTHAL — BLESSING OF THE RINGS

In the first part of the service, the couple becomes betrothed by the church. The priest blesses the rings and touches the foreheads of the bride and groom with them. Making the sign of the cross above their heads with the rings, he proclaims to each of them, "The servant of God [name] is betrothed to the servant of God [name] in the name of the Father, and the Son, and the Holy Spirit." The rings are put on the right hands, and the official sponsor — *koumbáros* (male) or *koumbára* (female) — exchanges the rings three times, symbolizing the complementary role of husband and wife.

THE WEDDING

The wedding proper then takes place, highlighted by the following:

The Candles

The bride and groom each hold a lighted candle during the service, similar to a parable in the Bible where five wise maidens prepare to receive Christ the Bridegroom by lighting their lamps with oil. The candles remind the couple of the light of Christ who is with them throughout the sacrament and their coming life together.

The Joining of Hands

The couple joins right hands as the priest appeals to God to make them one in spirit and flesh and grant them the joy of children.

The Crowning

Crowns (*stéphana*) joined with a ribbon are worn by the bride and groom who are to be respected as king and queen in their home and family. As this crowning takes place, the blessing of God is invoked upon the couple. "O, Lord our God, crown them with honor and glory." As these words are sung, the *koumbáros/a* exchanges the crowns three times.

The Readings

There are two designated readings from the scriptures. In the Epistle of St. Paul to the Ephesians, Paul talks of love and respect. The husband should love his wife and be prepared to give his life to protect her as Christ gave his life out of love for the church. The wife should respect her husband as the church honors and respects Christ and should submit herself to him. The second reading from the Gospel of St. John relates the story of Christ at the wedding in Cana of Galilee and his miracle of changing water into wine.

The Common Cup

Just as wine was drunk at the wedding in Cana, the bride and groom share a common cup of unconsecrated wine, symbolizing the sharing of all that life will bring — the joys, sorrows, love, and pain.

The Dance of Isaiah

Led by the priest, the couple circles the small table while wearing their crowns and holding hands. The *koumbáros(a)* follows them, holding the ribbon that joins the crowns. The dance proclaims the church's joy at the new union, similar to the joy of Isaiah the prophet who saw the Messiah in a vision nine hundred years before Christ's birth. In Greece, guests shower the couple with rose petals and rice during the dance.

Near the end of the ceremony the priest removes the crowns, charging the newlyweds: "Be magnified, O bridegroom, as Abraham, and blessed as Isaac, and increased as was Jacob. Go your way in peace, performing in righteousness the commandments of God. And you, O bride, be magnified as was Sarah, and rejoiced as was Rebecca, and increased as Rachel, being glad in your husband, keeping the paths of the law, for so God is well pleased."

The bride and the groom are proclaimed as husband and wife, at the conclusion of the service. Just before the crowns are removed from their heads, the priest invokes God's blessings once more. "O Lord, bless these your servants who, by your providence, are now joined in the communion of marriage."

[End of ceremony]

THE ENGAGEMENT PERIOD

The wedding ceremony is the culmination of an intense time of anticipation and planning before the marriage. The engagement period and the process of organizing the wedding test the bond, commitment, and values of the future husband and wife. During this time they work with their families and church, preparing for their life together.

PARENTAL PERMISSION

Unlike Greek couples generations ago, whose marriages were arranged by their parents, women and men today meet, fall in love, and choose each other. Although parents play a lesser role now, it is respectful to seek the parents' permission to marry. The prospective groom should discuss his plans with the prospective bride's parents. This is also an American tradition and begins the formal relationship on a positive note.

Many years ago Greek parents prearranged their children's marriages. Marriage was a practical business based on the background of the families, calculated prospects for success and happiness, old promises between families, and even the amount of a dowry (*príka*). Sometimes a matchmaker (*proksenitís* [m] or *proksenítra* [f]) facilitated the prearranged marriage (*proksenió*), even negotiating terms of the agreement. In Constantinople, the matchmaker would come to make an offer wearing one slipper and one shoe!

RINGS

Traditions vary regarding the rings. In America, a man sometimes gives the woman an engagement ring with a precious stone that she wears on the third finger of her left hand. The wedding bands for the bride and groom are usually inscribed with a variety of information: initials, names, dates of either the engagement or wedding. This is a matter of personal preference. In Greece, a gold band serves as both the engagement ring and the wedding ring for the man and the woman. For the engagement, the ring is worn on the left hand, but moved to the right after the marriage. The right hand is considered stronger because in the Bible it performed miracles.

ENGAGEMENT PARTY

Like Americans, Greeks celebrate the good news with an engagement party. The focal point is the blessing of the engagement and wedding rings by the priest. Prepare for the blessing by setting a table with an icon and a silver tray layered with *kouféta* (candied almonds). Put the rings on the *kouféta* for the blessing. This blessing takes the place of the binding betrothal service which is now the first part of the marriage sacrament. *Kouféta* are placed in candy dishes for the guests or distributed as *bonboniéres* (see below). Guests generally bring gifts to the party, and well-wishers congratulate the couple with, "*Kalá stéphana*" ("Good crowning") or "*Syncharitíria*" ("Congratulations").

You may want to adopt a lively tradition from some parts of the Peloponnesus. A large sweet bread shaped like a ring and decorated with fresh flowers is baked for the engaged couple. They pull it apart, and whoever gets the larger piece will have the upper hand in the marriage!

In some villages in Cyprus, the *sympethéres* (mothers of the bride and groom) invite guests to the wedding by going together from house to house. They sprinkle the invitees with rosewater from a small decorated container and give them white candles to bring to church to light in the narthex on the day of the wedding.

PRE-MARITAL COUNSELING AND INTER-CHRISTIAN MARRIAGES

The Greek Orthodox church in the United States requires premarital counseling, although the extent differs from one diocese to another. It is advisable for couples who are contemplating marriage to consult their priest immediately following the engagement. In addition to providing emotional support, he can answer questions about church guidelines. The church welcomes to the sacrament of marriage a partner of a different Christian faith and recommends that the couple and their families read *When You Intermarry: A Resource for Inter-Christian Intercultural Couples, Parents and Families* by Rev. Fr. Charles J. Joanides.[1]

GREEK ORTHODOX CHURCH GUIDELINES

The Orthodox church promulgates strict guidelines for marriage, concerning membership standing, the *koumbáros/a*, marriage to a non-Orthodox, etc. Certain criteria must be met before the priest can perform the marriage. (See "Guidelines for Marriage in the Greek Orthodox Church" below.) Be aware that the church does not recognize marriage outside the Orthodox church. If you marry in a non-Orthodox ceremony, you excommunicate yourself and are barred from the sacraments, from becoming a sponsor at a wedding or baptism, and from receiving an Orthodox funeral.

WEDDING SHOWER

American Etiquette

At a wedding shower the bride receives gifts for her new house-hold and/or herself, depending on the kind of shower being given. Since this is an American custom, check with a wedding book for further details concerning types and etiquette.

Greek Customs Today and Yesterday

The traditional candy for weddings, *kouféta*, may be distributed in small candy dishes or as *bonboniéries*. An appropriate Greek gift is a case (*stephanothíki*) for the marriage crowns (*stéphana*) usu-ally given by a close relative such as the mother of the bride, an aunt, or sometimes the *koumbáros/a*. According to a folk belief, if you receive scissors or knives as a gift, you should give money (like a penny or nickel) to the person who gave you the gift to avoid a quarrel!

In most cultures, women begin collecting bedding, kitchenware, and household items before the marriage. Americans call this a "hope chest." At one time young Greek women sewed, embroi-dered, and crocheted linens for their *príka* (dowry) and proudly displayed their work just before the wedding.

The *príka* was the money, land, and possessions a woman's family promised to bring to the marriage. The *príkes* ranged widely in value. The Greek-American author, Harry Mark Petrakis, listed his mother's *príka* in 1908 in *Stelmark: A Family Recollection*: "2,000 gold drachmas, an orchard of 37 olive trees, free and clear of debt, some adjoining orange and peach trees, and assorted household items, bedding, spreads, pots and pans, knives and forks."[2]

A woman's marriage depended on the size of her *príka*, resulting in many cruel ramifications. The birth of a girl was bemoaned because it meant providing a *príka*. Failure to provide one re-sulted in a loss of honor (*philótimo*) for the entire family. Brothers were pressed to earn *príkes* for their sisters before they themselves could marry. In fact many Greek men came to America simply to earn money for such obligations. Today parents of the bride in Greece help as much as they can, but it is voluntary and not legally required.

Planning the Wedding

Most Greek Orthodox weddings in the United States combine Greek and American customs. Use an American wedding etiquette book as a basic planning guide. Such books are available for purchase or may be checked out of a local library. Add the Greek customs included here — *bonboniéres*, *stéphana*, *bouzoúki*, and *baklavá* — for a unique and joyous Greek-American wedding!

SETTING THE DATE

Marriages cannot be performed on certain church feast days and during some periods of Lent. For example, do not plan to marry during Great Lent and Holy Week. (See "Guidelines for Marriage in the Greek Orthodox Church" below)

SELECTING THE *KOUMBÁROS(A)* AND OTHER ATTENDANTS

The *koumbáros* (male) or *koumbára* (female), the official sponsor of the marriage, must be Orthodox and in good standing with the church. Generally there is only one *koumbáros(a)*, but some priests permit couples (*koumbári*). (In formal Greek the word *paránymphos* is used for *koumbáros[a]*.)

Traditionally the groom's godparent is asked to serve first and then the godparent of the bride. If neither of them participate, ask a close friend or family member. Remember, this is an important relationship lasting a lifetime. *Koumbári* become almost like family. Consider also the suitability of the *koumbáros(a)* as a godparent, since he or she usually baptizes the first child.

The *koumbáros(a)* can be the best man or maid of honor, but this does not have to be the case. No other attendants, except the *koumbáros(a)*, are required to be Orthodox.

RESPONSIBILITIES OF THE *KOUMBÁROS(A)*

The *koumbáros(a) stephanóni* the couple. *Stephánoma* is the act of exchanging the wedding crowns three times above the heads of the bride and groom during the service.

The *koumbáros(a)* should provide the following for the marriage ceremony (see explanations below):

- Proof of good standing in an Orthodox church (a letter from the parish priest)
- Marriage crowns (*stéphana*)
- Wedding tray layered with *kouféta* and rice
- Two candles
- Wedding rings (purchased by the couple)
- Gratuities to the priest, chanter, and sexton
- *Optional*: Wine goblet

Marriage Crowns (*Stéphana*)

The crowning of the bride and groom during the church ceremony is a highlight of the Orthodox service.

In most instances, the *koumbáros(a)* provides the *stéphana*. Selection of the *stéphana* is a matter of personal choice. Some *koumbári* buy the crowns without consulting the bride and groom. Others may go with the bride to the specialty shop and make the selection together.

Crown styles change frequently. The church requires only that they be round and joined together by ribbon. Traditional crowns are delicate and simple, a weaving of white wax flowers with beading and white leaves, linked together with a white satin ribbon (see *illustration*). They may be purchased through a Greek specialty store, a catalog, in Greece, or from an individual who makes them. Elaborate crowns are becoming more common, featuring intricate beading or metal work with designs that match the bride's gown. These can be quite expensive, however, and are not necessary. Some couples use their parents' *stéphana*, but most have their own for permanent display at home.

Wedding Tray

Put the *stéphana* on top of a tray covered with a single layer of *kouféta* and rice. The priest places the tray on a small table at the front of the church for the ceremony. The tray, usually the wedding gift from the *koumbáros(a)* to the couple, is traditionally made of silver and may include a tea and coffee service. This is changing, however, and less formal trays such as mirrored vanity sets and serving pieces make suitable wedding presents.

Candles

Decorating the candles is optional. These may be prepared at a Greek specialty store or made by tying large bows with streamers on the candles and attaching artificial flowers to them.

Gratuities

The *koumbáros(a)* customarily thanks the priest, chanter, and sexton for their services with a gratuity. Amounts vary with each parish.

Optional: Purchase of a wine goblet to be kept by the newlyweds is not required since the church provides the chalice used during the ceremony.

WEDDING GOWN AND HEADPIECE

Select a wedding gown or dress appropriate to the time and style of the wedding. Consult an American etiquette book. But keep in mind two Greek traditions during the ceremony: The *koumbáros(a)* simultaneously switches the *stéphana* three times above the heads of the bride and groom during the ceremony. The headdress should not interfere with the exchanging. Also, you will have to go around a table three times during the ceremony and may want to avoid a large, bulky dress.

Greek Americans from Constantinople write the names of unmarried female friends of the bride on the lining of the train or back hem of the wedding dress to bring them good luck in finding a husband. The names are in back of the bride, so that the friends will follow her footsteps to the altar!

In some areas of Greece it is traditional for the groom to buy the bride's entire wedding outfit. In Athens, brides usually rent modern gowns, but in remote villages elaborate native costumes are worn.

BRIDAL BOUQUET

In Epirus the bride's bouquet includes a tiny pair of scissors to cut the power of the evil eye from envious guests!

BONBONIÉRES

Bonboniéres (favors of *kouféta*), are given to guests after the wedding. The bride's parents usually provide them, but in some regions they are the responsibility of the *koumbáros(a)*. Traditionally, the bride and her bridesmaids make them together. Like the *bonboniéres* for a baptism, they can be simple, with netting and an interesting decoration or much more elaborate (see *illustration*). The almonds are always white and uneven in number, usually five or seven. Each family decides its own style and amount to spend. Traditionally each guest receives a favor, but it has become common practice at weddings to give one to female guests only. In Cyprus, *loukoúmia* (little sugar-covered shortbreads with almonds and hazelnuts in the center) are given for favors instead of *bonboniéres*.

Bonboniéres

There are numerous ways of distributing the *bonboniéres*. In the United States the newlyweds sometimes hand them out at the reception, or the bridesmaids may do so. The bride and groom go from table to table with a nicely decorated basket greeting their guests and distributing *bonboniéres*. If the wedding is large and time does not permit personal distribution, the *bonboniéres* may be left at the table place settings. Sometimes each favor has a card with the guest's name and table number on it. In this case, all the favors are placed on a general table outside the hall, and guests find their table assignments by picking up their favor.

MARRIAGE SERVICE

Language

The ceremony, lasting about forty-five minutes to one hour, may be performed in both Greek and English, in whatever combination is comfortable for the couple and the priest. However, the content and wording cannot be changed in any way. Modern "I do" vows are not part of the service and cannot be added. Neither can phrases be eliminated. Couples concerned about the wording, "Wives, be subject to your husbands," should understand that this is the Orthodox approach to marriage. According to church doctrine, the husband is the head of the household, but the mother has a revered position as the cornerstone of the family and is responsible for maintaining the family unit. According to a popular folk custom, if the bride can step on the groom's foot first while this passage is being read, she will be the head of the house!

Wedding Program

A printed program that explains the Orthodox service is very helpful to your guests. You may reprint the "Sacrament of Marriage" in this chapter or ask your priest to supply text. Also include in the program the names of the bride and groom, the date, time and place, the name of the priest, names and titles of the wedding party, and special performers such as musicians.

Music

The church likes to maintain a Greek Orthodox atmosphere throughout the ceremony. It requires, for example, that only the chanter provide responses to the priest. Any singers other than the chanter and any instruments other than the organ can be used only with permission of the diocesan bishop. It has become acceptable to play appropriate, non-Orthodox music while the guests arrive, during the wedding party entrance, and as the guests leave.

Church Decorations

Consult your priest about placement of flower arrangements and other decorations. The table with the *stéphana*, arranged by the priest, is the focal point. You may also want to consider using a decoration common in Greece: two candles joined with fabric to symbolize the uniting of the man and the woman. Place a large candle stand with lighted candles behind and on either side of the small *stéphana* table. Connect the two candles with a large white drapery and have a young child stand by each one throughout the ceremony. The bride keeps the material and may have it made into a dress, tablecloth, or any item she chooses.

COMMUNION

It is suggested the couple take communion the Sunday before the wedding, each in his or her respective church if one of the partners is not Orthodox. Communion is not given during the ceremony. The bride and groom drink wine from a common cup to commemorate the Biblical wedding in Cana.

WEDDING BED AND SHAVING THE GROOM

If convenient, single women friends of the bride (often the bridesmaids) prepare the wedding bed. An old custom is to roll a young child on the bed and then scatter *kouféta*, rice, and money on the top for wishes of fertility and good fortune. In some small Greek villages, the marriage bed is decorated and paraded around the village before the ceremony. In Cyprus, the groom's face is ritually shaved in his house by the other groomsmen on the day of the wedding.

WEDDING RECEPTION

Delicious food, a table laden with sweets, *bouzoúki* music, and lines of laughing dancers complete the day. Most wedding receptions are a combination of American and Greek food, music, and dancing. The music alternates between modern American songs, current Greek pop favorites, and folk music for dances like the *hasápiko* and the *kalamatianós*. Traditionally the Greek dancing begins with the bride leading a *kalamatianós* (if she wishes) with her husband next in line. Then the family members and close friends take turns "dancing the bride" by assuming the lead at the head of the line, starting with the father. The most popular wedding song is *"Oréa ine i Nyfi Mas"* ("Beautiful is our Bride"). In addition to the wedding cake, it is customary to have an assortment of Greek sweets including *baklavá* and *kourabiéthes*. Be sure to have the priest bless the food before eating. Add whatever American customs you wish — such as a receiving line, toasts by the best man and maid of honor, tossing the bride's bouquet — and enjoy!

AFTER THE WEDDING

PRESERVING THE MARRIAGE CROWNS — *STEPHANOTHÍKI*

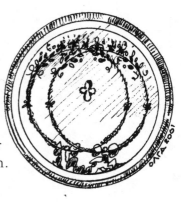

The *stéphana* are one of the most important symbols of the marriage. They remind the newlyweds that they are united in their own kingdom with the blessing of God, and they have a chance to build their own home and family together. The crowns deserve to be properly preserved. Place the crowns in the home *ikonostási* or in a special case called a *stephanothíki* (pron. *stephanoTHíki*).

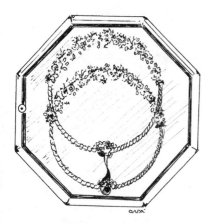

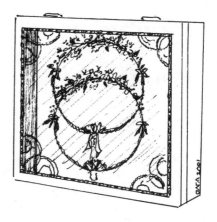

Stephanothíki

The case, handmade or purchased through a Greek specialty store or catalog, may be round, rectangular, or octagonal, made of wood with a glass front (see *illustration*). Some contain an electric light and an icon of the Virgin Mary inside. Keep the *stephanothíki* by the *ikonostási* or above the marriage bed.

In some places in Greece, the crowns are brought to the church after the wedding and left on the altar for eight days for a special blessing.

SUPERSTITIONS

Kouféta under the Pillow

It is said that a single woman will dream of her future husband if *kouféta* from a *bonboniéra* are put under her pillow. If *kouféta* from the wedding tray are placed under her pillow, her chances of finding a husband greatly improve — the Greek equivalent of catching the bouquet!

Preserving the Candle Wicks

At the end of the ceremony, cut the tips off the two candles from the table with the *stéphana*. These should be saved by the bride and groom. Some say that a jealous person can take them and cast *máya* on the couple, preventing consummation of the marriage.

SPECIAL SITUATIONS

MARITAL RELATIONS

Birth Control

The church leaves the decision to use birth control up to the couple but disapproves of any device that aborts life. The church maintains that the main purpose of sexual intercourse is procreation.

Abstinence

The church recommends abstinence from sex before communion and during Holy Week.

DIVORCE

The parish priest must exert every effort to reconcile the couple and avert a divorce. However, should he fail to bring about a reconciliation, after a civil divorce has been obtained, he will transmit the petition of the party seeking the ecclesiastical divorce, together with the decree of the civil divorce, to the Spiritual Court of the Diocese. The petition must include the names and surnames of the husband and wife, the wife's surname prior to marriage, their addresses, the name of the priest who performed the wedding, and the date and place of the wedding. The petitioner must be a member in good standing with the parish through which he or she is petitioning for divorce. Orthodox Christians of the Greek Orthodox Archdiocese who have obtained a civil divorce but not an ecclesiastical divorce may not participate in any sacraments of the Church or serve on the Parish Council, Diocesan Council or Archdiocesan Council until they have been granted a divorce by the Church.[4]

SECOND AND THIRD MARRIAGES

Second or third marriages are allowed by the church, but only if both civil and ecclesiastical divorces have been granted, or if a spouse has died. A fourth is forbidden. The wedding in such circumstances is usually handled in a subdued manner with less elaborate food and clothing. Even the marriage service is different and more somber. Check with your priest and an American etiquette book for the proper approach.

GUIDELINES FOR MARRIAGE IN THE GREEK ORTHODOX CHURCH

The following guidelines are excerpted from the Greek Orthodox Archdiocese of America's *Yearbook 2006*.[3] If you have any questions, consult your priest.

WEDDINGS

For the union of a man and woman to be recognized as sacramentally valid by the Orthodox Church, the following conditions must be met:

1. The Sacrament of Matrimony must be celebrated by an Orthodox Priest of a canonical Orthodox jurisdiction, according to the liturgical tradition of the Orthodox Church, in a canonical Orthodox Church, and with the authorization of the Archbishop or Metropolitan.

2. Before requesting permission from his Archbishop or Metropolitan to perform the marriage, the Priest must verify that: a) neither of the parties in question are already married to other persons, either in this country or elsewhere; b) the parties in questions are not related to each other to a degree that would constitute an impediment; c) if either or both parties are widowed, they have presented the death certificates(s) of the deceased spouse(s); d) if either or both of the parties have been previously married in the Orthodox Church, they have obtained ecclesiastical as well as civil divorce(s); e) the party or parties who are members of a parish other than the one in which the marriage is to be performed have provided a certificate declaring them to be members in good standing with that parish for the current year; and f) a civil marriage license has been obtained from civil authorities.

3. No person may marry more than three times in the Church, with permission for a third marriage granted only with extreme oikonomia.

4. In cases involving the marriage of Orthodox and non-Orthodox Christians, the latter must have been baptized, in water, in the Name of the Father and the Son and the Holy Spirit. The Church cannot bless the marriage of an Orthodox Christian to a non-Christian.

5. The Sponsor (koumbaros or koumbara) must provide a current certificate of membership proving him or her to be an Orthodox Christian in good standing with the Church. A person who does not belong to a parish, or who belongs to a parish under the jurisdiction of a bishop who is not in communion with the Greek Orthodox Archdiocese, or who, if married, has not had his or her marriage blessed by the Orthodox Church, if divorced, has not received an ecclesiastical divorce, cannot be a sponsor. Non-Orthodox persons may be members of the wedding party, but may not exchange the rings or crowns.

DAYS WHEN MARRIAGE IS NOT PERMITTED

Marriages are not performed on fast days or during fasting seasons or on the feasts of the Church as indicated: September 14 (Exaltation of the Holy Cross), December 13-25 (Nativity), January 5 and 6 (Theophany), Great Lent and Holy Week, Pascha (Easter), Pentecost, August 1-15 (Dormition Fast and Feast), and August 29 (Beheading of St. John the Baptist). Any exceptions are made only with the permission of the respective hierarch.

INTER-CHRISTIAN MARRIAGES

It is a fact that the more a couple has in common, the more likely they are to live together in peace and concord. Shared faith and traditions spare couples and their children, as well as their extended families, many serious problems and help to strengthen the bonds between them. Even so, the Orthodox Church will bless marriages between Orthodox and non-Orthodox partners, provided that:

1. The non-Orthodox partner is a Christian who has been baptized, in water, in the Name of the Father, and the Son, and the Holy Spirit.
2. The couple should be willing to baptize their children in the Orthodox Church and raise and nurture them in accordance with the Orthodox Faith.

A baptized Orthodox Christian whose wedding has not been blessed by the Orthodox Church is no longer in good standing with the Church, and may not receive the Sacraments of the Church, including Holy Communion, or become a Sponsor of an Orthodox Marriage, Baptism or Chrismation.

A non-Orthodox Christian who marries an Orthodox Christian does not thereby become a member of the Orthodox Church, and may not receive the Sacraments, including Holy Communion, or be buried by the Church, serve on the Parish Council, or vote in parish assemblies or elections. To participate in the Church's life, one must be received into the Church by the Sacrament of Baptism or, in the case of persons baptized with water in the Holy Trinity, following a period of instruction, by Chrismation.

INTER-RELIGIOUS MARRIAGE

Canonical and theological reasons preclude the Orthodox Church from performing the Sacrament of Marriage for couples where one partner is Orthodox and the other partner is a non-Christian. As such, Orthodox Christians choosing to enter such marriages fall out of good standing with their Church and are unable to actively participate in the life of the Church. While this stance may seem confusing and rigid, it is guided by the Orthodox Church's love and concern for its member's religious and spiritual well-being.

PROHIBITED MARRIAGES

The following types of relationships constitute impediments to marriage:

1. Parents with their own children, grandchildren or great grandchildren, or godchildren of the same parents.
2. Brothers-in-law with sisters-in-laws.
3. Uncles and aunts with nieces and nephews.
4. First cousins with each other.
5. Foster parents with foster children or foster children with the children of foster parents.
6. Godparents with godchildren or godparents with the parents of their godchildren.

[End of "Guidelines" Excerpt]

---

1. C. J. Joanides, *When You Intermarry: A Resource for Inter-Christian, Intercultural Couples, Parents and Families.* (New York: Greek Orthodox Archdiocese of America, 2002).
2. Harry Mark Petrakis, *Stelmark: A Family Recollection* (New York: David McKay Company, 1970), 21.
3. Greek Orthodox Archdiocese of America, *Yearbook 2006* (New York: Greek Orthodox Archdiocese of America, 2006), 272-273.
4. Ibid., 263.

CONFESSION

While men and women of the Orthodox faith can express their contrition to God and beg his forgiveness at anytime or in any place, this is not always effective. Therefore loving guidance and direction may be sought in the formal sacrament of confession (*exomológisis*).

THE SACRAMENT OF CONFESSION

A person in emotional turmoil because of sins committed may need to talk to someone on a higher spiritual level with a special degree of authority who will say, "You are forgiven." Jesus knew this human weakness and established the sacrament of confession after the Resurrection:

> "Peace be with you. As the Father has sent me, even so I send you." And when he had said this, he breathed on them, and said to them, "Receive the Holy Spirit. If you forgive the sins of any, they are forgiven; if you retain the sins of any, they are retained." John 20:21-22.

During a sacramental confession, the penitent and the priest are alone in the church, usually standing side by side before the icon of Christ at the *ikonostásion* (altar screen). The priest is a witness, not a judge, and is required to keep everything in strict confidence. Three basic elements are involved: recognition of the sins, repentance, and absolution. The penitent must confess all and completely repent before forgiveness can be granted.

After confession, kneel or bow your head so that the priest may put his hand and stole on your head while repeating the prayer of absolution:

> May God Who pardoned David through Nathan the Prophet when he confessed his sins, and Peter, weeping bitterly for his denial, and the sinful woman weeping at his feet, and the publican and the prodigal son, may that same God forgive you all things, through me a sinner, both in this world and in the world to come, and set you uncondemned before His terrible Judgment Seat. Having no further care for the sins which you have confessed, depart in peace.[1]

PRELIMINARIES

WHO CAN CONFESS AND TO WHOM

Only baptized Orthodox can participate in the sacrament of confession, starting at age seven. Ideally, confess to your own priest. However, if this makes you uncomfortable, arrange to see another.

WHAT AND WHEN TO CONFESS

Grave sins such as murder, apostasy (abandoning of one's belief), adultery, and transgressions that cause extreme discord in your relationship with other people and with God should be brought before a priest immediately. Other sins can be saved until your next confession, repented in your own prayers, or confessed during the Divine Liturgy.

The frequency of sacramental confession varies greatly, and the church has no strict rule regarding this. Once a year is the minimum, but more often is recommended. Many people choose the time of Great Lent, a period of reflection and cleansing. Confession is an integral part of taking communion, and should be said, either in private or to a priest, before receiving the Gifts (see "Private Confession" below).

Although it is one of the seven sacraments of the Orthodox church, sacramental confession before a priest is not widely practiced. Even some of the most devout do not participate, despite the fact that the church considers baptism, chrismation, confession, and communion essential for complete participation in the church.

PREPARATION

An honest self-examination is essential before confession with the priest. Two Greek words associated with confession, *metánia* and *exomológisis* (pron. *eksomológisis*), describe the process of introspection. *Metánia* means a "change of mind" and therefore repentance. You acknowledge both that you are wrong and that you have had a change in your heart and mind. *Exomológisis* means "expressing it in words," i.e., an unburdening of the soul.

PENANCE AND EXCOMMUNICATION

PENANCE

Penance is not a part of the sacrament of confession, but the priest may prescribe remedies such as fasting, charitable works, restraint from communion, or additional prayers.

EXCOMMUNICATION

The harshest punishment for the Orthodox Christian is excommunication, literally the breaking of communion. Communion and all other basic aspects of religious life such as being a godparent, sponsor at a marriage, and receiving a church funeral service are denied. One breaks communion with the faith by adopting another faith, like Islam or Judaism, or marrying outside the Orthodox church. The Greek Orthodox Archdiocese of America, however, considers each case separately and is very careful in imposing such a severe penalty.

Although the church appears to excommunicate, actually it is the sin of the unrepentant person that puts that person out of communion with the church. There is an ancient ritual of excommunication, but the church does not exercise that rite in modern times.

PRIVATE CONFESSION

Private confession occurs between the penitent and God, whenever you feel the need, at any time or place. This personal acknowledgement of sin is not a substitute for the sacrament of Holy Confession. However, you should always confess before taking communion. Follow carefully the Communion Prayer said during The Divine Liturgy after the priest pours water in the communion cup.

---

1. N. M. Vaporis, ed., *An Orthodox Prayer Book* (Brookline, Mass.: Holy Cross Orthodox Press, 1977), 136-137.

Receiving Communion

COMMUNION

The sacrament of communion is the most important act in the liturgical life of the church. Jesus asked his followers to remember him by participation in this dramatic ritual where the transformation of ordinary bread and wine into the actual parts of a sacred human body represents the greatest mystery of the Christian faith.

THE SACRAMENT OF COMMUNION

Communion is given at every Divine Liturgy and at the Liturgy of Presanctified Gifts. This reenactment of Christ's Last Supper with his disciples restores spirituality and renews faith. By partaking of the Body and Blood of Christ (Eucharist or Gifts), the faithful come closer to union with God (*théosis*).

While parishioners are kneeling during the Divine Liturgy, the Holy Spirit transforms the wine and bread into the Eucharist. After the priest takes communion, he stands at the altar gate with the chalice and invites parishioners to come forward by saying: "Approach with the fear of God, faith, and love."

Participants walk slowly toward the priest. Women should remove their lipstick. When you reach the priest, make the sign of the cross, and tell him your baptismal name. Hold the red cloth of the chalice under your chin as the priest puts the spoon containing the holy Gifts in your mouth. He will say: "The servant of God [baptismal name] receives the Body and Blood of Christ for forgiveness of sins and eternal life."

Hand the chalice cloth to the person behind you and make the sign of the cross again. Take bread from the altar boy and return to your seat.

PRELIMINARIES

ELIGIBILITY

Only baptized and chrismated Orthodox are eligible to take communion. Those who have committed extraordinary sins such as murder, adultery, and incest should consult with their priest before taking communion. Penance, including a period of abstinence from communion, may be required.

FREQUENCY

The frequency with which church members take communion has varied since the beginning of the church. For the first three hundred years every member took communion each time the Divine Liturgy was performed. However, participation declined as the worthiness of the individual was emphasized more. Later, to encourage participation, a canon was adopted in 1819 stating that the faithful should receive communion with each liturgy. Yet to this day, very few do. Why? Orthodoxy emphasizes the proper preparation of the individual to receive the holy Gifts, and strict compliance can be rigorous and inhibiting. (See "Preparation" below)

Most priests today encourage parishioners to partake more often and not feel compelled to comply with every custom of preparation such as formal confession to a priest. Thus, there has been increased participation over the widespread practice of taking communion four times a year in conjunction with the four major fasting periods in the church year: Christmas Lent, Great Lent, Holy Apostles Lent, and Dormition of the Mother of God Lent. Many parishioners take communion at a Divine Liturgy conducted during these fasting periods or on the feast day that ends the fast: the Easter Resurrection service (date varies), June 29 or 30 (Saints Peter and Paul or Holy Apostles), August 15 (The Dormition of the Mother of God), and December 25 (Christmas). In addition to these special days, parishioners should take communion as often as they wish after proper preparation.

PREPARATION

The Orthodox faith places great emphasis on the spiritual, emotional, and physical preparation to take communion. This is not a creation of the church but rather an apostolic directive, specifically passed to the church by St. Paul in his first epistle to the Corinthians.

> Whoever, therefore, eats the bread or drinks the cup of the
> Lord in an unworthy manner will be guilty of profaning the

Body and Blood of the Lord. Let a man examine himself, and so let him eat of the bread, and drink of the cup. For any one who eats and drinks without discerning the body eats and drinks judgment upon himself. I Cor. 11:27-29

Developing this directive, Father George Mastrantonis, a Greek-American priest, gives this advice in "Holy Communion, the Bread of Life":

Strengthen your belief in Communion. Apply the Christian principles of self control and sympathy for others; pray constantly; ask the Lord to guide you; avoid temptation; keep your stomach light, your mind sober, your flesh pure, your relations calm — humbly in the name of the Lord. Recognize your sins and avoid them — especially sins of neglect. Live in prayer, alms giving, forgiveness, and good will.[1]

Physical preparation for communion, specifically fasting, varies throughout the United States. All authorities agree that except in health-threatening situations, NO FOOD OR LIQUIDS MAY BE CONSUMED AFTER MIDNIGHT BEFORE TAKING COMMUNION, and social activities should be moderated the prior evening. However, some communicants follow a strict fast at least three days before receiving communion. Others fast every Wednesday and Friday, according to Orthodox tradition, and take communion frequently. (See *Fasting*) Consult with your parish priest. Before an evening service, church authorities request no food or water for six hours prior to communion. Ask forgiveness of those with whom you are in disharmony.

A controversial canon prohibits a woman from taking communion while she is menstruating. However, there is a movement within the church to change such thinking on "cleanliness." Most priests recommend that each woman decide for herself. Many women raised with this tradition are uncomfortable taking communion during that time, but many others are uncomfortable with the idea that menstruation renders a woman "unclean."

At one time, all makeup was prohibited, but today only lipstick is discouraged while taking communion. An unadorned face reflects the clean state of the mind and body prepared for the holy Gifts. From a practical standpoint, lipstick accumulates on the common spoon and chalice cloth, possibly offending fellow parishioners.

COMMUNION AT NON-ORTHODOX CHURCHES

Orthodox cannot take communion at non-Orthodox churches. Major differences in the faith prevent sharing of the common cup.

CONTRIBUTING TO THE EUCHARIST

The Orthodox church invites its members to contribute the bread (*prósforo*) and wine needed for the Eucharist. You may bring these items along with a list of names of living and deceased persons you would like the priest to commemorate in the Divine Liturgy. In the closing prayer of the preparation service (*proskomidí* — pron. *proskomithi*) during the *órthros* service and during the Divine Liturgy, the priest asks God to bless those who offered the gifts and those requested to be remembered.

You may want to bake the *prósforo* yourself — a satisfying and rewarding tradition. See *Religious Breads* for the recipe and special instructions. There are no specifications regarding the wine, except that it be red; a sweet dessert wine such as mavrodaphne is customary.

Be sure to notify the priest that you would like to bring the bread. The priest will need it before the *órthros* service that precedes the Divine Liturgy.

---

1. George Mastrantonis, "Holy Communion, The Bread of Life (St. Louis, Mo.: Ologos, n.d), 10.

HOLY UNCTION

Orthodox believe in the power of God to heal both the body and the spirit. In this sacrament, the Holy Spirit is invoked to bless olive oil, an ancient Greek balm, and the ill person is anointed. Most parishioners receive the sacrament once a year on Holy Wednesday of Holy Week, but it also may be administered privately.

THE SACRAMENT OF HOLY UNCTION

The sacrament of holy unction provides both physical and mental healing with holy oil (*efchéleon*) blessed by the Holy Spirit. The oil carries God's grace both to renew the body and to cleanse the spirit. The service follows the apostolic tradition mentioned in the Gospels. "...Let him call for the elders of the church, and let them pray over him, anointing him with oil in the name of the Lord; and the prayer of faith will save the sick man, and the Lord will raise him up; and if he has committed sins, he will be forgiven." James 5:14-15

The service is composed of Psalms from the Old Testament, hymns of direct supplication to God, and prayers to saints to intercede for the petitioner. In addition, there are seven readings from the Gospels preceded by seven other New Testament writings, notably the epistles of St. Paul and St. James. After each set of scriptural readings, a prayer is offered on behalf of the penitent by the priest asking for forgiveness and the sanctification of the oil.

At the end of the service, the priest puts holy oil on the forehead, cheeks, chin, and hands of the parishioner in the form of a cross, saying: "O Holy Father, physician of our souls and bodies, heal your servant [name] from every physical and emotional affliction."

Holy unction is a sacrament of great comfort to the faithful. It provides uplift and asks for patience to accept the will of God whatever the physical outcome. HOWEVER, IT SHOULD NOT BE USED AS A SUBSTITUTE FOR MEDICAL TREATMENT.

HOLY WEDNESDAY SERVICE

On Holy Wednesday of Holy Week, sick and healthy alike attend church to receive the sacrament of holy unction. Holy Week is a time of repentance, confession, and forgiveness. Parishoners must prepare themselves, ideally through confession, to receive the oil with a clean heart. At the end of the service, each parishioner walks to the front of the church, and the priest puts a small amount of holy oil on his or her head and hands as described above. The dispensing cotton swabs are collected in the back of the church to be disposed of in a proper manner. Consecrated oil should not be taken out of the church and dispensed by lay people. Holy Unction is a sacrament that only a priest can administer.

PRIVATE SERVICE

When a person is very ill — physically, mentally, or both — a private service can be held at any time at home, church, or hospital. If possible, the recipient should prepare with confession, repentance, and fasting (health permitting) to receive the sacrament with a pure heart and faith in the power of God to heal. The private service is conducted by one or more priests. In an earlier time, seven priests participated, but this requirement has been dropped for practical reasons.

Have ready for the priest on a table:
- An icon (preferably Christ or the Virgin Mary)
- A Bible
- A bowl containing five cups of flour
- Seven candles placed in the bowl of flour
- A lighted wick floating in olive oil
- Small measure of wine
- Incense
- Cotton balls or swabs

A shorter version of the Holy Wednesday service is performed; a candle is lit after each Gospel reading. The oil with the floating wick becomes holy oil, symbolizing the grace of God, and is used by the priest for anointing. You may want to thank the priest for his services with a small gift or remuneration.

After the service, the candles and floating wick should continue to burn until consumed. Dispose of the cotton properly by burying it or its ashes where no one will step on them. Do not put it in the garbage. Traditionally *prósforo* (bread for the holy communion) should be made from the flour and taken to church the following Sunday along with a list of names of living family members (including the sick individual) that you want remembered in the Divine Liturgy. If you ask the priest, he will save a portion of the *prósforo* for you. (See *Religious Breads* for recipe)

Greek Orthodox Clergy

HOLY ORDERS

Occasionally Americans see Orthodox holy men in full black regalia: a tall hat with veil, long beard, and flowing black robes. The effect is startling. As the figure floats among those in Western dress, an air of mysticism surrounds him. While few Orthodox priests in America today dress like this, they still have a spiritual aura and are respected by their people. As guardians and teachers of the Orthodox Christian faith, their induction into the priesthood is one of the most sacred rites of the church, bestowed by holy sacrament.

THE SACRAMENT OF HOLY ORDERS

The vital work of the church was begun by Christ who appointed twelve apostles to assist in the ministry of Christianity. Fifty days after his Resurrection, the apostles received the Holy Spirit at Pentecost to continue Christ's work. They in turn anointed others. This continuous line of holy men anointed by other holy men is known as the apostolic succession, a direct link with the original apostles, and one of the most important concepts in Orthodox priesthood. The sacrament of holy orders repeats this tradition.

Ordination in the service of God can be on various levels in the Orthodox church, major and minor. Members of a major order — bishop, priest, and deacon — are ordained during a Divine Liturgy by a bishop. During the service, a priest leads the candidate around the altar three times while hymns are sung. The candidate then kneels and rests his head on the altar. The bishop puts his stole and right hand over the candidate's head as the candidate receives the Holy Spirit. The entire congregation witnesses the ordination and proclaims its consent by shouting in unison, *Áxios!* (Worthy! — pron. *Áksios*) The bishop bestows sacred vestments on the new priest, who then receives communion and recites a special prayer.

Minor orders, including subdeacons, readers, chanters, and acolytes (altar boys), are ordained by a bishop outside the framework of a Divine Liturgy outside the sanctuary (altar area).

The elaborate ceremonial vestments worn by the church hierarchy lend dignity and solemnity to Orthodox services. The striking tall hat, a *kalimáfchion*, can be worn by all priests. Unmarried priests and bishops wear a veil over it making the hat an *epáno-kalimáfchion*. The tall hats, a carry-over from Byzantine society where they were worn by the clergy and laymen, are worn mainly by bishops in the United States, but are very common in Greece.

THE PRIESTHOOD

QUALIFICATIONS

Candidates for holy orders must have a firm faith, exemplary conduct, and theological training commensurate with their duties. Ordained positions are for males only. If priests and deacons marry, they must do so before being ordained. Only unmarried priests may become bishops.

Priests who have their own parishes must be well educated. In addition to an undergraduate degree, a graduate degree from an approved theological school is desired. It is the principle of the Greek Orthodox Archdiocese of America that its priests graduate from an Orthodox theological school, and the vast majority of its priests have done so. In the United States there is one Greek Orthodox theological school open to men and women, Holy Cross Greek Orthodox School of Theology, in Brookline, Massachusetts, under the Archdiocese. For additional Orthodox theological schools in America and around the world, see *The Historic Orthodox Church* — "Theological Schools, Seminaries, and Institutes."

RESPONSIBILITIES

Many demands are made on the local priest, who serves as a celebrator, educator, counselor, and administrator. As a representative of Christ, his religious responsibilities include preserving the correct faith, administering sacraments, conducting services, and educating his people about Orthodox tradition and living as good Christians. Parishioners look to him for advice and counsel about their daily lives. In addition, he must possess administrative, management, and political skills if his church is to run smoothly and successfully.

PRIESTS AND LAITY

RELATIONSHIP WITH PRIEST

Because of the emphasis on family in Orthodoxy, the priest becomes well acquainted with his parishioners and their personal lives. Parishioners invite him to their homes for special celebrations, such as the blessing at Epiphany or an engagement, and for parties or a simple dinner. Ideally the priest becomes a spiritual father, an old Orthodox tradition.

Traditionally, people stand when the priest enters a room, and kiss his right hand when greeting or receiving something from him. It is through his hands the sacraments are received. It has become customary for parishioners to give the priest remuneration or a small gift for personal services such as conducting a wedding, funeral, house blessing, etc.

PROPER FORMS OF ADDRESS

The following forms should be used when addressing the Ecumenical Patriarch and the clergy of the Greek Orthodox Archdiocese of America. Use the title in third-person situations such as addressing a letter or listing in a printed program. Use the salutation when speaking to the individual or as a greeting in a letter.[1]

His All Holiness [first name]
Archbishop of Constantinople and Ecumenical Patriarch
    Salutation: Your All Holiness

His Eminence Archbishop [first name]
Primate of the Greek Orthodox Church in America
    Salutation: Your Eminence

His Eminence Metropolitan [first name] of [name of metropolis]
Presiding Hierarch
Holy Metropolis of [United States location]
    Salutation: Your Eminence

The Right Reverend (Rt. Rev.) Bishop [first name] of [name of ancient see]
[Alternate title: His Grace Bishop [first name] of [ancient see]
    Salutation: Your Grace

The Very Reverend (V. Rev. Fr.) [first and last name] — (archimandrite)
    Salutation: Reverend or Father

Reverend Father (Rev. Fr.) [first and last name] — (priest)
    Salutation: Reverend or Father

Reverend Father (Rev. Dn.) [first and last name] — (deacon)
    Salutation: Reverend or Deacon

Since the Greek word for "priest" is *"presvytéros,"* his wife is called *"presvytéra."*

THE ROLE OF WOMEN IN THE CHURCH

Women have a limited official role in the Orthodox church. Their greatest limitation is exclusion from the priesthood. The church reinforces this position with various arguments. Since Jesus was a man, the priest should also be a man — the image or icon of Christ. Therefore when conducting the Divine Liturgy, culminating with communion, the priest must symbolically represent Jesus offering the Last Supper to his apostles. In addition, Christ chose men, not women, to be his disciples, establishing the tradition known as apostolic succession.

Advocates for changing this position argue that the essential icon image of Christ is his humanness, not his maleness. God became human to show that both men and women could be saved and return to the divine image within them. Challengers also point out that Christ did not ordain his apostles. This was done at Pentecost by the Holy Spirit. Women were present at the time, and the Holy Spirit continues to descend on male and females alike. The Orthodox church recognizes a number of women saints as apostles, including the "apostle to the apostles," Mary Magdalene. (See Eva Catafygiotu Topping, *Holy Mothers of Orthodoxy: Women and the Church*[2])

Orthodox women today are raising questions about the traditional role and status of women in the church in writings and conferences. Many conferences have been held, some exclusively dedicated to the issues of women and others with those matters as part of a broader agenda. The first to be held was the "Consultation on the Role and Participation of Women in the Orthodox Church" in Agapia, Romania, in 1976. In Rhodes, Greece, in 1988, at the "Inter-Orthodox Theological Consultation" of the fourteen autocephalous and anonymous Orthodox churches convened by the Ecumenical Patriarchate of Constantinople, the Consultation declared that it did not foresee the ordination of women as priests and bishops, but "formally and unanimously advocated the restoration of the order of the women deacons."[3] A Second International Women's Consultation was held in 1990 in Crete and another major consultation in 1997 in Constantinople. Conferences with various groups dealing with a variety of subjects take place almost yearly.

Significantly, in 2004 the Church of Greece restored the order of the diaconate for women, although no women have been ordained yet. In Greece nuns will be the first women to serve, but it is expected that other qualified women will eventually be ordained. As with male deacons, ordination will take place in the altar area duing a Divine Liturgy. A deaconess' ministry will include instructing and guiding others in the Christian faith, helping with social and pastoral care, and bringing Holy Communion to members unable to participate in the Divine Liturgy. For historical background on the participation by women as deacons, apostles, evangelists and teachers read *The Female Diaconate* by Matushka Ellen Gvosdev[4] and *Women Deacons in the Orthodox Church* by Kyriaki Karidoyanes FitzGerald.[5] Their work has contributed to the momentum in Greece and the United States to reinstitute the order.

MONASTIC ORDERS

The monks and nuns of the Orthodox church take special vows and occupy a unique position within the church. Each monk and nun strives to achieve union with God through prayer, fasting, poverty, and celibacy, undistracted by the temptations of the secular world.

St. Anthony, the father of Orthodox monastic life, lived in the third and fourth centuries. He is typical of the anchorite monk who lives alone but comes together with others for work and worship. The cenobitic monks reside and worship in organized monasteries as defined by St. Basil. Solitary monks (eremites or hesychasts) live completely alone in isolation. The largest and most famous Orthodox center of monasticism is at Mt. Athos, Greece, with twenty active monasteries.

---

1. Greek Orthodox Archdiocese of America, *Yearbook 2006* (New York: Greek Orthodox Archdiocese of America, 2006), 275.

2. Eva Catafygiotu Topping, "Orthodox Women and the Iconic Image of Christ," and "Orthodox Eve and the Royal Priesthood," 103, in *Holy Mothers of Orthodoxy: Women and the Church* (Minneapolis: Light and Life Publishing Company, 1987).

3. Kyriaki Karidoyanes FitzGerald, *Women Deacons in the Orthodox Church: Called To Holiness and Ministry* (Brookline, Massachusetts: Holy Cross Orthodox Press, 1998), 162.

4. Matushka Ellen Gvosdev, *The Female Diaconate: An Historical Perspective* (Minneapolis: Light and Life Publishing Company, 1991).

5. Kyriaki Karidoyanes FitzGerald, *Women Deacons in the Orthodox Church.*

St. George the Great Martyr

✤ *Saints*

Icons of saints with penetrating eyes and flowing robes dominate the interior of Orthodox churches. Infants receive the names of saints at their baptisms, and festivals celebrate saints' feast days. To the Greek Orthodox, saints are extended family with whom to share worship, holidays, and intimate moments.

SAINTS AS MODELS AND PROTECTORS

Saints serve as examples of the heights each individual can reach. They are human beings who have achieved a goal that seemed unattainable, people who tried to imitate the life of Christ. Just as Christ was not held back by adversity and hurdles but continued walking the road set by God, so the saints accepted with patience all adversities to reach their goal, union with Christ (*théosis*). For this the saints not only receive honor and recognition in the Christian community but serve as models to a Christian person.

Saints also protect and assist the faithful like extended family. Just as you might turn to a family member for help and guidance, you may pray to a saint for assistance. The saint intercedes on your behalf with God, acting as a petitioner and a defender. This tradition comes from the Orthodox belief that everyone, here and in heaven, is a vital part of the family of God.

CHOOSING SAINTS

Generally, there are three main categories of Orthodox saints: martyrs who died for Christianity; ascetics such as nuns and monks; and men and women who were major figures in church history. Today, an Orthodox saint is chosen by a special committee that studies, searches, prays for guidance, checks every detail of a candidate's life, and looks for signs of holiness after death. Then the Ecumenical Patriarchate in Constantinople issues a special letter to recognize the person, making him or her a saint.

One of the most recent saints is St. Nektarios, who died in 1920 and was canonized in 1961. A noted writer and educator, he founded the Convent of the Holy Trinity for nuns on the Greek island of Aegina. His shrine there at St. Nektarios chapel at the convent is the object of many pilgrimages for healing and miracles. When near his tomb, believers smell a beautiful fragrance, a sign of his holiness.

Another sign of saintliness is the preservation of the body after death without embalming. For example, the body of St. Spyridon who lived in the fourth century is still intact without artificial means in St. Spyridon Cathedral in Corfu, Greece. Nuns and monks are usually buried in the ground in a shroud only, and their condition is revealed after exhumation in three years.

PATRON SAINTS

A patron saint is someone with special significance for you, your family, organization, cause, or city. For a family, it is often the saint for whom the head of the house is named. An organization may choose a saint who is helpful to its cause. For example, St. Basil Academy, a residential childcare center in New York, is so named because St. Basil founded the world's first orphanage and was famous for his philanthropic work with poor children.

The Orthodox believe that saints can intercede with God for general and specific concerns. Sometimes God works through them to perform miracles, especially healing. The faithful may pray directly to a specific patron saint for help in a specific situation.

ILLNESSES	SAINTS
Birthmarks	St. Symeon
Childbirth	St. Eleftherios
Eye disease	St. Paraskevi
Fertility	St. Anna
Headaches	St. Paraskevi
Illness (general)	Ss. Cosmas and Damian (best known)
	St. Nektarios
	St. Panteleimon
	St. Spyridon the Miracle Worker
Retarded and incurable children	St. Marina

SPECIAL SITUATIONS

Children	St. Basil the Great
	St. Nicholas
	St. Stylianos
Crops	St. Demetrios the Great Martyr
Education	The Three Hierarchs:

- St. Basil the Great
- St. Gregory the Theologian
- St. John Chrysostom

Godparents	St. John the Baptist
Lost property	St. Phanourios
Orphans	St. Basil the Great
Peace	St. Irene
Pious parents	Ss. Joachim and Anna
Poor	St. Basil the Great
	St. George the Great Martyr
Rain, thunder and lightning	St. Elias the Prophet
Roads	St. Barbara
Sailors	St. Nicholas
Scholars	St. Katherine
Shepherds	St. Demetrios the Great Martyr
	St. George the Great Martyr
Warriors	St. George the Great Martyr
	St. Procopius
	St. Theodore Tyron
	St. Theodore Stratilates

INTERACTING WITH SAINTS

TÁMA (VOW)

A *táma* is a combined prayer and vow to a saint. As you pray for help, you promise to give or do something. For example, you may ask for protection during a storm or for the cure of an illness. In turn you vow, for example, to give money to the church or help someone in need. (See *Birth* and *Special Blessings, Prayers, and Appeals.*)

WAYS TO HONOR SAINTS

The Orthodox honor their saints through prayers, icons, and special observances.

Prayers and Prayer Services

Saints are praised and prayed to frequently. A prayer service *(paráklisis)* for a specific saint may be offered, particularly those known to perform miracles, such as St. Paraskevi for healing eyes. Make arrangements with your priest. The two most popular services, the Great Paraklisis and the Small Paraklisis, honor the Virgin Mary, during the first fifteen days of August. (See *Special Blessings, Prayers, and Appeals*)

Veneration of Icons

Saints are represented on icons that are venerated and handled with great respect. (See *Icons* and *The Church of the Home*)

Feast Days

Both the church and individuals honor the saints on their feast days. Celebrations include going to a church service, attending a name day party, baking bread for communion or for an *artoklasía* service, baking sweets, attending a festival, or observing regional customs.

Relics in Church Altars

Relics of a saint (vestments and/or remains) are usually buried in the altar of each Orthodox church. During the consecration of a church, a bishop conducts an elaborate service to sanctify the altar where the Eucharist is performed. The bishop places in a small crypt, usually in the center of the altar, a box made of gold or silver containing relics of a saint and then seals it. This tradition derives from the practice of using tombs of the early Christian martyrs as eucharistic tables.

Roadside Shrines in Greece

While traveling in Greece, you may notice shrines the size of birdhouses that contain icons, incense, and *kandíli*. These are usually erected by the side of a road where a life has been spared during an accident. The shrine honors a saint who may have helped save an individual. It may also be erected in memory of someone who died. You are welcome to stop at the shrine, venerate the icons, and light the *kandíli*.

Naming after Saints

The church encourages its parishioners to name their children after an Orthodox saint, a significant feast day, or a Christian symbol, such as the cross (*stavrós*). The patron saint provides the individual a role model and protector for life. (See *Selecting a Name*)

WELL-KNOWN SAINTS OF THE GREEK ORTHODOX CHURCH

Listed below are some of the most celebrated saints for whom Greek Americans are named. The brief list includes basic information each individual should know about his or her patron saint. The name day is the one most frequently celebrated. Some of the information may conflict with what you have heard because historical records for early Christians are not completely accurate or consistent. The dates of death and some of the information on relics come from the writings of George Poulos, author of numerous books on Orthodox saints.[1]

Only proper names are listed even though nicknames are very common. For example, "Tasios" and "Stacy" are short for "Anastasios." Note that three times as many male saints as female saints are listed. A woman's name is frequently a feminization of a male saint's name, such as "Demetra" for "Demetrios." For more information about female saints see *Saints and Sisterhood: The Lives of Forty-eight Holy Women* by Eva Catafygiotu Topping.[2]

St. Alexander

Name Day: August 30

Alexander lived in the third and fourth centuries and is known for his successful opposition to Arius, a man who heretically preached that Christ was inferior to God the Father.

Greek: Alexandra (f) and Alexandros (m)

English: Alexandra (f) and Alexander (m)

Anastasios

Name Day: Easter (moveable)

Anastasios means "one who shall rise again" or "of the Resurrection," referring to the church's most important feast day, Easter.   Numerous saints (male and female) are named after this great event, but the name day most commonly celebrated is Easter.

Greek: Anastasia (f) and Anastasios (m)

English: Anastasia (f) and Anastasios (m)

St. Andrew the Apostle (*Protóklitos*)

Name Day: November 30

St. Andrew   (*Protóklitos* — first chosen) was the first apostle selected by Christ.   A vigorous orator, he converted thousands to Christianity in Greece, Asia Minor, and Byzantium and was crucified upside down on an X-cross in Patras in the first century.   Patron saint of Patras, Greece, and Cyprus

Relics: Mt. Athos; Cathedral of St. Andrew, Patras, Greece

Greek: Andreana (f) and Andreas (m)

English: Andrea (f) and Andrew (m)

St. Anna

Name Day: December 9

St. Anna is the mother of the Virgin Mary.   This date honors her conception, but she is also honored with her husband, St. Joachim, on September 9, and on her date of death, July 25. Together they are known as the saints of pious education for the religious instruction they provided their daughter. St. Anna is also the patron saint of fertility.

Relics: Mt. Athos; Island of Patmos; Tomb in the Garden of Gethsemane in Jerusalem

Greek: Anna (f) (no masculine)

English: Anna (f) (no masculine)

St. Anthony the Great

Name Day: January 17

St. Anthony is considered the father of monastic life. He sold everything he owned and lived alone in the Egyptian desert until many followers settled nearby and emulated his example of asceticism. He formed the first monastery and died at the age of 105 in 356 A.D.

Greek: Antonia (f) and Antonios (m)
English: Antonia (f) and Anthony (m)

St. Athanasios the Great

Name Day: January 18

St. Athanasios, Patriarch of Alexandria, was influential in defining the early doctrines of the Christian faith, especially the belief that Christ is one in essence *(homoousis)* with the Father. Although exiled ten times for his beliefs, he died peacefully in 373 A. D.

Relics: Mt. Athos; St. John Monastery, near Dimitsana (Northwest of Tripoli, Peloponnesus)
Greek: Athanasia (f) and Athanasios (m)
English: Athanasia (f); Athan and Arthur (m)

St. Barbara

Name Day: December 4

St. Barbara was an intelligent, beautiful woman who was kept in seclusion in a tower by her father. When he discovered her conversion to Christianity, she was violently tortured, but Christ appeared to her in jail and healed her wounds. Refusing to accept the Roman pagan idols, she was subsequently beheaded by her father in the third century. St. Barbara is the patron saint of roads.

Relics: Rousanou Monastery, Meteora; Kechrovounion, Tinos
Greek: Barbara (f) (no masculine)
English: Barbara (f) (no masculine)

Saints Constantine and Helen

Name Day: May 21

St. Constantine the Great was the first Roman Emperor to be converted to Christianity after seeing a cross in the sky saying, "In this sign you shall conquer." His Edict of Milan in 313 sanctioned religious tolerance, ending the persecutions of Christians. In 330 he moved the capital from Rome, renamed it Constantinople, and established the Byzantine empire. He convened the First Ecumenical Council that laid the basis for Christianity's beliefs with the first seven articles of the Nicene Creed. Although he died in 337, and his mother, St. Helen, died in 338, they share the same feast day.

Relics: Mt. Athos; Panagia Tourliane Monastery, Mykonos; St. John of Ipselou Monastery, Mitilini

Greek: Konstantina (f) and Konstantinos (m)

English: Constance (f) and Constantine (m)

St. Helen, the mother of St. Constantine, made a pilgrimage to Jerusalem where she discovered, under a sweet basil plant, the cross on which Christ was crucified. She erected a shrine there and churches over Christ's tomb, his birthplace, the mountain of Ascension (Mt. of Olives), and a monastery at Mt. Sinai. She is considered one of the most important female saints in the church. She was born in 255 and died in 328.

Greek: Eleni (f) (no masculine)

English: Helen and Elaine (f) (no masculine)

St. Demetrios the Great Martyr

Name Day: October 26

St. Demetrios, an officer in the Roman army, was put into prison for converting soldiers to Christianity in Thessaloniki in the early fourth century. He urged his friend, Nestor, to fight a famous gladiator and prove that, through prayer, the power of God could make him victorious. When Nestor killed the gladiator, the emperor was so angry, he ordered both Nestor and Demetrios executed. For many in Greece, October 26 also signifies the end of summer when the shepherds come down from the hills for the winter. St. Demetrios is the patron saint of shepherds, crops, and the city of Thessaloniki.

Relics: Mt. Athos; St. Demetrios Church, Thessaloniki; procession and celebration in Thessaloniki on October 26

Greek: Demetra (f) and Demetrios (m)

English: Demetra (f); Demetri and James (m)

St. Elias (Elijah) the Prophet
Name Day: July 20

Elias lived in the ninth century B.C. and was one of the greatest prophets of the Old Testament. He is most renowned for convincing the Israelites to stop worshiping the God of nature, Baal, and return to one true God. He was taken to heaven in a chariot, and thunder and lightning are said to be St. Elias traveling across the sky in his chariot. He is the patron saint of rain, thunder, and lightning.

Pilgrimages: Chapels on mountain tops throughout Greece, especially at Mt. Taygetus near Sparta.

Greek: Elias (m) (no feminine)
English: Elias and Louis (m) (no feminine)

Evangelismos (Annunciation)
Name Day: March 25

On March 25 the church celebrates the Evangelismos, the Annunciation to the Virgin Mary that she will be the Mother of God. Many men and women are named for this event and most celebrate their name day on this date.

Greek: Evangelia (f) and Evangelos (m)
English: Evangeline (f); Evan and Angelo (m)

St. George the Great Martyr
Name Day: April 23 (If during Holy Week, celebrate the first Monday after Easter.)

This saint, one of the most popular, dared to be a Christian in the Roman army. A popular myth says he slew a dragon just before a princess was about to be sacrificed to it — thus St. George is frequently depicted on a horse with a lance and dragon. He is seen as a defender of good over evil. St. George was tortured and beheaded in 303. He is famous for healing and is the patron saint of the poor, shepherds, and warriors.

Relics: Mt. Athos; Church of the Metamorphosis, Plaka, Athens; Benaki Museum

Greek: Georgia (f) and Georgios (m)
English: Georgia (f) and George (m)

St. Gregory the Theologian
Name Day: January 25

St. Gregory is one of the great church fathers who built the foundations of the Orthodox faith. While Patriarch of Constantinople, he presided over the Second Ecumenical Council in which the Nicene Creed was completed. He was born in 329 and died in 390. He is known as the patron saint of education along with St. Basil the Great and St. John Chrysostom.

Relics:	Mt. Athos; Church of Evangelismos, Peristeri, Athens; St. Stephen Monastery, Meteora
Greek:	Gregoria (f) and Gregorios (m)
English:	Gregoria (f) and Gregory (m)

St. Helen (see Saints Constantine and Helen)

St. John the Baptist
Name Day: January 7

St. John, an ascetic and great prophet, baptized Christ and became one of the most revered saints in the Greek Orthodox church. He was later beheaded by Herod in the first century to satisfy the request of his stepdaughter, Salome, and wife Herodias. Because he baptized Christ, he is the patron saint of godparents.

Relics:	St. Demetrios Church, Neo Phaleron, Piraeus; Benaki Museum, Athens; Topkapi Museum, Constantinople; Umayyad Mosque in Damascus, Syria
Greek:	Ioanna (f) and Ioannis (m)
English:	Joanna (f) and John (m)

St. Katherine
Name Day: November 25

St. Katherine is renowned for her intellect, wisdom, and persuasive oratory. A princess in Alexandria and highly educated in the classics and Christian theology, she was ordered at age eighteen by Emperor Maxentius to worship the Olympian gods. She refused to do so and at her trial debated at least fifty philosophers, converting all of them to Christianity. Placed in jail, she converted the empress and many soldiers. Tortured on a wheel, she was released by an angel, but was eventually beheaded in 311. St. Katherine is the patron saint of scholars.

Relics:	St. Nicholas Church, Kato Patissia, Athens; Zerbitsa Monastery, Sparta; St. Katherine Monastery at Mt. Sinai, Egypt
Greek:	Ekaterini (f) (no masculine)
English:	Katherine (f) (no masculine)

Mary (Panayia)

Name Day: August 15

The Virgin Mary is the mother of our Lord God and Savior Jesus Christ and the most highly honored and beloved saint. She has four names in the Greek Orthodox church: Theotokos (Mother of God), Panayia (All Holy), Aiparthenos (Ever Virgin), and Despina (Our Lady). August 15 is one of the most important church holidays.

Pilgrimage sites:
- Mary's tomb at the foot of the Mount of Olives, Jerusalem
- Miraculous icon at the Church of the Evangelistria on the island of Tinos

Greek: Maria, Panayiota, and Despina (f); Panayiotis (m)
English: Mary and Maria (f); Panayiotis (m) and Peter (popular but incorrect)

Saints Michael and Gabriel (the Archangels)

Name Day: Nov. 8

Saints Michael and Gabriel are the two archangels of God. St. Michael is popularly believed to conduct souls to God after death. St. Gabriel announced the Virgin birth to the Theotokos. Gabriel is not a common Greek name.

Pilgrimage: Miraculous icon at the Panormitis Monastery on the Dodecanese island of Simi

Greek: Michailia (f) and Mihael (m)
English: Michele (f) and Michael (m)

St. Nicholas

Name Day: December 6

Bishop of Myra in Lycia (now southeast Turkey) in the fourth century, St. Nicholas was tortured and imprisoned for his faith. But with the ascendancy of Constantine and the toleration of Christianity, he attended the First Ecumenical Council. He was admired for his love of giving presents to poor children and families. In northern Europe, Santa Claus became the name for St. Nicholas. St. Basil is also known for giving gifts; it is on St. Basil's name day in Greece, not Christmas, when gifts are given to children. St. Nicholas is the patron saint of children and sailors.

Relics: Mt Athos; Barlaam Monastery, Meteora; St. Nicholas Monastery, Vlasia (Peloponnesus); St. Nicholas Cathedral, Bari, Italy
Greek: Nicoleta (f) and Nikolaos (m)
English: Nicole (f) and Nicholas (m)

St. Paul the Apostle

Name Day: June 29

St. Paul was the greatest missionary of the church. Formerly a fervent Jew named Saul, he was converted to Christianity by a blinding light on the road to Damascus and proceeded to convert thousands to Christ. His extensive writings (almost half of the New Testament) have greatly influenced Christian thought. He is considered by some to be the single most influential Christian after Christ himself. A "pillar of the church," he was beheaded in Rome circa 67.

Relics: St. John Monastery, Patmos; Taxiarchon Monastery, Digiatia (Peloponnesus)

Greek: Pavlos (m) (no feminine)

English: Paula (f) and Paul (m)

St. Peter the Apostle

Name Day: June 29 (popularly celebrated August 15)

St. Peter is considered the leader of Christ's apostles. He conducted an extensive ministry and founded the church in Antioch and Rome. He is popularly known as "the rock" for the firm foundation he gave Christianity. He fearlessly proclaimed God's word and baptized three thousand people on Pentecost.

Relics: Mt. Athos; St. Nicholas Church, Chalandri, Athens; Eisodia Monastery, Oblon (Peloponnesus)

Greek: Petroula (f) and Petros (m)

English: Petroula (f) and Peter (m)

St. Sophia

Name Day: September 17

St. Sophia had three daughters, Faith, Hope (Elpitha), and Love (Agape). In the second century, her daughters, ages nine, ten and twelve, were thrown into a boiling vat of tar and asphalt by the Emperior Hadrian. The emperor then had them beheaded. The mother prayed for her own death, died, and was buried next to her daughters. Women named Elpitha and Agape also celebrate this name day. (Churches named St. Sophia [Holy Wisdom] celebrate their feast day the Monday after Pentecost, not on September 17).

Greek: Sophia (f) (no masculine)

English: Sophia (f) (no masculine)

St. Spyridon the Miracle Worker

Name Day: December 12

St. Spyridon was a simple shepherd from Cyprus who had no formal education. He memorized the Bible, however, and became a bishop who attended the First Ecumenical Council. Many miracles have been attributed to him, including healing the Emperor Constantine. A patron saint of illness, it is believed that he often leaves the church at night to perform miracles for those who invoke his name. It is said that the shoes by his casket are periodically worn out from his travels and have to be changed each year. He died in the mid-fourth century.

Relics:	St. Spyridon Cathedral, Kerkyra, Corfu. Casket opened by special request, and pieces of his slippers may be purchased. Procession and celebration on December 12.
Greek:	Spiridoula (f); Spyridon and Spiros (m)
English:	Spiridoula (f); Spyridon and Spiros (m)

Stavros

Name Day: September 14 (The Exaltation of the Holy Cross)

"Stavrós" means "cross," the most important symbol in all of Christianity. Many people are named after this symbol and celebrate their name day in commemoration of St. Helen's discovery on September 14, 325, of the true cross on which Christ was crucified. The return of the captured cross from the Persians to Constantinople in the seventh century is also remembered at this time.

Relics:	To prevent its capture again, the cross was split and taken to Mt. Athos, Rome, Alexandria, Constantinople, and Antioch. Other churches claim splinters also.
Greek:	Stavroula (f) and Stavros (m)
English:	Stavroula (f) and Stavros (m)

St. Stephen the Protomartyr

Name Day: December 27

St. Stephen the Protomartyr, the first Christian martyr and deacon, was stoned to death in the year 36 in Jerusalem. He was one of seven assistants to the apostles in their ministry.

Relics:	Mt. Athos; Kykko Monastery, Cyprus; St. Stephen Monastery, Meteora
Greek:	Stephania (f) and Stephanos (m)
English:	Stephanie (f) and Stephen (m)

St. Theodore

Name Day: Third Saturday of Souls (first Saturday of Lent — moveable)

The church honors two Theodores on this Saturday along with the miracle of the *kóllyva* (boiled wheat). Theodore Tyron and Theodore Stratilates both appeared in a vision to a Patriarch in the fourth century, warning him of contamination of the food for Lent and urging the Christians to eat boiled wheat instead. (See *Easter Season*) Some individuals celebrate the fixed name days: Theodore Tyron (February 17) or Theodore Stratilates (February 8).

Relics: Meteora Monastery, Meteora; St. Bessarion, Pyli (Thessaly); Nea Moni Monastery, Chios

Greek: Theodora (f) and Theodoros (m)

English: Theodora (f) and Theodore (m)

All Saints Day

Date: Sunday after Pentecost (moveable)

If you are unable to find the name day for a specific saint, celebrate on All Saints Day when every saint in the church is honored.

---

1. George Poulos, *Orthodox Saints: Spiritual Profiles for Modern Man,* 4 vols., (Brookline, Mass.: Holy Cross Orthodox Press, 1976-82), and *Lives of the Saints and Major Feast Days* (1981; reprint, Brookline, Mass.: Greek Orthodox Archdiocese of North and South America, 1989).

2. Eva Catafygiotu Topping, *Saints and Sisterhood: The Lives of Forty-eight Holy Women* (Minneapolis: Light and Life Publishing Company, 1990).

⚜ *Name Days*

Many Greek Americans describe with nostalgia the old days when family members and friends gathered together to celebrate a name day. Along with Easter and Christmas, name days were among the most joyous occasions in the family, especially the name day of the male head of the family. The name day, not the birthday, was remembered.

Name day celebrations gave the immigrants a continuity with the customs of Greece. A typical party in Greece, even today, is an open house with different kinds of food and drink, especially brandy. An invitation is not required. For example, on St. Basil's name day (January 1) every household with a member named Basil, celebrates. One simply drops by different homes to wish the honoree, *"Chrónia pollá"* ("Many years").

Such spontaneous visits are the exception in America. If a name day party is held here, guests attend by invitation only. Perhaps a greater appreciation of the name day's significance will revive the joyous tradition of celebrating name days.

Chrónia Pollá

RELIGIOUS SIGNIFICANCE

A person's name day is the feast day of a major church event or of the saint for whom he or she was named. In most cases the feast day is the anniversary of the saint's death. This tradition began during the first century when Christians prayed to God in the catacombs on the anniversary of the martyr's death, thanking God for the martyr's example and asking him through the saint's intercessions to guide and direct their lives. Frescoes depicting such gatherings still exist in some of the catacombs. According to the church, saints come to earth on their name days. A common bond exists among people with the same name and guardianship by the same saint. The people are *synonómati*, sharers of the same first name.

CELEBRATING IN AMERICA

WHEN TO CELEBRATE

If named after a church event, such as Anastasi, celebrate on the feast day of the event. If named after a saint, the name day to celebrate may not be as obvious. Saints with the same name may be celebrated on different days. How do you know which day to observe? Most people remember the name day of the person for whom they were named. For example, a *yiayiá* and her granddaughter with the same name would remember the same day.

If your family does not keep this tradition, check the alphabetical listing in *Saints* or the chronological listing below. If your saint is not listed, talk with your priest or check an Orthodox calendar and reference books. Be careful when selecting the date. Over the years, social and church tradition favor one saint over another. For example, there are approximately fifty saints named "John," but most people with that name celebrate January 7, the Feast Day of St. John the Baptist. You can, however, choose another St. John, such as one from your region of Greece, and be perfectly in order with the church.

Women named after male saints usually celebrate on the male name days. Women named "Georgia" and "Alexandra" remember April 23 and August 30, respectively. However, there was a St.

Georgia (August 11) and a St. Alexandra (April 21). Those name days could be used instead, and there are hundreds of women saints from whom to choose.

Sometimes there are different celebration days for the same saint. For example, the majority of Orthodox remember the Virgin Mary on August 15 (The Dormition of the Mother of God), but a few choose to celebrate her name day on September 8 (The Nativity of the Mother of God).

If determining the name day becomes too complicated or the information cannot be found, celebrate on All Saints Day — a time when every saint in the Greek Orthodox church is honored. This is a moveable date, the Sunday after Pentecost.

WHAT TO SAY

Wish the celebrant either: *"Chrónia pollá"* ("Many years") or *"Ke tou chrónou"* ("And to next year").

WAYS TO CELEBRATE

Attend Church

Divine Liturgies are celebrated for the well-known saints. A church will always hold a service for its patron saint, and you are welcome to attend those services. If a special service is not conducted nearby, attend church on the nearest Sunday to the name day and take communion.

Make a Phone Call

Today most name days are remembered with a simple phone call and a wish of *"Chrónia pollá"* or *"Ke tou chrónou."*

Have a Party

Parties are usually by invitation and range from an open house with appetizers and sweets to a sit-down dinner.

Bake Bread or Sweets

Make bread for communion or the *artoklasía* service. (See *Religious Breads* for details and recipes.) Some people also make sweets for the church coffee hour following services.

Take your Godchild to Church

If it is your godchild's name day, attend church together and discuss the life of the saint.

Attend a Church Festival or Celebration

A church may hold a Greek festival in honor of its name day. This is a replica of the festival (*paniyíri*) that most small villages in Greece hold on a name day. Typically there is an abundance of Greek food and dancing. Many churches also give dances or dinners.

Decorate Icons

Some parishioners place a single flower or small bouquet by the saint's icon at church and at home.

CELEBRATING IN GREECE

PILGRIMAGE TO CHURCH

Many Greeks and Greek Americans make pilgrimages to churches in Greece where the relics of saints are kept. Relics (the body, bones, or vestments of saints) are believed to emit God's grace and have healing powers. Pilgrimages may also be made to locations where a miracle involving the saint is said to have taken place. (See *Visiting Greece*)

ATTEND A *PANIYÍRI*

Find a village, town or church celebrating its name day with a *paniyíri*. The festival usually lasts three days in the *platía* (town square) with Greek food, music, and dancing at its best! Many who have moved away from the village come back at this time as a homecoming. Sometimes major cities will also hold special celebrations. For example, Thessaloniki, the second largest city in Greece, honors its patron saint, St. Demetrios, on his feast day, October 26, with a procession of his relics through the streets. A similar celebration takes place for St. Spyridon on December 12 in Corfu.

GREEK SECULAR CUSTOMS

Many secular customs are observed on saints' name days. For example, shepherds traditionally break winter camp on St. George's day. In the villages of northern Greece on January 18, St. Athanasios Day, no work is done because it is considered bad luck. On July 17, St. Marina's Day, at Metrae, Thrace, the villagers cut the first bunch of grapes of the season.

POPULAR NAME DAYS

People usually celebrate the following name days (see "When to Celebrate" above):

September 14	Stavroula/Stavros [from *stavrós* (cross) — Exaltation of the Holy Cross]
September 17	Sophia (St. Sophia)
October 26	Demetra/Demetri and James (St. Demetrios the Great Martyr)
November 8	Michele/Michael (Saints Michael and Gabriel the Archangels)
November 9	Nektarios (St. Nektarios)
November 25	Katherine (St. Katherine)
November 30	Andrea/Andrew (St. Andrew the Apostle)
December 4	Barbara (St. Barbara)
December 6	Nicole/Nicholas (St. Nicholas)
December 9	Anna (St. Anna)
December 12	Spiridoula/Spyridon and Spiros (St. Spyridon the Miracle Worker)
December 25	Christine and Emmanuela/Chris and Emmanuel (The Nativity of Jesus Christ)
December 27	Stephen (St. Stephen the Protomartyr)

January 1	Vasilia/Basil and William (St. Basil the Great)
January 6	Photini/Photios [from *ta phóta* (the light) — Epiphany]
January 7	Joanna/John (St. John the Baptist)
January 17	Antonia/Anthony (St. Anthony the Great)
January 18	Athanasia/Athan and Arthur (St. Athanasios the Great)
January 25	Gregory (St. Gregory the Theologian)
First Saturday of Lent	Theodora/Theodore (St. Theodore)
March 25	Evangeline/Angelo (from Evangelismos [Annunciation])
Easter	Anastasia/Anastasios (from Anastasi [Resurrection])
April 23	Georgia/George (St. George the Great Martyr — if during Lent, celebrated Monday after Easter)
May 21	Constance/Constantine (Constantine the Great) Helen (St. Helen)
June 11	Bartholomew (St. Bartholomew the Apostle)
Sunday after Pentecost	All Saints Day
June 29	Paula/Paul and Peter (Saints Peter and Paul)
July 20	Elias and Louis (Elias the Prophet)
July 26	Paraskevi (St. Paraskevi)
August 15	Mary, Maria, Panayiota, Despina/Panayiotis [and Peter — popular but incorrect] (Mother of God)
August 30	Alexandra/Alexander (St. Alexander)

The Mother of God and Jesus Christ
(Wall painting from St. George's Chapel,
Monastery of St. Paul, Mt. Athos, 16th Century)

✤ *Icons*

The pensive faces and flat bodies of Orthodox icons, flickering in candlelight, have an unreal quality compelling the viewer to contemplate the world of the divine. They inspire ritualistic customs: kissing, decorating, and honoring. Their presence and inspiration are an integral part of Orthodox worship.

MEANING AND PURPOSE

Mystical Byzantine icons contrast with the religious art of the Western renaissance that depicts important Biblical characters and scenes with great realism. The contrast comes from the different theological traditions of the Latin West and the Orthodox East. Catholics stress that God became man, and the Orthodox emphasize that man is to become like God (*théosis*).

It is this profound concept of the sacred image of God within humans that underlies the meaning and purpose of an icon, which means "image." Icons are sacred images of extraordinary human beings who have become godlike and achieved divinity through grace. An icon is a window to the spiritual world, revealing the heavenly possibilities for each viewer on earth and providing models to imitate. The unearthly appearance of the icon subjects is intentional, pushing the viewer beyond the real world. As such, they play a critical role in worship and Orthodox theology. Most icons depict individual saints, but they may also represent significant events such as the Annunciation and the Nativity of Christ.

HISTORICAL CONTROVERSIES

Icons appeared during the time of Christ, but it took 800 years to define their role in church tradition. Controversy often raged over the depiction of the divine. In keeping with Old Testament tradition, the depiction of God was forbidden. How should Christ be shown? Was he God (and forbidden), or was he human? The controversy was not resolved until 692 when the church agreed upon the dual nature of Christ. The Quinisext Council declared that Christ was both divine and human and should be depicted as a human, not symbolically as a lamb or fish. This canon became the theoretical basis for Orthodox liturgical art. Art must reflect divine revelation and the kingdom of God.

The popularity of icons greatly increased. Some factions of the church believed icons were worshiped like idols, a practice forbidden by the Bible. In addition some still could not accept the depiction of the divine Christ. The iconoclasts (image breakers) triumphed when the Imperial Edict of 726 prohibited religious images, and many icons were destroyed. For 157 years icons were banned, except for a brief time of restoration. But in 843 through the efforts of Empress Theodora, a church council condemned iconoclasm for the last time. On the first Sunday of Great Lent there was a great procession to St. Sophia Cathedral in Constantinople bringing back the icons. The return of the icons is still commemorated in the church on the first Sunday of Lent (Sunday of Orthodoxy) with a procession of icons.

CREATING AND RESTORING

ICONOGRAPHERS

Iconographers translate revealed scripture and divine truths into visual images, writing — not painting — the icon with consecrated brushes, paints, and materials. Ideally, they should be pious individuals trained by holy fathers. Monks and nuns, therefore, have traditionally been the primary source of icons. Most iconographers outside of monasteries today have commercialized the sacred art of iconography.

Iconographers should pray, fast, and avoid worldly excitement during their work. Individual interpretation should be kept to a minimum as their task is to pass on tradition by replicating previous icons within proscribed limits. Works should remain anonymous, but if signed, be inscribed with the words, "By the hand of [name]."

MEDIA

Theology and history dictate that icons be two-dimensional. Three-dimensional art (sculpture) is not allowed to avoid the appearance of an idol and sensual realism. Icons may be executed in a variety of media such as wall frescoes, moveable paintings on wood and canvas, mosaics, on eggs (Russian) and lacquer boxes (Slavic), etc. In the United States, large mosaics are being installed in churches, particularly in the dome and altar area, in a revival of the Byzantine mosaic tradition like that at St. Sophia Cathedral in Constantinople. The stained glass windows in some Orthodox churches are not traditional.

Techniques for small, moveable icons also vary. The classic medium for an icon on wood is egg tempera which gives a unique richness, depth, and softness to the icon. Oil and acrylic also are common. Sometimes silver pounded in the form of a picture covers all of the icon except specific body parts, usually the head and hands. This gilding tradition originated with the custom of giving precious metal to a saint to fulfill a *táma* (see *Special Blessings, Prayers, and Appeals*). The least expensive icons are paper reproductions laminated on wood.

CHARACTERISTICS

Certain characteristics give icons their unique, mystical look. Subjects appear flat and may have exaggerated features such as large eyes to reveal the soul and high foreheads to emphasize the spirit. An unrealistic appearance reveals the divine, spiritual nature the saints have achieved. Inverse perspective may be employed where certain subjects thrust themselves forward on the viewer, emphasizing their importance. This contrasts with the linear perspective of realism that shows vanishing points and three dimensions. Certain colors are symbolic. For example, gold, a primary background color, represents the divine light of God's world.

There are strict formal rules of composition. Fixed patterns in a repetitive design and craftsmanship must be exact. Oral tradition, descriptions in scripture, church writings, canons, and manuals prescribe how icons should look. Depictions of saints generally appear a certain way: the Virgin Mary with the Christ Child, Saints Cosmas and Damian together with medical instruments, and Mary Magdalene with a red Easter egg and myrrh bottle.

INSCRIPTIONS

The saint's name and/or initials seen in the upper corners of the icon tell the viewer who or what they are seeing. For example, the icon of Christ is always shown with "IC" (Jesus) in the upper left corner and "XC" (Christ) in the upper right. Or there may be a brief title of an event like Metamorphosis, Greek for Transfiguration.

STYLISTIC HISTORY

Despite the conformity and anonymity in iconography mandated by the church, artistic styles have changed through the centuries ranging from realistic to the mystical. With the fall of Constantinople in 1453, regional styles gained prominence with the rise of such centers as Crete, Cyprus, the Balkans, Mt. Athos, and Russia. In Russia, Theophanes the Greek and his pupil, Andrei Rublev, at the Novgorod school produced some of the most famous icons in the world during the late fourteenth and fifteenth centuries.

In the twentieth century, iconography took a dramatic turn back toward the strict religious Byzantine tradition, led by Photios Kontoglou in Greece and Leonid Ouspensky, a Russian in Paris. (This revival is now favored in America also.) Kontoglou returned to the original intent of the church fathers and established strict rules and standards for iconographers. Ouspensky and Vladimir Lossky wrote the definitive books on icons, *The Meaning of Icons* and *Theology of the Icon*.[1] An American professor, John Yiannias, in "Orthodox Art and Architecture" in *A Companion to the Greek Orthodox Church*, suggests outstanding examples of Byzantine icons that can be seen in Greece, Turkey, Italy, Cyprus, Egypt, Russia, Yugoslavia, Bulgaria, and Rumania.[2] (See also *The Historic Orthodox Church* — "Orthodox Sites to Visit.")

RESTORATION

The restoration of an historic icon should be done by an experienced iconographer. The process may be too complicated for an artist who is not an icon specialist. Contact a reputable icon dealer for references.

VENERATION

The Orthodox draw a clear line between venerating and worshiping icons. Worship would constitute idolatry, whereas veneration is respect and reverence for the subject of the icon, such as the person of Christ or St. Sophia. Icons help the petitioner visualize the living saint in heaven. It is that represented person toward whom appeals and thanksgiving are directed, not the icon itself. For example, when taking a journey, people customarily kiss an icon and ask the saint's assistance in safe travel.

In the church the most common form of veneration is to light a candle, bow slightly as you make the sign of the cross, and kiss the icon. The icons in the narthex are always venerated. If no service is in progress, you also may venerate any of the icons in the *ikonostásion*.

Icons relating to special feast days are placed in the narthex or sometimes at the front of the nave. For example, an icon of the Annunciation will be displayed on March 25. The church usually decorates these icons with fresh flowers. Parishioners also may bring a single flower or tiny bouquet and place it by the icon. The Sunday of Orthodoxy commemorates the restoration of the icons to the church in 843 with a procession around the church.

MIRACLES

Through the centuries many miracles have been attributed to the power of personal and famous icons. The first icon is said to be that of Christ himself when he placed a linen cloth on his face, and his image immediately transferred. The holy cloth was taken to King Abgar of Edessa who was healed by its miraculous power.

HEALING ICONS

During an illness, believers often bring icons into a sick person's room. Harry Mark Petrakis, in *Stelmark: A Family Recollection* describes the role of icons during his mother's struggle with typhoid fever when she was two years old.

[The doctor] offered scant hope that the child would survive. My grandparents prayed to my mother's patron saint
and placed small icons in the four corners of the child's
sick room… An icon of St. Luke in a nearby monastery was
reported to have supernatural powers… They carried the
icon back to my mother's room… my grandfather raised
my mother in his arms. "Come, child, kiss the icon and it
will make you well." My mother claims to this day she
remembers those words spoken to her, and the cool feel of
the icon under her lips. Afterwards, miraculously, she
recovered.[3]

ACQUIRING AND SELLING

INHERITANCE AND GIFTS

Orthodox families treasure their icons. With love and reverence
they are passed on to other family members, usually after someone dies. It is common, for example, for the icon of the patron
saint of a deceased grandmother to be given to her granddaughter
with the same name. People also give icons to newborns and the
afflicted.

CONSIDERATIONS FOR PURCHASE

Identify the Occasion

Before buying an icon, clearly define why you are purchasing it.
Is it a gift of a patron saint for a newborn or a name day? Is it for
your home *ikonostási*? Is it an aid for a specific cause? Does it
simply appeal to you?

Learn about the Saint

Research the life of the saint, including how the saint is traditionally depicted. For example, Saints Constantine and Helen are
always shown together. If St. Helen is shown alone, this is
incorrect. Depictions can vary, however, and still be correct. For
example, St. George most often rides a horse while slaying a
dragon, but he may also appear alone holding a spear.

Train your Eye

Observe a variety of icons in churches, on the covers of the Sunday bulletin, in books, etc. Which ones conform to Orthodox theology and Byzantine tradition as described above?

Determine your Budget

In a religious sense, a "value" cannot be placed on an icon. Its value comes from its purpose, meaning, and sentimentality. In this sense, many icons are priceless. Nevertheless, you may find yourself in the market for icons, and prices vary greatly. The least expensive and most readily available icons are mass-produced photographs of historic icons, without backing or laminated on wood. Hand-painted icons of acrylic or oil are generally moderately priced. Somewhat more expensive are icons painted in the traditional medium of egg tempera. The price of icons that are covered with precious metal varies, depending on the quality of the particular covering —for example, brass and silver plate versus sterling silver and gold. In general, the most expensive icons are antiques more than one hundred years old and made with egg tempera or with precious metals. These icons are rare, and when found, can cost thousands of dollars.

BUYING IN THE UNITED STATES

Mail Order and Internet

Contact the following distributors for their icon catalogues: Holy Cross Bookstore (Brookline, Massachusetts), Holy Transfiguration Monastery (Brookline, Massachusetts), Light and Life Publishing Company (Minneapolis, Minnesota), and St. Isaac of Syria Skete (Boscobel, Wisconsin). For contact information see *The Historic Orthodox Church* — "Orthodox Internet Websites — Books, Icons, Devotional Items, and Other Products."

Bazaars, Conventions, and Shops

For hands-on shopping, look for moderately priced icons at church bazaars, Greek-American conventions, and in Greek specialty stores. For expensive antique icons, some may be found on rare occasions at an auction house, through an antique dealer, or through a general art dealer. The most dependable sources are antique icon dealers, only a small number of whom are in the United States. A reputable icon dealer will be willing to provide you with a list of client references and provide a written guarantee of the icon's authenticity. Good dealers can be trusted; however, you may also want to confirm authenticity of the icon by having it professionally appraised. Look for a museum staffed with people who are knowledgeable about icons. Fake antiques have become a problem.

Commission

Commissioning an icon requires research, time, patience, and money. Of utmost importance are the religious qualities an icon projects and the iconographer's method. Are they in keeping with the meaning and purpose of icons discussed here? Theoretically the iconographer remains anonymous and icons are not purchased because of the iconographer's reputation. As a practical matter, however, your priest may be able to help you locate a trustworthy iconographer. Another source is exhibits of icons at church festivals and Greek-American conventions.

BUYING IN GREECE

In Greece, a wide variety of icons are available on the street, in shops, churches, and especially monasteries. Most of the religious stores are located on Mitropolis Street behind the Mitropolis Cathedral in Athens. Check also with the Byzantine Museum on Sophias Street in Athens and ask your family and friends who live in Greece.

There is usually no problem in taking new icons out of the country. Some icons are stamped, "Approved for Export." Historic icons are another matter. It is illegal to remove these from Greece without an export permit. Be aware that even old family icons could be seized by customs officers. See *Visiting Greece* for detailed customs information.

BLESSING BEFORE USE

Be sure that each icon is blessed by the church. When you purchase one, ask if it has been consecrated. Many are, especially if they were prepared at a monastery. If the icon has not been blessed or you are uncertain, take it to your church and ask your priest to consecrate it by saying a prayer for hallowing icons or keeping it in the altar area for forty days and saying a special blessing.

SELLING

The church considers it sacrilegious to buy and sell icons for purposes of investment alone; icons should be part of worship, not a financial portfolio. (Of course, if the funds are needed for an emergency, this is understood.) When this is not the case, but you want to sell an icon, consider donating the money realized for a worthy cause. If it is an historic icon, you may want to sell it directly to or put it on consignment with a good dealer. Another option is to sell it through a reputable auction house.

---

1. Read Leonid Ouspensky, trans. E. Meyendorff, *Theology of the Icon* (Crestwood, N.Y.: St. Vladimir's Seminary Press, 1978) and Leonid Ouspensky and Vladimir Lossky, *The Meaning of Icons,* rev. ed. (Crestwood, N.Y.: St. Vladimir's Seminary Press, 1982).

2. John Yiannias, "Orthodox Art and Architecture," in *A Companion to the Greek Orthodox Church,* ed. Fotios K. Litsas (New York: Department of Communication, The Greek Orthodox Archdiocese of North and South America, 1984), 104-105.

3. Harry Mark Petrakis, *Stelmark: A Family Recollection* (New York: David McKay Company, 1970), 17-18.

Home Ikonostási

✤ *The Church of the Home*

Many Greek-American homes contain a little corner of serenity and holiness to house the family's icons and religious effects. A soft light bathes the holy items, inviting the making of the sign of the cross or the murmur of a prayer. This is the *ikonostási*, the place where icons and other religious items are displayed. It is the physical religious center of the church of the home.

The concept of the church of the home (*kat' íkon ekklisía*) is an old Orthodox tradition. The name, coined by St. Paul in the first century, refers to the gathering of Christians in a private home in the days when there were no churches. Today the term refers to the spiritual atmosphere created by a positive Christian way of living and respect for the following traditions.

THE *IKONOSTÁSI*

CONTENTS

The *ikonostási*, the physical religious center of the house, may contain the following items:

- Icon of Christ
- Icon of the Virgin Mary
- Icon of the family patron saint
- Optional: Other icons such as those of saints of family members and significant church events
- A cross
- A prayer book
- The Bible
- Seasonal items from church holidays:
  - First piece cut from the Vasilopita at New Year's
  - Holy water from the Epiphany church service
  - Palms from the Palm Sunday service
  - Flowers from special services: Good Friday, etc.
  - Easter egg
- Seal (*sfrayítha*) for communion bread
- Censer (*thimiató*) with incense and charcoal pellets
- Light or candle (*kandíli*)
- Optional: Marriage crowns

Icon of the Family Patron Saint

Generally the patron saint of the family is the saint for whom the head of the family is named. It could also be a saint of special significance such as the patron saint from your region of Greece, for instance St. Michael for individuals from the island of Simi.

Vasilopita

Each family cuts a Vasilopita (bread for St. Basil) on New Year's Day in honor of St. Basil's name day. The first piece is always cut for Christ, wrapped in foil, and put at the *ikonostási*. (See *New Year*)

Easter Egg

Many people save either the first egg removed from the dye on Good Thursday (the egg of the Virgin Mary) or an egg from the Easter midnight service. The eggs are said to have protective power against the evil eye. (Yes! It will miraculously last all year — the inside evaporates.)

Seal (*Sfrayítha*) for Communion Bread

The church encourages members to make *prósforo*, the bread for communion. The seal (*sfrayítha*) imprints a religious design on the dough before baking (see *Religious Breads*).

Censer (*Thimiató*)

The *thimiató* (pron. *THimiató*) is a small metal container used for burning incense on charcoal pellets during prayers at the *ikonostási*. It may be carried from room to room as prayers are being said to bless the house (see "Censing the Home" below).

Light or Candle (*Kandíli*)

A lit candle, symbolic of the light of Jesus, should constantly be burning as a reminder that Christ is in the home. The traditional *kandíli* is a glass holder suspended by a chain with a wick attached to cork floating in oil on top of water. A wax candle may be used, but it cannot burn continuously and must be watched closely. Electric candles or lights, while not as aesthetically pleasing, are convenient and safe — accounting for their great popularity.

Disposal of Seasonal Items

Seasonal items from the previous year such as the Vasilopita, palms from Palm Sunday, flowers from special services, and the Easter egg should be disposed of on Holy Thursday by burning them in a metal container or foil. Bury the holy remains outside the house in a place where no one will walk.

LOCATION AND ARRANGEMENT

If possible, locate the *ikonostási* on an east wall of the house so that you face east while praying. According to Orthodox belief, Christ, the light of the world, will come again from the East. Choose a relatively private area conducive to prayer but accessible to all of the family. Some people prefer an upstairs hallway; others select the parents' bedroom. The choice is yours.

There are many ways to arrange the *ikonostási*. The items may go into a glass-enclosed cabinet, on open shelves, and/or hung on the walls above a small table.

USING THE *IKONOSTÁSI*

The *ikonostási* is your family's place of worship. Traditionally the *kandíli* is kept lit, but some prefer to light it only during special occasions such as:

- Daily prayer — individually and as a family.
- On Sunday. Since the church day begins at sunset the night before, light the *kandíli* on Saturday evening.
- Prayers for illness, thanksgiving, etc.
- Forty days of mourning.
- Major holiday seasons, such as Exaltation of the Cross, Christmas, Theophania, and Easter. At Easter light the *kandíli* with the flame brought home from the midnight service. Add an icon of the feast day if possible.
- Any other special occasions, such as name days, the birth of a baby, etc.

CASE FOR MARRIAGE CROWNS (*STEPHANOTHÍKI*)

The case for the marriage crowns (*stephanothíki* — pron. *stephanoTHíki*) preserves and displays the marriage crowns, a symbol that the husband and wife are the king and queen of their own kingdom. The case is usually placed by the *ikonostási*. Sometimes a case is not used, and the crowns are put with the other *ikonostási* effects.

ICONS

Icons are revered and treasured in the Greek-American home. Small or large, old or new, elaborate or simple, they remind the faithful of the holy presence of God and the saints. (See *Icons*)

WHERE TO DISPLAY

In addition to icons at the *ikonostási*, it is common to have icons in other parts of the house. For example, you may want to put an icon of each family member's saint in their respective bedrooms.

SPIRITUAL USE

The Orthodox use icons as a part of personal worship in times of crisis, celebration, and regular devotion. For example, icons may be decorated with flowers on a feast day or brought into a sick person's room to invoke a saint's help.

Censer

CENSING THE HOME

Incense contributes to the mystery of the Orthodox church service. The fragrant smoke symbolically carries prayers to God, an ancient tradition described in the Old Testament: "Let my prayer be counted as incense before Thee, and the lifting up of my hands as an evening sacrifice." Ps. 141:2

You may want to duplicate this church tradition in your home. In addition to burning incense at the *ikonostási*, you can say prayers throughout the house, using the censer (see *illustration*). Light the censer by igniting a charcoal pellet in the bottom of the censer with a match. Add the incense and when it becomes fragrant and smoky, lift the censer, making the sign of the cross with it. Go through the house asking for God's blessing and mercy, especially at each family member's bedroom. A common prayer for the front door is, "May only good things come through my front door." Censing can be done at any time, the beginning of the Sabbath on Saturday evening, when making a prayer, when someone is ill, or before a name day or a feast day. The very devout cense twice a day, in the morning and before going to bed at night.

SPIRITUAL ATMOSPHERE

The *ikonostási* acts as the physical religious center of the church of the home, providing a place of worship and prayer. It is only a part of the Christian atmosphere of the entire household. The home, along with the church, must nurture religious values. You lay a solid Christian foundation through positive examples of worship and conduct.

✤ *Special Blessings, Prayers and Appeals*

The Orthodox acknowledge God's presence and importance in all aspect of their lives, turning to him for protection and strength. The church recognizes this need, providing various blessings, prayers, and appeals for many situations: a new home or business, an illness, times of trouble, and thanksgiving. Devout Greek Americans frequently involve their church and priest in the matters of everyday life.

SPECIAL BLESSINGS

Recognizing the benefits of God's watchful presence, many call upon their priest to bless and say prayers in various situations: communion for the sick; the beginning of church school; a time of thanksgiving; installation of officers; adoption of a child; blessing of homes, icons, cars, anniversaries, medals, or any object the petitioner wishes. A few of these blessings are detailed below.

NEW HOME

Whenever you move into a new residence, it is advisable to have the priest come and give a special blessing. The service includes sprinkling the entire house with holy water and reciting prayers asking God to "keep safe also from harm them who now desire to dwell here. . . and bless this their home and dwelling, and preserve their life free from all adversity."[1]

Prepare for the service by cleaning the house and having all the rooms open and lit. The service should be conducted by the family *ikonostási* on a small table upon which a clean bowl of water, candle, icon, and incense burner have been placed. The priest sanctifies the water (*ayiasmós*) by dipping a cross and a small bunch of flowers, preferably basil, in it three times while singing the hymn, "Lord Save your People." Each person kisses the cross and receives a sprinkling of water. If possible, have the entire family at home to walk in a procession led by the priest

through the house as he blesses each room. Save the holy water
for the next morning and have each family member drink a little
before eating or drinking. Thank the priest with a small gift or
remuneration. The same procedure is followed at the beginning
of each year (see *Epiphany*).

VEHICLE

The blessing for a vehicle asks God to "send down upon it Thy
guardian Angel, that all who desire to journey therein may be
safely preserved and shielded from every evil end."[2] Popular customs include putting a blessed icon or medal somewhere in the car.

*Religious
Medal*

ICON

Icons must always be blessed to be complete. If purchased at a
monastery, an icon will have been blessed already. However, if
you are unsure of its origin, take it to church, and the priest will
keep it on the altar for forty days, blessing it with this prayer:
"Bless and make holy this icon unto Your glory, in honor and
remembrance of Your Saint (name); and grant that this sanctification will be to all who venerate this icon of Saint (name), and
send up their prayer unto You standing before it."[3]

SPECIAL PRAYERS

PARÁKLISIS AND AGRYPNÍA

Paráklisis are prayers of supplication asking a saint, especially the
Virgin Mary, for assistance in praying to God for strength, healing,
and guidance. The Great and Small Paraklisis are offered the first
two weeks of August before The Dormition of the Mother of God
on August 15. You may also ask your priest to conduct a private
paráklisi in your home or at the church for illness or other difficulties. This intimate approach can be helpful and comforting. For a
large group concerned about a common problem such as a lost
child or extrordinary illness, prayers may be said at an extended
night vigil (*agrypnía*).

DISPELLING THE EVIL EYE

The church acknowledges the evil eye (*vaskanía*) as legitimate and believes in the power of Christ and the cross to dispel it. The evil eye stems from a consuming jealousy that creates a powerful evil. The envious person may knowingly or unknowingly bring bad luck, illness, or even death to the envied person. Young children up to adolescence are especially vulnerable making parents wary of such phrases as, "What a smart little girl." Effects of the evil eye can vary in severity: lethargy, illness, misfortune in life. If you suspect the presence of the evil eye, talk with your priest. He can say a prayer to dispel it. This redress differs from an exorcism performed by a specially trained priest in rare, extreme circumstances. For popular folk remedies see *Superstitions*.

SPECIAL APPEALS

TÁMA

A *táma* combines prayer and a vow to a saint while appealing for help and assistance. The petitioner vows to give or do something as he or she prays to a saint in times of need. Sometimes the petitioner fasts before making the *táma*.

A *táma* is personal and private. A father while praying for the safe birth of his child might promise to give money to a church in the name of St. Eleftherios. Someone may ask St. Nektarios to heal her cancer and volunteer to make hospital visits or donate something to the church. In Tinos, Greece, a typical pledge to the Virgin Mary is to crawl from the boat dock to the Church of the Evangelistria on hands and knees carrying olive oil on your back! It is also a common custom to promise a gift of precious metal. Jewelry and money are traditional. Originally people covered icons with metal to fulfill a *táma*, but this rarely happens today. In Greece the object of the request may be replicated in metal. For example, if a ship is in danger during a storm, a *táma* asking for the ship's safekeeping could be fulfilled by bringing a miniature silver boat to be hung in a church. Many churches in Greece have hundreds of metal objects hung from their ceilings. A small metal rectangle called a *táma* or *aphiéroma* embossed with a facsimile of a leg, a house, a baby, etc., may be used and is placed on the altar or in front of the church icons either before or after fulfillment (see *illustration*).

You must always satisfy a *táma* regardless of the outcome. Sometimes the *táma* is fulfilled in anticipation of the favor. Ignoring the *táma*, however, invites a lifetime of question and possible distress. The Greeks have an expression emphasizing this belief, "Do not make a pledge to a saint or to a small child unless you are sure you will fulfill it."

Some people travel extraordinary distances to the most famous church of the saint to make the *táma*. When the wish has been granted, they travel back — sometimes years later — to fulfill it. This, however, is not necessary. A *táma* can be made and satisfied any time, anywhere.

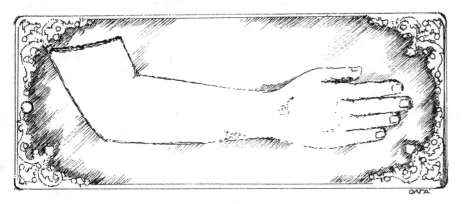

Táma

PHANOUROPITA

If you have lost something, try baking Phanouropita (cake for St. Phanourios — pron. *Phanourópita*) St. Phanourios, the patron saint of lost articles, helps people find anything from a missing piece of jewelry to good health and happiness. *"Phanoúrios"* comes from the Greek word, *"phaneróno"* (I reveal). During the baking of the cake, say a prayer for St. Phanourios' help and for the soul of his mother, a troubled woman. Share the cake with seven or more people, but do not reveal what you are trying to find.

121

PHANOUROPITA

1 cup sugar

1 cup vegetable oil

2 cups orange juice

¾ cup light or dark raisins

¾ cup chopped walnuts

1 teaspoon baking soda

1 teaspoon vanilla

4 cups flour

Beat sugar and oil together until creamy yellow. Dissolve baking soda in orange juice and pour slowly into sugar mixture. Add other ingredients and pour into a 9" x 13" greased pan. Bake at 350°F for 45-50 minutes or until an inserted toothpick pulls out cleanly. Cut into squares for serving.

---

1. N. M. Vaporis, ed., *An Orthodox Prayer Book* (Brookline, Mass.: Holy Cross Orthodox Press, 1977), 154.

2. Ibid. 155.

3. Ibid. 153.

✦ *Religious Breads*

The church invites parishioners to prepare bread for several of its church services: communion and the *artoklasía*. The communion bread *(prósforo)* becomes the Body of Christ for your fellow church members at the Divine Liturgy. The loaves of bread for the *artoklasía* service commemorate Christ's miracle of feeding thousands of people with five loaves of bread.

PRÓSFORO (COMMUNION BREAD)

Communion is the most important rite of the Orthodox church. During this sacrament, wine and bread become the Blood and Body of Christ. The *prósforo*, meaning "offering," becomes the Body of Jesus, the bread of life. You are encouraged to bring the *prósforo* and red wine to church for this holy sacrament.

WHEN TO BRING TO CHURCH

The *prósforo* can be made for any number of occasions: a Divine Liturgy (particularly if you and your family take communion that day), name day, memorial, feast day, etc. Ask the priest if you may provide the bread and what time he will need it. It must arrive before *órthros*, the service in which the priest divides the bread for the Divine Liturgy.

THE RELIGIOUS SEAL (*SFRAYÍTHA*)

A religious seal (*sfrayítha*) stamps a special design on the *prósforo* before baking (see *illustration*). During preparation of the Eucharist, the priest conducts the *proskomithí* in which he first cuts out the center of the stamped design that says *"IC, XC, NIKA"* ("Jesus Christ Conquers"). It becomes the Body of Christ (the Lamb). Then the large triangle on the left is cut in honor of the Virgin Mary. The nine small triangles on the right are cut to commemorate the angels, prophets, apostles, holy fathers and prelates, martyrs, ascetics, holy unmercenaries, Joachim and Anna, and all saints, including the saint of the day's liturgy. The last cuts are tiny squares to remember specific names of the living and the dead.

The *sfrayítha* has two sides. One side features the full seal described above, and the other side has a smaller circle with the letters, "*IC XC NIKA*" (see *illustration*). When a large number of people are expected for communion, prepare extra bread, making imprints with the small seal around the large circle or on separate loaves.

Purchase the seal at a Greek specialty store or order from a catalogue and keep it in your home *ikonostási*.

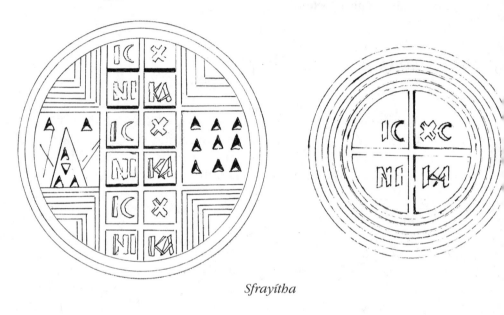

Sfrayítha

LIST OF LIVING AND DECEASED

Take the *prósforo* to church with a list of names for the priest to mention during the Divine Liturgy. Put the first names of the living in one column of your note (including those who have baked the bread, and others you want remembered) and the names of any deceased in another column. The priest cuts the *prósforo* in their honor and recites their names during the service.

Prósforo

$\frac{1}{2}$ cup lukewarm water	4 cups bread flour
1 teaspoon sugar	$\frac{1}{2}$ teaspoon salt
1 package dry yeast	*sfrayítha* (seal)
1 cup water	

Dissolve the yeast in $\frac{1}{2}$ cup lukewarm water with sugar and let rise until bubbly. Mix liquid ingredients. Slowly add 3 cups flour, while continuing to mix. Work the sticky dough until it forms a loose ball. Turn out on a floured surface and add additional flour until a stiff dough is formed. Knead a few minutes. Make two balls, and place one on top of the other in a cake pan that has been floured, not greased. (The double layer represents the dual nature of Christ.) Press out to edge of pan. Sprinkle the top lightly with flour. Place the *sfrayítha* in the center and press down as far as possible. Remove seal and make holes about an inch apart with a toothpick around the edge of the design. Cover the bread with a dry cloth, and let rise in a warm place until double in size. Open the holes with a toothpick again. Before baking make the sign of the cross over the bread and say the "Lord's Prayer" and/or a short prayer for those for whom you are baking the bread. Bake at 375°F for about 35 minutes. Reduce oven to 250°F and bake another 30 minutes or until hollow when tapped.

Bread for *Artoklasía* Service

THE *ARTOKLASÍA* SERVICE

The service of *artoklasía* (breaking of bread) is both a gesture of thanksgiving for God's blessings and a commemoration of the miracle of Christ's multiplying five loaves of bread to feed five thousand.

Five loaves of bread are brought to church, blessed, and distributed to the congregation in a short service of blessings and prayers for health and prosperity. Bread, wine, olive oil, wheat, and candles grace the service table. The priest blesses the food, considered the basic elements necessary for life by the Greek Orthodox:

Lord, Jesus Christ our God, You blessed the five loaves in the wilderness and from them five thousand men were filled. Bless now these loaves (the wine and oil) and multiply them in this holy church, this city, in the homes of those who celebrate today, and in your whole word. And sanctify Your faithful servants who partake of them.[1]

The congregation shares the bread, and the church keeps the remaining items. A church may hold an annual *artoklasía* service on its name day. Individuals or organizations may also sponsor an *artoklasía* on special occasions such as Greek Letters Day to honor the Three Hierarchs of Education.

ITEMS FOR THE SERVICE

Prior to the Divine Liturgy bring the following items for the sexton or priest to arrange on a small table at the front of the church:

- Five loaves of bread
  (see recipe below)
- One bottle of sweet red
  wine, such as mavrodaphne
- One small bottle of olive oil
- One small jar of wheat
- List of living persons to
  be commemorated

Bread for *Artoklasía*

5 packages dry yeast	3½ cups milk
½ cup warm water	1 teaspoon *machlépi*
1 tablespoon sugar	½ teaspoon *mastícha*
1 cup butter	4 eggs
2½ cups sugar	5 lbs. bread flour (15 cups)

Dissolve yeast in ½ cup warm water with 1 tablespoon sugar and let stand for 5 minutes. In a pot warm the butter, sugar, and milk to dissolve. Add *machlépi* and *mastícha* and cool. Beat the eggs and add them and the yeast to butter mixture. Slowly add ⅔ of the flour with other ingredients. Work the sticky dough until it forms a loose ball. Turn out on a floured surface and work in additional flour until a stiff dough is formed. Knead a few minutes. Shape into five round loaves, place in greased pans, cover with a dry cloth, and let double in a warm place. Before baking, brush with water. Make the sign of the cross and say a prayer for those you are honoring with the bread. Bake at 350°F for 35 minutes. Reduce heat to 250°F and bake another 35 minutes or until hollow when tapped. (See "Easter Bread" concerning spices)

(Lenten bread: Eliminate the butter, milk, and eggs; substitute 2 teaspoons salt and about 6 cups of water. Grease pans with vegetable shortening.)

---

1. Members of the Faculty of Hellenic College/Holy Cross Greek Orthodox School of Theology, trans. *The Divine Liturgy of Saint John Chrysostom* (Brookline, Mass.: Holy Cross Orthodox Press, 1985), 56.

✤ *Fasting*

The word "Byzantine" accurately describes fasting *(nistía)* in the Greek Orthodox church, since the complexity can confuse even the most devout with its required days, food prohibitions, and exceptions. Strict fasting in the Orthodox church is so demanding that only a minority of Orthodox believers practice it to the letter.

Few topics generate more opinions from a group of Greek Americans than the subject of fasting. Through the centuries priests and laypeople have developed their own customs. Each has his own rules from the church and from his mother or *yiayiá*. For example, one family always ate fried potatoes cooked in olive oil at noon the Saturday before taking communion; family members did not feel prepared unless they had done this. Your family may have similar customs that are meaningful for you.

The customs below may not conform to your traditions because practices vary greatly. Try to remember that the focus should always be on the purpose of fasting, not the regulations themselves.

PURPOSE

Fasting is a form of self-control over temptations, impatience, sin, and material urges, such as food. Its purpose is to discipline and cleanse the soul and body regularly. A change in diet signals a change in errant ways and assists the penitent in achieving higher and loftier goals as stated in one of Orthodoxy's Lenten hymns: "...the casting off of evil, the bridling of the tongue, the cutting off of anger, the cessation of lusts, evil talking, lies, and cursings. The stopping of these is the fast true and acceptable."

DEMEANOR

Fasting should be done privately without boasting, in keeping with the Biblical teaching:

And when you fast, do not look dismal, like the hypocrites, for they disfigure their faces that their fasting may be seen by men. Truly, I say to you, they have received their reward. But when you fast, anoint your head and wash your face, that your fasting may not be seen by men but by your Father who is in secret; and your Father who sees in secret will reward you. Matt. 6:16-28

DIETARY RESTRICTIONS

Most confusion over fasting comes from what should or should not be eaten. The canons and rules concerning this are complicated and in some cases obsolete.

Different levels of fasting are practiced: severe, strict, and moderate. Severe fasting permits no eating or drinking. Strict fasting (called *xeropháyi* — dry eating) prohibits meat, fish (with backbone), animal products (cheese, milk, butter, eggs, lard), olive oil, and alcohol (wine in moderation allowed). Shellfish, fruit, vegetables, bread, legumes, and vegetable margarine/oil may be eaten.

The very observant comply with strict fasting rules on the days specified below in "Days to Observe." In general, however, people follow a strict fast a few times a year: during the weekdays of the first week of Great Lent, Holy Week, January 5 (the day before Epiphany), and the first fifteen days of August before The Dormition of the Mother of God. In practice, most Orthodox do moderate fasting where they give up some foods, especially meat, on the specified days.

Before evening liturgies, the church authorities suggest no food or water for a minimum of six hours prior to the service.

DAYS TO OBSERVE

The observant Orthodox fasts on Wednesdays and Fridays throughout the entire year. Christ was betrayed by Judas on Wednesday, a day to evaluate one's commitment to Christ. On Fridays the crucifixion of Christ is remembered. Such regular fasting focuses the individual on a Christian lifestyle.

The church specifies four major fasting periods of varying length: Great Lent (49 days), Holy Apostles Lent (length varies), Dormition of the Mother of God Lent (14 days), and Christmas Lent (40 days). The longest fasts imitate Christ's fast for forty days in the wilderness in which he overcame temptation by the devil. These and individual fasting days are specified in "Days to Observe" below. A Lenten period is called "Tessarakosti" (formal) and "Sarakosti" (informal). Before a fasting period, people wish each other, *"Kali Sarakosti."*

The fasting periods and individual fast days listed below are reprinted from the *Yearbook 2006* the Greek Orthodox Archdiocese of America.[1] For a detailed listing, see a book of Lenten services called *The Lenten Triodion* by Mother Mary and Kallistos Ware.[2]

The following are fast days and seasons:

1. All Wednesdays and Fridays, except for those noted below;
2. The day before the Feast of Theophany (January 5);
3. Cheesefare Week (the last week before the Great Lent, during which meat and fish are prohibited, but dairy products are permitted even on Wednesday and Friday);
4. Great Lent (from Clean Monday through the Friday before Lazarus Saturday, olive oil and wine are permitted on weekends);
5. Great and Holy Week (note that Great and Holy Saturday is a day of strict fasting, during which the faithful abstain from olive oil and wine);
6. Holy Apostles' Fast (from the Monday after All Saints' Day through June 28, inclusive);
7. Fast for the Dormition of the Mother of God (August 1-14, excluding August 6, on which fish, wine and olive oil are permitted);
8. Beheading of St. John the Baptist (August 29);
9. Exaltation of the Holy Cross (September 14); and
10. Nativity Lent (November 15-December 24, although fish, wine and olive oil are permitted, except on Wednesdays and Fridays, until December 17).

The following are fasting days on which fish, wine and olive oil are permitted.

1. The Feast of the Annunciation (March 25, unless it falls outside the Great Lent, in which case all foods are permitted);

2. Palm Sunday;

3. The Feast of the Transfiguration (August 6); and

4. The Feast of the Entry into the Temple of the Mother of God (November 21).

On the following days, all foods are permitted:

1. The first week of the Triodion, from the Sunday of the Publican and the Pharisee through the Sunday of the Prodigal Son, including Wednesday and Friday;

2. Diakainisimos (Bright) Week, following the Sunday of Pascha;

3. The week following Pentecost; and

4. From the Feast of the Nativity of the Lord (December 25) through January 4.

CHURCH FLEXIBILITY

While fasting serves a vital purpose in the Orthodox lifestyle, the church today shows flexibility and understanding on the issue. All of the canons are not followed. For example, Canon LXIV of the Holy Apostles suggests that any holy men who do not fast for Lent or on Wednesdays and Fridays be deposed and that laymen should be excommunicated.

This canon is not adhered to today, and the church fathers themselves question strict observance of every rule. St. John Chrysostom, one of the most important church fathers from the fourth century, defended himself after being criticized for giving communion to people who had already eaten: "…consider Christ Himself, who gave the Communion to the Apostles right after supper." (Concord to Canon XXIX of the Sixth Ecumenical Synod)

---

1. Greek Orthodox Archdiocese of America, *Yearbook 2006* (New York: Greek Orthodox Archdiocese of America, 2006), 274.

2. Mother Mary and Kallistos Ware, *The Lenten Triodion* (London: Faber and Faber, 1978), 35-37.

✤ *Death and Mourning*

The death of a beloved family member or friend is difficult to accept. The pain and sense of loss can overwhelm even the most positive and optimistic. However, the Orthodox church through its beliefs and rituals offers the bereaved a solid structure to deal with grief and the reality of death.

ORTHODOX BELIEFS OF DEATH AND AFTERLIFE

The Orthodox belief in eternal life provides the base for many traditions relating to death and mourning. For example, cremation is forbidden by the church because it is believed that the physical body is eternal and will be reunited with the soul during the Last Judgment. Therefore, the body is not to be destroyed. The church discourages the practice of excessive wailing during a funeral because it contradicts the positive side of death: the deceased is alive with God. Also, memorial prayers seeking God's mercy for the departed are said by the living. This tradition comes from the belief that all Christians, living and dead, are united together in one church, and there is interaction between the two worlds. Finally the traditional memorial dish, *kóllyva*, made of boiled wheat mixed with sugar and other spices, symbolizes the eternal cycle: people, like wheat, must be buried to grow and have new life.

Traditions also are patterned after Christ's life. After His Resurrection, Christ ascended to heaven after forty days. In remembrance of this significant event, one of the most important memorials for the deceased is held on or before forty days after death. Through these rituals the church tries to help the parishioners to achieve *théosis*, becoming like God, even in death.

LAST COMMUNION

If death appears imminent, call a priest to administer communion. However, communion can only be given to an aware, conscious person. If possible, have the person prepare for the sacrament with confession.

IMMEDIATELY AFTER DEATH

TRISAGION SERVICE

After a person dies, call the priest immediately to say the Trisagion service over the deceased. The title "Trisagion" (three Holies — pron. *trisáyion*) comes from the repetition three times of the opening phrase of the service, "Holy God, Holy Mighty, Holy and Immortal, have mercy on us." This service may be repeated for a loved one in church or at the grave throughout the first year: at the time of death, the third day, the ninth day, the fortieth day, six months, one year, and any time one feels the need.

OFFERING SYMPATHY

See *As the Greeks Say* for commonly expressed sentiments to the family and other mourners.

Sympathy can be offered in many ways: Visiting the home with food for the family; attending the viewing, funeral, and after meal; sending a sympathy card, flowers, or contribution. Many families now request that contributions be made in memory of the deceased. This is in keeping with the longstanding Greek tradition of giving to the poor or doing good works when someone dies. St. John Chrysostom said, "Do you wish to honor the departed? Honor him by giving alms and by doing works of benefaction." Specifics about sending contributions and flowers should be published in the notice of death. Flowers may also be sent to the home any time during the forty-day mourning period.

Customarily close friends and family visit the grieving family throughout the forty-day mourning period. Guests are served brandy, coffee, and small, hard toast called *paximáthia*. Always call first. If the family does not want visitors, respect their wishes.

When discussing someone's death, people use a phrase to ward off a similar fate, *"Ékso apó ethó ke makriá"* ("Out of here and far away"). In Greece, you sometimes hear the phrase, "His thread is cut," referring to the ancient myth that the three "Fates" spun, measured, and cut a person's life in the form of a thread.

MOURNING CLOTHES AND DEMEANOR

The church's official mourning period lasts forty days, and the family should dress in dark clothing during that time. Women generally wear all black with little or no makeup and jewelry. People also combine black with white, the latter a symbol of new life. Close family members should conduct themselves with decorum: no dancing, loud partying, or celebrating. Some continue this during the first year.

Years ago in Greece social custom dictated that widows wear black the rest of their lives, and daughters for three years. Today, such extremes are rarely observed. A widow may wear black for a year at the most, but this is up to each individual. At one time the widow(er) wore the wedding band of the deceased mate along with his or hers on the right-hand ring finger, the finger used for the wedding ring in Greece. Other expressions of grief included soaping or covering mirrors, and men not shaving or cutting their hair for forty days. In Greece today black banners are hung on the front door or on the balcony of an apartment.

VIEWING, FUNERAL, BURIAL, AND *MAKARÍA*

ELIGIBILITY FOR ORTHODOX FUNERAL

Any person baptized in the Orthodox church is entitled to a funeral service, with some exceptions. Individuals who are in severe violation of canon law may have a prayer said after death but not a complete service. Severe violations include marriage outside of the Orthodox church, cremation, or suicide (unless caused by certified insanity). A recent ruling of the Ecumenical Patriarchate allows the local bishop to use his discretion in deciding cases where mercy should be shown. If, for example, there have been signs of remorse given publicly or in confession to the priest, these severe rules may be bent.

SELECTING A FUNERAL HOME

The funeral home helps with many details of the funeral, including a checklist of things to do, and official papers and documents required by the government, such as the death certificate. If a

funeral home in the community is Greek-owned or -managed, that
can be helpful in integrating Greek traditions.

SCHEDULING

Contact a priest immediately to make arrangements. His schedule
and the church calendar must be taken into consideration. Funeral services are permitted on any day of the year except for
Sundays and Holy Friday, unless permission is granted from the
diocesan bishop. In the United States, a viewing is usually held at
a funeral home for several hours during an afternoon and again in
the evening. (All-night vigils in a home are rarely practiced as they
were in Greece.) Since embalming is tacitly accepted in the
church, the body does not have to be buried within a twenty-four-
hour period, and the funeral is often delayed to accommodate
those coming from out of town. The interment and meal usually
follow immediately after the funeral.

NOTICE OF DEATH AND OBITUARY

In small Greek villages, the slow, somber ringing of church bells
alerts the community to a death. Residents run to the center of
town, and the word is passed by mouth. However, in the United
States it is customary to put a notice of death in the newspaper.
The funeral home assists you with this task. The paid notice is
usually short including date and place of death, names of the
immediate family, times and places of the viewing, funeral and
burial, and information regarding flowers or contributions.

An obituary is a longer article describing more about the deceased's
life, accomplishments, cause of death, and surviving family. Such
biographical information can be submitted to the paper(s), but
each newspaper has its own policy regarding publication.

BURIAL SITE

The body should be buried under ground with the eyes of the
deceased looking East for the Second Coming of Christ. The
ground must be consecrated (blessed) by a priest, usually at the
time of the burial. The site does not have to be in an Orthodox
cemetery or section. However, some churches in large Greek-

American communities buy land within a cemetery, designating it for burial of their fellow Orthodox. Orthodox theology emphasizes the unity of its members in life and in death, and an Orthodox section keeps the community together. In Greece the deceased are not embalmed, but exhumed after three years, and the bones of the family are kept together. This is not possible in the United States, where exhuming is prohibited by law except in extraordinary cases.

SELECTING A GRAVE MARKER

You may want to inquire about the kind of headstones permitted at the cemetery. Some cemeteries only allow stones set flush to the ground for ease of maintenance. Others allow upright monuments but charge a high fee that includes perpetual maintenance. Decide on the style you would like and select the burial site accordingly. The marker is usually selected after the funeral. A Greek or Byzantine cross is frequently engraved on the marker.

PREPARING THE BODY

Religious beliefs govern preparation of the body for burial. In keeping with the Orthodox goal of *théosis* (man becoming like God), an Orthodox should be buried like Christ according to the Old Testament tradition. "...for out of [the ground] you were taken; you are dust, and to dust you shall return." Gen. 3:19

Cremation

The church forbids cremation because the body is expected to be rejoined with the soul at the Last Judgment. No funeral service or burial rites can be held for a cremated person. However, a prayer can be said at the wake if the priest or bishop so decide. Exceptions to cremation are made if state laws prohibit burial (as in Japan) or the community's health is at risk from disease.

Embalming

The church accepts this practice since most funeral homes require that a body for public viewing be embalmed.

CLOTHING FOR THE DECEASED

The family usually selects a favorite article of clothing for the deceased. At one time, if the departed was young and single, a *stéphano* would be placed on the head. The family dressed the man as a groom and the woman in white as a bride. If the widow(er) is old, the ring is removed from the deceased and worn by the living spouse. Some people tape a paper icon by the deceased's heart.

In some areas people put a sheet-like shroud called a *sávano* on the body under the outer clothing. Although seldom practiced, this tradition emulate's Christ burial in white linen. In Mitilini, they use the departed's white baptismal sheet. An ancient pagan tradition is to put a coin between the deceased lips or on the eyelids to pay Charon (the ferryman to Hades) for his future services. This is rarely done in the United States and Greece.

TRANSFER OF THE DECEASED TO GREECE

The funeral home can handle the transfer of remains to Greece. The body must be embalmed. The local Greek consulate will tell you the necessary requirements, including copies of the death certificate, certification from the city health department that the deceased did not die of a communicable disease, and proof from the funeral home that proper hygienic regulations have been met.

CASKET

Style

In accordance with the Orthodox belief that the human body returns to dust, a wooden casket is preferable to a metal one so that the body can decompose more quickly. This is especially important in Greece where relatives exhume the body after three years to wash and store the bones (see "Third-Year Anniversary" below).

Additions

For the viewing and funeral, place an icon in a corner of the casket by the deceased's head or in the hands of the deceased for guests to kiss. Choose a saint with meaning for the deceased, either the namesake or someone who has been particularly important. The icon can be buried with the deceased, but this is not necessary.

Burying the *stéphana* (marriage crowns) with the deceased is an optional social custom. If the departed has been married, the *stéphana* are sometimes put into the casket for burial with the deceased spouse. Or cut the ribbon that joins the two *stéphana* and bury one crown with each of them.

Sometimes a white sheet is put in the casket to pull over the departed's face at the end of the funeral service. This is an optional social tradition also.

Open Casket

Whenever possible, the casket should be left open for the viewing and the funeral to acknowledge the reality of death. In addition, the funeral service concludes with a "last kiss" by each visitor.

OPTIONAL: ICON CARDS

The funeral home can prepare icon cards for distribution to guests at the viewing and funeral. Choose a Byzantine icon with special meaning for the deceased, if possible the patron saint. The card may include any of the following information: the deceased's name, dates of birth and death, a prayer, pallbearers, etc.

FUNERAL CLOTHING

The immediate family should dress in black for the viewing and funeral. If possible, close male relatives wear black ties. Guests are not required to wear black but should dress conservatively. Black and white are also acceptable. Black signifies mourning, and white symbolizes new life. At one time men wore black arm bands, but this is done infrequently today (see "Mourning Clothes and Demeanor" above).

SELECTING PALLBEARERS AND USHERS

Select six to eight pallbearers to escort the casket into the church. They should be individuals who have been especially meaningful to the deceased, such as grandsons and nephews. Children and spouses should never serve.

VIEWING

In Greece it is customary to have a twenty-four-hour vigil by the body. In the United States, however, most Greek Americans hold a viewing of the deceased at a funeral home for several hours one afternoon and evening. At the viewing, friends and family join together to comfort each other in their time of sorrow.

Visitors at the viewing should sign the guest book, pick up an icon card if available, and pay their respects to the deceased by going to the casket, saying a short prayer and kissing the icon or the deceased. If the priest is scheduled to come, stay for the Trisagion service. The short service pleads for the forgiveness of sins and the repose of the deceased's soul in heaven. Visitors express their condolences to the family.

Today's subdued service contrasts with some wakes and funerals held primarily in Greece years ago. These were dominated by women wailing funeral dirges (*miralóyia* — words of fate) for the deceased.[1] However, the church discourages loud moaning and muttering because such despair contradicts the positive Christian message of life after death.

The church also discounts the superstition of keeping newlyweds and pregnant women from the viewing and funeral because it is considered bad luck. This custom has no religious basis.

FUNERAL SERVICE (*KITHÍA*)

The Orthodox funeral service emphasizes the reality of death and the new life of the deceased. It is a positive service featuring prayers for forgiveness and repose of the departed's soul. Some priests wear white to symbolize new life.

Before the service at the church, the priest repeats the Trisagion service at the funeral home. The deceased and the family then go to church where the priest begins the service by meeting the family, friends, and casket at the front door of the church. Chanting, he leads them into the sanctuary for the service. Guests who have waited outside enter the church, signing a guest book in the narthex. The family sits in the front row before the icon of Christ in the *ikonostásion*. The open casket is arranged so that the eyes of the deceased look east towards the altar, the direction from which Christ will rise again.

The priest leads the bereaved in hymns, scriptures, readings, and prayers, asking God to give rest to the departed's soul and forgive all sins.

The priest then invites the visitors to "Come and kiss the one that was with us a short time ago." Starting from the rear of the church, guests go row by row, to the casket. Except for the immediate family and exceptionally close friends, mourners kiss the icon in the casket. They pass by the family expressing their sympathy. Then the entire family gathers around the casket for the last kiss and the concluding ritual.

To conclude the priest sprinkles oil on the body in the form of a cross, saying, "Wash me with hyssop [a plant in the mint family], and I shall be pure, cleanse me and I shall be whiter than snow." The casket is closed and the service ends.

The priest may make brief remarks about the individual. Remarks by the family and friends may be done only with the permission of the authorities, and no music except for chanting is allowed. The body is carried out first and normally taken immediately to the cemetery for burial.

In some Greek villages, pottery will be thrown out of the windows as the body is taken to the cemetery. The breaking of pottery symbolizes that something has ended.

BURIAL (*ENDAPHIASMÓS*)

The funeral home transports the body and the immediate family to the cemetery. The priest says the Trisagion service for the last time and sprinkles dirt on the closed casket in the form of a cross with the words, "The earth is the Lord's and the fullness thereof, the world and those who dwell therein; you are earth and to earth shall you return." This seals the grave. Sometimes each guest puts a flower on the casket. In America people usually leave and do not watch the lowering of the casket into the ground. If the family has prepared a *makaría* (see below), the priest announces the time and location after the prayers are completed.

MAKARÍA

Mourners share a somber meal called a *makaría* to bless the deceased. It provides an opportunity for relatives and friends to refresh themselves and remember their loved one in an informal setting.

Time and Location

The family usually holds a *makaría* after the funeral, but sometimes after the forty-day memorial. The meal is a social custom that has come to be expected but is not required by the church; some people do not hold one. It can be held at a home, in the church hall, or in a restaurant, depending on the circumstances. Sometimes the Ladies Philoptochos Society (the women's philanthropic organization) of the church caters such occasions.

Menus

Menus for the *makaría* range from simple to elaborate according to the family's circumstances. The simplest menu traditionally includes brandy, coffee, and *paximáthia*. The brandy is always served to the guests as they arrive. *Paximáthia* (pron. *paksimáthia*) are traditional because they are dry, like bones, and not too sweet (see recipe below). Sweets are considered a sign of celebration. *Baklavá*, for example, would be inappropriate.

A moderate menu includes the above, plus sandwiches. A typical full meal consists of brandy, fish, salad, rice or potatoes, green beans, cheese, olives, rolls, wine, coffee, and *paximáthia*. Fish, the symbol of Christianity, is the most traditional entree, but this varies according to regional custom.

ACKNOWLEDGMENTS

Thank you notes for help, flowers, donations, and expressions of sympathy should be sent.

MEMORIAL SERVICES

PURPOSE AND ORTHODOX THEOLOGY

The Orthodox believe that intercessions on behalf of the dead are possible through the fervent prayers of those remaining on earth. Individuals who die go to a state of blessedness or damnation, but the Last Judgment is to be made at the Second Coming of Christ. Through the memorial prayers the living seek mercy and forgiveness for all of the deceased's transgressions.

While the Orthodox hold memorial services at many different times, the most widely observed service is the forty-day memorial based on the last days of Christ. After his Resurrection, Christ remained on earth for forty days: "To [the apostles] he presented himself alive after his passion by many proofs appearing to them during forty days, and speaking of the kingdom of God." Acts 1:3

While it is popularly believed that the deceased's soul also remains on earth for forty days, this is not a belief of the Greek Orthodox church.

MEMORIAL SERVICE *(MNIMÓSINO)*

The memorial (*mnimósino* — calling to mind) recalls the deceased to God, the heavenly host, family, and friends. The service begins with an appeal to God to restore the departed to the divine image in which he or she was created. The priest asks God to forgive every sin and give rest to the deceased. In the service Christ, the Virgin Mary, and the saints, including the Old Testament patriarchs Abraham, Isaac and Jacob, and Christ's friend Lazarus, are asked to intercede for forgiveness and repose of the soul. The service ends with the well-known refrain, "Eonia i Mnimi."[2]:

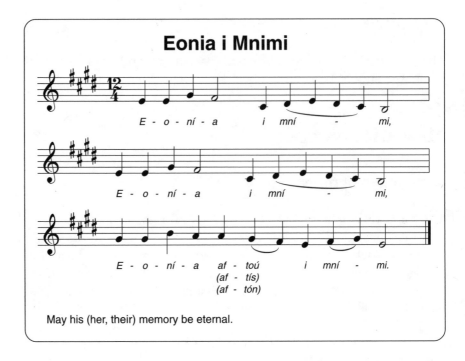

May his (her, their) memory be eternal.

Family and friends comfort the mourning family with similar words: *"Eonía i mními"* ["Eternal be (his/her) memory"]. (See *As the Greeks Say* for additional sentiments.)

It is traditional for the family to sit in the front row of the church before the icon of Christ during the service. The family provides a wheat dish called *kóllyva,* a symbolic custom based on two scriptures concerning eternal life:

> But someone will ask: "How are the dead raised? With what kind of body do they come?" You foolish man? What you sow does not come to life unless it dies: And what you sow is not the body which is to be, but a bare kernel, perhaps of wheat or of some other grain. But God gives it a body as he has chosen, and each kind of seed its own body. 1 Cor. 15:35-38

> Truly, truly, I say to you, unless a grain of wheat falls into the earth and dies, it remains alone; but if it dies, it bears much fruit. John: 12:24

The Christian message of everlasting life and hope is symbolically represented by the white mound of *kóllyva* on a tray bearing a cross and the deceased's initials in Greek (see *illustration*). The tray rests on a small table with candles in front of the church *ikonostásion* during the memorial service. After church the family shares the *kóllyva* with the rest of the congregation. (See recipe below.) If you are unable to make the *kóllyva*, contact your church for the name of an individual or an organization that will make the preparations.

Additional tributes on that day may include making the *prósforo*, donating altar flowers and/or candles, and bringing refreshments for the coffee hour after church, such as the traditional *paximáthia*. If possible, relatives visit the grave site that day.

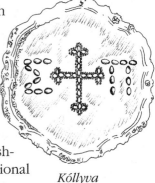

Kóllyva

MEMORIAL DATES

The most common times to offer individual memorials are the fortieth day following the death, at six-months, the first-year anniversary, the third-year anniversary, and Saturday of Souls (see below). You may hold more memorials if you wish. Most individual memorial services are held on Sundays after the Divine Liturgy, except on any of the feast days of the Lord and the Mother of God, or from the Saturday of Lazarus (one week before Easter) through the Sunday of Thomas (one week after Easter).

DURING THE FIRST YEAR

Memorial prayers may be said at the following times:

Immediately after Death

   If possible, have the priest say the Trisagion service immediately over the deceased.

Third Day after Death

   The priest says the Trisagion service for the deceased as a reminder that Christ remained dead for three days. In America this most likely will occur at either the viewing or funeral.

Ninth Day after Death

The Trisagion service is said on the ninth day to recognize that the spirit of the deceased has now joined the nine choirs of holy angels. In some regions in Greece *kóllyva* made on this day is taken to the church for a blessing, divided into nine portions, and distributed to nine people to eat.

Fortieth Day after Death (Saránta)

The forty-day memorial must be observed, even if this means holding it a few days before the forty days have passed. The official mourning period ends after the forty days.

Six-Month Anniversary

Repeat "Memorial Service" above.

First-Year Anniversary

Repeat "Memorial Service" above.

THIRD-YEAR ANNIVERSARY

Repeat "Memorial Service" above.

In Greece, families traditionally exhume the bodies of their deceased after three years. The deceased are not embalmed and by then only bones remain. This is a church custom with Biblical underpinnings:

The hand of the Lord was upon me, and he brought me out by the spirit of the Lord, and set me down in the midst of the valley; it was full of bones. And he led me round among them; and behold there were many upon the valley; and lo, they were very dry. And he said to me, "Son of Man, can these bones live?" And I answered, 'O Lord God, thou knowest.' Ezek. 37:1-3

The family members wash the bones in water mixed with wine or vinegar and place them in a special container. In some villages the container is placed in the narthex for a number of days for sanctification before being reburied or placed in a building called the *kimitírion* (sleeping place). If possible the bones are stored with those of other family members.

The tradition may be an ancient one. The bones in the tomb of Philip of Macedon, father of Alexander the Great, at Verginia are stained with wine.

OTHER YEARLY ANNIVERSARIES

Many people hold memorials on other yearly anniversaries also, such as the tenth or twentieth. This is optional. You can also remember a loved one each year during the Saturday of Souls service described below.

SATURDAY OF SOULS (PSYCHOSAVATO)

Traditionally, the Orthodox remember the dead on a Saturday, the day Christ lay in his tomb. Four times a year parishioners assemble to pray for all their deceased loved ones. These general memorial services, known as Saturday of Souls (Psychosavato — pron. *Psychosávato*) take place the two Saturdays that precede the beginning of Great Lent, the First Saturday of Great Lent, and the Saturday before the Feast of Pentecost.

If you would like to offer prayers for the deceased, write their first name(s) on a slip of paper, and the priest will read the list toward the end of the service. Submit names only once for the first three consecutive Saturdays as the names are read even if you are not present. Put the list in an envelope with a small remuneration for the priest. You may want to bring a small bowl or platter of *kóllyva*. (See below) A few parishioners also bake *prósforo*.

Following the service all the *kóllyva* is combined, symbolizing the mixing of souls in heaven. Parishioners share the *kóllyva* and greet each other with, "*O Theós na tous anapáfsi*" ("May God forgive the souls of the dead.")

OTHER WAYS TO REMEMBER THE DECEASED

- Visit the grave site.
- Light a candle in the narthex at any time or donate candles for the altar and holy *proskomithí* table where the bread and wine are prepared for communion.

- Donate altar flowers
- Remember the deceased's name day by:
  - Making the altar bread (*prósforo*) for communion or bread for an *artoklasía* service, giving the priest the name of the deceased to be read during the service
  - Making sweets to share with the congregation at the coffee hour
  - Offering a memorial

SPECIAL SITUATIONS

TRANSPLANTS AND DONATION OF ORGANS AND BODY

The Orthodox church believes the body to be the temple of the Holy Spirit and therefore its integrity should be maintained. However, the church does not oppose transplants now, and in many cases endorses and encourages the decision. In some cases organ donation is quietly accepted because many Orthodox also are beneficiaries of the new scientific and medical advances. In dealing with the question of organ donation in the "Tell Me Father" column of the *Orthodox Observer,* George Papaioannou strongly recommends, "…we should support and encourage people to sign up as organ donors. Consult your parish priest; discuss it with your family; and after prayerful evaluation, please sign up."[3]

Because there is no similar recent ruling regarding body donation for research, this is still officially prohibited. Any Orthodox Christian who wants to make such an arrangement should discuss it with his priest before deciding to do so.

AUTOPSY

A medical examiner is allowed to proceed with an autopsy in questionable circumstances of death, and for medical and scientific reasons.

RECIPES

KÓLLYVA

(FOR INDIVIDUAL MEMORIAL)

Start preparation of *kóllyva* two days in advance and assemble the day of the memorial.

4 cups (2 pounds) shelled wheat
½ cup granulated sugar
1½ cups finely chopped walnuts
1½ cups slivered almonds
1 cup pine nuts
2 cups white raisins
2 teaspoons cinnamon
2 teaspoons coriander
2 teaspoons cumin
2½ cups powdered sugar
2 cups finely ground zwieback toast
Optional: Seeds of one pomegranate and 1 cup chopped fresh parsley

Decoration: Whole blanched almonds without skins, white candied almonds, large silver dragees, white paper doilies

Distribution: Small plastic bags and spoons

Rinse the raw wheat until water is clear. Then cover the wheat with 2 quarts of water and soak overnight. Drain and rinse. Cover with 4 quarts of water in a large heavy pot and bring to a boil. Reduce heat and simmer uncovered several hours, keeping the wheat covered with water and stirring occasionally, until wheat becomes puffy and tender. (Cooking time varies with time of soaking.) Drain in a colander, rinse, and drain again. Spread the wheat out on a smooth dish towel to dry overnight. (If desired, burn a *kandíli* beside the wheat as it dries.)

Prepare all other ingredients but do not assemble until the day of the memorial to prevent mush-like texture.

On the day of the memorial light a censer and *kandíli* while making the *kóllyva.* Cover a large tray approximately 20" x 13" with wax paper and then paper doilies that extend over the edge about an inch and a half. Combine all the ingredients except the powdered sugar, zwieback crumbs, and decorations. Put combined mixture on a tray and mold into a heaping mound toward the center, pressing it smooth. Spread crumbs evenly over the top, making sure the wheat is thoroughly covered, and press down. (This layer keeps the wheat mixture from bleeding through to the top layer of powdered sugar.) Sift powdered sugar over the mound and press smooth with wax paper.

Make a cross in the center with large silver dragees. With blanched almonds form the initial of the first name of the deceased on the left side of the cross, and the initial of the last name on the right, preferably using Greek letters (see *Pronunciation Guide*). Decorate the edges as desired.

Take the *kóllyva* to church where it will be placed on a small table by the icon of Christ at the *ikonostásion*. If the table does not have candles, put one or three in the *kóllyva* to be lit during the memorial service. After the service put about ¼ cup of *kóllyva* in small plastic bags for distribution to parishioners. Eat with spoon or fingers. In Greece relatives take *kóllyva* to the grave site and distribute to passers-by.

The ingredients have symbolic meaning: wheat for everlasting life, raisins for sweetness, pomegranate seeds for plenty, powdered sugar for the sweetness of heaven, and parsley for the green of the earth.

———⯈•○•⯇———

KÓLLYVA
(FOR SATURDAY OF SOULS)

Make one-fourth of the above recipe. (Note that the cooking time for the wheat may be reduced.) Put the *kóllyva* in a bowl or on a small plate. Decorate the top with a cross and border design, not initials of the deceased since *kóllyva* for Saturday of Souls is generally made for more than one person.

Put a candle in the center of the *kóllyva*. Take it to church where it will be placed on the memorial table with the *kóllyva* from other parishioners. At the end of the service, all the plates of *kóllyva* are combined in a large bowl and distributed. In Greece parishioners pinch *kóllyva* from each other's dish, mixing it by hand.

Paximáthia

(Allow two days to prepare)

2 cups warm water	1 cup vegetable shortening
1 teaspoon sugar	5 teaspoons anise seed
5 packages dry yeast	1 teaspoon *mastícha*
5 pounds flour (15 cups)	½ cup sugar
½ teaspoon salt	1 quart water

Dissolve yeast and 1 teaspoon sugar in water and let sit until foamy. Combine the yeast and all ingredients except flour. Slowly add 10 cups of flour. Work the sticky dough until it forms a loose ball. Put on a floured surface and add additional flour until a stiff dough is formed. Knead several minutes. Place in a large bowl greased with shortening. Cover with a cloth for an hour, kneading for a few minutes every 15-20 minutes (minimum of 3 times). Remove from bowl and place dough on floured surface. Cut dough into 10 portions. Cover again and let sit for 15 minutes. Form 10 oblong pieces approximately 1" high and 1½" wide. Place on baking sheets, leaving adequate space between loaves for dough to rise. Cut half way through each oblong with a sharp knife at ½" intervals. Let loaves rise until double in size. (Do not cover in summer; in winter cover with clean cloth and plastic over cloth.) Bake at 375°F on middle oven rack about 25 minutes or until golden brown. Remove loaves to racks to cool overnight. The next day, cut each loaf into pieces and place each piece flat on baking sheet. Bake at 350°F until slightly brown and then turn over to brown other side. Makes appoximately 14 dozen.

---

1. The *miolóyia* (words of fate) is an ancient funeral dirge that originated in pagan times. One of the earliest examples is the lament of Hector's body by his wife, Andromache, in *The Iliad*. The *miolóyia* is a long extemporaneous poem about the deceased's life sung by female relatives and friends over the body during the wake, funeral, and burial.

2. "Eonia i Mnimi" adapted from Nick and Connie Maragos, eds., *Sharing in Song,* 4.

3. George Papaioannou, "Tell Me Father," *Orthodox Observer,* 11 February 1987.

PART TWO

Greek Customs of Everyday Life

✤ *Greek-American Values*

Greek Americans are proud of their individuality. After all, their ancestors were the first in Western civilization to elevate and glorify the individual. Yet Greek Americans maintain a common identity. They share values deeply rooted in Greek Orthodoxy, in a classical heritage from Greece, and in a dynamic American society. Each individual finds a personal balance of those influences — some people are more Greek; some are more American — thereby defying sociologists who try to profile a typical Greek American. Each, however, is influenced in some way by the following common values.

FAMILY

Most Greek Americans hold religion and family in the highest esteem. Closely linked, the two mutually reinforce each other as the Greek Orthodox church emphasizes the family, and the family emphasizes the church. In 1972 Archbishop Iakovos of the Greek Orthodox Archdiocese of North and South America explained the connection in an encyclical letter concerning National Family Week:

> Home and family life [are] the bedrock of our Greek Ortho-dox life-style. The spirit that binds us together as a people finds its deepest roots in the home where the tenderest values of human existence, love, compassion, forbearance, and mutual helpfulness thrive in abundance... Marriage is holy. The home is sacred. Birth is a miracle. In these we find the very meaning of life itself.

The ideal family is close-knit and loving with a sense of mutual obligation among generations. Parents feel great love for their children and willingly sacrifice for their children's well-being and education. Deference to authority is important, and children are taught to respect their parents and other elders. Many children stay home until married. Sometimes aging parents move into a child's home. However, these last two traditions are being modi-fied as Greek Americans become more assimilated, mobile, and affluent.

The church advocates the traditional patriarchal family consisting of father, mother, and children, an ideal strongly recommended by St. Paul in the first century. In the marriage ceremony, the wife accepts the husband as head of the house. "Wives, be subject to your husbands as to the Lord; for the man is the head of the woman…" The husband is a strong authority figure and sometimes a strict disciplinarian. Some people view this patriarchal approach as chauvinistic, while others argue that the wife does not take second place in the family. In many ways she is the cornerstone of the family, and is charged with the most important responsibility: keeping and maintaining intact the fabric of the family. Greek Americans view mothers with feelings of respect and reverence because of women's central role. Until recently, the wife assumed almost complete responsibility for housework and child rearing even if she worked outside the home. Earlier generations referred to her as the "good mistress of the house" (*kalí nikokirá*). The husband was known as the "master of the house" (*nikokíris*) which lead to interesting personal dynamics. A popular old folk saying captures the situation: "The husband is the head, but the wife is the neck that decides which way the head will turn!"

Greek Americans highly value family honor and community approval. The imprudent acts of one family member can affect the entire family's reputation; therefore each person is responsible for maintaining both personal honor and family honor. Greek Americans' concern for protecting the family reputation is one of the main reasons they are seldom involved in criminal activity.

Of course, it is difficult to maintain these values in a modern society. In fact, earlier generations feared the negative influence of other nationalities on their children. Non-Greeks were referred to as *xeni* (foreigners or strangers — pron. *kséni*). Great efforts were made to preserve the language, traditions, and purity of the family. Marriages between Greeks and non-Greeks were discouraged, even by the church. However with the defection of young people from the church and a decline in the marriage rate, in 1948 the church reversed its policy.[1] From 1980 to 2004 inter Christian marriages fluctuated between fifty-nine and sixty-seven percent.[2]

The Greek-American family is subject to the same strains that weaken the American family. But the Greek love of family, nurtured for so many centuries, stands as a bulwark to many assaults, and there is hope that family values will prevail.

RELIGION

Greek Orthodoxy provides a spiritual base for Greek people and affects their life style and outlook. Much of their social life consists of celebrations that are religious in nature, such as marriages, baptisms, and holidays. In a crisis, God and the saints are often their refuge. In general, Greek people's optimism stems from their positive Christian outlook. Yet religion is treated as a natural part of an everyday life filled with many secular interests.

Many Greek Americans attend church to fulfill not only religious, but also social and cultural needs. Their approach to church contrasts with the situation in Greece where family and friends are accessible on a daily basis. In America, the church plays a more comprehensive role. Early Greek immigrants, isolated from their loved ones, turned to the church to serve all their needs, which is not as true today with second and third generations. However, even for those generations, the church remains not only a house of worship, but often the primary place to be with other Greek people and to enjoy various religious and secular events.

A close relationship between the church and Greek culture has existed since the beginning of Christianity. The New Testament was written in Greek. Much of Christian doctrine was formulated by church fathers trained and inspired by the philosophy and spirit of ancient Greece. Concepts regarding the origin of the soul, individual redemption, a human's personal relationship with God, and the ideal spiritual world are Greek in origin. The relationship between being Greek and being Christian is so deeply rooted in the Greek psyche that centuries later during the 400-year-rule of Greece by the Ottoman Empire, attempts by the conquerors to uproot this unity of religion and culture failed. The church assumed responsibility in maintaining Greek culture. Hidden or secret schools (*krifá scholiá*) conducted by the church at night in basements, monasteries, and caves have become legendary.

When transplanted to America, the Greek Orthodox church continued to safeguard religion, language, and culture. The more Americanized second and third generations, however, have pressured the church to downplay the Greek language and culture. Each parish and its priest makes its own accommodation on these issues. Some parishes are more "Greek" than others, but all value and respect this cultural component of Orthodoxy.

Estimates range from a little over half a million to two million Greek Orthodox in the United States. The conservative estimate includes the 140,000 households of four that regularly contribute to the parish churches of the Greek Orthodox Archdiocese of America.[3] The two million figure is an estimate from *Orthodox Christians in America* by John Erickson.[4]

ETHNIC PRIDE

Greek Americans have cherished their Greek heritage since the first Greek immigrants arrived in the United States. Just as their Byzantine ancestors developed the early Christian faith, their Greek ancestors developed models and standards of thought and conduct acknowledged as the basis of Western civilization. The architects, philosophers, mathematicians, poets, dramatists, politicians, scientists, and historians of classical Greece remain some of the most influential men of recorded time.

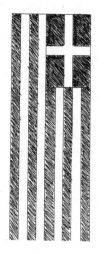

To be Greek *and* American creates a special pride of its own. The world looks to America as a model of democracy and to ancient Greece as democracy's birthplace. Pride comes from knowing that the founders of the United States reached back over 2,000 years to the Greeks for their inspiration and wisdom concerning the relationship of government to its people.

Parents make a special effort to educate their children about their heritage, sending them to Greek language classes, dressing them in national costumes for programs and parades, attending Greek festivals, and visiting Greece. Increased travel and cultural exchanges over the past twenty-five to thirty years have tightened the link between Greece and America.

Greek Americans are concerned about contemporary Greece and help with a variety of causes from improvements of family homes to restoration of antiquities. Their interest also extends to politics, as they press for the rights of Greece in the world arena.

Greek Americans point with pride to any success of other Greek Americans. The emergence of some national leaders of Greek descent has stimulated the interest of the younger generation, which feels proud to be of the same ethnic background. Scholars, musicians, and business leaders are applauded for their success, which reflects well on everyone in the group. Always ethnically conscious, they continuously scan names in newspapers, books, movie credits, and other public sources, noting with delight when the name is Greek.

More than one million Americans claim Greek ancestry. According to both the 1990 U.S. Census and the 2000 U.S. Census, just over one million people claimed Greek ancestry.[5]

EDUCATION

Greek Americans highly value education for themselves and their children. Through knowledge people find their place in, and shape civilization. Ancient Greeks articulated this universal truth centuries ago. Their methods of observing, analyzing, questioning, and synthesizing provided the model for Western education still used today. Plato founded the first institution of higher learning, the Academy. The Orthodox church continued this tradition by emphasizing religious and secular education. On Greek Letters Day, January 30, the church honors the patron saints of education, the Three Hierarchs: St. Basil the Great, St. Gregory the Theologian, and St. John Chrysostom.

These saints serve as models of intellectual excellence. Ancient Greeks believed that one of the best ways to learn is by imitating an ideal model. Even during difficult circumstances, such as the Ottoman oppression, Greeks continued to educate themselves and their children by attending the *krifá scholiá* (hidden schools).

When they arrived in America, most Greek immigrants did not have the luxury of educating themselves. Their poor English skills and the necessity of earning a living meant working long hours in semiskilled jobs with no opportunity to go to school. However, they understood the importance of education and knew that dignity and freedom came from educational excellence. They were determined to educate their children. In fact the word "education" *("paedía")* comes from the ancient Greek word for "child."

Greek-American parents sacrificed greatly to send their children to institutions of higher learning. Those children lived up to their parents' expectations, often moving, in one generation, from laborers to professionals such as doctors, lawyers, scientists, engineers, business people, professors, and heads of universities and colleges.

Personal Honor — *Philótimo*

Greek Americans highly value personal honor, or *philótimo* (love of honor). *Philótimo* stems from a respect for oneself, and from it flow many other positive attributes: dignity, generosity, hospitality, consideration and love of others, and a sense of right and wrong.

Individuals are judged as having *philótimo* (or not) by their willingness to be loving and caring toward other people, even strangers. A person who lacks those qualities, therefore, lacks a basic, if not the most basic, human value. No matter how intelligent or how wealthy, an individual without *philótimo* will not have the respect of others. Conversely, a poor person (or family) with *philótimo* is held in high regard in the community.

HOSPITALITY — *PHILOXENÍA*

Greek hospitality, known as *philoxenía* (friendship to strangers or guests —pronounced *philoksenía)* dates back to ancient times. Travelers appeared without notice, and before being asked their names were accorded baths, a place of rest, and food. A guest never left without gifts. This extraordinary treatment mentioned in both *The Iliad* and *The Odyssey* by Homer most likely came from the desire to please the gods, especially Zeus. "Zeus himself is the [protector]. . . of guests. . . . Guests are august, and Zeus goes with them." *The Odyssey,* Book 9.269-270.

Centuries later in *Report to Greco*, the modern Greek author, Nikos Kazantzakis, writes that his grandfather in Crete, "...took his lantern each evening and made the rounds of the village to see if any stranger had come. He would take him home, feed him, give him a bed for the night, and then in the morning see him off with a cup of wine and a slice of bread."[6]

Unfortunately, changes in American and Greek society preclude such blind faith in strangers today. To Greek Americans, *philoxenía* means hospitality and generosity among acquaintances, friends, and newcomers. Greek Americans graciously extend their hospitality with warmth and sincerity. Great effort is put into making guests feel welcome and at home.

GREEK-AMERICAN WORK ETHIC

Most Greek immigrants moved to the United States for economic reasons. For generations America has opened its doors to people from around the world, offered economic opportunity, and promised material success for individuals willing to work hard. The relationship between economic success, hard work, and the individual was stated by Max Weber, a German economist and sociologist, who in 1904 linked the success of capitalism to the Protestant work ethic and individualism. The three ingredients were interdependent. As noted by George Papaioannou in his book *The Odyssey of Hellenism In America*, such an economic and social system was ideally suited to the Greek immigrant who came from a culture that had emphasized and prized the individual for centuries.[7] Greek immigrants adapted naturally, and each person worked long hours to achieve success. This work ethic is a key value for Greek Americans and one of the reasons for their success.

For decades most Greek immigrants were employed in mass industries such as the textile mills of New England, railroad construction in the West, and steel mills. Many immigrants became entrepreneurs, running businesses such as restaurants, shoe repair shops, boats to collect sponges, dry cleaning stores, theaters, and florist shops. Charles Moskos in *Greek Americans: Struggle and Success* states that by the end of World War I a substantial middle class existed[8] and after World War II a professional class emerged.[9] Many professionals learned the value of hard work while helping in their parents' business. They passed that work ethic on to their children.

1. Athenagoras, "An Encyclical on Marriages and Family," 27 September, 1948.

2. *Yearbook 2006* (New York: Greek Orthodox Archdiocese of America, 2006), 122.

3. Interview with Public Affairs Office, Greek Orthodox Archdiocese of America, 2006.

4. John H. Erickson, *Orthodox Christians in America* (New York: Oxford University Press, 1999), 129-130.

5. U.S. Bureau of the Census, "1990 Detailed Ancestry Groups for States," CP-S-1-2, 3 (1.10 million); U.S. Bureau of the Census, QT-02 "Profile of Selected Social Characteristics: 2000" (1.18 million).

6. Nikos Kazantzakis, *Report to Greco,* trans. P. A. Bien (1965; reprint, New York: Bantam Books, 1966), 171-172.

7. George Papaioannou, *The Odyssey of Hellenism in America* (Thessaloniki, Greece: Patriarchal Institute for Patristic Studies, 1985), 69.

8. Charles C. Moskos, *Greek Americans: Struggle and Success,* 17.

9. Ibid. 52.

❖ *Birth of Children*

The Greek family welcomes a new baby with tremendous joy — children are prized, pampered, and most of all, loved. Familiar terms of endearment such as *"petháki mou"* ("my little child"), *"angeloúthi mou"* ("my angel") and *"hrisó mou"* ("my golden one") are used constantly by doting relatives and friends to convey affection and tenderness. A new child is considered a blessing that bonds the family together.

In fact, the central role of children is clear from the beginning of marriage. During the Greek Orthodox wedding ceremony, the priest often refers to procreation and implores God to let the couple "rejoice with the sight of sons and daughters" and "behold their children's children like newly-planted olive trees around their table." Such emphasis on family is a basic Greek value giving rise to many customs and traditions.

BEFORE THE BABY ARRIVES

THE EXPECTANT MOTHER

It is customary to wish an expectant mother, *"Kalí leftheriá"* (Safe delivery — literally, "good liberation!") Similarly, any prayers or promises for the health of the mother and child often are directed to St. Eleftherios, the patron saint of childbirth. In some parts of Greece, it is believed that an expectant mother will have an easier delivery if she is touched with *váya*, a cluster of bay or myrtle leaves blessed by the priest on Palm Sunday.

CHOOSING A NAME

Originally, the godparent selected the child's name and gave it at baptism. In the United States today, the parents select the name before the child is born since the hospital requires the name for the birth certificate. If the godparent has been selected before birth, discuss the name selection together out of courtesy. (See *Selecting a Name*)

THE BABY SHOWER

The baby shower is an American custom that has been adopted by many Greek Americans. Guests, generally female friends and relatives, bring gifts for the expected baby.

MALE AND FEMALE CHILDREN

In the Greek family, a desire still lingers for the birth of at least one male, primarily to carry on the grandfather's name. The historically negative reaction to females has been eased with the ending of the dowry practice. That custom required the bride to bring money and property into the marriage. Girls meant burden and expense; boys meant income. At one time girls were so unwelcome that a popular wish for a married woman was "May you have male children and female sheep!" This attitude no longer prevails, and daughters are equally loved. In some families the pressure to produce a son still exists, although this is not an exclusively Greek phenomenon.

TÁMA (VOW) FOR CONCEPTION AND DELIVERY

Sometimes a couple may have difficulty conceiving a child and bringing it to term. In such cases a common practice is to pray to a saint for assistance, making a *táma* (vow) to give or do something. Vows might include naming the child after the saint, giving a precious object or money to the church, or performing a good work (see *Special Blessings, Prayers, and Appeals*).

WELCOMING THE NEWBORN

WHAT TO SAY

When the baby arrives, parents and other family members — grandparents, sisters, brothers, aunts, and uncles — happily congratulate each other with, *"Na mas zísi"* ("May he/she live for us"). Acquaintances say, *"Na sas zísi"* ("May he/she live for you") or *"Na zísi"* ("May he/she live").

CIRCUMCISION

Circumcision is not a religious practice of Orthodoxy. The church does not oppose it, however, and leaves the decision to circumcise up to the parents and their physician.

SPECIAL PRAYERS AND BLESSINGS

First-day Prayer

You may wish to ask your priest to visit the hospital or home soon after birth to offer the first-day prayer for mother and child. However, this has become less common in America because of time, distance, and the needs of larger parishes.

On the island of Sifnos, Greece, the priest blesses water in the home, and visitors must first wash their hands with the holy water before holding the baby.

Eighth-day Prayer

There is an official prayer for the newborn on the eighth day after birth that comes from the Jewish tradition of giving the name and performing a male child's circumcision on that day. (Luke 2:21: And when eight days were completed for the circumcision of the Child, His name was called Jesus.) For Christians, a prayer of birth is given instead. The baby may be named at this time. Few Greek Americans observe the eighth-day prayer. For those who do, the priest may go to the home or the newborn may be brought to the church by the intended godparent, a relative, or a friend since the mother may not enter church for forty days.

Forty-day Blessing (see below)

TRADITIONAL SWEETS

After the baby's birth, you may want to serve traditional sweets typical of your family's region of Greece to visitors who come to the home during the forty-day period. On the island of Kastelorizo, guests receive *yennitoúria,* a small potpourri of walnuts, raisins, and dried fruit wrapped in tulle tied with a little ribbon and a saint's medal. *Loukoumáthes,* deep-fried pastry puffs, symbolize sweetness and joy on the island of Mitilini.

GIFTS FOR THE NEWBORN

Silver or Gold

A beautiful custom followed in Greece and America is to *asimósi
to pethí* (to silver the child). When you visit a baby for first time,
bring a silver coin or a gift made of silver and place it in the
baby's crib. Silver is the most common precious metal. In Mitilini,
when the relatives come on the third day to watch the midwife
bathe the baby for the first time, they place gold coins on a pillow
by the child's crib. In Crete, visitors customarily put a gold coin,
small crosses, or zodiac signs.

Filaktó

Filaktó

This is a small religious medal or tiny cloth pouch that may be
pinned to an upper-back shoulder of the baby's clothing to protect
against evil. The square or triangular pouch, measuring about an
inch on each side, contains sacred items such as holy flowers.
Decorations sometimes include beaded edges and an embroidered
cross or the "eye of God." They may be made by hand, purchased in monasteries in Greece, or sometimes obtained through a
Greek specialty store. Older children and adults may also wear or
carry *filaktó*.

Máti

Mati

Some children receive a *máti (matopiástra* - formal), a small pin
or medallion of blue stone with a black eye in the center. The
child wears the *mati*, a common folk remedy to ward off the evil
eye, on the upper back.

Toys, Clothing, Icons, and Accessories

These items are also commonly given to newborns and are thoughtful
and appropriate.

SUPERSTITIONS

At one time in certain regions of Greece, new parents put bread
under the newborn's pillow and covered the mirrors in the house

to deflect evil influences. New mothers wore only white for forty days. An even more obscure tradition appeased the "Fates" that supposedly visited a newborn on the third day. The "Fates" in the form of three women gathered around a newborn's cradle to write the child's destiny. To secure a favorable outcome, sweets were left on a table in the same room. Although most Greeks do not observe these customs, some do believe in predestination. For example, if a tragic event happens to someone, they often remark, *"Étsi ítan graftó."* ("That's the way fate was written.")

THE FORTY-DAY BLESSING (CHURCHING)

The most important custom for the newborn and the mother is the forty-day blessing (*sarantismós*), a reenactment of Mary's bringing Jesus to the temple on the fortieth day after his birth (The Presentation of Jesus Christ in the Temple). The mother brings her baby to church on the fortieth day (or the closest following Sunday) for a brief service of purification and to formally bring the baby into the church. Call your local priest to arrange a convenient time.

According to tradition, this is the first time that the new mother and the baby are allowed to enter the church. (In the past some people believed that going outside the house before the prescribed forty days would bring bad luck.)

The mother and child remain in the church narthex and do not enter the nave until the priest has offered a prayer. Then the priest carries the baby to the front of the church, followed by the mother and sometimes other participants. The priest proclaims: "The servant of God is brought within the church in the name of the Father, and the Son, and the Holy Spirit. Amen."

Male children are carried around the altar. Females must remain at the altar gates in keeping with the Orthodox practice that only males may enter the sanctuary area. (This tradition is controversial, and some change is taking place. Many priests and bishops take female children into the altar area — the new practice has not been challenged by the Greek Orthodox Archdiocese of America.) After the forty-day blessing, close family members say, *"Na mas zísi"* ("May he/she live for us") and acquaintances offer congratulations with *"Na sas zísi"* ("May he/she live for you") or *"Na zísi"* ("May he/she live"). Since the mother and child are still in delicate condition, no celebration or reception afterwards is necessary.

The prohibition of a new mother from entering the church for forty days after birth stems from the church's policy on cleanliness. According to the Old Testament, women were considered unclean after childbirth. A period of purification lasting forty days was required before entering the church, a controversial tradition today. Many women do not consider themselves "unclean" from giving birth and are pressuring the church for change.

SPECIAL SITUATIONS

BIRTHDAYS

In the United States, the one-year birthday comes after twelve months. However, in Greece a child is considered to be "walking" into the second year on the first birthday, sometimes creating confusion when Greeks and Greek Americans discuss age. In Greece, name days, not birthdays, are celebrated.

ABORTION

Abortion is forbidden by the church unless the mother's life is in danger.

ADOPTION

The church will bless the union of the parents and the new child with a special prayer to bind them together.

MISCARRIAGE

In the event of this misfortune, a special prayer can be said by the priest for the mother. As in giving birth, the mother cannot enter the church until she has received the forty-day blessing.

❧ *Selecting a Name*

Many Greek names have a timeless quality. Maria, John, Peter, Helen, Christine, and Paul are names used again and again throughout the centuries for family and religious reasons. Both grandparents and saints can be honored when naming your children. Selecting a name is easy, and if you follow tradition to the letter, your child's godparent will even do it for you!

FAMILY CUSTOMS

In the Greek family, it is customary to give the grandchildren the first names of their grandparents. The middle name is usually the father's first name. This tradition preserves the continuity of the family, creating a link between the present generation and its ancestors and honors the grandmothers and grandfathers, who enjoy having namesakes. If you do not follow this tradition, be sure to discuss the matter with your parents to avoid any hurt feelings. To some it is an insult to neglect to name the grandchildren after them.

FIRST NAME

A child's first name is the first name of either a paternal or maternal grandparent — the custom varies from region to region. The first two methods closely follow the Greek tradition of always naming the first male after the paternal grandfather. The third method is more American.

Method A
> First male child named after paternal grandfather
> First female child named after paternal grandmother
> Second male child named after maternal grandfather
> Second female child named after maternal grandmother

Method B
> First male child named after paternal grandfather
> First female child named after maternal grandmother
> Second male child named after maternal grandfather
> Second female child named after paternal grandmother

Method C

First child named after either paternal grandfather or grandmother
Second child named after either maternal grandfather or grandmother
Subsequent children's names repeat pattern of naming after
    paternal then maternal grandparents

Of course, there are exceptions to the above custom. A paternal grandfather may already have a grandchild named after him, and is willing to have the child named after the other grandfather. A promise may have been made to a saint to name the child after that saint *(na to táxis to pethí)*. The non-Orthodox grandparents in an interfaith marriage may not be as concerned about the naming tradition. And if you have more than four children or more than two of the same sex, the choice is left to you and the godparents.

MIDDLE NAME

The middle name is usually the first name of the father, used as a possessive in Greek, i.e., you are the son or daughter of your father. This name is also known as the patronymic and probably comes from the Greek law requiring the father's name for the transfer of property for both males and females. The tradition also prevents confusion among grandchildren. Two grandsons could have the same name as their grandfather: Emanuel Rouvelas. The first name of the father in the middle differentiates them. For instance, Emanuel Nicholas Rouvelas is the son of Nicholas; Emanuel Eleftherios Rouvelas is the son of Eleftherios. In America, boys customarily take the father's name as the middle name, but girls rarely do. They sometimes take a feminine middle name, or none at all. For example:

Grandfather:	Eleftherios Emanuel Rouvelas
Son:	Emanuel Eleftherios Rouvelas
Grandson:	Eleftherios Emanuel Rouvelas
Grandmother:	Mary Rouvelas
Mother:	Marilyn Sue Rouvelas
Granddaughter:	Mary Pauline Rouvelas

RELIGIOUS TRADITIONS

NAME SELECTION BY GODPARENT

Traditionally the godparent alone has the right to name the child. Today, however, godparents and parents have modified tradition somewhat and collaborate in advance so the name will be available for the birth certificate issued at the hospital.

In Greece the child is called "baby" until baptized, and the legal name is the one given at the baptism. In America, this need not be the case. A child may have one name on the birth certificate and another on the baptismal papers. Converts to Orthodoxy take a religious baptismal name, but retain their prior legal name.

NAME OF SAINT OR BIBLICAL EVENT PREFERRED

The church prefers the baptismal name to be that of a saint in the Greek Orthodox church, a significant feast day (such as Anastasios), or symbol such as the cross. This is neither canon law nor a directive. The tradition began in the fourth century in Antioch when people began naming their children after St. Meletios, who led a model Christian life. Parents wanted their children to inherit some of his saintly, exemplary qualities. Today it is still hoped that the child's behavior will be inspired by the saint's life. The namesake also becomes the child's patron saint, providing protection from danger and acting as the child's messenger to God.

CHOOSING A SAINT

Because this custom has been in effect for centuries, the grandparent's name usually will already be the name of a saint. This simplifies the selection process, satisfying both the religious and family requirements. If a specific saint and name day are not a family tradition, determine who would be a good role model and patron saint. For example, "Joanna" is the feminine of "John," and most women celebrate the name day of St. John on January 7. But one of the myrrh-bearing women who anointed Christ after his crucifixion is St. Joanna, and her feast day is June 27. This name day could be chosen instead. More options are open to women now with the recent scholarship about female saints.

Sometimes an individual is named after the saint whose feast day
is closest to the date of baptism and chrismation. A man chrismated
in late October might take the name "Demetrios" for St. Demetrios
whose feast day occurs on October 26. For further information
see *Saints* and *Name Days* and consult with your priest.

BLENDING FAMILY AND RELIGIOUS TRADITIONS

Many Greeks have ancient or mythological names such as Sophocles,
Aphrodite, or Agamemnon. When the grandparent's name is not
that of a saint, conflict may arise between the wishes of the
grandparent and the church. Some priests accept nonreligious
names for baptism, others will not. Some priests allow combined
religious and secular names, for example, "Persephone Panayiota."
It is wise to discuss this question well in advance of the baptismal
ceremony to prevent problems. If the name presented to the
officiating priest at the time of the sacrament is not an acceptable
one, the priest may demand that the parents and godparent make
another selection on the spot!

CONVERTING NAMES

A "two-letter" rule has been commonly adopted in converting
Greek names to English. In general, two letters are taken from the
Greek name, and an English name with the same two letters is
found. For instance, the "Ha" from the name "Haralambos" are
the first two letters of the English name "Harry."

There are countless variations on the formal names of the saints.
The endings change according to gender; names are shortened,
expanded, and transformed beyond recognition. One of the most
popular examples is the beloved "Panayia," one of the names for
the Virgin Mary. Males are called "Panayiotis" and females,
"Panayiota." Female names include Panayiotitsa, Pitsa, and Yota.

❧ *Greek School*

Adult Greek Americans love to recount their childhood Greek school experiences with humor and affection. Like taking piano lessons, they begrudgingly went because their parents insisted. Those who attended long enough to read, write, and speak are glad they did; those who did not, regret their lack of knowledge. Most then have children who feel the same way!

HISTORIC HIDDEN SCHOOLS

For many Greek Americans, afternoons at Greek school are as much a part of the ethnic experience as eating *baklavá* or dancing a *hasápiko*. For generations, parents and the church stressed the importance of learning the language, culture, and faith at classes taught in a church after school and/or on weekends. Greek classes sponsored by the church are an old tradition dating back at least to the Turkokratia (Turkish rule), when Greece was dominated by Turkey from the fifteenth to the nineteenth centuries. The hidden schools (*krifá scholiá* – also pronounced *scholía*) in Greece and Greek communities in Turkey were located in caves and secret places where priests taught children at night, to their peril. "My Bright Shiny Moon," a child's poem memorized by thousands of Greek-American children even today, describes the experience:

Fengaráki mou lambró	My bright shiny moon
Fénge mou na perpató	Light my pathway
Na piyéno sto scholió	To walk to school
Na maTHéno grámmata	To learn to read and write
Grámmata spouthágmata	Letter and studies —
Tou THeoú ta prágmata	God's things!

Φεγγαράκι μου λαμπρό
Φέγγε μου να περπατώ
να πηγαίνω στο σχολειό
να μαθαίνω γράμματα
γράμματα σπουδάγματα,
του Θεού τα πράγματα.

"My Bright Shiny Moon"

Years later the American Greek schools also sought to preserve the language, heritage, and faith. But in the United States practical considerations mattered too. Children needed to learn to read and write Greek in case they visited Greece or went there to live some day. In addition, keeping the children "Greek" was a way for the parents to maintain the Greek heritage in an alien land.

EARLY GREEK SCHOOLS IN AMERICA

Although well meaning and adamant about their goals, the early Greek schools were far from perfect. Teachers were not adequately trained and used old-fashioned methods. Texts were slavishly copied or memorized by rote. Classrooms and materials were inadequate. The resistant pupils themselves did not make things easy. Greek school was conducted two or three times a week, and students resented the extra work and time away from other friends. Teachers were strict disciplinarians, and many a disruptive student was labeled a *zóon tis kinonías* (animal of the society). Greek-American historian Theodore Saloutos attended Greek school in the twenties and recounted it with discomfort:

> I suppose one reason I hated Greek school was because it gave me little time to play or do the things I wanted to do as a youngster. Imagine a grade school youngster coming home from the public school in late afternoon, then having to ready himself for a school he had no desire to attend, and which he attended often under protest, haunted with the thought he would be reprimanded by the teacher for coming to school unprepared, taking with him often a piece of Greek bread or some other edible to curb his growing appetite, often sitting in bleak, uncomfortable and sometimes cold surroundings totally different from what he knew in the public school, and forced to have a late supper... the Greek language school was a nightmare.[1]

Parents and teachers jokingly reminded the children that they were still better off than their forebears in the *krifá scholiá!* But the church took the complaints seriously, and in the early 1930s Archbishop Athenagoras made Greek education a top priority, urging every parish to have a Greek school whether there was a church building or not. By the 1936-37 school year, the number of Greek schools (450) and pupils (25,000) had roughly doubled since 1932-33.[2] In 1944 Athenagoras established the St. Basil Academy in New York to train new teachers. But World War II disrupted the growth, and momentum was not regained despite Archbishop Iakovos' efforts to keep education at the top of the church's agenda. In 1970 he declared the old system a failure and insisted that the latest teaching methods be employed to revitalize the program and that teachers have training and attend workshops. While significant progress has been made, the Greek Orthodox Archdiocese of America released another major report in 1999, noting the loving atmosphere in the schools, but calling for improved facilities, higher salaries for teachers, better textbooks, and increased parental participation.[3]

GREEK SCHOOLS TODAY

For the 2002-2003 school year, there were approximately 340 afternoon Greek schools serving 30,000 students ages six to fifteen. The Archdiocese school system also includes preschools, kindergartens, adult language classes, and twenty-seven parochial day schools in the United States.[4] Of the twenty-seven day schools, most are accredited to meet government standards and offer a complete education, including classes on the modern Greek language, culture, and faith. Most of the schools are sponsored and financially supported by churches. Some are independent entities.

PURPOSE AND CURRICULUM

The purpose of Greek schools is to transmit the Modern Greek language, history, culture, and Greek Orthodox faith. Each Greek-American child should develop an awareness and pride in the contributions made to the world by his or her Greek ancestors. Individuals with a basic knowledge of the language can participate more fully in the church service and contribute their talents as members of the choir. In addition, proficient individuals may now obtain an official Certificate of Attainment in Modern Greek issued by the Ministry of Education of Greece which is recognized in Greece, Cyprus, and the European Community.[5] Holding the certificate has numerous advantages: proficiency is required for most jobs in Greece and for admittance to many Greek institutions of higher learning. In some states in America students receive high school and college language credit if proficiency can be proven.

The spoken everyday language of Greece known as demotic is now taught. This language was recognized by the Greek government in 1976 as the official language in place of a stiff, formal Greek named *katharévousa* developed from the Greek spoken in classical Athens after independence in the nineteenth century.

STUDENT PROGRAMS

The cultural programs staged for the community by the children of the Greek school delight and please their elders. They proudly watch the young people dressed in national costumes recite poems in Greek, perform plays, and dance to Greek folk music. At Christmas, they sing the *kálanda* (carols); on Oxi Day (October 28) they remind everyone of Greece's resistance to the Germans in World War II. On Greek Independence Day (March 25) they stir patriotic feelings with recitations that celebrate the end of Turkey's rule. For months, the children rehearse diligently for these events.

PARENTAL INVOLVEMENT

The most successful Greek schools are those that are enthusiastically supported by the parents. Their active interest in the schoolwork and progress of their children is vital. They must convince the children of the value and advantages of knowing the Greek language and heritage now and in the future. They can supplement the schooling by speaking Greek at home, if possible, watching direct broadcasts from Greece on television or the Internet, enjoying Greek videotapes, and reading books for pleasure. At-home tutors are also popular and are a long tradition in their own right.

---

1. Theodore Saloutos, "Growing Up in the Greek Community of Milwaukee," *Historical Messenger of the Milwaukee County Historical Society* 29, no. 2 (Summer, 1973), 52, quoted in Alice Scourby, *The Greek Americans,* 42.

2. Athenagoras, "Encyclical on the Greek Language Schools," 7 August, 1937, quoted in George Papaioannou, *The Odyssey of Hellenism in America,* 391.

3. "The Future of the Greek Language and Culture in the United States: Survival in the Diaspora" [The Rassias Report], (New York: Greek Orthodox Archdiocese of America—Greek Education Department, 1999).

4. Greek Orthodox Archdiocese of America, *Yearbook 2006* (New York: Greek Orthodox Archdiocese of America, 2006), 111.

5. Examinations for the Certificate of Attainment in Modern Greek are organized by the Center for the Greek Language in Thessaloniki by order of the Greek Ministry of Education at various locations throughout the United States. Exams are both oral and written for four specific levels of proficiency. For further information, contact the Greek Embassy, Office of the Educational Counselor, Washington, D.C, at www.greekembassy.org.

Ke sta thiká sou (And at yours [wedding] —
said to single women and men)

Ke sta pethiá sou/sas (May your children get
married and to theirs — said to married
couples with children [formal/informal])

Memorial	*Eonía i mními* (Eternal be [his/her] memory) See also "Death" above
Misfortune	*Étsi ítan graftó* (That's the way fate was written)
Name day	*Chrónia pollá* (Many years)
	Ke tou chrónou (And to next year)
New Year	*Chrónia pollá* (Many years)
	Kalí chroniá (Good year)
Pregnant woman	*Kalí leftheriá* (Safe delivery)
Saturday of Souls	See "Memorial" above
Sneeze	*Yiá sou/sas* (To your health — formal/informal)
So so	*Étsi k' étsi* (So so)
Toasts	*Yiá sou/sas* (To your health — informal/formal)
	Is iyían (To health)
	Yiá chará (Health and joy)
To avoid a problem	*Ktípa ksílo* (Knock on wood)
Trip	*Kaló taksídi* (Good trip)
Yippee!	*Ópa!*

The following phrases are commonly used to respond in many of the above situations:

- *Efcharistó* (thank you)
- *Epísis* (and to you too)
- *Ke tou chrónou* (and to next year)

Be careful! You would not say, *"Epísis"* when someone says, *"Kalí lefteriá."*

SPECIAL PEOPLE

Greek grandparents love to be called *"yiayiá"* and *"papoú."* The terms add to the joy of grandchildren and confirm a respect for their heritage. Other common relationships are listed below.

The form used in this listing is for direct address. The first ending in a word is masculine; the ending after a slash is feminine.

Aunt	*Thía* (pron. *THía*)
Brother	*Adelphé* (pron. *athelphé*)
Child	*Pethí*; *petháki* (diminutive)
Countryman	*Patrióti* (from same region of Greece)
Cousin	*Eksáthelphe/eksathélphi*
Daughter	*Kóri* or *thigatéra* (pron. *THigatéra*)
Father	*Patéra*; *Babá* (affectionate)
Father-in-law	*Patéra or Babá* (Use *peTHerós* for third person)
Godfather	*Nouné* (*nounó* — popular usage)
Godmother	*Nouná*
Grandfather	*Papoú*
Grandmother	*Yiayiá*
In-law(s)	*Sympéthere/sympethéra* (pron. *sympeTHéra*) *Sympétheri* (plural)
Mother	*Mitéra*; *mamá* (affectionate)

Mother-in-law	*Mitéra* or *mamá* (Use *peTHerá* for third person)
Mr.	*Kírie*
Mrs.	*Kiría*
Priest	*Páter*
Priest's wife	*Presvytéra*
Relation by baptism or marriage	*Koumbáre/a (Koumbáro* – popular useage*)*
Sister	*Adelphí* (pron. *athelphí*)
Son (my son)	*Yié mou*
Uncle	*Thíe* (pron. *THíe*) (*Théo* – popular useage)

❧ *Food and Drink*

Delicious food is one of the great pleasures of Greek culture, and today the general public enjoys many Greek specialties. *Baklavá, moussaká, souvláki,* and the *gýro* (pron. *yíro*) have found their way into the American mainstream. For Greek Americans, food goes beyond these popular images. It is an integral, emotional part of their ethnic identity and one of their most satisfying traditions.

CUSTOMS AND TRADITIONS

An old Greek proverb says, "If the pot boils, friendship lives." Social life often revolves around the table where families bond together and friendships are solidified. Here, amid large platters of food, values are transmitted, old times recounted, politics discussed, and differences aired. Hours pass by as friends and family talk together. Sharing a meal is the most common Greek social activity.

Both the quantity and the quality of the food are important. A heavily laden table suggests well-being and generosity. Large quantities of food entice guests to eat as much as they want, and running out of food is considered a great embarrassment. Guests are continually urged to eat and to take second helpings. Increasingly, however, Greek Americans are becoming more aware of the effects of certain foods. In today's world, favorite old recipes have been modified to lower fat and cholesterol. Olive oil, a Greek mainstay, has no cholesterol and is low in saturated fat.

On religious holidays special food brings a renewed appreciation of tradition. During Lent, *fasolátha* (bean soup) reminds one of sacrifice and restraint. At Easter the traditional red eggs, Easter bread (*tsouréki*), a soup called *mayerítsa,* and roasted lamb enhance the joy of the Resurrection of Christ. Cracking red eggs symbolizes Christ's emergence from the tomb. The cutting of the New Year's Vasilopita (bread for St. Basil) and finding the lucky coin focuses everyone on the coming year. Eating and sharing *kóllyva* (boiled wheat) following a memorial service for a departed loved one reinforces the hope of afterlife. These special foods strengthen beloved Greek traditions.

ORIGINS

Greek cuisine today is a blend of old and new. The old goes back to classical Greece where sophisticated Athenians analyzed and enjoyed certain dishes. Food and dining became an art form like drama, sculpture, and architecture. Greek cuisine spread to other countries, and the Romans were known to import Greek chefs. Later there was substantial Middle Eastern influence due to Greece's proximity to the Middle East, its ties to the Byzantine Empire, and its subjugation to the Ottoman Empire for centuries. Yet, even during the occupation, much of Greek cuisine was preserved. Greek chefs fled to Orthodox monasteries to preserve their culinary traditions. They wore tall white hats to be distinguished from the priests wearing black ones — and from this began the practice of chefs' donning high white hats. It is difficult to determine exactly how many dishes are of Greek origin, since some Greek foods such as *baklavá* have Turkish names. Despite the names, however, the fact remains that many countries in the Middle East share similar foods with the Greeks.

THE GREEK TASTE

Certain ingredients and flavors distinguish Greek food. Their complexities and subtleties must be discovered at the table and in the numerous cookbooks available. Excellent books may be purchased at bookstores and through Philoptochos societies of many Greek Orthodox churches. Consult these books for a more complete discussion of ingredients, recipes, and serving suggestions. The following tips deal with some of the most popular elements of Greek cuisine.

OLIVE OIL

The foremost ingredient of Greek cooking is olive oil, a splendid greenish-gold liquid that threads its way through a variety of dishes, enhancing the flavor of vegetables, stews, and meats. It tastes best, perhaps, alone with chunks of hearty bread. Greeks love to recount the famous myth where the city of Athens conducted a contest to see which god or goddess would be its patron, depending on who gave the most valuable gift. Athena was chosen for giving the olive tree, useful for its oil, fruit, and wood.

It outranked Poseidon's gift of a spring of sea water. The finest olive oil is cold pressed extra-virgin, generally used for eating. A less refined oil may be used for cooking.

OLIVES

Greece is one of the largest olive producers in the world. Luscious black, green, or brown olives appear as a side dish on most Greek-American tables, eaten before and during meals. Different regions produce different types; some are picked earlier than others; some cracked open. The most famous is the large black Kalamata olive, but be adventurous and try some of the other kinds. Look for olives that are firm and not too salty. If you prefer, lessen the salty taste by soaking the olives in water for several days, changing it periodically; draining; drying; and adding olive oil, red wine vinegar, garlic, and oregano as a marinade.

CHEESES

Féta, *kasséri*, and *kefalotíri* are among the most popular Greek cheeses available in the United States. *Haloúmi*, a rubbery textured cheese, is the pride of Cyprus. *Féta* (meaning "slice") remains the best known. Traditionally made by shepherds in the mountains of Greece, the most popular variety comes from the milk of sheep and is white, flaky, and slightly salty. *Féta* made from goat's milk is harder and sharper. Avoid the inferior *féta* made from cow's milk. Freshness is essential. Always ask the grocer for a little taste to make sure it has not become rubbery and tasteless. Keep the cheese fresh in the refrigerator by storing it in an airtight container completely submerged in its natural brine, if possible. Eat within several weeks of purchase.

SPICES, HERBS, AND FLAVORINGS

Certain spices, herbs and flavorings predominate in Greek cooking. Fresh parsley, mint, and dill are used generously, and a variety of wild oregano from Greece called *rígani* is preferred. (Basil, an herb with religious significance, is rarely used in cooking.) Generous quantities of fresh garlic season lamb, stews, and the antisocial *skorthaliá* (garlic sauce). Lemons are a key ingredient in the popular *avgolémono* (egg-lemon) sauce that can be added to a soup. Wedges of fresh lemon come with most meals. Cinnamon appears in both tomato sauces and pastries. The most famous honey, a common sweetener, comes from thyme-covered Mt. Hymettus in Attica, Greece.

PHÍLLO

Many Greek dishes are constructed with layers of *phíllo*, paper-thin sheets of dough. A variety of fillings from spinach and cheese to egg custard and nuts are sandwiched in between the layers to make *spanakópita* (spinach pie), *galaktoboúriko* (milk custard between *phíllo*), and *baklavá*. To the novice, working with the fragile pastry sheets seems nothing short of miraculous until you see an experienced cook deftly handle the sheets, rapidly applying butter to each one. *Phíllo* (sometimes called strudel leaves) is now sold in many supermarkets in the freezer section. Try to find recently made dough. Work with it at room temperature, keeping the unused dough on the side under a slightly damp towel to prevent drying.

BEVERAGES

Wines

Greece is more famous for its god of wine, Dionysos, than the wines themselves. Recently, however, as Greece attempts to become competitive in the aggressive world of wine production, wine regions have been formed and standards set. The most distinctive Greek wine is *retsína*, a white wine made by adding a small amount of pine resin at the beginning of fermentation. If properly made, the resin taste can be pleasing, but even many Greeks have failed to develop a taste for it. Only Greek wineries produce *retsína*, a name protected by law.

Oúzo

Oúzo, is said to be the national drink of Greece, although most Greeks in Greece prefer Scotch whiskey. *Oúzo* is a clear, anise-flavored aperitif that tastes like licorice and is most often taken with *mezéthes* (appetizers), especially grilled octopus. There are many brands of *oúzo*, but the island of Mitilini claims to be the best producer. An acquired taste for many, *oúzo* may be drunk straight or with ice. Most popular is a mix of one-part *oúzo* to two-parts water. When water is added, the *oúzo* becomes a milky white color.

Brandy

Many companies produce brandy, but Metáxa brand remains the preferred Greek brand. There are three qualities from which to choose: three, five and seven-stars (seven is the best). Brandy is served to toast a special occasion or served after dinner. Following a death it is customarily served at the *makaría* (the meal following a funeral) and to guests who visit the grieving family during the forty-day mourning period.

Coffee

Potent and strong, Greek coffee is served black with foam on the top, in a small demitasse cup called a *flintzáni*. Since sugar is brewed together with the coffee, declare your preference when you order: *skéto* (plain), *métrio* (medium), or *glikó* (sweet). Avoid drinking the thick coffee residue remaining in the bottom of the cup. One or two cups may be made at a time in a small, long-handled pot called a *bríki*. (Consult a Greek cookbook for directions.)

Reading coffee cups is a favorite pastime. After drinking, the coffee cup is turned over, and the residue forms patterns on the inside of the cup that can be read to predict the future.

A TYPICAL TABLE

Mealtime provides an opportunity for good company and good times. A wide variety of delicious foods may be presented, but certain side dishes always complement the fare. Just as Americans automatically place salt and pepper shakers on the table, Greeks put out little dishes of olives, sliced cheese, wedges of lemon, and carafes of olive oil, and red-wine vinegar.

Appetizers are called *mezéthes*. Popular ones include *tiropitákia* (little cheese pies) and *keftéthes* (meatballs), dips made of fish roe (*taramosaláta*) and eggplant (*melitzanosaláta*), and pickled vegetables. Sometimes a sampling of these little snacks make a repast known as the *mezé*, often accompanied by *oúzo*.

Meals often begin with the light and tasty *avgolémono* (egg-lemon) soup. *Pítes* (pies) made with *phíllo*, meat, vegetables and/or cheeses are standard fare. Artichoke and eggplant are among the most popular vegetables, along with roasted potatoes and the typical Greek village salad of cucumbers, tomatoes, and *féta*. Rice prepared as *piláfi* and hearty bread may accompany the meal. Chicken roasted with lemon, lamb grilled on skewers (*souvláki*), and baked fish are favorites. Lamb has a special status in Greece because of its association with the biggest holiday, Easter, when it is roasted on an outdoor spit. Other times of the year lamb makes excellent stews and casseroles. Popular dishes in Cyprus include *sheftaliá* (grilled rolls of spiced meat) and *koúpes* (wheat tubes stuffed with minced meat).

Fruit marks the end of the meal. Elaborate sweets are served later. Standard favorites include *galaktoboúriko*, and nut cakes and tortes drenched with sweet syrup. Some sweets are associated with certain times of the year and occasions. Christmas and New Year treats include *baklavá*, *melomakárona*, *thíples*, and *kourabiéthes*. *Halvá* is served during Lent. *Baklavá* and *kourabiéthes* are popular at weddings and christenings. Sweets symbolize joy and good wishes. Greek guests customarily bring sweets when visiting someone's home to "sweeten" the friendship.

Greek food tastes best in its cultural context: after a glorious wedding, with a family gathered around the table, at a church bazaar, or at a *tavérna* by the sea. Then you experience the true Greek tradition of food. *Kalí órexi* (Bon appetit)!

❧ *Popular Music*

The many moods of Greek music fascinate the Western ear — the lamenting of the clarinet, the exuberance of the *bouzoúki*, the mystery of the minor key. To the uninitiated, the music invites images of intriguing places, food, and people. For the Greeks the sounds and rhythms express their very essence: their dreams, sorrows, joys. Add dancing and nothing more need be said. Two families whose children have just married share their happiness after the wedding by joining hands in one large circle to dance together. A proud grandfather dances alone, arms outstretched, to show his pleasure at his grandson's baptism. Through music and dancing, Greeks express *kéfi*, their pleasure and satisfaction with life.

There are three major categories of popular Greek music: *dimotiká* (pron. *thimotiká*), *laiká*, and *Evropaiká*. Understanding the categories will help you know what you are hearing, what to request, and what recordings to buy.

DIMOTIKÁ

Dimotiká are traditional rural folk songs with a non-Western sound. They are often played by a small ensemble of instruments such as the clarinet, lute, violin, dulcimer, and drum. A single voice sings the words, the rhythms have complex times like 7/8, 9/8 or 5/8, and the mode is usually in minor key. These songs go back centuries, perhaps even as far as classical Greece. Music historians, however, have been unable to establish a direct connection between folk music and that of the ancient Greeks.

Bouzoúki

The influence of both Byzantine church music and the Middle East is unmistakable. While the rhythms are not ecclesiastical, the distinct, single melodic line in minor key that dominates most folk songs resembles the monophonic Byzantine chant still heard in Orthodox churches today. The early church encouraged secular music at the feast day celebrations, and the priest would even start the first dance. The music of the Middle East has used similar instrumentation and rhythms for centuries. Greek folk songs remained a combination of Byzantine and Middle Eastern music, untouched for the most part by Western influence during the four-hundred years of domination by Turkey that ended in the nineteenth century. (The Ionian islands closest to Italy are an exception.) Common themes include love, politics, war, and lamention.

With Greek independence from the Ottoman Empire in 1821, Greece became receptive to Western influences. The tango and fox trot began making their way into *dimotiká*. Each region of Greece had its own style that still exists today. Songs of the islands are more lighthearted than those of the mainland. The Ionian islands show Italian influence with their serenades (*kantáthes*). The Aegean islands are famous for improvisations before the main song, instrumental (*taxím*) and vocal (*amané* — Turkish for "alas"). Cretan music is highly syncopated. On the mainland, the Peloponnese have a strong vocal tradition heard in the heroic *kléftica* songs, music composed by the resistance fighters who fought the Turks in the mountains. Thracean music has a lively tempo while that of Epirus is slower, a characteristic especially evident in its instrumental laments called *mirolóyi* (words of fate).

Patriotic songs (*patriotiká*) are a special kind of *dimotiká*. Most of these songs tell stories of heroic deeds and tragedies relating to the Ottoman occupation and to the revolution.

Dimotiká are still popular today, and their rhythms provide the base for popular folk dances like the *kalamatianós, sirtós, tsámiko, zeibékiko, hasápiko,* and *tsiftetéli* (see *Folk Dancing*). Bands today often substitute the electric guitar, electric keyboard, and a set of drums for the traditional equivalents.

LAIKÁ (GENERAL *LAIKÁ*, *REBÉTIKA*, *ELAFROLAIKÁ*, AND MODERN *ELAFROLAIKÁ*)

Laiká are urban songs of various styles: general *laiká*, *rebétika*, *elafrolaiká*, and modern *elafrolaiká*.

General *laiká* developed after the turn of the twentieth century. This urban folk music was greatly influenced by *rebétika,* a sound that began in the early 1900s in *cafe amans* and back city streets. Small nightspots called *cafe amán* became very popular in Asia Minor and the urban centers of Greece. A cross between a coffee house and a nightclub, the *cafes* featured Turkish-style songs played on the *bouzoúki* and *baglamá*. Beginning in 1922 a great influx of Greeks arriving from Asia Minor after the war between Turkey and Greece brought more Middle Eastern influence.

Meanwhile a new sound was emerging in the back streets of Aegean seaports such as Piraeus, home to destitute people called *rebétes*. Others were criminals who composed music while in jail. Many were refugees living on the fringe of society. They lived in an underworld where smoking hashish was commonplace and part of the music scene. Musicians there began playing a kind of soulful folk music also featuring the *bouzoúki* and *baglamá*. Similar to American blues, the close harmony, low-life lyrics, and emotionalism proved captivating. Combined with the influences of Asia Minor, a soulful folk music called *rebétika* evolved. Despite its allure, *rebétika* was not acceptable to the government nor the middle and upper classes because of its sometimes crude themes and Turkish sound. In the thirties *rebétika* began moving out of the hashish houses, resulting in classic *rebétika*. When the government closed the houses in the late thirties, many *rebétika* musicians became part of the established music scene incorporating the *bouzoúki* and *rebétika* sound into urban folk music.

After World War II, music featuring the *bouzoúki* became the rage all over Greece. Respectable composers like Mikis Theodorakis and Manos Hatzidakis began using the tantalizing sound. Popularly referred to as *bouzoúki* music, nightclubs called *bouzoúkia* flourished and continue to do so today. Most *laiká* music today features the *bouzoúki* sound. For further reading, see *The Road to Rembetika* and *Theodorakis: Myth and Politics in Modern Greek Music* by Gail Holst-Warhaft.[1]

The *bouzoúki* is now considered the premier Greek instrument. With electrification, the power and force of the *bouzoúki* evokes an extreme range of emotions. During a solo *taxím*, the *bouzoúki* takes the listener from painful loneliness to exuberant happiness. Like the violin, it possesses a haunting quality.

A lighter *laiká*, known as *elafrolaiká*, comes from the *laiká* tradition, but the sound is softer and more modern. These are easy-listening songs popular with the general public. Modern *elafrolaiká* is far removed from general *laiká* and *elafrolaiká*. These songs have a faddish quality, absorbing the latest Western sounds from Europe and the United States.

EVROPAIKÁ

Evropaiká has a distinct European flavor but with Greek words. After the revolution of 1821, European music gained enormous popularity. At that time, the *kantátha* (an Italian and German hybrid) and waltz were the rage. The sound remained Greek, often retaining some traditional instruments such as the clarinet and *bouzoúki*, but blending several cultures. Easy listening and fun to dance to, *evropaiká* is still popular especially with the older generation. Today's Greek singers, such as Giannis Parios, tend to revive old songs, including ballads about love, loneliness, and gambling.

GREEK MUSIC IN AMERICA

In the Greek-American community, music trends basically follow those of Greece. During the forties, some Greek-American music was heavily influenced by the big-band sound. In the fifties, two major trends emerged: the *rebétika* sound and a return to more *dimotiká* especially at baptisms, weddings, and dances. Today the Greek-American public enjoys a variety of Greek music.

At one time Greek-American musicians and composers recorded with such companies as RCA Victor, Columbia, Capital, Balkan, and Astro. Their recordings of *rebétika* before World War II are particularly valuable since recordings were restricted in Greece. They also continued to record *dimotiká* when it was considered unsophisticated by the urban population in Greece. Most recordings of Greek-American music today, however, are made in Greece. For further reading on the history of Greek music in America, read articles by Steve Frangos.[2]

BUYING RECORDINGS

If you are unfamiliar with Greek music, listen to it with someone who can identify the above types. Discover what you like and learn some of the key vocabulary that may appear on recording labels. Some catalogs organize the music by categories: *dimotiká*, *laiká*, and *elafrolaiká*. If you want traditional dance music, look for words such as *kalamatianós*, *sirtós*, *tsámiko*, *zeibékiko*, and *hasápiko*. You might also look for some of the well-known composers and performers who have remained popular through the years (listed below).

Finding a good selection of recordings may prove difficult. Many Greek Americans therefore buy Greek music when they visit Greece. In the United States, general music shops carry a limited selection of Greek recordings. Greek specialty stores have a wider choice, depending on the size of the Greek community. Ask to see the specialty store's mail-order catalog or obtain one through advertisements in a Greek-American newspaper. The largest distributor in the United States is Greek Music and Video Superstore, Inc, in Astoria, New York. Their catalogue identifies artists by music category such as *dimotiká* and *laiká*. A performer may have recordings in more than one category.

WELL-KNOWN PERFORMERS AND COMPOSERS

The following performers and composers have established reputations in Greek music. Some are from an earlier era; some are contemporary. Although they are listed in specific categories, be aware that many are versatile and perform more than one style of music. Some performers use only one name.

Dimotiká

Hronis Aidonidis
Yiorgios Anestopoulos
Rena Dalia
Rosa Eskenazi
Tassos Halkias
Kitskais
Oi Konitopouleoi (family)

Yiannis Konstantinou
Georgia Mittaki
Giorgos Papasideris
Vasilis Saleas
Sofia Vembo
Tacia Vera
Nikos Xilouris

Laiká

Haris Alexiou
Antipas
Sotiria Bellou
Grigoris Bithikotsi
George Dalaras
Litsa Diamanti
Stratos Dionisiou
Glikeria
Manos Hatzidakis (composer)
Stelios Kazantzidis
Stamatis Kokotas

Marinela
Dimitris Mitropanos
Poli Panou
Giannis Parios
Katerina Stanisi
Mikis Theodorakis (composer)
Prodomos Tsaousakis
Vasilis Tsitsanis
Markos Vamvakaris
Stavros Xarhakos (composer)

Evropaiká

Nikos Gounaris
Tonis Maroudas

Nana Mouskouri

---

1. Gail Holst, *Road to Rembetika: Music from a Greek Sub-culture* (Athens: Anglo-Hellenic Publishing, 1975) and Gail Holst-Warhaft, *Theodorakis: Myth and Politics in Modern Greek Music* (Amsterdam: Adolf Hakkert, 1980).

2. The leading authority on Greek music in America is Steve Frangos whose articles appear in various publications such as, *Resound, a Quarterly of the Archives of Traditional Music* (Indiana University, Bloomington) and *Greek American Review* (New York).

⚜ *Folk Dancing*

For centuries, infectious Greek songs with their insistent rhythms have lured listeners to dance — to celebrate happy occasions, bond together in wartime, and even express loneliness. Communal dancing appears on ancient Greek vases and in Byzantine frescoes. One dance, the *tsakónikos* from the Peloponnesus, allegedly represents the mythical king Theseus threading his escape through the labyrinth of the minotaur in Crete.

GEOGRAPHIC DIVERSITY

There are hundreds of traditional Greek folk dances. Each region boasts its own favorites and has certain characteristics. Cretan dances are proud and vigorous. The dances of the plains of Thessaly are controlled and composed, and some mountain people dance with wide steps and leaps. Even cold weather can affect dance style when heavy clothing is worn, as evident in northern Epirus. Some dances are named for their locality (*rodítikos* from Rhodes) or a profession (*hasápiko* from the word for butcher, *hasapis*). Names are also derived from a city, an event, or a special person. Many dances are related to each other, with individual variations.

Greeks and Greek Americans enjoy non-folk dancing also, such as the tango, waltz, disco, rock, and the latest trend. The danger of forgetting the traditional dances always exists, but they continue to survive along with the modern. Greek Americans like to mix contemporary and traditional dancing when they celebrate.

DANCE TIPS

The great fun of most Greek dancing is its communal, inclusive nature. With the exception of a few solo and couples' dances, everyone joins in the serpentine lines that whirl and weave around the floor: the reluctant novice, the two-year-old, the dance expert, the irritable grouch.

Anyone can join an open-circle dance by grabbing someone's hand at the end of the dance line or by breaking into the middle. You are swooshed into the heady whirl, taking lessons on the spot just by imitating the person next to you. People tend to be patient and encouraging with beginners, pleased that you want to learn. You will be criticized more for not trying than for making mistakes.

Leaders of the line, however, are expected to know the basic steps and variations, so the front is not a comfortable position for a novice. A good leader puts on a show. Partially suspended from a handkerchief held by the next person in line, the leader performs variations on the basic steps, sometimes leaping into the air. Others in the line show their approval by shouting, *"Ópa,"* or making a hissing sound through closed teeth. After a brief time in the spotlight, the leader moves down the line, letting another dancer take over the lead.

In contrast, dances like the *zeibékiko* and the *tsiftetéli* are intended for one or two people. To be strictly traditional, no one would join in and distract from the dancer(s). At most Greek-American functions, however, many individuals and couples dance the *zeibékiko* and *tsiftetéli* while others are also on the floor. If you are uncertain, always wait and watch what others do.

At one time, certain dances like the *hasápiko* and the *zeibékiko* were reserved for men. Even the dancing styles for men and women were different. Men were open, vibrant and virile, performing leaps and turns, improvising complicated steps. Women danced modestly with eyes downcast. This, however, is not true today. Women lead lines and frequently dance a *zeibékiko*.

Appreciative spectators sometimes throw money on the floor, but it is meant for the band, not the dancers. In Greece the old practice of dashing plates to the floor has been prohibited, and in the big nightclubs, flower petals are scattered instead.

THE DANCES

The following six dances are the basics of the Greek-American dance floor. Learn these and you will rarely miss a beat. It is highly recommended that you take Greek dancing lessons from an experienced individual or perhaps a class sponsored by a church. Taking Greek dancing lessons has become a Greek-American tradition of its own! Imitating a dancer in line or watching videotapes are the next best ways of learning.

KALAMATIANÓS (OPEN CIRCLE)

If a Greek national dance was declared — unlikely, given the regional rivalries — the *kalamatianós* might be the choice. Easy and extremely popular, it is danced everywhere and has twelve basic steps in 7/8 time. Contrary to popular belief, it did not begin in the town of Kalamata (although one version did), but was derived from a very old dance, the *sirtós*.

SIRTÓS (OPEN CIRCLE)

It is believed that the *sirtós* is the oldest dance, and many dances are variations of it. In fact the ancient Greeks called all circular dances "*sirtós.*" In a *sirtós* the feet "drag" along the floor with a controlled reserve and tension even when the beat is fast. Twelve basic steps are executed in 2/4 time.

TSÁMIKO (OPEN CIRCLE)

Some describe the *tsámiko*, a stately warlike dance, as the most handsome in Greece. It originated in the Tsamouria area in Epirus and was originally danced only by men. Also called the *kléftikos*, it was danced by the *kléftes*, the fighters and rebels of the revolution of 1821. The dance showcases the leader's ability. Each area dances it a little differently.

HASÁPIKO AND *HASAPOSÉRVIKO* (OPEN LINE)

The *hasápiko* is a lively, hopping-style dance that dates back to Byzantium when it was danced exclusively by butchers in Constantinople. Influenced by *rebétika* music and enjoyed by many Greek sailors, it became the "sailors' dance." Its lively 1-2-3 kick step is danced arm-over-arm. When danced fast, the dance is called a *hasaposérviko* and resembles the Jewish hora. However, the hora moves clockwise, and the *hasaposérviko* moves counter-clockwise. The *sirtáki* combines the *hasápiko* and the *hasaposérviko*, beginning slowly and ending in a frenzy.

TSIFTETÉLI (ONE OR TWO PEOPLE)

The *tsiftetéli* originated in the Middle East where it is danced by belly dancers. The undulating hips and provocative style evoke images of a harem. Greeks and Greek Americans do the dance in a restrained yet seductive way either with one person or together as a couple.

ZEIBÉKIKO (SOLO)

The *zeibékiko* is an intensely personal dance executed with great restraint and control. The dancer with lowered head and drooping outstretched arms is totally self-absorbed, performing alone on the floor. Traditionally, no one interrupts the dancer's trance-like movements. Today, however, many individuals dancing the *zeibékiko* may ocupy the dance floor at the same time. The steps are improvised, making each dance different. Sometimes the dancer performs stunts such as dancing with a glass of wine on the head, or circling a glass of wine on the floor and then picking it up by the teeth and drinking it without hands. A small table is sometimes picked up in the teeth.

Brought by Greek immigrants from Asia Minor, the *zeibékiko* flourished in the underclass world of *rebétika* before World War II and was danced originally only by men. It gained widespread popularity with both men and women, however, after the rise of *bouzoúki* music.

VIEWING TRADITIONAL FOLK DANCING

America may be one of the best places to see a variety of Greek folk dancing since people from all over Greece may come to a single Greek-American dance. Many churches and organizations sponsor Greek dancing classes whose participants wear authentic costumes and perform at church bazaars and special programs.

The best dancing may be seen at the annual Greek Orthodox Folk Dance Festival sponsored by the Diocese of San Francisco of the Greek Orthodox Archdiocese of America. (Locations vary each year.) Dancers from seven western states perform in authentic costumes at the four-day competition.

In Greece, Dora Stratou's National Dance of Greece Ensemble performs daily in their theatre on Philopappou Hill across from the Acropolis. Performances are also sponsored in Greece and abroad by the Lyceum Club of Greek Women (*Lykeion ton Ellinidon*). The Club, with forty-eight chapters in Greece and seventeen around the world, is an authority on dances and related customs, costumes and music. Traditional dances and songs are being recorded for posterity in projects headed by Simon Karas at the Society for the Dissemination of National Music in Athens and the Lyceum Club.

❧ *Proverbs and Sayings*

The Greeks are full of wisdom and humor, from the loftiest sentiments to the earthiest folk advice. Aristotle reminded his fellow
Greeks that "Dignity does not consist of possessing honors but in
deserving them." In modest contrast, an old proverb advises, "If a
dog doesn't bite, let it bark with all its might!"

The following proverbs and sayings were collected from Greek
families, friends, and written sources.[1] They represent treasures
remembered and loved.

Apó to stóma sou stou theoú to aftí.
From your mouth to God's ear.

Yírise o tétsiras ke vríke to kapáki.
The pot rolled around until it found the lid.
(That person found the right match.)

To krasí ke ta pethiá léne tin aliTHia.
Wine and children speak the truth.

Ópou akoús polá kerásia, mikra kaláTHia vásta.
When they brag of many cherries, bring along a small container.

Pan métron áriston.
Moderation in all things is excellent.

Yiátrepse ta páTHi sou keh ystera ta thiká mou.
Mend your own faults, then look at mine.

Ekí pou íse ímouna, ke ethó pou íme THa élTHis.
Where you are, I have been; and where I am, you will be.

Káne to kaló ke ríchto sto yialó.
Do a good deed and cast it to the sea.

Áplose ta póthia sou óso fTHáni to páplomá sou.
Extend your legs only as far as your coverlet reaches.
(Live within your means)

O kalós fílos, stin anángi fénete.
A true friend proves himself when needed.

Prépi na vális tin perispoméni?
Do you have to add the accent?
(Must you have the last word?)

I kalí méra apó tin avgí fénete.
A fine day from dawn shows itself.

To mílo THa pési káto apó tin miliá.
The apple will fall under the apple tree.

To éma neró then yínete.
Blood cannot become water.
(Blood is thicker than water)

Mazí miláme ke hória katalavénoume.
Together we speak but apart we understand.
(We are not communicating.)

Páre papoútsi apó ton tópo sou ke as íne baloméno.
Take a shoe from your own country or town even if it is patched.
(The known is better than the unknown.)

Pes mou piós íne o fílos sou na sou ipó piós ise.
Tell me who is your friend, and I shall tell you who you are.
(You are judged by the company you keep.)

Ótan mbis sto horó prépi na horépsis.
When you get into the dance, you must dance.
(When you get involved you, are committed to perform.)

Píga na káno to stavró mou ke évgala to máti mou.
I tried to make my cross and poked my eyes.

---

1. Compiled by Helen Panarites from various sources, including
   Greek Proverbs, by Steven G. Economou, N.p., 1976.

⚜ *Superstitions*

Greeks love garlic — in sauces, dips, stews, roast lamb, and even in their pockets!. A popular superstition says that garlic protects against the evil eye. If a child looks attractive, inviting the envy of others, the mother may take a little precaution by tucking a clove of garlic in the child's pocket.

Such folk superstitions are common among Greeks and many other nationalities. The superstitions below probably span thousands of years and thousands of miles. Most Greek Americans view them as fun and colorful — a form of amusement — yet many give lip service to at least a few!

PREVENTING MISFORTUNE

JINXING

Do not spoil a good thing by bragging or predicting success. Overconfidence can bring failure. For example, never brag that you will get an "A" on a test before it is returned or make a million when the deal is closed. If you boast ahead of time, you may fail. Even in ancient times, myth had it that the gods chastised those who became too over confidant. When the triumphant Agamemnon returned home as a conquering hero from the Trojan War, he walked on a purple carpet reserved only for the gods. His arrogance offended them, leading to his downfall.

KNOCK ON WOOD *(KTÍPA KSÍLO)*

Knock on wood to keep a good thing from going wrong. This is a cousin to the idea of jinxing. If you must predict that something will go well, for example, "It looks like the sun will shine for the wedding," knock on wood several times to keep away the rain. This custom may have religious origins. Many early Christians carried pieces of wood believed to be part of the original cross. When in danger, they touched the wood, receiving God's protective power.

PREVENT THIRD MISFORTUNE

Some believe bad things happen in three's. After two bad things have occurred (such as two funerals) say, *"Na min tritósi"* ("May it not triple") to prevent a third unfortunate event.

EVIL EYE: IDENTIFICATION AND FOLK REMEDIES

Contrary to popular opinion, the evil eye *(vaskanía)* is recognized by the church as a legitimate religious phenomenon. It is part of a larger picture of evil generated by the devil. For a more detailed description see *Special Blessings, Prayers, and Appeals*. The church helps its parishioners exorcise the evil eye with a prayer offered by the priest. Some people practice the following folk remedies, even though the church discourages their use.

IDENTIFICATION

A popular folk method to determine if someone has the evil eye is to put three drops of oil in a glass of water. If the oil stays separate from the water, you do not have it. If the oil blends with the water, you do.

PREVENTING THE EVIL EYE

Ptoú, ptoú

> The most common protection against the evil eye is the simple phrase, *"Ptoú,* ptoú, *"* said immediately after receiving a complement. A cautious Greek parent upon hearing, "Your daughter is so smart," would counter with *"Ptoú, ptoú"* to keep the evil eye from harming her. Or it might be said by the person who gives the compliment. The phrase is a verbalizing of spitting to scare away evil spirits. In the Orthodox baptismal service, the godparent spits three times and denounces Satan.

***Na mi se matiáso* (Not to eye you)**

> One way of giving a compliment without bringing on the evil eye is to end the remark with, *"Na mi se matiáso"* or *"Ptoú, ptoú, na mise matiáso."* This lets the person know that you are not putting on the evil eye.

Eye over the Door

Some homes keep a picture of an eye over the main entryway to dispel envy brought in from the outside.

Matí

The *matí* ("eye") is a folk talisman made of blue stone, glass, or plastic with a black eye in the center. It is commonly given to newborn babies and pinned to clothing at the upper back. Adults also wear it as a pin, a necklace, on a charm bracelet, and even on the same chain as their cross. Although frequently viewed with amusement, the *matí* evokes a skeptical respect from even the most sophisticated!

Máti

Layman's Prayer *(Ksemátiasma)*

Another folk remedy employed by the Greeks to dispel the evil eye is a ritual prayer *(ksemátiasma)* that is passed on orally. The prayer cannot be written, or, legend says, it will lose its power. If you are a woman, you must learn it from a man; if you are a man, from a woman. It is passed on when the bearer is old as the bearer's power is lost once the prayer is revealed.

MISCELLANEOUS

USE THE SAME DOOR

Use the same door when entering and leaving someone else's house. To not do so, invites bad luck on an impending matter, such as a marriage proposal or a business deal.

READING COFFEE CUPS

After finishing a cup of Greek coffee, swirl the dregs, turn the cup over into a saucer and cool. The grounds form unique patterns inside the cup that are then read by a fortune teller *(kafetzoú)*. This is a common form of entertainment.

BEWARE OF KNIVES

Do not hand a knife directly to someone, or you will have an argument. Lay it down, and have the person pick it up. If you hand a knife, say *"Ptoú, ptoú."*

RINGING EARS

You will hear some news

SNEEZE

If you sneeze, you are telling the truth, or someone is talking about you.

RECEIVING SOAP, KNIVES, COLOGNE, AND HANDKERCHIEFS

If you are given a handkerchief, cologne, or a knife, hand the person a penny to avoid an argument and loss of friendship. Never give a friend soap as a gift or hand it to them. It washes away the friendship.

FOLD IN BEDSPREAD

Fold up the corner of the bedspread before going on a trip, so that you will return safely.

FOR SPECIAL OCCASIONS

For superstitions relating to holidays and special events, see: Christmas, New Year, and Epiphany *(kalikántzari);* marriage; and the birth of a child.

⚜ *Community Life*

In explaining the greatness of classical Athens, the statesman Pericles in his speech "Funeral Oration," said, "Here each individual is interested not only in his own affairs but in the affairs of the state as well." Pericles was referring to government, but he went on to explain that Athenians also cared about all aspects of their community: the law, meritocracy, beauty, discussion, recreation, kindness toward others, and free trade. This legacy of concern for building a worthwhile community continued with the early immigrants to America and the subsequent generations.

While involved in the broader society, Greek Americans still maintain a wide range of Greek organizations to preserve the Greek ethos, a system of values transplanted to America built on the dual foundations of the Greek Orthodox faith and Hellenism. The early immigrants began by building Greek Orthodox churches as centers for religious, cultural and social needs. In addition, they established secular Hellenic organizations dedicated to regional, cultural, professional, and personal needs. These efforts sustain the transplanted ethos and strengthen the whole community in new and diverse ways.

THE GREEK ORTHODOX CHURCH

With 541 parishes, chapels, and missions, the Greek Orthodox church is the largest organization in the Greek-American community[1], with 140,000 households that regularly contribute each year.[2] The parishes are located in eight metropolises headed by metropolitans. One Direct Archdiocese District is headed by the Archbishop who also leads the entire church in America from the national headquarters in New York. The Greek Orthodox Archdiocese of America comes under the political and spiritual guidance of the Ecumenical Patriarchate in Constantinople. (See *The Historic Orthodox Church*.)

For more details on church departments and programs, individual parishes, monasteries, the Ecumenical Patriarchate, statistics, and Greek-American secular organizations, see the Greek Orthodox Archdiocese of America *Yearbook* in your church office, order a copy from the Archdiocese in New York, or visit its website. The church's monthly newspaper, the *Orthodox Observer,* provides timely news articles about church and community life. Greek Orthodox Archdiocese of America, 8-10 East 79th Street, New York, New York, 10021, www.goarch.org.

CHURCH PROGRAMS

The primary purpose of the church remains a place for religious worship, administering the sacraments, education about Greek Orthodoxy and Hellenism, and ministering to the needs of the faithful and the wider community. Thousands of dedicated workers, both paid and voluntary, give time and talent to meet these goals in established church organizations such as the local parish council, Ladies Philoptochos Society, the Archdiocesan Council, Leadership 100, Archons of the Ecumenical Patriarchate, Young Adult League, Greek Orthodox Youth of America, summer camps, retreat centers, the Ionian Village in Greece for teenagers and young adults, Greek-American day schools and afternoon Greek language programs, and the National Forum of Greek Orthodox Church Musicians. Every two years the clergy and laity gather for a meeting. Major philanthropic projects include St. Basil Academy (for children), St. Michael's Home (for the aged), and Trinity Children and Family Services. The Greek Orthodox church helps support two major international groups under the auspices of the Standing Conference of Canonical Orthodox Bishops of America (SCOBA): the Orthodox Christian Mission Center and International Orthodox Christian Charities.

CHURCH FESTIVALS

Each year most parishes sponsor a Greek festival *(paniyíri)*, patterned after those typically held by churches, cities, and towns in Greece to celebrate the name day of the entity's patron saint. The public is invited to browse for Greek crafts, books, and artwork, hear Greek music, dance, and eat traditional foods, such as lamb roasted on spits, *moussaká, spanakópita,* and deep-fried *loukoumáthes.* The *paniyíri* presents Greek culture to the broader community and gives Greek Americans a chance to celebrate their heritage. Usually the largest project of the year with the most volunteers, the church festival has become a Greek-American tradition of its own.

HELLENIC ORGANIZATIONS

In addition to the Greek Orthodox church, secular organizations play a significant role in preserving the Hellenic heritage. Countless individuals involved with regional societies, national groups, academia, writing, publishing, museums, and the media contribute to this dynamic community life. The following list provides a sampling of the activities. For additional organizations and contact information, see *The Greek Diaspora* — "Greek Diaspora Internet Websites — Organizations."

AHEPA

AHEPA (American Hellenic Educational Progressive Association), established in 1922, has become the largest Hellenic heritage organization, with members worldwide, chapters in America, Canada, Greece, and independent chapters in Australia and New Zealand. While its early purpose was to help Greek immigrants participate in non-Greek society, it has broadened its scope to become a major philanthropic organization and promoter of Hellenism. Philanthropic projects include granting scholarships for college students, fundraising for medical causes, and building housing for low-income seniors through ANHC (AHEPA National Housing Corporation). Individual chapters across the country help support Hellenic awareness projects such as an annual float in the Rose Bowl Parade in California, the Classic Greek Theatre of Oregon in a summer drama festival, and a Greek Studies Fellows program in Newton, Massachusetts, which conducts seminars for teachers in the classics. Its annual national convention with its ancillary organizations, Daughters of Penelope, Sons of Pericles, and Maids of Athena, continues to be the largest Greek-American gathering, and its annual congressional dinner the largest political event. AHEPA, 1909 Q Street, NW, Washington, DC, 20009, www.ahepa.org.

REGIONAL SOCIETIES *(TOPIKA SOMATIA)*

Some Greek Americans belong to regional societies *(topiká somatía)* consisting of individuals from the same area of Greece or Asia Minor. For example, former residents and their descendants from the island of Icaros belong to the Pan-Icarian Brotherhood of America, a society with twenty-five local chapters across the United States, a national magazine, and an annual convention. While its original goals included helping new immigrants in America and meeting needs on Icaros, it has broadened its philanthropic reach. Plans include endowing a Hellenic studies chair at a university.

Most regional societies sponsor a variety of social, cultural, and educational events. The Greek Orthodox Archdiocese of America *Yearbook* lists the umbrella organizations under "National Organization/Federations" for Arcadia, Constantinople, Crete, Cyclades, Cyprus, Dodecanese, Epirus, Icaros, Laconia, Macedonia, Messinia, Pontia, Rhodes, and Chios.

OTHERS

Hundreds of other groups organize according to special interests. Doctors, dentists, business-people, bankers, and educators form professional networking organizations such as the Hellenic American Professional Society (San Francisco), Greek American Women's Network (New York), Hellenic American Women's Council (Washington, DC), Hellenic Link-Midwest (Chicago), and Hellenic Professional Society of Texas (Houston).

Numerous intellectual societies and literary groups focus on ancient and modern Hellenism, such as Hellenic Society Paideia (Storrs, Connecticut), Hellenic University Club of Southern California (Los Angeles), Hellenic University Club (Philadelphia), and Society for the Preservation of the Greek Heritage (Washington, DC).

Community service organizations such as the Hellenic American Neighborhood Action Committee (HANAC) in Astoria, New York, and the Hellenic Foundation in Chicago provide immigration counseling, senior services and housing, family counseling, and youth services. Funded with government money and corporate and private donations, they assist the Greek community and beyond.

Since the invasion of Cyprus in 1974, Greek Americans have become more active in formulating and expressing views on American foreign policy relating to Greece, Cyprus, Southeastern Europe, and the Eastern Mediterranean. Groups concerned with foreign policy include organizations such as AHEPA Public Affairs Committee, American Hellenic Institute (AHI) Public Affairs Committee, National Coordinated Effort of Hellenes (HEC), and the Pan-Epirotic Federation of America.

Some regions of the country have formed federations to coordinate local organizations for special events and causes. Examples include the Federation of Hellenic American Societies of New England, Federation of Hellenic Societies of Greater New York, Federation of Hellenic Societies of the Greater Baltimore-Washington Region, and United Hellenic Societies of Northern California.

Many private and public foundations contribute to causes within the Greek and American communities, including churches, scholarships, endowed chairs at universities, museums, medical benefits, cultural events, and lectures. For example, the American Foundation of Greek Language and Culture (AFGLC) of Tampa, Florida, is endowing Hellenic professorships at the University of

South Florida, in Tampa. The Karakas Family Foundation of St. Louis promotes Greek studies and culture. The Cyprus Museum in Jacksonville, North Carolina, houses written documents and artifacts from Cyprus. See *The Greek Diaspora* — "Foundations" for activities of the largest private foundations in Greece contributing abroad: the Alexander S. Onassis Public Benefit Foundation and the Stavros S. Niarchos Foundation.

Not to be overlooked are the numerous <u>individual philanthropists</u> who generously contribute to such worthwhile causes as the permanent exhibits at the Metropolitan Museum of Art in New York: "Mary and Michael Jaharis Gallery" for ancient Greek art; the "Mary and Michael Jaharis Galleries for Byzantine Art;" "Evanthea & Leo Condakes Greek Gallery" at the Boston Museum of Fine Arts, and the "Kyriakos Tsakopoulos Chair in Hellenic Studies" at Columbia University (Angelo Tsakopoulos).

GREEK-AMERICAN MUSEUMS

In a tribute to their ancestors and immigrant heritage, some communities have begun small museums relating to the Greek-American experience: St. Photios National Shrine at 41 St. George Street, St. Augustine, Florida; the Hellenic Cultural Museum at Holy Trinity Cathedral, 279 South 300 West in Salt Lake City, Utah; and the Hellenic Museum and Cultural Center currently at 801 West Adams, Chicago, Illinois. Future address: 333 South Halsted Street, Chicago. www.hellenicmuseum.org. The Greek Museum in New York City is in the planning stage: www.greek-museum.org.

HIGHER EDUCATION

CLASSICS, EARLY CHRISTIAN, BYZANTINE, AND MODERN GREEK STUDIES

In the forefront of educating and preserving the culture are the following American colleges and universities with the most extensive course offerings in the classics, early Christian (patristic), Byzantine, and modern Greek studies. This list is subject to change and is not comprehensive, especially in the classics where most colleges and universities offer courses. Also missing are some institutions with recently established chairs where departments are just getting started. (For Orthodox studies, see *The Historic Orthodox Church* — "Theological Schools, Seminaries, and Institutes.")

Boston College, Boston, (classics, modern Greek studies)
Boston University, Boston, (classics, modern Greek studies)
Catholic University, Washington, DC (early Christian, Byzantine)
Columbia University, New York (classics, modern Greek studies)
Dartmouth College, Hanover, New Hampshire (classics)
Harvard University, Cambridge, Massachusetts (classics, early Christian, modern Greek studies). Research libraries in Washington, DC, at the Center for Hellenic Studies (classics) and Dumbarton Oaks (Byzantine)
Hellenic College/Holy Cross School of Theology, Brookline, Massachusetts (classics, early Christian, Byzantine, modern Greek studies)
Kent State University, Kent, Ohio (classics, modern Greek studies)
New York University, New York, (classics, Byzantine, modern Greek studies)
Ohio State University, Columbus, Ohio (classics, Byzantine, modern Greek studies)
Princeton University, Princeton, New Jersey (classics, Byzantine, modern Greek studies. Also headquarters for American School of Classical Studies, Athens)
Queens College, City University of New York, Flushing, New York (classics, Byzantine, modern Greek studies)
Regis College, Weston, Massachusetts (classics, modern Greek studies)
Richard Stockton College, Pomona, New Jersey (classics, Byzantine, modern Greek studies)
Rutgers University, New Brunswick, New Jersey (classics, Byzantine)
San Francisco State University, San Francisco, (classics, modern Greek studies)
Tufts University, Medford, Massachusetts (classics)
University of Arizona, Tucson, Arizona (classics, modern Greek studies)
University of Chicago, Chicago (classics, Byzantine)
University of Florida, Gainesville, Florida (classics, modern Greek studies)
University of South Florida, Tampa (classics, Byzantine and modern Greek studies)
University of Michigan, Ann Arbor, Michigan (classics and modern Greek studies)
University of Minnesota, Minneapolis (classics, modern Greek studies and Byzantine)
University of Missouri at St. Louis — St. Louis, Missouri (early Christian classics and modern Greek studies)
University of New Hampshire, Durham, New Hampshire (classics)
University of Notre Dame, Notre Dame, Indiana (early Christian)
University of Wisconsin, Madison, Wisconsin (classics, Byzantine)
Wayne State University, Detroit Michigan (modern Greek studies)

ACADEMIC ASSOCIATION WEBSITES

www.apaclassics.org   American Philological Association (classics)
www.mgsa.org   Modern Greek Studies Association
www.patristics.org   North American Patristics Society
www.sc.edu/bsc/usnat/ U.S. National Committee for Byzantine Studies

ACADEMIC JOURNALS

Arethusa (classics), *Greek Orthodox Theological Review, The Journal of Byzantine and Modern Greek Studies, The Journal of Early Christian Studies, Journal of the Hellenic Diaspora, Journal of Modern Greek Studies, Journal of Modern Hellenism,* and *St. Vladimir's Theological Quarterly*

MODERN GREEK STUDIES

Modern Greek studies deal primarily with Greece since independence in 1821 and its Diaspora. It has become an established discipline in some American educational institutions of higher learning, with courses on the modern Greek language, political history, and literature. A typical literature class might include reading works by two Greek poets awarded the Nobel Prize in Literature, Laureates Giorgos Seferis (1963) and Odysseus Elytis (1979), and the renowned author of *Zorba the Greek,* Nikos Kazantzakis. Modern Greek studies also encompasses the study of Greek Americans.

GREEK-AMERICAN STUDIES

Very few courses are devoted to Greek-American studies, so the discipline falls under modern Greek studies. The first major scholarly work, *The Greeks in the United States,* by Theodore Saloutos, was published in 1964 based on a collection of primary documents now housed at the Immigration History Research Center at the University of Minnesota in Minneapolis. Other books include *Greek Americans: Struggle and Success* by Charles Moskos; *The Odyssey of Hellenism in America* by George Papaioannou; *The Greek Americans* by Alice Scourby; *Studies on Greek Americans by* George Kourvetaris; *American Aphrodite* by Constance Callinicos; *Greek American Families: Traditions and Transformation,* edited by Sam Tsemberis, Harry Psomiades, and Anna Karpathakis; and *New Directions in Greek American Studies ,* edited by Dan Georgakos and Charles Moskos. Histories of local areas, such as *Education and Greek Immigrants in Chicago, 1892-1973,* by Andrew Kopan, are also being written.[3] Recently academics have begun asking for primary documents from communities such as commemorative albums, publications, and videos. The modern Greek studies program at Ohio State University started the "Greek American Communities Library Collection," and San Francisco State University established the "Northern California Greek American Archive."

Popular Greek-American Writing

Up until the end of World War II writings about the experiences of Greek Americans were mostly limited to diaries, journals, and newspapers. However, one of the first <u>novels</u> with Greek-American themes, *Gold in the Streets* by Mary Vardoulakis, was published in 1945. Other novels include *America, America* by Elia Kazan, *A Dream of Kings* (one of eight) by Harry Mark Petrakis, *The Time of the Little Blackbird* by Helen Papanikolas, and *The Priest Fainted* by Catherine Temma Davidson. Well-known <u>short stories</u> include *The Chronicle of Halsted Street* (one collection of six) by Theano Papazoglou Margaris, *Pericles on 31st Street* (one collection of four) by Harry Mark Petrakis, and *Small Bird, Tell Me* (one collection of two) by Helen Papanikolas. Nicholas Samaras' *Hands of the Saddlemaker* and Penelope Karageorge's *Red Lipstick and the Wine-dark Sea* relate their cross-cultural experiences in <u>poetry.</u>[4]

Even more plentiful are <u>memoirs</u> about life in Greece, immigration, coping in America, and reactions of subsequent generations such as: *Eleni* and *A Place for Us* by Nicholas Gage, *Stelmark: A Family Recollection* by Harry Mark Petrakis, *Emily-George* by Helen Papanikolas, *Not Even My Name* by Thea Halo, and *Growing Up Greek in St. Louis* by Aphrodite Matsakis.[5]

Community organizations such as the Greek Women's University Club in Chicago are gathering <u>biographies</u> of local figures in such books as *Greek-American Pioneer Women of Illinois.*[6] Self-published books and private family videos have fueled an explosion of primary data for historians.

Greek-American Media

The Greek-American media facilitate communication within the community in both Greek and English languages.

NEWSPAPERS

Check *Yearbook 2006* of the Greek Orthodox Archdiocese of America for a more comprehensive list of newspapers and monthly publications. Some of the most prominent national <u>newspapers</u> are (in alphabetical order): <u>In Greek</u>: *Ethnikos Kiryx (National Herald)* (daily from Long Island City, New York). <u>In English</u>: *The Greek Star* (weekly from Chicago); *Hellenic Journal* (monthly from Oakland, California); *Hellenic Times* (biweekly from New York); *The Hellenic Voice* (weekly from Lexington, Massachusetts); *National Herald (Ethnikos Kiryx)* (weekly from Long Island City, New York); *Orthodox Observer* (monthly from the Greek Orthodox Archdiocese of America, New York, primarily English)

MAGAZINES

Prominent magazines include: *The AHEPAN* (quarterly, Washington); *Greek-American Review* (monthly magazine, New York); *Greek Circle* (quarterly, Chicago); *Greece-in-Print* (monthly literary review, River Vale, New Jersey); and *Odyssey: The World of Greece* (bimonthly magazine covering Greece and the Diaspora, Athens)

RADIO

Greek Americans have a variety of choices for radio programming. Local American-produced shows broadcasting news, announcements, Greek music, and Greek Orthodox church services, are available at limited hours in limited geographic areas, using both Greek and English. The *Yearbook 2006* lists 35 shows in twelve states.[7] Many incorporate programming directly from Greece. Increasingly, programming from Greek American Educational Public Information System, Inc. (GAEPIS) (Brooklyn) and "Come Receive the Light" (Fort Lauderdale), Florida, are building a national audience by webcasting on the Internet. Listeners who want direct access to broadcasting from Greece may tune in via the Internet at any time.

TELEVISION

Twelve Greek-American local television shows using Greek and English are produced for limited hours in seven states.[8] Greek Orthodox Telecommunications produces videotapes of Greek Orthodox and Hellenic programs for sale from the Greek Orthodox

Archdiocese of America in New York. Increasingly, Greek Americans pay for programming directly from Greece via cable or satellite dishes. To subscribe, check with your local companies about their services. Some of the more popular television stations broadcasting directly from Greece include Antenna, ERT, Mega, STAR, and Alpha TV.

INTERNET

Access to information about Greece and Orthodoxy has broadened dramatically with the Internet. Information ranging from the ancient Olympic Games to dining in Athens to a Greek Orthodox church festival in Australia appears in seconds on a computer monitor. For sites on Orthodoxy, see *The History of the Orthodox Church* — "Orthodox Internet Websites," and for sites on Hellenism see *The Greek Diaspora* — "Greek Diaspora Internet Websites."

GREEKTOWNS, USA

ASTORIA, NEW YORK

The largest concentration of Greek Americans lives in the Astoria section of Queens, a borough of New York. The area has a mix of apartment buildings, attached row houses, shops, restaurants, a Hellenic Cultural Center, three Greek Orthodox churches (St. Demetrios Cathedral, St. Catherine-St. George, and St. Markella), and the Patriarchal Monastery of St. Irene Chrysovalantou. In warm weather, the ambiance is typical of big-city life in Greece: bustling and congested with outdoor eateries. Astoria can be reached by cab or a twenty-minute subway ride across the river from Manhattan. The subway runs along Thirty-first Street, the main location for the Greek restaurants and stores; but establishments are sprinkled throughout the large rectangular neighborhood formed by Steinway, Thirty-first Street, Ditmars Boulevard and Broadway. The character of the neighborhood has been gradually changing to Asian and Hispanic as the second generation of immigrants from Greece in the 1960s and 1970s has moved to the suburbs.

The New York area, however, remains the "capital" of Greek America, with about 250,000 Greeks, including all the boroughs but not the suburbs.[9] The major daily Greek-language newspaper,

Ethnikos Kiryx (National Herald), is published there, and the vast majority of Greek food, music, and specialty items are distributed through New York companies. The headquarters of the Greek Orthodox church and the national cathedral, Holy Trinity, are located in Manhattan.

BALTIMORE, MARYLAND

Baltimore, with approximately thirty thousand Greek Americans in the area,[10] now boasts the only Greektown between New York and Florida. An estimated six hundred families of Greek heritage live in this approximately 122-square block, racially mixed neighborhood bounded by LeHigh, Umbra, Lombard and O'Donnell streets.[11] The Greek Orthodox Church of St. Nicholas, 520 South Ponca Street, with its village-style plateía for festivals and other celebrations, anchors the community. Greek restaurants, bakeries, shops and businesses between 4600 and 4900 Eastern Avenue provide a commercial base. Annual community events include a Greek Independence Day parade and the St. Nicholas festival held the second weekend of June. The city of Baltimore in cooperation with the state of Maryland, has begun to work in partnership with the community to preserve and improve the neighborhood. The Greektown Community Development Corporation and St. Nicholas Church are in the forefront of revitalizing the community.

CHICAGO, ILLINOIS

A substantial Greek-American community of about 110,000 resides in the Chicago area.[12] Most of the original Greektown clustering around Halsted Street has been displaced by the University of Illinois at Chicago, and the Greek population has dispersed throughout the city and suburbs. However, Halsted Street between Randolph and Van Buren streets still has the largest concentration of Greek restaurants, nightclubs, and grocery stores. Recently, the city of Chicago, as part of its effort to celebrate its ethnic populations, helped with the Greektown Re-Development Project on Halsted Street by building gateways to Greektown with classic Greek columns and pediments. The Hellenic Museum and Cultural Center, 801 West Adams Street, receives thousands of visitors who enjoy its exhibits and cultural events relating to Greece and Greek-American life. Eventually the museum will be housed in its own building in Greektown at 333 South Halsted. www.hellenicmuseum.org

DETROIT, MICHIGAN

Approximately forty thousand people of Greek heritage live in the Detroit area.[13] At one time Greektown was the home of many residents and commercial Greek establishments. Surrounded today by municipal buildings, Greektown consists of two blocks of Greek restaurants and shops on Monroe Street anchored by the Greek Orthodox Church of Annunciation at the intersection of LaFayette and Monroe streets. The annual March 25 Independence Day parade has been revived, and the Greek Merchants Association sponsors three annual events: the Greektown Glendi following Orthodox Easter, Greektown Art Festival, and the Harvest Festival. A recent addition to the community is the "Greektown Casino" with Greek decor.

TARPON SPRINGS, FLORIDA

Tarpon Springs is part of a Greek community of about thirty thousand living in the St. Petersburg-Tampa-Tarpon Springs area in southwest Florida.[14] Tarpon Springs is the most reminiscent of a Greek island village with its outdoor tables, white stucco buildings, tin cans of flowers, and a lovely setting by the ocean. In 1905 immigrants from the Dodecanese Greek islands started the natural sponge industry, and a Greek community quickly developed and thrived. With the invention of synthetic sponges, however, the market changed. This, together with the red tide scourge that killed sponges in the late 1940s, crippled the sponge economy. Today tourism is the primary industry and much of the Hellenic culture has been preserved. The annual celebration of Epiphany on January 6, starting in St. Nicholas Cathedral and culminating on the waterfront, is the premier Greek event in Tarpon Springs.

---

1. *Yearbook 2006* (New York: Greek Orthodox Archdiocese of America, 2006), 187-211.

2. Interview with Public Affairs Office of the Greek Orthodox Archdiocese of America, 2006.

3. **Greek-American Studies.** Theodore Saloutos, *The Greeks in the United States* (Cambridge: Harvard University Press, 1964); Charles C. Moskos, *Greek Americans: Struggle and Success,* 2d ed. (New Brunswick, N.J: Transaction Publishers, 1989); George Papaioannou, *The Odyssey of Hellenism in America* (Thessaloniki, Greece: Patriarchal Institute for Patristic Studies, 1985); Alice Scourby, *The Greek Americans* (Boston: Twayne Publishers, 1984); George Kourvetaris, *Studies on Greek Americans* Boulder, Colo.: University

of Colorado, 1997); Constance Callinicos, *American Aphrodite: Becoming Female in Greek America* (New York: Pella Publishing Company, 1990); Sam Tsemberis, Harry Psomiades, and Anna Karpathakis, eds., *Greek American Families: Traditions and Transformation* (New York: Pella Publishing Company, 1999); Dan Georgakas and Charles Moskos, eds., *New Directions in Greek American Studies* (New York:Pella Publishing Company, 1991); and Andrew Kopan, *Education and Greek Immigrants in Chicago, 1892-1973* (New York, Garland Pub., 1990).

4. **Novels, short stories, and poetry.** Mary Vardoulakis, *Gold in the Streets* (New York: Dodd, Mead, 1945); Elia Kazan, *America, America* (New York: Stein and Day, 1962); Harry Mark Petrakis, *A Dream of Kings* (New York: David McKay Company, 1966); Helen Papanikolas, *The Time of the Little Blackbird* (Athens, Ohio: Swallow Press/Ohio University Press, 1999); Catherine Temma Davidson, *The Priest Fainted* (New York: Henry Holt and Company, 1998); Theano Papazoglou Margaris, *The Chronicle of Halsted Street* (Athens: Fexis, 1962); Harry Mark Petrakis, *Pericles on 31st Street* (Chicago: Quadrangle Books, 1965); Helen Papanikolas, *Small Bird, Tell Me: Stories of Greek Immigrants* (Athens, Ohio: Swallow Press/Ohio University Press, 1993); Nicholas Samaras, *Hands of the Saddlemaker* (New Haven: Yale University Press, 1992); Penelope Karageorge, *Red Lipstick and the Wine-dark Sea* (New York: Pella Publishing Company, 1997).

5. **Memoirs.** Nicholas Gage, *Eleni* (New York: Random House, 1983); Nicholas Gage, *A Place for Us* (Boston: Houghton Mifflin Company, 1989); Harry Mark Petrakis, *Stelmark: A Family Recollection* (New York: David McKay Company, 1970); Helen Papanikolas, *Emily-George* (Salt Lake City: University of Utah Press, 1987); Thea Halo, *Not Even My Name* (New York: St. Martin's Press Inc., 2000); and Aphrodite Matsakis, *Growing Up Greek in St. Louis* (Chicago: Arcadia Publishing, 2002).

6. **Biographies.** Elaine Thomopoulos, ed. *Greek-American Pioneer Women of Illinois* (Chicago: Arcadia Publishing, 2000).

7. Greek Orthodox Archidiocese of America, *Yearbook 2006* (New York: Greek Orthodox Archidiocese, 2006), 250-251.

8. Ibid., 251-252.

9. Charles Moskos, "The Greeks in the United States," in *The Greek Diaspora in the Twentieth Century*, Richard Clogg, ed., (New York: St. Martin's Press, Inc., 1999), 106.

10. Ibid.

11. Greektown Community Development Corporation interview, November 2001.

12. Charles Moskos, "The Greeks in the United States," 106.

13. Ibid.

14. 1bid.

GREECE

❖ *Visiting Greece*

Images of classical antiquity, ancient gods and goddesses, intense blue skies, and whitewashed buildings lure thousands of tourists to Greece each year. For Greek Americans, the reasons for visiting go beyond those of the typical tourist. It is a chance to renew family ties and touch the roots of their rich heritage.

THEN AND NOW

Today many Greek Americans of different generations enjoy being with their families, relaxing, brushing up on language skills, visiting historic sites of their ancestors, and making religious pilgrimages. The wide use of commercial airplanes has reduced the time and expense of a once arduous trip made by a limited few. The Greek-American tradition of visiting Greece is changing.

In an earlier time, such trips could be a financial and emotional trauma for first-generation immigrants. Many who intended to stay in the United States for only a few years to earn money ended up staying for their entire lives. Some were expected to return with substantial wealth to disperse to the relatives. If they had not been back for many years, their friends and family were much older and in some cases gone. After their arrival back home, some experienced a sense of alienation because of contrasting cultures and values. Although very welcomed, in Greece they were considered Americans, and in America they were considered Greeks. Many felt caught between both countries. They did not feel they belonged in either place, despite their longing for Greece and intense feelings of exile in a foreign land (*xenitiá* — pron *ksenitiá*). Most desired to go back permanently or to visit. The Greek poet George Drosinis expressed their feelings:

> And should it be my fate —
> A black and desolate fate —
>   to leave and never to return,
> I will finally ask you to forgive me.

> (George Drosinis, "The Soil of Greece")

Such emotionalism is generally less dramatic today, depending on each individual situation. There is better communication by telephone, trips are more frequent, and the two cultures have more in common as economic disparities have lessened. For most Greek Americans, going to Greece is a positive, rewarding experience. They feel at home in both countries.

VISITING THE FAMILY

A primary aim of the trip is visiting the family. Word of a visit spreads quickly, and relatives throw open their doors and hearts. Hospitality (*philoxenía*) remains a national characteristic, a point of honor; and a guest is well attended to, well fed, and pampered. The table is laid and many inquiries are made about other family members. Often visitors are plied with gifts: a bunch of basil, a batch of fresh figs, brandy, sweets, and Greek recordings.

GIFTS

Customarily Greek Americans take presents to their families, ranging from inexpensive tokens to extravagant gifts, depending on the circumstances and number of relatives. Popular items include cosmetics, clothing, and money. (Children especially enjoy having money pressed into their hands.) Some Greek Americans bring substantial sums for a variety of reasons: helping family members in need, building and restoring residences, commissioning icons in a local church. This custom began when early immigrants came to the United States primarily to make money to send back to Greece. However, a trip should not be postponed or canceled because it is believed the gifts would be inadequate. Such a delay is a loss for both the families in America and Greece.

ACCOMMODATIONS

Most Greek Americans stay with their families if they have room. Family frequently takes care of family, and failing to stay with them could embarrass your Greek relatives. While traveling there are many hotels, and people in small towns often take guests in their homes. If you like local color, the Greek government has restored and developed some traditional accommodations. Contact the Greek National Tourism Organization (see "Sightseeing" below).

REUNION IN THE VILLAGE

Many Greek Americans emigrated from small villages and enjoy returning there for family reunions. The village (*horió*) is often the central meeting place for those who emigrated from Greece and for Greeks who left the village for larger cities, such as Athens and Thessaloniki, after World War II. The village remains a touchstone and has become a popular summer vacation spot for Greek city residents. Village life is simpler with its fresh air and produce, olive trees, flowers, and extended family of uncles, aunts, cousins, *yiayiáthes,* and *papoúthes.*

Many plan their visit to coincide with the *paniyíri*, the celebration of the feast day of the village's patron saint. The *paniyíri* becomes a "homecoming" with celebrations lasting for several days, including church services, music and dancing in the village square, and plenty of delicious food.

In some Greek villages, summer attracts the most visitors and, in effect, traditional villages are becoming summer resorts. As a result, some villages are losing their year-round economic base and population. However, it is becoming increasing popular for Greek Americans to build new or restore old houses in their family villages. Eleni Gage in *North of Ithaka* describes contemporary village life during the year she spent in Lia rebuilding her grandmother's home.[1]

Village Life

RELAXING

The slower Greek life style appeals to many Greek Americans looking for a change from the hectic pace of the United States.

LEISURE ACTIVITIES

In addition to sightseeing, Greece offers many leisure activities such as cruises, beach lounging, tours of wineries, tennis, hiking, festivals, health spas, and horseback riding. Information regarding these activities may be obtained from the Greek National Tourism Organization, a commercial travel agency, or a guidebook.

DAILY ROUTINE

Greeks stop their morning activity around one or two o'clock in the afternoon for a large meal and a rest. At one time everything — shops, businesses, restaurants — closed until around four o'clock in the afternoon. With the increased tourist trade, particularly in the summer, these hours are being modified. (Check with your relatives or hotel concierge.) After the afternoon meal and rest, Greeks often consume thick black coffee and a piece of pastry and begin what seems like a second day of work. Shops stay open until around eight, and dinner is late, between nine to eleven at night. In warm weather, Greeks love to eat outdoors at sidewalk tavernas and restaurants crammed with people. The favorite social activity in the evening is to sit at an outside cafe and people-watch. Those who are energetic go to nightclubs, staying until the early hours of the morning.

SPECIAL PLACES TO EAT AND CELEBRATE

Try some of the special restaurants and nightclubs with a unique Greek flair. A *psistariá* features meat roasted on spits, especially succulent pork, lamb, and chicken. A *psarotavérna* specializes in fresh fish and seafood. The most famous ones are in Piraeus in an area called Mikrolimano (formerly called Tourkolimano). If you cannot read the menu, act like the Greeks: go to the kitchen, look in the pots, and point out what you want!

For a leisurely break, enjoy coffee at a *kafenío* or *oúzo* at an *ouzerí*. Traditionally the *kafenío* has been for men only. Men would gather there to smoke, play cards, and discuss business and politics while clicking their *kombolói*, a string of worry beads worked with the fingers. The men-only rule has been modified, but in some places women still do not "violate" this male preserve. People sip *oúzo*, beer, and wine at an *ouzerí*, while nibbling on tidbits of food.

For late night fun and great music, try a *bouzoúkia*, a nightclub featuring music played on the *bouzoúki*, the predominant Greek instrument. The loud and raucous clubs are the most popular form of entertainment.

SIGHTSEEING

Greeks are justifiably proud of their rich and diverse heritage. With pride they walk the same places where democracy began and worship at churches where Christianity first flourished. World-famous historical attractions are everywhere. For an entertaining and thoughtful overview of Greek life today in its historical context, read *Hellas: A Portrait of Greece* by Nicholas Gage.[2] Commercial guidebooks provide the best overview of what to do in Greece: sights, leisure activities, travel tips, lodging, restaurants, festivals, and summer events. You can also contact the Greek National Tourism Organization (GNTO), with offices throughout Greece and the world, at www.gnto.gr. For additional website addresses, see *The Greek Diaspora* — "Internet Websites — Travel to Greece."

Guidebook information will not be duplicated here, but listed below are the essential highlights of ancient Greece, Byzantine/Orthodox heritage, and modern Greece.

ANCIENT GREECE

The ancient Greeks shaped much of Western civilization contributing in every area: politics, art, architecture, philosophy, science, drama, mathematics, medicine, law, literature, and language. Prepare for your trip by reading some of the many books available, including histories and the primary works of Homer, Hippocrates, Aristotle, Socrates, Plato, Herodotus, Sophocles, and Euripides. Children can be introduced to their heritage with stories of the myths and explanations of the Greek way of life. *Book of Greek Myths* by Ingri and Edgar Parin d'Aulaire remains the best-known source for young children on the Greek gods and goddesses.[3] The myths come to life at the temple for Athena in Athens (the Parthenon) and at Delphi, home of Apollo's most famous oracle. To see the place where the goddess of love, Aphrodite, was born in the sea, you must travel to the ocean cliffs south of her temple at Palaepaphos, Cyprus.

Essential ancient sites to visit:

Athens	Knossos	Sparta
Delphi	Mycenae	Santorini
Delos	Olympia	Vergina
Epidaurus		

Essential museums to visit in Athens: the National Archeological Museum, the Benaki Museum, and the Nicholas P. Goulandris Foundation-Museum of Cycladic Art.

BYZANTINE/ORTHODOX HERITAGE

The Byzantine empire spanned many countries and one thousand years from the fourth to the fifteenth centuries. During that time, the Orthodox faith developed along with Byzantine architecture and art, especially icons. (See *The Historic Orthodox Church.*) Some of the most outstanding examples of that tradition in Greece are listed below.[4] Use a guidebook for further information and attend a service if you are visiting a church:

- *Benaki Museum.* Houses Byzantine miniatures and icons. Located at Vasilisis Sofias Avenue and Koumbari Streets, Athens.

- *Byzantine Museum.* Houses a reproduction of a Byzantine Orthodox church, icons, frescoes, and ecclesiastical vestments. Located at 22 Vasilisis Sofias Avenue, Athens.

- *Meteora Monasteries.* Six monasteries set atop mountain pinnacles of Meteora. Located 200 miles northwest of Athens.

- *Mistra.* A well-preserved, deserted, Byzantine town featuring architecture and mosaics of the thirteenth to fifteenth centuries. Located approximately three miles west of Sparta.

- *Monastery of Daphni.* Superb eleventh-century architecture and mosaics. Located approximately seven miles northwest of Athens.

- *Monastery of Nea Moni.* Excellent example of eleventh-century mosaics. Located at Nea Moni Church on the Island of Chios.

- *Monastery of Ossios Loukas.* Outstanding eleventh-century architecture with beautiful mosaics. Located southeast of Delphi.

- *Mt. Athos.* The holy mountain of Greek Orthodoxy. Monasteries of special interest: Dionysiou, Megisti Lavra, and Stavronikita. Located on the eastern finger of the Chalkidiki peninsula southeast of Thessaloniki. Only men can visit and special permission must be obtained (see "Pilgrimages" below).

- *Thessaloniki Churches.* Outstanding fifth-century-style architecture and seventh-century mosaics at rebuilt St. Demetrios church. Fourteenth-century architecture and mosaics at the Church of the Holy Apostles.

MODERN GREECE

The following tourist attractions relating to the war of independence from the Ottoman Empire begun in 1821 are of special interest:

- The Ayia Lavra (Holy Laura) monastery near Kalavrita is the primary location for honoring Greek independence. Here you can see the banner raised on March 25, 1821 (Greek Independence Day) by Bishop Germanos of Patras and read the names of the revolutionary heroes inscribed on a large plaque. You may also want to visit Patras, about an hour and a half northwest of Kalavrita. A statue of Bishop Germanos has been erected in Patras' main square, Psila Alonia. (See "Greek Independence Day")

- Messolongi is the burial place of the partial remains of the great English poet Byron, who died here in 1824 while in Greece to support the revolution. Visit his tomb and statue in the Heroes Burial Garden and the Lord Byron exhibit in Old City Hall.

> The mountains look on Marathon —
> And Marathon looks on the sea;
> And musing there an hour alone,
> I dreamed that Greece might still be free,
> For standing on the Persians' grave,
> I could not deem myself a slave.
>
> (George Gordon, Lord Byron, *Don Juan*, Canto iii)

For pleasure reading related to modern Greece, explore the works of some of Greece's most famous writers: Constantine Cavafy, Odysseus Elytis (1979 Nobel Prize for Literature), Nikos Kazantzakis, Yannis Ritsos, and George Seferis (1963 Nobel Prize for Literature). For the perspective of Philhellenes about modern Greece, read Lawrence Durrell and Henry Miller.

PILGRIMAGES

Greeks and Greek Americans often make religious pilgrimages to churches for retreats, to honor saints, worship, and fulfill or make a *táma* (vow). Thousands of pilgrims visit the following sites each year where healing icons and saints' relics may be located. In some cases, you can spend the night. (See *Saints* – "Relics" for additional sites.)

- *Aegina.* Major site to honor St. Nektarios, a modern-day saint known for healing many ailments. St. Nektarios is buried at St. Nektarios chapel at the Convent of the Holy Trinity on Aegina, an island located south of Piraeus in the Saronic Gulf.

- *Kerkyra, Corfu.* Major site to honor St. Spyridon, patron saint of numerous ailments. He is buried in St. Spyridon Cathedral in Kerkyra, the capital of Corfu, an island in the Ionian Sea, west of mainland Greece.

- *Mt. Athos.* The largest and most important community of Eastern Orthodox monks in the world. Located on Chalkidiki peninsula southeast of Thessaloniki. A limited number of men only may visit for up to four days. Men should apply three or four months in advance by sending a request to: The Ministry of Northern Greece, Directorate for Cultural Affairs, Diikitirion Square, 54623 Thessaloniki, Greece. Include in your request a declaration of intent to be a pilgrim, the date you would like to visit, a letter of recommendation from your consulate, and a copy of your passport. You will be notified in writing that your permit has been approved, but it must be picked up in person in Thessalonika.

- *Patmos.* The sacred island where St. John wrote the Book of Revelation. The monastery of St. John houses an important Byzantine library and the relics of sixty saints. Located northwest of Rhodes in the Dodecanese Islands.

- *Simi.* Major site to honor St. Michael at the Monastery of Panormites. A miraculous icon of St. Michael is housed at the monastery. Located in the Dodecanese islands near Rhodes.

- *Tinos.* Major site to honor the Virgin Mary. Church of the Evangelistra houses a miracle-working icon of the Theotokos. An Aegean island located northwest of Mykonos.

- *Thessaloniki.* Major site to honor St. Demetrios who is buried in St. Demetrios Church. Located in northern Greece.

STUDY AND ENRICHMENT PROGRAMS

Many opportunities for enrichment and study in Greece are now available. These programs go beyond brief sightseeing excursions and include such diverse options as summer camp, language classes,

and Fulbright scholarships. Such opportunities provide participants with a deeper understanding of the Hellenic and Orthodox
heritages. For example, the Greek Orthodox Archdiocese of America
sponsors the Ionian Village in Bartholomio, a seaside summer
camp south of Patras for children ages twelve to eighteen and
young adults nineteen and older. The Athens Centre provides
Greek language and cultural enrichment classes, and the Theatre
Dora Stratou in Athens gives one-week workshops on Greek folk
dance. In addition to some Greek colleges that welcome students
from abroad, a number of American universities have year-abroad
programs for college credit. For further information, see *The
Greek Diaspora* — "Internet Websites — Study and Enrichment
Programs in Greece."

EXTENDED STAY

If you have the good fortune to extend your stay and live in
Greece, even part-time, you might find the following two re-
sources helpful. *Living in Greece* published in English by The
American Women's Organization of Greece in Athens (contact
through the American Embassy in Athens). The General Secre-
tariat for Greeks Abroad (a department of the Hellenic Republic
Ministry of Foreign Affairs) provides a "Manual on Returning to
Greece." ("Manual" in Greek only at www.mfa.gr/ggae.)

SHOPPING

Information from the Greek National Tourism Organization and
commercial guide books give tips on shopping for clothing, home
furnishings, and handicrafts. The following tips relate to the customs and traditions in this book.

TRADITIONAL HANDICRAFTS IN ATHENS

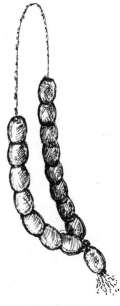

Komboloi

Embroidery, worry beads (*komboloi*), Greek hats, copper ware,
Greek costumes (including *foustanéles*), and other interesting mer-
chandise may be purchased throughout Athens. If you have time
to browse, start at Monastiraki, the largest flea market, at Ermou
and Athinas streets near the ancient agora. Then walk east to
Plaka at the base of the Parthenon and browse through its charm-
ing shops, the Center for Folk Art and Tradition, and The Greek
Folk Art Museum. Visit also in other parts of Athens, the National
Welfare Organization, the Lyceum Club of Greek Women, the Greek
Women's Institution, and the Hellenic Artisan Trades Cooperative.

RELIGIOUS ITEMS

Icons and *filaktá* may be purchased at monasteries throughout Greece. In Athens the largest selection of religious items (including icons, censers, crosses, and liturgical supplies) may be found on the streets behind Mitropolis Cathedral in Plaka.

CERAMICS, SCULPTURE, AND JEWELRY

Most museum shops have beautiful, authentic reproductions of these items.

EXPORTING ANTIQUES AND ARTIFACTS

Genuine antiques and artifacts (including sculpture, ceramics, icons, and furniture) are illegal to export without a permit. Be aware that Greek customs has the right to seize suspect items. To obtain a permit, submit a letter describing the object, its origin, and purpose for export, along with a photograph to the Directorate of Antique Shops and Private Collections, 13 Polygnotou Street, Athens. The letter will be reviewed by the Archaeological Council of the Ministry of Culture to decide whether to issue a permit. If a permit is denied, the state must purchase the antiquity at 50 percent of declared value. An export tax of 50 percent of declared value must be paid if a permit is issued. In effect, the laws are prohibitive, giving rise to a vigorous black market.

---

1. Eleni N. Gage, *North of Ithaka* (New York: St. Martin's Press, 2004).

2. Nicholas Gage, *Hellas: A Portrait of Greece,* 3d. ed. (Efstathiadis Group, 1987)

3. Ingri and Edgar Parin d'Aulaire, *Book of Greek Myths* (Garden City, N.Y.: Doubleday and Company, 1962).

4. With the exception of the Byzantine and Benaki Museums, the church and monastery list was compiled from an article by John Yiannias, "Orthodox Art and Architecture," in *A Companion to the Greek Orthodox Church,* ed. Fotios K. Litsas (New York: Department of Communication, Greek Orthodox Archdiocese of North and South America, 1984), 104-105.

PART THREE

Feast Days, Fasts, and Holidays

Greeks are forever celebrating — personal occasions, feast days, festivals, and political triumphs. Life is a celebration! They offset these jubilant times with interludes of soul-searching and spiritual cleansing through fasting. The intermingling of festivities and quiet contemplation brings a balance to life expressed by the ancient Greeks: *Pan métron áriston* (Moderation in all things is excellent).

The following feast days, fasts, and secular holidays are the most significant in the Greek Orthodox church, however these occasions are not equally observed by Greek Americans. The most commonly observed are described extensively below.

Greek Americans enjoy these holidays within their own community, whereas in Greece the entire country celebrates religious holidays together. The constitution of Greece mandates Orthodoxy as the official faith of the country. This official status makes major religious observances legal holidays. The entire country stops work and spends the day in religious devotion and recreation. For example, on the first day of Lent (Clean Monday) families traditionally go picnicking and fly kites. National legal holidays in Greece are: Oxi Day, Christmas, New Year's Day, Epiphany, Annunciation/Greek Independence Day, First Day of Lent, Good Friday, Easter, May 1 (Flower Festival), and The Dormition of the Mother of God.

The church year begins on September 1, the day Christ began his public ministry to the world by preaching in the synagogue. The Ecumenical Patriarchate in Constantinople observes the event with great ceremony. The following calendar does not include the feast days of many popular saints, except when it is a part of a larger observance, such as St. Basil's day. For additional feast days see *Name Days*.

ANNUAL CALENDAR

AUTUMN	September 8	The Nativity of the Mother of God*
	September 14	The Exaltation of the Holy Cross*
	October 28	Oxi Day
	November 15	Christmas Lent begins, ending the eve of December 24
	November 21	The Presentation of the Mother of God in the Temple*
WINTER	December 25	Christmas — The Nativity of Jesus Christ*
	January 1	Circumcision of Jesus Christ
		Feast Day of St. Basil the Great
		New Year's Day
	January 6	Epiphany — The Baptism of Jesus Christ*
	January 7	Feast Day of St. John the Baptist
	January 30	Feast Day of the Three Hierarchs
	February 2	The Presentation of Jesus Christ in the Temple*
SPRING	†	Triodion begins three weeks before Great Lent
	†	Great Lent begins seven weeks before Easter
	March 25	The Annunciation of the Mother of God* and Greek Independence Day
	†	Palm Sunday — The Entry of Jesus Christ into Jerusalem* (one week before Easter)
	†	Holy Week (precedes Easter)
	†	Holy Pascha (Easter) — The Resurrection of Jesus Christ
	†	The Ascension of Jesus Christ*
	†	Pentecost* (Fifty days after Easter)
SUMMER	†	Holy Apostles Lent begins the Monday after All Saints Sunday, ending the eve of June 28
	June 29	The Feast Day of Saints Peter and Paul the Apostles
	June 30	The Feast Day of the Holy Apostles
	August 1	Dormition of the Mother of God Lent begins August 1, ending the evening of August 14
	August 6	The Transfiguration of Jesus Christ*
	August 15	The Dormition of the Mother of God*

---

* One of the Twelve Great Feast Days; eight are events in the life of Christ, and four are in the life of the Mother of God. Easter is not included. It stands alone as the most important Orthodox holiday.

† Moveable date set in relation to Easter.

Autumn

The Nativity of the Mother God
September 8

The church honors the Virgin Mary on the day of her birth, for it was through her that God became man. Mary's parents, Joachim and Anna, who had been married for twenty years, had no children. One day an angel appeared in a separate vision to each of them, announcing that they would have a daughter whom they should dedicate to God. Her nativity is celebrated with a Divine Liturgy and hymns composed in her honor.

The Exaltation of the Holy Cross
September 14

The Exaltation of the Holy Cross is one of the most revered observances in all of Orthodoxy. In 325 A.D., after the persecutions against the Christians had just ended, Christians were free to express their religious feelings and to adorn their places of worship with symbols of the faith, such as the cross. Empress Helen, a devout Christian and mother of the Emperor Constantine the Great, went to Jerusalem to undertake a mission to retrieve the cross upon which Christ had been crucified. After a futile search, the Empress was attracted by the scent of a plant called *vasilikós* (basil) in the area where Jesus had been put to death. She ordered excavation, and three crosses were unearthed. A paralyzed person was positioned on each of the crosses to determine the cross upon which Christ had died. When the person was placed on the true cross, he recovered miraculously and walked. On September 14, the event was celebrated. Patriarch Makarios, who had also witnessed the miracle at the historic site, raised the cross and blessed the people with it as they responded, "Lord, have mercy" (*"Kýrie, eléison"*).

Orthodoxy honors this event on September 14 at a special service in which the priest carries a small cross on a tray decorated with *vasilikós* in procession throughout the church (see *illustration*). *Vasilikós*, the traditional flower of the Orthodox church, is also

The Exaltation of the Holy Cross

used during the feast days of Epiphany, the Veneration of the Holy Cross, and any time the service of *ayiasmós* (blessing of the water), takes place.

The church has established September 14 as a day of fasting equal to that of Good Friday, as a reminder that Christ died on the cross; many parishioners take communion that day. The Gospel reading at the Divine Liturgy describes the Crucifixion of Christ. After the service, each parishioner receives a basil sprig.

Oxi Day
October 28

Oxi Day is a national secular holiday in Greece commemorating its resistance to Axis (Italian) forces during World War II. On October 28, 1940, Benito Mussolini, the dictator of Italy, demanded that Greece give free passage to Italian troops through Greek territory. The Greek Prime Minister, Ioannes Metaxas, responded with a resounding *"Oxi!"* (No! — pron. *Óchi*) Although outnumbered, the Greek forces fought valiantly for six months, routing the Italians, who retreated into Albania. The victory was the first Allied success against the Axis countries and aroused great ethnic pride. Winston Churchill said of the victory: "Hence we will not say that Greeks fight like heroes but that heroes fight like Greeks."

In America, Oxi Day is remembered at church with a special doxology, a service of thanksgiving and glorification held after the Divine Liturgy. Dignitaries attend, and poems are usually recited in Greek by children. The congregation stands to sing the Greek National Anthem, "Hymn to Liberty" ("Se Gnorizo Apo Tin Kopsi"). (See *Greek Independence Day* for lyrics.) In many communities a separate program also takes place where poems are recited, songs connected with the event are sung, and plays are presented. These programs may be sponsored by the Greek school of the parish or other Greek-American organizations.

Oxi, the day of defiance, is still widely celebrated on October 28 as a national holiday throughout Greece. Homes fly the Greek flag, and villages and towns are draped in blue and white bunting. Similar to Veteran's Day in America, it is a day to remember those who died in military service. Many people attend church where there is a liturgy and memorial for soldiers. A wreath is placed at the tomb of the Unknown Soldier, and military parades are common. Since most of the fighting in 1940 took place in northern Greece, Thessaloniki has the largest parade. In Athens an electric sign saying, "*Oxi*," shines over the city from Lycabettus Hill during the last few days of October.

CHRISTMAS LENT
November 15 - December 24

Christmas is preceded by a forty-day period of fasting. For the devout Greek Orthodox, Christmas Lent should be somber, unlike the secular pre-Christmas period of parties and excessive eating. The Orthodox way demands fasting, prayer, and alms, similar to Great Lent that precedes Easter. In practice, however, most Greek Americans do not strictly observe this fast. The Christmas Lenten period begins on November 15 and ends the eve of December 24.

THE PRESENTATION OF THE MOTHER OF GOD
IN THE TEMPLE
November 21

At the age of three, Mary's parents, Joachim and Anna, dedicated her to God and presented her to the temple. As was customary, dedicated children stayed with holy men of the temple for twelve years, receiving the finest education. At fifteen, Mary came home to her parents, and was visited soon thereafter by the Archangel Gabriel, announcing that she would be the Mother of Christ. She and her parents are honored with special church hymns and writings.

Ή ΧΡΙΣ͂Υ ΓΈΝΝΗΣ

The Nativity of Jesus Christ

⚜ *Winter*

Christmas, New Year, and Epiphany (Dodecameron)

December 25, January 1, and January 6

The Greek Orthodox combine the holidays of Christmas, New Year, and Epiphany into a period called the Dodecameron (twelve days — pron. *thothecámeron*). The period starts with Christmas on December 25 and ends January 6 with Epiphany. Once Christmas starts, the season is one of continuous celebration (except for one day of fasting in January), to commemorate some of the year's most important holidays.

Christmas

CHRISTMAS LENT

For the devout Orthodox, the Christmas season begins with Christmas Lent (November 15 to December 24), a subdued period observed by only a few. Most Greek Americans celebrate Christmas the American way, participating in a flurry of activities during the month of December, including decorations, Santa Claus, parties, and rich food. However, except for preparing food and purchasing a few gifts, this is not in keeping with the Orthodox tradition of fasting and reflection before the major feast day of Christmas. Many of the faithful, however, fast and take communion during the week before Christmas.

SIGNIFICANCE AND CHURCH SERVICES

Christmas commemorates the birth of Jesus Christ. The story of the Annunciation to the Virgin Mary, the journey with Joseph to Bethlehem, and the birth of Jesus in a stable is retold to worshipers each year. The story reminds the faithful that God sent his Son to save the world and that they, too, can find new life through Christ.

At one time the Christmas church service began at midnight, but this has changed in many American churches to attract greater participation. Now the Divine Liturgy may be offered early Christmas Eve and again on Christmas Day. In the Divine Liturgy the hymns and the Biblical readings declare the Christmas message of hope and renewal. Instead of a pastoral sermon, a message from the Archbishop of America is usually read from the pulpit. Christmas pageants of the Nativity may also be presented by the children. The pageant is not typically Greek, but rather an adaptation of a European tradition.

Parishioners may sing both English and Greek carols at the end of the service. The Orthodox carols are rich in theology, and the best known religious Greek carol is "I Yennisis Sou" ("Your Birth, O Christ").[1] (See below)

Another beautiful hymn comes from *The Festal Menaion*:

Kontakion

Today the Virgin gives birth to Him who is above all being, and the earth offers a cave to Him whom no man can approach. Angels with shepherds give glory, and Magi journey with a star. For unto us is born a young Child, the pre-eternal God.[2]

I Yennisis Sou

I - yén - ni - sís sou Chri - sté o THe ós i-
món. a - né - ti - le to kó-smo to fos to tis
gnó - se - os en af - ti gar i tis á - stris la-
trév- on- des i- po a - sté- ros e - thi - thá- skon- do.
Se pro-ski - nín ton í - li - on tis thi- ke- o-
sí - nis ke se yi - nó - skin ex i - psous a-
na - to- lín. Ky - ri - e, thó - xa si.

Your birth, O Christ our God, brought to the world the light of knowledge. For through it those who had adored the stars were taught by a star to worship you, the sun of righteousness, and to know you as the dawn from heaven, O Lord, glory to you.

CHRISTMAS FOOD AND FESTIVITIES

THE *KÁLANDA*

On Christmas Eve Day in Greece, young people, carrying triangles, small drums, and harmonicas, go in groups from house to house, singing the *kálanda* (carols) about the birth of Christ. (See "Kalanda Christouyennon" below) Before singing the children ask the traditional question, *"Na ta poúme?"* ("May we sing it for you?"). (The question is asked so that songs will not be sung at a house in mourning.) Some children carry small ships of cardboard, wood, or tin in honor of St. Basil who came to Greece by sea from his home in Caesarea to bring presents to the children. Decorated with the Greek flag and the word "Ellas," the ships hold the sweets and money given to each caroler at the end of the *kálanda*. Sometimes the children are welcomed into the house for treats. In America, this is a popular activity for Greek school students.

SWEETS

The most traditional Christmas cookies are the white, powdery *kourabiéthes* and the rich, brown *melomakárona*. The cloves in the *kourabiéthes* represent the spices of the wise men.

CHRISTMAS BREAD (CHRISTOPSOMO)

Christmas bread (Christopsomo — pron. *Christópsomo*) or *kouloúra tou Christoú* (round bread of Christ) graces the Christmas table. It is usually a round loaf often made with the same ingredients as Easter bread. Nuts and dried fruits may be added. Some families attend church on Christmas Eve and return home for a meal that begins with the cutting of the Christopsomo by the head of the household. Others wait until a main meal on Christmas Day. The head of the house makes the sign of the cross on the bread with a knife while saying, "In the name of the Father, the Son, and the Holy Spirit," and then cuts a piece for each person with a wish of *"Kalá Christoúyena"* ("Good Christmas") or *"Chrónia pollá"* ("Many years"). (See recipe below)

In Cyprus, special bread and pastries covered with sesame seeds and a cross on top are prepared. For blessings on the house, one will be hung from the beam of a ceiling or maybe in front of the home *ikonostási* through Christmas or New Year's Day.

Kalanda Christouyennon
(Christmas Kalanda)

1.Ka - lín es - pé - ra - n ár - chon -
2. ná - te sí me -

tes, ki a - n i - ne
ron stin vi - THle -

o - ri - smós sas, Chri - stoú ti
é - m tin pó - li, i ou - ra -

THí - a yén - ni - si
ní a - gál - lon - te

na i - pó st'ar - chon - ti - kó
ke ke her' - i phí - sis

sas. 2.Chris - tós yen - ó - li.

1. Good evening, noble folk. if you so command,
   I will tell your noble household of the birth of Christ.
2. Today Christ is being born in Bethlehem,
   and the heavens rejoice along with all of nature.

✦

CHRISTOPSOMO OR *KOULOÚRA TOU CHRISTOÚ*

Make a half recipe of Easter bread (see *Easter Season*). Add:

¼ cup toasted pine nuts	1 cup golden raisins
¾ cup chopped walnuts	½ cup chopped dried apricots
or blanched almonds	

Soak dried fruit for one hour and drain. (Candied fruit may be substituted.) Follow Easter bread recipe, adding the fruit, nuts, and extra flour if needed. Shape into one ball for a greased 14" round cake pan or form two balls for two greased 8" round cake pans. Omit the red eggs and decorate with sesame seeds or sliced blanched almonds and/or a cross made of dough.

CHRISTMAS DINNER

Christmas menus vary from region to region, but turkey or pork is the most common main course.

❧

CHRISTMAS DINNER

Grape leaves, small pies, meatballs
Christopsomo and *avgolémono* soup
Roast pork or stuffed turkey
Roasted potatoes and Greek salad
Spinach and cheese pies
Fruit
Melomakárona, kourabiéthes, thíples, and *baklavá*

❧

GREETINGS

Wish someone a Merry Christmas with *"Kalá Christoúyena"* ("Good Christmas") or *"Chrónia pollá"* ("Many years") or *"Ke tou chrónou"* ("And to next year").

GIFTS

Most Greek Americans exchange gifts on Christmas Eve or Christmas Day, not at New Year's as in Greece. Greek-American youngsters look to Santa Claus, not St. Basil, for their presents.

NAME DAY CELEBRATIONS

In Greece Christmas Day is a very popular time to hold open-house name day parties to honor persons with names such as Chris, Christos, Christine, Emmanuel, and Emmanuela. This is not widely done in the United States.

KALIKÁNTZARI SUPERSTITION

An old folk belief in Greece holds that mischievous goblins called *kalikántzari* appear during the Dodecameron. The *kalikántzari* live beneath the surface of the earth and chop away at a large tree trunk, the foundation of the earth. With their chopping they attempt to destroy God's work. They almost succeed when they hear the noise created by the birth of Christ. They come to earth on December 25 to disrupt people's lives with pranks and tricks such as spilled milk, disappearing keys, and broken glass. It is common to blame mishaps this time of the year on the *kalikántzari*.

Fire, light, and holy water protect people from the *kalikántzari*. On Christmas Eve some people in rural Greece light a fire to prevent them from coming down the chimney. This Christ log (*skarkántzalos*) burns until Epiphany. Sometimes large bonfires are built in the villages of Greece, and people carry a candle with them at night for protection. The little imps roam the earth until Epiphany when holy water cleans them away.

New Year

NEW YEAR'S EVE

CARD PARTIES

Greek Americans love to party and play cards on New Year's Eve. It is said that you sample your luck for the coming year on the last day of the old. Card playing may follow a dinner party or just be combined with coffee and sweets, especially *loukoumáthes*. Generally, just before midnight the lights are turned out and then turned on again at twelve to shouts of *"Kalí Chroniá"* ("Good year"), "Happy New Year," and *"Chrónia pollá"* ("Many years"). It is customary to cut a Vasilopita at this time.

VASILOPITA

The most popular New Year's custom is the cutting of the Vasilopita (bread for St. Basil — pron. *Vasilópita*). Everyone hopes to get the lucky coin baked inside the *píta*.

Legend of the Vasilopita

The Vasilopita commemorates a miracle performed by St. Basil while serving as a bishop. The legend varies as to how St. Basil became the guardian of the gold, silver, and jewelry of the people of Caesarea. Some say thieves had taken the valuables from the village, and they were recovered. Others say it was a tax the government asked St. Basil to collect, but then decided to cancel. In either case, St. Basil became responsible for returning the riches to the people. However, they could not agree on the rightful owners. St. Basil suggested that the women bake the valuables inside a large *píta*. When he cut the *píta*, each owner miraculously received the right valuable. Today a single coin is baked inside each loaf to honor this miracle, and the recipient has good luck for the coming year.

Cutting the Vasilopita

Greek Americans enjoy Vasilopita for most of the month of January. They cut the first *píta* at midnight on New Year's Eve and repeat the ritual at social occasions and community functions throughout the first half of January. Before the cutting, everyone sings the *kálanda* ("Kalanda Protochronias") announcing the new year and St. Basil.

A short poem popular in Constantinople may also be said by one of the children:

Pérno thíno to mahéri	I take the knife and put it
Stou Babáka mou to héri,	in my father's hand,
Yia na kópsi tin pitítsa	So he can cut the Vasilopita
Na mou thósi miá fetítsa!	and give one slice to me!

Kalanda Protochronias
(New Year's Kalanda)

1.Ar - chi - mi - niá ki ar - chí - chro-
2.A - yio va - sí - lis ér - che-

niá, psi - lí - mou then - dro-
te, ár - chon - tes ton ka-

li - va - niá, Ki ar-
té - che - te, a -

chí ki'ar - chí ka - lós mas chró - nos, ek - kli-
pó a - pó tin Ke - sa - rí - a, si'se ar-

siá ek - kli - siá me - t'á - yio THró - nos.
chó si'se ar - chon - ti - sa ky - ri - á.

1. (It's the) start of the month and the start of the year,
   Oh, my tall rosemary tree, and the start of a happy new year,
   Oh, church of the holy throne.
2. St. Basil is coming, as you noblemen know, from Caesarea.
   You, my lady, are a noblewoman.

The head of the household makes the sign of the cross on the *píta* with a knife while saying, "In the name of the Father, the Son, and the Holy Spirit, Amen." Pieces are cut in a specific order. Protocol varies, but the first piece is always for Christ. It should be wrapped and placed in the home *ikonostási.* The second and third pieces are usually for the Virgin Mary and St. Basil, and the fourth for the poor. The head of the house receives the next piece and the rest of the family according to their ages, including those members who are not at home. Then pieces should be cut for guests according to their place of honor, mentioning those of highest esteem first. The person cutting the Vasilopita wishes each recipient, *"Chrónia pollá"* ("Many years") or *"Kalí chroniá"* ("Good year"), while distributing each piece. (In Greece a little Vasilopita and other food may be left out for St. Basil just as Americans leave food for Santa. St. Basil visits each house on his name day, January 1, to bring gifts to the children.)

At a public Vasilopita observance, Christ, Mary, St. Basil, and the poor are recognized before the members of the community. Then those of highest esteem are mentioned, such as the archbishop, priest's wife, presidents of the parish council and Philoptochos, and other dignitaries.

Vasilopita (Bread or Cake)

Vasilopita may be either a bread or a cake, depending on the region of Greece from which your family originated. Some regions use the recipe for Easter bread but decorate the top differently. Others make a rich, sweet cake. All versions are round and include a lucky coin. Arrange greens, nuts, and fruit (fresh and dried) around the loaf or cake.

VASILOPITA (BREAD)

Make a half recipe of Easter bread (see *Easter Season*). Shape into one ball for a greased 14" round pan or two smaller balls for two greased 8" round pans. Hide a coin somewhere in the dough. Omit the red eggs, and decorate with blanched almonds or strands of dough spelling out the year.

VASILOPITA (CAKE)

1 cup regular butter	1 cup milk (room temperature)
2 cups sugar	1 cup crushed almonds
7 eggs separated	1 tablespoon *machlépi*
1 teaspoon almond extract	1 scant teaspoon *mastícha*
2 teaspoon vanilla	¼ cup slivered almonds (top)
3 cups flour, sifted	1 coin
3 tablespoon baking powder	

Cream butter and sugar for ten minutes. Add egg yolks and flavorings. Add remaining ingredients, alternating milk with the flour. Fold in stiffly beaten egg whites until blended. Grease and flour a 14" round cake pan or two 8" round cake pans. Insert coin in batter and sprinkle top with crushed almonds or slivers. Bake in 350°F oven for 45 minutes. Cake is ready when an inserted toothpick removes cleanly. If more baking is required, put aluminum foil lightly over the top to prevent burning and continuing baking. Makes one large *píta* or two small.

NEW YEAR'S DAY

CHURCH SERVICES

The church celebrates two special events on January 1: The Circumcision of Christ and the Feast Day of St. Basil.

Circumcision of Christ

As a member of the Jewish religion, Christ was circumcised on the eighth day after his birth and given his name. This important event is commemorated in a church service. "And at the end of eight days, when he was circumcised, he was called Jesus, the name given him by the angel…" Luke 2:21

Feast Day of St. Basil the Great

The Orthodox observe the name day of St. Basil The Great on January 1 with a Divine Liturgy written by him. St. Basil, widely honored and revered, is one of the three great church hierarchs along with St. Gregory the Theologian and St. John Chrysostom. St. Basil lived in the fourth century working as a missionary, monk, and philanthropist. He prescribed rules of monasticism and began institutions of care for the sick, elderly, underprivileged, and orphaned. The Vasilopita, gifts, the *kálanda,* and name day parties are in his honor.

FESTIVITIES

Greetings

"Kalí chroniá" ("Good year") and *"Chrónia pollá"* ("Many years")

Name Day Celebrations

This is a popular day to hold name day parties for persons named Vasili, Basil, Vaso, Vasiliki, William, and Bill. It combines the joy of the new year with honoring St. Basil and his namesakes.

Traditional Food

Pork and turkey are the most popular main courses. In one region of Greece, a rooster is killed on the house's threshold to make the house strong; then *avgolémeno* soup and chicken are served. If the Vasilopita was not cut the night before, it is cut at the main meal and given to any guests who come to visit.

Superstitions

People associate luck and good fortune with the start of the new year. Some Greek Americans better their chances with a few of the following practices on New Year's day:

- Open the windows at midnight to let out the evil spirits.
- Say *"kaló potharikó"* (good omen) when the first person enters the house after midnight. Good luck for the year is related to that first person who must enter with the right foot (*póthi* or *pothári*). Many families select someone, such as the head of the house, the oldest son, or the youngest child. Families who have not been out of the house, hope someone strong and healthy will enter first, and they welcome the person with

sweets and/or money. Some people prefer an icon to enter the home first. An individual holds the icon in outstretched arms so that it crosses the threshold before anyone.

- Try to be the first to hear something good and happy.

- Eat something sweet at breakfast to sweeten the new year.

- Be happy and positive. Do not quarrel, cry, or lose anything. Whatever you do this day, it is said you will do all year.

- Set an abundant table of food to assure plenty.

- Wear new clothes, to be bright and clean all year.

- Break a pomegranate on the threshold of the front door. The scattered seeds symbolize that life takes many directions. The more seeds that scatter, the greater the prosperity for the household.

Epiphany (Theophania)

The holiday season ends with the great feast of Epiphany or Theophania (God appears). It ranks after Easter and Christmas in importance. The faithful especially appreciate the custom of receiving blessed holy water. The events are remembered on three separate days: January 5, Eve of Theophania (Lesser Blessing of the Water); January 6, Theophania (Greater Blessing of the Water); and January 7, Feast Day of St. John the Baptist.

FASTING

For the Orthodox faithful, fasting is widely practiced the day before Theophania. Fasting prepares the body and mind to receive the holy water distributed at the church service. Since services are held on January 5 and January 6, fasting may be on January 4 or 5, depending on which service you attend. Most Greek Americans attend the service on January 6 and fast January 5.

SIGNIFICANCE AND CHURCH SERVICES

Theophania celebrates God's first public revelation of the identity of Jesus, the manifestation of the Godhead as three persons (the

Father, Son, and Holy Spirit), Christ's baptism, and beginning of Christ's public ministry.

> In those days Jesus came from Nazareth of Galilee and was baptized by John in the Jordan. And when he came up out of the water, immediately he saw the heavens opened and the Spirit descending upon him like a dove; and a voice came from heaven, "Thou art my beloved Son, with whom I am well pleased." Mark 1:9-11

The special services commemorating these events on January 5 (Lesser Blessing of the Water) and January 6 (Greater Blessing of the Water) are the same despite their names.

During the service, the Holy Spirit is invoked to sanctify the water (*ayiasmós*), and the cross is dipped into it three times, symbolic of Christ's own immersion into the Jordan river. The holy water sanctifies and heals the faithful. Parishioners then come to the front of the church to be blessed by the priest, who dips a large sprig of basil or evergreen into the water and touches the parishioner's head saying, *"Chrónia pollá."* The parishioner kisses the cross and the priest's hand before receiving a small bottle of holy water to take home.

EVE OF THEOPHANIA

ATTENDING CHURCH

On January 5, parishioners may attend a Divine Liturgy and the Lesser Blessing of the Water service. Most Greek Americans fast on January 5 and attend the service on January 6.

THE *KÁLANDA*

Children in Greece also sing the *kálanda* on this day, announcing the baptism of Christ.

Epiphany has come — illumination of the world — and great rejoicing in the Lord. By Jordan River — stands our good Mary — and thus she begs St. John — "St. John Baptist — it is in your power — to baptize the child of God." [3]

EXORCISING THE *KALIKÁNTZARI*

On the eve of Theophania, young men in northern Greek villages dress in frightening masks and costumes and wear jingling bells to imitate the *kalikántzari* and scare them away. Large bonfires are also lit on the eve of Theophania to expel evil spirits. In Cyprus, families make *loukoumáthes* (fried pastry puffs with sweet syrup) for the coming feast day. But before serving, they throw a few on the roof to keep the *kalikántzari* from coming in the house.

Greek village priests often visit each home that evening, sprinkling holy water in all the rooms with a sprig of basil. This is the only method approved by the church for ridding the house of evil spirits.

THEOPHANIA: THE FEAST OF LIGHTS (TON PHOTON)

ATTENDING CHURCH

On January 6 the faithful attend a Divine Liturgy and the Great Blessing of the Water service to celebrate Theophania, also called "Ton Photon" ("Feast of Lights") with reference to the spiritual illumination of the Holy Spirit. The service commemorates the baptism of Christ and the manifestation of God in three persons as described above.

Large numbers of people attend church to be blessed and to receive holy water which they take home in small bottles provided by the church. Some parishioners bring their own bottles often made specifically for holy water. In most churches in America the blessing is held indoors, and the water is contained in a large urn.

OUTDOOR BLESSING SERVICES

After the Divine Liturgy in the church, some communities hold the Blessing of the Water service outside by a body of water. In the United States, the most famous outdoor service is conducted each year by the Archbishop of the Greek Orthodox Church of America in Tarpon Springs, Florida.

In Tarpon Springs a great procession of altar boys, children dressed as angels, young people in Greek costumes, political dignitaries, and church officials carrying large icons makes its way from the church to the bay on streets decorated with flags, pennants, and flowers. At noon the archbishop blesses the water, and a white dove is released. The archbishop throws a cross into the water while church bells ring, and boats blow their whistles. Young men dive into the water to retrieve the cross; the diver who recovers it is formally blessed back at the church and is said to have good fortune for the year. After the ceremony, a festival features traditional Greek food, dancing, and music. Many similar services are held by parishes, such as Holy Apostles in Kenmore, Washington (Lake Washington), and St. Nicholas in Manhattan (New York City Harbor/Battery Park). In Greece, the largest service is held at Piraeus (port city of Athens) and attended by the prime minister and the archbishop of Greece.

In Cyprus, people take fruits, vegetables, and their seeds for planting wrapped in cloth napkins to the church service. They dip the bundles in the blessed water to ensure a good harvest. Upon returning home, they eat the blessed food and plant the seeds.

HOLY WATER

BLESSING OF THE HOME

It is customary to invite your priest to bless your home with holy water within a few weeks following Theophania. Prepare by cleaning the house, opening and lighting all the rooms. Place a clean bowl of water, *kandíli*, icon, and incense burner on a small table. The priest will bless the water by dipping a cross in it and repeating a blessing. Using a basil or evergreen sprig dipped in water as a sprinkler, he will go to each room and sprinkle it in the four corners, exorcising evil spirits. Save some of the holy water in a bottle in your *ikonostási* and pour the remainder on plants.

PERSONAL USE

According to Orthodox doctrine, holy water has the power to sanctify and heal. Have each family member drink a small amount of the holy water from Epiphany and/or the home blessing. Keep the unused holy water in your home *ikonostási* for future use: times of adversity, before starting a new venture or trip, to give thanks, or when someone is ill. You may drink it and/or put it on an afflicted part of the body. To rid the house of evil spirits, it should be sprinkled in the four corners of each room, so no one will step on it. (In rural Greece the holy water is sprinkled in the fields and on the animals.)

FEAST DAY OF ST. JOHN THE BAPTIST

On January 7 the church honors St. John the Baptist. St. John's baptism of Christ has made him one of the most significant saints in Orthodoxy. The patron saint of godparents, he always stands on Christ's left side at each church *ikonostásion*.

John is one of the most popular Greek names. Most people named John (including Yianni, Joanna, Yiana) celebrate their name day on January 7. In Greece many homes are open for parties — the last festive occasion of the Dodecameron. So many families choose this name that there is an old Greek expression, *"Spíti horís Yiánni prokopí then káni."* (A home without a person named John will not succeed.)

Other Winter Feast Days

FEAST DAY OF THE THREE HIERARCHS
January 30

Three outstanding hierarchs, St. Basil the Great, St. Gregory the Theologian, and St. John Chrysostom, are honored as patron saints of education and culture on January 30. They are among the early church fathers who recognized the importance of the Greek language and culture in developing and advancing Orthodoxy.

In formulating Christianity, the church fathers questioned the compatibility of pagan classical thinking and Christianity. Should the heritage of the Greco-Roman world into which Christianity emerged be discarded and condemned? Church fathers such as St. Basil the Great, St. Gregory the Theologian, and St. John Chrysostom reasoned it should not. St. Basil advised that virtue could be found in classical thinking. One should "look for the honey and avoid the poison." [4]

These church fathers understood the importance of letters and that through the universal language of Greek, the Gospel could be spread to many. The Christian faith was developed in the Greek language and Greek thought. Instead of being discarded, ancient Greek concepts concerning the nature of the soul, man's personal relationship with God, and the ideal spiritual world, became part of Christianity.

The Greek Orthodox church still cherishes the Hellenistic influence and makes every effort to preserve it. Most Greek schools in America are sponsored by churches, and every year the Archdiocese of America proclaims the week around January 30 as the week of Greek Letters. Greek school teachers are honored and recognized with a short program. Some churches hold an *artoklasía* service in honor of the Three Hierarchs.

The Presentation of Jesus Christ
February 2

Forty days after the birth of Christ, his parents brought him to the temple in accordance with the Jewish custom of offering the first male child to the service of God. Christ was received by Simeon, an elderly prophet whom God had promised would not die before seeing the Messiah. Simeon's prayer is repeated during the service: "Lord, now lettest thou thy servant depart in peace, according to thy word; for mine eyes have seen thy salvation which thou hast prepared in the presence of all peoples, a light for revelation to the Gentiles, and for glory to thy people Israel." Luke:2:29-32

Today each newborn child is brought to church after forty days, reenacting the journey of Christ and the Virgin Mary. (See *Birth of Children*)

The Resurrection of Jesus Christ

❖ *Spring*

The Easter Season

Easter, the celebration of the Resurrection of Christ, is the most important Greek Orthodox holiday. The season culminates with a midnight service in a darkened church illuminated by hundreds of candles. Later the faithful feast on red Easter eggs and succulent spring lamb. Preceding this celebration is a somber period of intense self-examination for the individual, a period of rejecting an old way of life to gain a new one.

The date of Orthodox Easter changes each year, usually occurring on a date different from that of the West. (Occasionally the dates coincide.) The Orthodox calculate the date according to a canon adopted in 325: Easter is determined on the old Julian calendar as the first Sunday after the first full moon following the vernal equinox. Passover must always come before Easter.

The Orthodox use the Julian calendar only for Easter and dates dependent on it, such as Lent and Pentecost. The Julian is thirteen days behind the new Gregorian calendar on which the rest of the Greek Orthodox year is based. The fixing of the Orthodox date for Easter was a political compromise so that all Orthodox churches, including those who use the Julian year-round (Old Calendarists), could celebrate Easter on the same day.

The Easter season spans eleven weeks: The Triodion (consisting of Pre-Lent, Great Lent, and Holy Week), Easter, and Bright Week. Participation in the traditions and customs over the entire period can give your Easter celebration profound meaning.

PRE-LENT

Two conflicting messages compete during the pre-Lenten season. The church stresses themes of repentance and sacrifice, urging its parishioners to prepare for the rigors of Great Lent. Secular society, however, indulges and parties during a three-week period called carnival before the long fast of Great Lent.

CARNIVAL (*APOKRIÁ*) — A SECULAR CELEBRATION

Pre-Lenten celebration is common throughout the world. Some of the most famous festivals are carnival in Rio de Janeiro and Mardi Gras in New Orleans, Louisiana. In Greece, carnival (*apokriá* — abstinence from meat) lasts three weeks: Announcing Week (beginning of carnival), Meat Week (last week to eat meat), and Cheese Week (last week to eat dairy products).

During those three weeks in Greece there are masked balls, parades, fireworks, and plays. Masquerading is very popular, and it is common for small bands in costume, playing musical instruments, to roam the streets. Short street plays and parodies are often performed in village squares. Hundreds of children dress in their best and stroll through the parks with their parents. Zappeion Gardens in Athens is one of the most popular spots for such a stroll. Patras in the Peloponnesus is reputed to have the largest and best carnival in Greece, including a large parade with floats. The most famous carnival in Cyprus in the city of Limassol, begins with a parade on Thursday before Great Lent and continues through Sunday with the Grand Carnival Procession with floats and costumes.

Carnival is not widely celebrated in the United States although masked balls, usually sponsored by Greek societies, are popular and enjoyed by many Greek Americans.

RELIGIOUS PREPARATION

In contrast to the secular celebrations, the church teaches its parishioners to prepare themselves for Great Lent and Easter with diet modification and themes of humility, judgment, repentance, and forgiveness. The Pre-Lenten period lasts three weeks, but includes four Sundays. Text for the following Sunday services may be found in *The Lenten Triodion* by Mother Mary and Kallistos Ware.[5]

SUNDAY #1 — THE PUBLICAN AND THE PHARISEE (LUKE 18:10-14)

The reading suggests that parishioners should emulate the humility of the publican, not the false piousness of the pharisee.

SUNDAY #2 — THE PRODIGAL SON (LUKE 15:11-32)

The reading implores the faithful to repent and return to God the Father, just as the prodigal son returned to his earthly father.

Meat Week (Kreatini)

Meat Week begins on Monday two weeks before Great Lent and is the last week to eat meat. Greek Americans do not cook special food, but in Greece roast pork is especially popular and tavernas are always packed on Tsiknopempti (Aromatic Thursday). In the villages this was the traditional week to slaughter the family pig that had been growing all year. Leftovers would be smoked and eaten after Easter.

First Saturday of Souls (Psychosavato)

The deceased are remembered at a special service called "Saturday of Souls" held four times a year: the two Saturdays prior to Great Lent, the first Saturday of Great Lent, and the Saturday before Pentecost. Orthodox believe that it is the duty of the living to remember and pray for the deceased. A general prayer is said for specific individuals and all unknown souls who have no one to pray for them. Parishioners bring small dishes of *kóllyva* to the church and submit a list of first names of deceased loved ones to the priest. For further details see *Death and Mourning*.

SUNDAY #3 — MEAT FARE SUNDAY — THE LAST JUDGMENT (MATTHEW 25: 31-46)

If strict fasting is observed, this is the last day to eat meat until Easter. The reading for the day states that an individual will be judged in heaven according to the kindnesses shown to others on earth.

Cheese Week (Tirini)

For the observant Cheese Week is the last week to eat animal products until Easter. Typical dishes include those made with milk, cheese, and eggs, such as macaroni and cheese, *tirópita* (cheese pie), and custards.

Second Saturday of Souls

See *Death and Mourning*.

SUNDAY #4 — CHEESE FARE SUNDAY — FORGIVENESS (MATTHEW 6:14-21)

Animal products are eaten for the last time this day if a strict fast is going to be kept. In some parts of Greece, the custom is to eat an egg at the end of the meal and say, "With an egg I close my mouth, with an egg I shall open it again." This refers to the red Easter egg eaten after the Easter Resurrection service.

The reading emphasizes the importance of forgiving others, stating that only those who forgive will be forgiven. It also suggests that fasting should be done in a private, humble manner — an appropriate suggestion for Great Lent that begins the next day.

GREAT LENT

The Orthodox observe Great Lent (Lent) more widely than the other three Lenten periods (see *Fasting*). Great Lent precedes the most important event in the church, Christ's Resurrection. For six weeks (seven including Holy Week), the faithful modify their diet and behavior to achieve spiritual renewal. Sometimes this goal gets lost in the flurry of cooking Lenten dishes, buying new outfits, and, in America, putting together Easter baskets. While all these activities are a part of the Easter season, the most important preparation for Easter should be spiritual.

PURPOSE

Great Lent is a tremendous spiritual challenge for each individual. Three basic components are emphasized: fasting of body and soul, prayer, and philanthropy. Through self-examination, fasting, and giving to charity the old way of life can be shed. Just as Christ received new life after his death, a new life is given at Easter to those individuals who have prepared themselves. The soul must be cleansed by genuine repentance, the breaking of sinful habits, forgiveness and reconciliation. The challenge is to recover the image of God within oneself (*théosis*). Lent and Easter offer each parishioner that opportunity.

Spring

SUGGESTED READING AND TRANSLATIONS

For a deeper understanding of the season, read *Great Week and Pascha in the Greek Orthodox Church* by A.C. Calivas and *Great Lent* by Alexander Schmemann.[6]   You may want to use English translations of the Greek services while attending church. For Pre-Lent, Great Lent, and Holy Week, the classic translation is *The Lenten Triodion* by Mother Mary and Kallistos Ware. *The Services for Holy Week and Easter* by Nomikos Michael Vaporis is published by Holy Cross Orthodox Press. The Easter service and the services of the week following Easter may be found in the *Pentecostarion*.[7]   Since most churches do not supply these books, parishioners buy their own copies and bring them to church.

You may be able to buy these and other appropriate books from your church, or you can order them from Holy Cross Orthodox Bookstore and/or Light and Life Publishing Company.[8]

DEMEANOR

You can observe Lent by attending church frequently, praying, fasting, giving confession, taking communion, giving to charity, and reading religious materials. Dress should be modest, especially in church. Certain social events such as large parties and dancing should be avoided. For this reason, the Orthodox church prohibits weddings and dances during Lent.

FASTING

The purpose of fasting is to prepare for communion and rebirth at Easter. Forgoing food is a tangible symbol of controlling indulgences, both physical and mental. Fasting should not become an obsession or an end in itself, as stated in a hymn from Cheese Fare Wednesday:

> In vain do you rejoice in not eating, O soul
> For you abstain from food,
> But from passions you are not purified.
> If you have no desire for improvement,
> You will be despised as a lie in the eyes of God.[9]

Fasting during Lent varies with each individual. A few parishioners observe a strict fast for the entire Lenten season: no meat, fish, animal products, olive oil, or alcohol. A less strict approach eliminates the above foods the first week of Lent, each Wednesday and Friday, and all of Holy Week. Note that fish is permitted on two days during Lent: The Annunciation of the Mother of God (March 25) and Palm Sunday.

You can prepare interesting Lenten food (Sarakostiana) from the allowed list of legumes, vegetables, fruit, and shellfish. These include the popular *spanakórizo* (baked spinach and rice), bean soup (*fasolátha*), eggplant casserole, and Lenten *koulourákia*. The following is a typical Lenten menu.

LENTEN MENU

Taramosaláta and bread
Vegetable relish tray
Fasolátha and salad
Fruit

WEEKLY SCHEDULE

Week #1 — Clean Week (Kathara Evdomada)

Clean Monday (Kathari Deftera)

Clean Monday is the first day of Lent, and individuals wish each other "*Kalí Sarakostí*" ("Good Lent"). In the United States, fasting begins and lasts all week. Many people take communion at the Divine Liturgy of the Presanctified Gifts on either Wednesday or Friday.

In Greece, however, Clean Monday is a national holiday, traditionally observed by picnicking in the countryside or city parks. Families pack large baskets of Lenten food: shellfish, *taramosaláta*, green onions, pickled vegetables, salad, fruit, halva and *lagána*, a special bread eaten only on Clean Monday (see recipe below). Flying multicolored kites is extremely popular, and the hallmark of the day. Although meat and dairy products are not eaten on this day, many view Clean Monday as the last day of carnival because it is festive and fun.

In Athens the day is called Koulouma because the most popular picnic area used to be by the columns of the temple of Zeus. In Lefkogia, Crete, a mock funeral procession is held for the king of carnival. In Thebes a famous comic parody of a peasant wedding takes place. Two shepherds arrange the marriage of their children including negotiating the dowry. The daughter is a man dressed as a woman, and the relatives ride donkeys backward.

Lagána
(Bread for Clean Monday)

1 package dry yeast	¼ cup vegetable shortening
1 cup warm water	2 tablespoons sesame seeds
1 teaspoon sugar	Pinch of salt
4 cups all-purpose flour	

Dissolve yeast and sugar in warm water. Mix dry ingredients with shortening. Add yeast solution and mix well, adding flour until dough pulls away from bowl. Knead for 10 minutes. Let sit for 30 minutes covered with a cloth. Knead again for 3 minutes and form into an oblong roll. Place on a 10" x 15" greased cookie sheet or large greased round baking tray. Press dough out and away from center. Brush flattened dough lightly with water. Sprinkle with sesame seeds. Let rise again, uncovered, for 45 minutes. Punch 6 holes throughout the dough to keep bread from popping as it bakes. Bake at 375°F on middle oven rack for 20 minutes. Remove immediately from pan and place on rack to cool.

Wednesday — The Liturgy of the Presanctified Gifts

The Liturgy of the Presanctified Gifts offers communion of the holy gifts (Eucharist) consecrated at the Divine Liturgy the previous Sunday. It is an opportunity to receive the sustaining spiritual strength of Christ during the difficult journey of Lent. Although the church forbids the celebration of the Eucharist on weekdays of Lent (except the Annunciation), it recognizes the need for spiritual food. The consecrated Gifts may be offered on Wednesdays and Fridays of Lent. (Check your local church calendar.)

Friday

Check local schedule for Divine Liturgy of the Presanctified Gifts.

On the first five Friday evenings of Lent, the Small Compline service and "The Akathist Hymn" honor the Virgin Mary. The Compline is a worship service with prayers and psalms. "The Akathist Hymn," one of the most beautiful and beloved hymns of Orthodoxy, is an ecclesiastical poem about The Annunciation of the Mother of God (which occurs during Lent) and The Nativity of Jesus Christ. Parishioners stand during the hymn; the word *"akáthistos"* means "not seated." The hymn contains twenty-four stanzas in order of the Greek alphabet. Each stanza begins with a letter of the alphabet starting with Alpha and ending with Omega. A different stanza (referred to as "Salutations to the Virgin Mary") is sung on the first four Friday evenings of Lent. On the fifth Friday, "The Akathist Hymn" is sung in its entirety.

Preamble to The Akathist Hymn

Rejoice, through whom joy shall shine forth;
Rejoice, through whom the curse shall vanish. [10]

Each service concludes with the singing of "Ti Ipermacho" ("The Invincible Commander") [11] by the entire congregation, a triumphant song about the Virgin Mary, the protector of Constantinople. During the seventh century, she appeared in Constantinople during a siege by the Persians. The enemy fled after its fleet had sunk, and the grateful citizens stayed up all night in church composing the following hymn in her honor. The most popular hymn in Orthodoxy, it is also sung along with the national anthem at major ethnic holidays and during times of crisis.

Saturday — Third Saturday of Souls (The Feast of Two Theodores and The Miracle of the Kollyva)

This is the third and most prominent Saturday of Souls. It celebrates the Feast of Two Theodores and the Miracle of the Kollyva. Saints Theodore Tyron and Theodore Stratilates are symbols of Christian obedience. During the fourth century, Emperor Julian the Apostate, in an attempt to break the Christian fast from meat, ordered the blood of animals to be sprayed on the food in the market. But the two Theodores appeared in a vision to the patriarch warning him of contamination and urging the Christians

Ti Ipermacho

Ti i-per-má-cho stra-ti-gó-ta
ni-ki-tí-ri-a. Os li-tro-
THí-sa ton thi-nón ef-cha-ri-stí-
ri-a. A-na-grá-fo si i
pó-lis sou THe-o-tó-ke. All' os
é-chou-sa to krá-tos a-pro-smá-
chi-ton, ek pan-dí-on me kin-
thí-non e-lef-THé-ro-son, i-na kra-zo
si; ché-re ním-fi a-ním-fef te.

To you we attribute victory, the invincible commander in chief, and sing praises of thanksgiving, O Theotokos. Keep us all unassailable and deliver us from all dangers that beset us that we may sing: Hail, O bride unwedded.

to eat *kóllyva* to remain clean. Commemoration of this miraculous vision reminds the faithful to obey the fast of Lent.

It has been traditional for Orthodox Christians to fast during the first week of Lent and receive communion on this third Saturday of Souls. Relatives visit the graves of the deceased taking flowers and *kóllyva*. (See *Death and Mourning*)

The majority of individuals named "Theodore" celebrate their name day on this day, although some honor St. Theodore Stratilates on February 8 and St. Theodore Tyron on February 17.

Week #2

Sunday of Orthodoxy

The Sunday of Orthodoxy celebrates the restoration of the icons to the church and the affirmed dogma of Christ's humanity as shown in the icons of Christ, the man. In 726 A.D. icons were banned because many believed that Christ as God should not be depicted and that icons were being worshiped as idols. In 843 the Empress Theodora ordered them restored. This event is commemorated each year with a procession of icons through the church and the reading of the Synodikon Proclamation of the Seventh Ecumenical Council:

> As the prophets beheld, as the Apostles have taught, as the Church has received, as the Teachers have dogmatized, as the universe has agreed, as grace has shown forth, as truth has revealed, as falsehood has been dissolved, as wisdom has presented, as Christ awarded: thus we declare, thus we assert, thus we preach Christ our true God and honor his saints in words, in writings, in thoughts, in sacrifices, in churches, in holy icons; on the one hand worshiping and reverencing Christ as God and Lord, and on the other hand honoring them as true servants of the Lord of all and accordingly offering them veneration.

> This is the faith of the Apostles, this is the faith of the Fathers, this is the faith of the Orthodox, this is the faith which established the universe. To these all, teachers of piety and faith, we cry out in brotherly love, "Memory eternal." Amen.[12]

Wednesday

Check local schedule for Liturgy of the Presanctified Gifts.

Friday

Check local schedule for Liturgy of the Presanctified Gifts. The "Salutations to the Virgin Mary" (second stanza) is sung during the evening.

Week #3

Sunday — Feast of St. Gregory Palamas

St. Gregory Palamas is recognized on this day for his scholarly contributions to the church and for his example of asceticism (praying and fasting), major components of Lent.

Wednesday

Check local schedule for Liturgy of the Presanctified Gifts.

Friday

Check local schedule for Liturgy of the Presanctified Gifts. "Salutations to the Virgin Mary" (third stanza) is always sung during the evening.

Week #4

Sunday — Veneration of the Holy Cross

The cross on which Christ died is honored this day, the most important Sunday of Lent. This is the half-way point of the long journey of fasting, prayer, and philanthropy. The Veneration of the Holy Cross reminds the faithful how Jesus carried the cross, letting no obstacle prevent him from carrying it to the end. It is the same with the life of the Christian during Lent. Easter is reached only through the crucifixion of one's passions.

A cross is carried in procession to the middle of the church during the Divine Liturgy and left there all week for veneration as a symbol of strength. At the end of the Divine Liturgy, everyone receives a flower from the cross to be saved at the home *ikonostási.*

Wednesday

Check local schedule for Liturgy of the Presanctified Gifts.

Friday

Check local schedule for Liturgy of the Presanctified Gifts. The "Salutations to the Virgin Mary" (fourth stanza) is sung during the evening.

During Lent two significant events celebrated on March 25 break the solemn mood: The Annunciation of the Mother of God and Greek Independence Day. March 25 is a fixed date, but the dates of Lent change each year. March 25 is inserted here arbitrarily.

THE ANNUNCIATION OF THE MOTHER GOD AND GREEK INDEPENDENCE DAY
MARCH 25

March 25, one of the most important Greek holidays, celebrates The Annunciation of the Mother of God and Greek Independence Day. Although one event is religious and the other secular, the two are linked together by the common themes of birth and liberty. One event marks the good news that the Virgin Mary will give birth to the Son of God. The other commemorates the birth of the modern Greek state in 1821 and the proclamation that freedom would come to the enslaved Greek nation.

THE ANNUNCIATION OF THE MOTHER OF GOD

The Annunciation is the revelation by the Angel Gabriel to the Virgin Mary, that she would become the Mother of God. It confirmed that Christ, born of a human mother, would also be

The Annunciation of the Mother God

human and elevated Mary to sainthood and the highest position in the Orthodox church.

> And [Gabriel] said to her, "Do not be afraid, Mary, for you
>   have found favor with God.
> And behold, you will conceive in your womb and bear a
>   son, and you shall call his name Jesus.
> He will be great, and will be called the Son of the Most
>   High; and the Lord God will give to him the throne of
>   his father David,
> And he will reign over the house of Jacob forever; and of
>   his kingdom there will be no end."
> And Mary said to the angel, "How shall this be, since I
>   have no husband?"
> And the angel said to her, "The Holy Spirit will come upon
>   you and the power of the Most High will overshadow
>   you; therefore the child to be born will be called holy,
>   the Son of God." Luke 1:-26-35

A Divine Liturgy always commemorates this major feast day. Annunciation falls during Lent, but fish may be eaten.

GREEK INDEPENDENCE DAY

HISTORY OF THE REVOLUTION

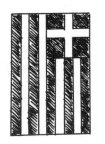

Bishop Germanos

March 25 is the Greek "Fouth of July." Greece's modern revolution began on March 25, 1821, with a declaration of independence from the Ottoman Empire and subjugation since the fall of Constantinople in 1453. While revolutionary ferment had been growing for some time, a Greek Orthodox clergyman, Bishop Germanos of Patras, is popularly credited as the first to declare Greece free when he raised a flag over the monastery of Ayia Lavra (Holy Laura) near Kalavrita. His declaration, *"Elefthería i thánatos"* (pron. *THánatos*) ("Liberty or death"), became the ralllying cry for the ensuing war.

Although independence was granted in 1829, fighting continued until 1833. The devastating war resulted in bloodbaths throughout the Ottoman Empire, including Smyrna, Cyprus, and Chios. The Greek cause eventually captured the imagination of Philhellenes (lovers of Greece) throughout the world who contributed money and time and sacrificed their lives to secure freedom for the birthplace of democracy. British romantic poets like Byron and Shelley inspired sympathizers with their poetry in *Don Juan* and *Hellas*, respectively. For Greeks today all around the world, the liberation from the Ottoman Empire evokes great pride and passion for their oppressed and courageous ancestors.

Greek Flag

INDEPENDENCE DAY AND THE CHURCH

The Archdiocese of America mandates a short service (doxology) and program in recognition of the church's vital role in preserving the Greek religion, culture, and language during the four hundred years of Ottoman occupation. The close relationship between church and state continues today. Orthodoxy is the state religion in Greece, and a cross graces the modern Greek flag.

Kolokotronis

Bouboulina

CELEBRATIONS IN AMERICA

In the United States, city, state, and national governments issue proclamations recognizing the day. Some communities with large Greek-American populations sponsor Independence Day parades such as: Baltimore/Washington, Boston, Chicago, Cleveland, New York, San Francisco, and Tarpon Springs, Florida. Churches, Greek schools, and secular Hellenic organizations sponsor a variety of events. A typical program includes speeches by dignitaries about Greek history and current issues. Children in national costumes recite patriotic poems in Greek.

While costumes vary from region to region, the most common are the *foustanéla* for a boy and the Amalia dress for a girl. The *foustanéla,* worn by military men in the Peloponnese and Central Greece, was adopted by King Otto (the first king of Greece, 1833-1862) as the formal court dress. The costume generally includes a white pleated skirt *(foustanéla),* a tasseled hat, blue jacket, and red shoes with pompoms *(tsaroúhia).* The soldiers known as *évzones,* who guard the Tomb of the Unknown Soldier in front of the parliament building in Athens today, wear this uniform. The Amalia costume, most often a blue skirt, white blouse, burgundy vest with gold trim, and tasseled beret, was also adopted as the formal court dress by King Otto's wife, Queen Amalia. There are many other popular costume styles from the other regions and islands. Most costumes are handed down through the generations or may be purchased in Greece.

Foustanéla

Pictures of revolutionary heroes such as Kolokotronis, Bishop Germanos, and Bouboulina decorate the walls, and Greek music and folk dancing often complete the program. Inspired audiences shout *Zíto i Ellás* (Long live Greece!) and robustly sing the Greek national anthem, "Ethnikos Imnos" by Greek poet, Dionysios Solomos.[13] Greek people popularly call it, "Se Gnorizo Apo Tin Kopsi" from the opening line, but the correct title is "Imnos is tin Eleftherian" ("Hymn to Liberty").

Amalia costume

271

Ethnikos Imnos
(Greek National Anthem)

Se gno - rí - z'a - pó tin kó - psi tou spa-

THioú tin tro - me - rí. Se gno - rí - z'a - pó tin

ó - psi pou me viá me - trái tin yí. Ap' ta

kó - ka - la vgal - mé - ni ton El - lí - non ta ie-

rá, ke san pró - ta an - thrio - me - ni ché - r'o

ché - re e - lef - THe - riá, ke san pró - ta an - thrio-

mé - ni ché - r'o, che - re'e - lef - THe riá, ke san

pró - ta an - thrio - mé - ni che - r'o che - re'e - lef - THe ria.

I know you by the cutting edge
of your dread sword;
I know you by your look
that fiercely scans the land.

Risen from the bones,
the sacred Greek bones,
and brave as of old,
Hail, O Liberty, Hail.

CELEBRATIONS IN GREECE

On March 25, white and blue bunting and flags decorate villages, towns, and cities throughout Greece. Greeks observe Independence Day with church services, parades, speeches, and parties. School children dress in their best clothes or in national costumes to participate in the marches. The festivities parallel America's Independence Day on the fourth of July.

The solemn atmosphere of Lent resumes as the devout continue preparing for Easter.

Week #5

Sunday — St. John of the Ladder

St. John Climacus is honored for the book he wrote for monks called *The Ladder of Divine Ascent.* It detailed the self-discipline, sacrifice, and hard work necessary to reach moral perfection. His example and wisdom in the seventh century are inspirational during the Lenten season.

Wednesday

Check local schedule for Liturgy of the Presanctified Gifts.

Friday

Check local schedule for Liturgy of the Presanctified Gifts. The entire "Akathist Hymn" is sung on the fifth Friday evening of Lent. During the four previous Fridays, "Ti Ipermacho" concludes the service, but on the fifth evening, the dismissal hymn, "To Prostachthen Mistikos," takes a place of prominence:

> When the bodiless learned of the secret command, he came in haste to Joseph's house and said to her who knew not wedlock: He who bowed the heavens by coming down is contained wholly and unchanged in you. Seeing him take the form of a servant in your womb, I stand in awe and cry out to you: Rejoice, O Bride unwedded.[14]

Week #6 — Week before Palm Sunday

Sunday — St. Mary of Egypt

Known as the penitent saint of the church, St. Mary is one of the church's most positive examples of repentance. Before conversion she lived a licentious life of pleasure pursued by many men. A turning point came, however, when she visited the Church of the Holy Sepulchre in Jerusalem and found it impossible to enter because of an unseen power. She immediately repented and then lived as an ascetic in the wilderness of Egypt for the next forty years. Her example reminds the faithful of the importance of the virtue of repentance.

After a quiet week, the celebratory services for the Saturday of Lazarus and Palm Sunday provide a distinct break between Lent and the sorrow of Holy Week.

Saturday of Lazarus

Church Service

On Saturday morning a Divine Liturgy commemorates the resurrection of Lazarus from the dead by Christ. This important miracle, sometimes called the "first Easter," previews Christ's own Resurrection that occurs the following Saturday. Christ brings Lazarus back to life in Bethany and leaves from there to enter Jerusalem the following day.

Food and Social Customs

Saturday of Lazarus is very significant in Cyprus. Lazarus came to Cyprus after Christ raised him from the dead, and later became the first consecrated bishop of the See of Larnaca. He died there, and part of his relics remain at the Church of St. Lazarus in Larnaca. On this day, young boys in Cyprus go from house to house singing a song about Lazarus' resurrection on this special Saturday. They are rewarded with uncooked eggs that are boiled and dyed red on Holy Thursday for the Anastasi service. In Mitilini, special buns called *lázari* are made for the day. The roll is long, thin, and crossed at the ends. A cross is made in the dough with currants. Children roll the buns down small hills, hoping to find a bird's nest where the buns stop.

Palm Sunday (The Entry of Jesus Christ into Jerusalem)

Word of the resurrection of Lazarus by Christ in Bethany spread quickly to Jerusalem, and Christ was triumphantly welcomed into the city by enthusiastic crowds the next day. The church commemorates this high point in Christ's public life at a Divine Liturgy in the church decorated with palms and/or laurel leaves. (Laurel is a symbol of triumph.) A procession through the church reenacts Christ's entry into Jerusalem, sometimes including children carrying lighted candles they have decorated. Small crosses made of palms are given to everyone at the end of the service and kept in the home *ikonostási.*

Fasting is modified because of the triumphant nature of Palm Sunday, and fish is permitted. *Bakaliáros* (fried cod) with *skorthaliá* (garlic sauce) and fried vegetables is a traditional dish, but any fish may be served.

Palm Cross

HOLY WEEK

PURPOSE

Holy Week serves as the ultimate preparation to face and worship the risen Lord. The joy of Easter cannot be complete without reliving the events that lead to it. During Holy Week all the passions and pathos of the last week of Christ's life are retold and reenacted. From Palm Sunday evening to Good Friday, the services recount everything Jesus endured to fulfill the will of the Father. On Good Friday God's will is completed on the cross and then with the Resurrection. By reliving Christ's experience of Holy Week, the faithful can be resurrected and come closer to becoming like God (*théosis*).

DEMEANOR

The faithful reaffirm their faith during Holy Week by preparing physically and mentally for Easter. Social activities are curtailed and marital relations avoided. Spiritual reading and acts of sharing should be substituted for plays, movies, and television. The somber demeanor parallels mourning for a deceased loved one.

In Greece, businesses shut down on Holy Friday, and people return to their family villages for the rest of the week. Many *kafenía* (coffee houses) hang the Jack of Spades from a light fixture during Holy Week, and card playing is suspended until the Monday after Easter.

FASTING

Most Orthodox fast in some way during Holy Week. The very devout follow a strict fast of no fish, meat, animal products, olive oil, and alcohol for the entire week. Others adopt a modified version for all or part of the week. Meals parallel those of Lent, utilizing legumes such as beans and lentils. Lentils are said to represent the tears of the Mother of God, and vinegar is added to the soup in remembrance of Christ's receiving vinegar instead of water while on the cross.

❧❀❧

TYPICAL HOLY WEEK MEAL

Lentil soup and bread
Olives and boiled vegetables
Halvah and fruit

❧❀❧

PREPARATIONS FOR EASTER

Cleaning, shopping, and food preparation for Easter is traditional, making this a hectic week. New outfits, symbolic of new life after the Resurrection, are purchased for the Anastasi service held at midnight on Saturday. Some godparents buy new clothing for a young godchild, along with an Anastasi candle decorated with a ribbon and flower.

Food preparation begins well in advance of Easter day. Of special note are the red eggs, *tsouréki* (bread) and *mayerítsa* (soup). The red eggs, always dyed on Thursday, have great symbolic significance (see "Holy Saturday"). The traditional *tsouréki* and *mayerítsa* appear on every table, as essential as red eggs and lamb. (See recipes below.)

CHURCH SERVICES

Since the church day always begins the evening before the secular day, confusion arises when scheduling and publicizing services. For example, the matins (morning service) of Holy Friday are sung on Holy Thursday evening. Thus the readings from the twelve Gospels are presented on Holy Thursday evening according to the secular calendar, but in the church it is Friday morning. Events and themes below are listed under the secular day or evening they occur.

The services of Holy Week contain some of Orthodoxy's most beautiful Byzantine poetry. You may want to purchase English translations of the services as mentioned above in "Suggested Readings and Translations."

Sunday

Evening Service — The Matins of Christ the Bridegroom

On Sunday evening, six days of sorrow begin. The service celebrates the allegory of the church (the people) as a bride and Christ as a bridegroom. Like a bride who must be ready to meet her bridegroom, the people must be prepared for an eternal union with Christ.

Two parables are told. One concerns the Old Testament figure of Joseph who was betrayed by his brothers, just as Jesus will be betrayed later in the week. The other makes an example of a fig tree destroyed for not bearing fruit. The faithful are reminded that they too will not have life if they ignore God's word.

The icon of Christ is carried through the church and placed in the center until Holy Thursday. Parishioners should venerate the icon at the end of a service and when entering the church if a service is not in progress.

Holy Monday

Evening Service — The Matins of Christ the Bridegroom

The theme of Christ as a bridegroom and the church (the people) as the bride is repeated again. Several parables are read, including that of the ten virgins. The virgins cannot meet Christ the bridegroom without lamps lit by oil, the oil of charity and love obtained only through the Holy Spirit. Likewise, the believer will not be ready for Christ at Easter without the genuine light of love.

Holy Tuesday

Evening Service — The Matins of Christ the Bridegroom

This service commemorates the anointing of Christ with myrrh by a sinful woman. While visiting the home of a Pharisee, Christ was approached by a woman who suddenly entered the house. While "...standing behind him at his feet, weeping, she began to wet his feet with her tears, and wiped them with the hair of her head, and kissed his feet, and anointed them with the ointment." (Luke 7:38) Despite the Pharisee's dismissal of her unworthiness to touch Christ, Jesus forgave her sins. She is presented to sinners as an example of how to repent and be saved. To honor this woman, one of the most beautiful and beloved hymns in the Byzantine repertoire, Kassiane's Hymn, is sung at the service. Written by one of only four Orthodox women hymn writers, Kassia the Melodos (ninth century), it relates the sinner's agony and repentance.

Holy Wednesday

Morning Service — The Liturgy of the Presanctified Gifts

Check local schedule.

Afternoon and/or Evening Service — The Sacrament of the Holy Unction

With compassion and mercy, the church offers the faithful the sacrament of holy unction on Holy Wednesday. Through this sacrament God provides both mental and physical healing with the administering of holy oil (*efchéleon*) for those in need:

> Is any one of you suffering? Let him pray. Is any one in good spirits? Let him sing a hymn. Is any one among you sick? Let him bring in the presbyters of the Church and let them pray over him, anointing him with oil in the name of the Lord. And the prayer of faith will save the sick man, and the Lord will raise him up, and if he be in sin, they shall be forgiven him. James 5: 13-15

At the end of the service, parishioners go to the front of the church where the priest with a cotton swab dipped in oil makes the sign of the cross on the forehead, cheeks, chin, and front and back of the hands of each parishioner. Upon request you may take additional oil home and keep it at the *ikonostási* for later use. In Greece, it is customary to send the swabs to men away at sea. (See *Holy Unction*)

Holy Thursday

Morning Service — The Divine Liturgy of St. Basil the Great

This Divine Liturgy by St. Basil the Great commemorates the first Eucharist when Christ and his disciples shared the Last Supper. He appealed to them to remember him by consuming bread and wine changed into his Body and Blood. This is a meaningful and popular time to take communion.

Dyeing Eggs

Red Easter eggs are traditionally dyed on Holy Thursday, also known as Kokkinopempti (Red Thursday). Red symbolizes the blood of Christ shed on the cross. (See "Holy Saturday") Some consider the first egg in the dye, the "egg of the Virgin Mary," and save it in their home *ikonostási* to protect the household from the evil eye. Others save the egg from the church service at Anastasi. Eggs can be dyed on Holy Saturday or any other day except Good Friday, the most intense day of mourning. (See recipe below)

Cleaning the Home Ikonostási

Holy Thursday is the traditional day to dispose of the previous year's degradable items at the home *ikonostási*: Vasilopita, palm cross, flowers, and Easter egg. Burn the items in a small metal container outside the house, burying the ashes in a location where no one will walk over them.

Evening Service — The Crucifixion

Holy Thursday evening (Friday morning on the church calendar) is the climax of Christ's suffering, his Crucifixion. The altar is draped in black, and twelve Gospel readings are delivered describing all the events: Christ's farewell at the Passover meal, the betrayal,

*Holy
Thursday
Cross*

arrest, trial, Crucifixion, death, and sealing of the tomb. A candle is lit after the reading of each Gospel. (A few parishioners practice the custom of knotting a small ribbon after each reading and using it later as a *filaktó*.) After the fifth Gospel, the cross is taken out of the altar area, carried in procession, draped with flower wreaths, and placed in the center of the church. At the end of the service, parishioners come forward, make the sign of the cross, and kiss the body or feet of Christ as he hangs on the cross. People wear mourning clothes, and in some churches an all-night vigil is held.

Holy Thursday is also known in English as "Maundy Thursday," the day Christ washed the feet of his disciples at the Last Supper. This act reveals Christ's great humility and teaches that the faithful should allow Christ to purify them from their sins. Some Orthodox churches commemorate this event with a reenactment. The priest imitates Christ and washes the feet of twelve boys or men seated in a semicircle. A play called *Niptir* (Washing) on the island of Patmos, Greece, has become one of the most famous reenactments. The washing takes place in the town square where a large wash basin is erected.

Holy Friday

Holy Friday, the most solemn day of the year, is a time of mourning and fasting. In Greece, it is a national holiday with no school or work, and flags are flown at half-mast. Church bells toll funeral knells, and the dead are honored at cemeteries. In Mitilini, Crete, and Thrace large bonfires are built, and Judas is burned in effigy. Many devout families in America take time off from work and school to emphasize the importance of the day and to attend church services.

Decorating the Kouvoúklion

Early Friday morning the women of each parish decorate the *kouvoúklion* (funeral bier) that will hold the *epitáphios* (an icon of Christ's burial embroidered on cloth). The women decorating the *kouvoúklion* represent the women who prepared Christ's body for the tomb. Hundreds of white, red, and purple flowers are used to cover the bier. Anyone can help with the decorating and/or contribute money for the flowers.

Attending Church

The devout reserve this day for church, attending three important services: The Reading of the Royal Hours, the Descent from the Cross, and the Matins of Lamentation. The dress for church is dark clothing. Upon entering the church (if a service is not in progress), venerate the cross in the center and the *epitáphios* with the sign of the cross and a kiss.

Morning Service — The Reading of the Royal Hours

Readings of prophecies from the Old Testament and church hymns relevant to the passion and death of Christ constitute this service.

Afternoon Service — The Descent from the Cross (Apokathilosis)

At this dramatic service, parishioners solemnly watch the priest take down the body of Christ from the cross, wrap him in a white sheet and place him on the black-draped altar. The priest reenacts the same steps taken by Joseph of Arimathea who took Christ's body to the tomb. The *epitáphios* is put in the decorated *kouvoúklion*. (People popularly refer to the *kouvoúklion* and *epitáphios* together as "the *epitáphios.*") Parishioners venerate the icon at the end of the service, and some children go under the *epitáphios* to show humility and to receive God's blessing.

The *epitáphios* remains at the front of the church for the entire afternoon and into the evening service. Parishioners come to church and pay their respects to the buried Christ, with the same regard accorded the viewing of a deceased family member or friend.

Evening Service — The Matins of Lamentation (Epitaphios)

A somber, sad atmosphere pervades this service, well attended by parishioners wearing dark clothing appropriate for mourning. Sorrowful funeral dirges, the "Encomia," are similar to those sung in ancient times. Young girls dressed in white stand at the *epitáphios*, like the women who guarded Christ's tomb. During the evening, the congregation joins the choir in singing one of the most famous Orthodox hymns, "Lamentations," presented in three stanzas: "I Zoi En Tafo" ("Thou, O Christ, the Life"); "Axion Esti Megalinin Se Ton Zoothotin" ("It is Meet to Magnify Thee, the Giver of Life"); and "E Genee Pase Imnon Ti Tafi Sou" ("All Generations Offer Adoration").

Kouvouklion

The procession with the *epitáphios* through the church is the high point, a solemn but extraordinary spectacle. Some churches hold the procession outside as the congregation follows with lit candles. The *kouvoúklion* is brought to the entrance of the church and raised high above everyone's head as the parishioners file underneath to receive God's blessing. To symbolize the death of Christ, the candles are extinguished and rosewater, representing tears, is sprinkled on the congregation.

At the end of the service, each person venerates the *epitáphios* and receives a holy flower. People customarily wish each other, *"Kalí Anastasi"* (Happy Resurrection) outside the church. After arriving at home, the holy flowers are placed at the *ikonostási*.

The procession with the *epitáphios* in Greece is held outside. From Athens to the smallest village, the procession winds through the streets. In large cities, bands play funeral marches, and in Athens the head of state and other dignitaries take part in the ceremony. In some places the bier is taken to the cemetery and carried over the graves. Effigies of Judas are hung in some towns or burned in bonfires.

Holy Saturday

Morning Service — The Descent into Hades and Anticipation of the Resurrection — The Divine Liturgy of St. Basil

The first service of Holy Saturday takes place in the morning and breaks the somber spell. Jesus' descent to Hades where he preached his message to the dead is observed. Those who believed in him received eternal life and salvation. The heavy sorrow of Good Friday begins to lift when the priest, wearing a bright robe, chants, "Arise, O God, to the world," while sprinkling bay leaves or flower petals throughout the church to celebrate the triumph over death.

EASTER

EVENING — THE MATINS OF EASTER SUNDAY AND THE RESURRECTION (ANASTASI)

The Anastasi service is the climax of the Orthodox year. Before midnight throngs of people dressed in new, bright clothing, especially red, arrive at church. Even those who do not attend religious services during the calendar year make an appearance. This is a universal event for believers and nonbelievers alike, those who observe Lent, and those who do not. They are brought together in a rare emotional harmony for Anastasi.

Participants buy white candles upon entering church or bring decorated ones of their own. Hymns of anticipation for the great event are sung at the matins before midnight as the church gets more and more crowded. A few minutes before twelve, the church is darkened to resemble a tomb. The only light in the church is that of an oil candle on the holy altar. At midnight the royal gates open, the chief celebrant (patriarch, bishop, or priest) appears holding a lighted candle and joyfully proclaims: "Come receive the light from the unwaning light, and glorify Christ who rose from the dead."

The light is given to the congregation, and parishioners pass it along to each other. In moments the church is aglow with the light of Christ. In the bright and colorful atmosphere the good news of the Resurrection is read from the Gospel, followed by the most joyful and triumphant hymn of Orthodox Christianity, "Christos Anesti" ("Christ is Risen").[15] The entire congregation sings while making the sign of the cross with their candles.

Christos Anesti

Chri - stós a - né - sti

ek ne - krón THa ná - to

THá - na - ton pa - tí-

sas ke tis en tis

mní - ma - si zo - in cha - ri-

sá - me - nos.

Christ is risen from the dead, trampling down death by death, and to those in the tombs granting life.

Many parishioners exit after lighting their candles, but they miss the true celebration of Anastasi that follows at the Divine Liturgy and a brief sermon written by St. John Chrysostom. The sermon explains that God welcomes, rewards, and comforts all of those who come to him, whether they have come early or come late. Christ has risen. Death and evil are conquered.

At the end of the service each parishioner receives a red egg sometimes wrapped in netting, a symbolic Orthodox tradition. The red color represents the blood shed by Christ for mankind, and the egg symbolizes the new life of the Resurrection. The enclosed shell is Christ's tomb; and when the egg is cracked, it represents Christ's emergence.

As everyone leaves the church, they greet each other with, "*Christós anésti*" (Christ has risen) and respond with, "*Alithós anésti*" (Truly he has risen) or "*Alithós o Kírios*" ("Truly the Lord") and exchange the kiss of the Resurrection. This is a time of forgiveness, peace, and joy.

Parishioners hurry home with their lit candles, trying to keep them from extinguishing. The light of Christ is used for three customs: To make a cross of smoke over the entryway of the home, to light the *kandíli* at the home *ikonostási*, and to light the candles on the dinner table. The holy light is believed to have miraculous powers of protection and to bring blessings for the entire year. If you wish to do so, save the candle and bring it back forty days later, on the day of Ascension or the Sunday following it. Light it and leave at church.

The traditions for Anastasi in Greece are similar, but include a grand public display at midnight. When the light is passed at church, fireworks explode, crowds cheer, bells ring, and ships and cars toot their horns. In Corfu an electric sign lights up the hillside, and in Athens, Lycabettus Hill glows with candle light as people wind down the slope from St. George's church.

ANASTASI MEAL

A delicious supper of traditional foods follows the service even though the hour is late. Instead of a prayer before the meal, "Christos Anesti" is sung three times in honor of the Trinity, and everyone chooses a red egg to crack with someone else. Eggs are cracked large end to large end and small end to small end with the competitors saying, *"Christós anésti"* and *"Alithós anésti,"* symbolizing Christ's emergence from the tomb. Through the process of elimination a "champion" unbroken egg is left. The holder is declared the winner and expected to have good luck all year. If complete fasting has been observed, the egg is the first food consumed, since it was the last thing eaten on Cheese Fare Sunday. ("With an egg I close my mouth, and with an egg I open it.")

The *tsouréki*, the Easter bread with a red egg peeking out from its three braids for the Trinity, is cut. The traditional Easter soup, *mayerítsa*, is shared. The delicate soup with its chopped lamb parts is considered a gentle way to introduce meat back into the diet. Some families share a modified menu similar to a light breakfast, serving Easter eggs, *tsouréki*, cheese, and hot chocolate. (Recipes for *tsouréki* and *mayerítsa* below.) Instead of *tsouréki* for Easter, Cypriots enjoy a unique pastry called *flaoúnes*. These are large squares or triangles of folded dough containing filling of *baloúmi* cheese, raisins and mint with sesame seeds on top.

Tsouréki

ANASTASI MEAL

Red Easter eggs, *tsouréki*,
and *mayerítsa*
Salad, cheese, olives, and wine
Fruit and *koulourákia*

EASTER SUNDAY (PASCHA OR LAMBRI)

The joyous day of Easter — a day of happiness, love, and delicious smells and tastes — finally arrives after the arduous journey through the Triodion.

Church Service — Great Vespers of Agape

The Great Vespers of Agape (God's love) takes place on Easter Sunday, encouraging love, forgiveness, and reconciliation: "...let us embrace one another. Let us, brothers and sisters, forgive all things to those who hate us..."[16]

The Gospel is read in as many different languages as readers can be found, showing the universality of God's message. After the service, the Kiss of Agape is exchanged.

The Greeks use the terms "Pascha" and "Lambri" interchangeably with "Easter." "Pascha" is from the Hebrew word for "Passover," referring to the Jewish holiday celebrating the deliverance of the Jews from slavery in Egypt. Christ was crucified during this holiday season. For Christians the passover is deliverance from death to life. "Lambri" ("Bright") describes the brilliant light of the resurrected Christ.

Easter Dinner

The Greek Orthodox literally feast on Easter Sunday. Even the church calls Pascha the most important feast day of the year, the Feast of Feasts, the Festival of Festivals. Spring lamb is the traditional meat along with a rich array of *pítes* and tasty *mezédes.* Some Greek Americans prepare the lamb outdoors on a spit as it is done in Greece, but more often it is roasted in the oven.

EASTER DINNER

Oúzo and wine
Taramosaláta, dolmathákia, kokkorétsi
Red Easter eggs and *tsouréki* • *Mayerítsa*, cheese, and olives
Roast lamb and roast potatoes • Salad with green onions and dill
Spinach and cheese *pítes*
Fruit and *Galaktoboúriko*

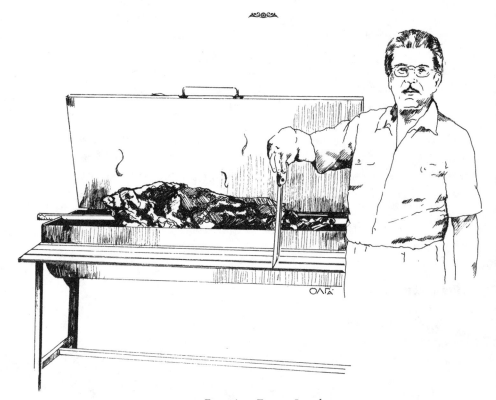

Roasting Easter Lamb

Easter Baskets and Easter Egg Hunts

Some Greek Americans give their children Easter baskets and conduct Easter egg hunts in keeping with American traditions. While these activities add to the festivities, they are secular, non-Orthodox customs.

AFTER EASTER

BRIGHT WEEK

The joy of Easter radiates into the following week, called "Bright Week," referring to the bright light cast by the Resurrection. For Greek Americans life returns to normal after Easter Sunday, except for the traditions mentioned below in "Forty-day Observances." There is no fasting during Bright Week as it is considered a time of complete joy. The doors of the church *ikonostásion* remain open for the week, symbolizing the open tomb of Christ.

In Greece the Easter celebration continues in the countryside for a week. In Megara on White Tuesday, for example, young and newly wed girls dance the famous "Dance of Trata," where they imitate fishermen pulling nets out of the ocean. At Karystos on Evia Island on New Thursday, a dance is done to appease the north wind. A common superstition is not to wash hair because it might turn white!

FORTY-DAY OBSERVANCES

The following customs should be observed for forty days after Easter, the time Christ was on earth before his Ascension.

Greetings	Say *"Christós anésti"* and *"Alithós anésti"* instead of "Hello" to fellow Orthodox.
Dinner	Light candles on the dinner table with the light from the *ikonostási kandíli* and sing "Christos Anesti" three times.
Liturgy	Do not kneel during the consecration of the Gifts during the Divine Liturgy. Christ's Resurrection provides the opportunity to rise, not fall. (Some theologians dispute this practice and recommend kneeling.)
Prayer	Sing "Christos Anesti" three times as a prayer.

RECINES

---•—⊷•⊶—•---

RED EASTER EGGS

3 dozen brown eggs (room temperature)
2 packages imported red egg dye from specialty store
1 cup white vinegar

Wash eggs with soapy water and rinse. (If you wish, make crosses on the eggs with white wax.) Dissolve the egg dye in a glass of warm water. Add dye mixture and vinegar to enough water to cover eggs. Bring the solution to a boil without eggs and simmer for about five minutes. Skim if frothy. Cool mixture by removing from heat and adding a few ice cubes. Add eggs to pot and return to heat, boiling gently for 15 minutes or until desired color. Remove eggs. While warm, wipe each egg with a lightly oiled soft cloth. Dye may be reused by adding a little more vinegar. To dye eggs for Easter bread, let uncooked eggs sit in cool dye until desired shade. (Boiled eggs baked in bread may crack open.)

Always use dye approved by the U.S. Food and Drug Administration. The practice of using textile dye is not recommended and could cause ill effects if consumed.

Easter Bread

(*Tsouréki* or *Lambrópsomo*)

2 envelopes dry yeast	1½ cups whole milk
1 tablespoon sugar	2 teaspoons *machlépi*
⅓ cup warm water	½ scant teaspoon crushed *mastícha*
1 cup unsalted butter	5 eggs
1½ cups sugar	9-10 cups flour

Decoration: 4 red eggs, uncooked
1 egg, plus 1 tablespoon of water for wash
⅓ cup of sesame seeds or ⅓ cup sliced blanched almonds

Mix yeast and 1 tablespoon of sugar in slightly warm water in a large cup. Cover, put in a warm place for 10-15 minutes until yeast activates (becomes bubbly). Warm the butter, sugar, milk, *machlépi*, and *mastícha* in a pan until the butter melts and sugar dissolves. Cool. Beat 4 eggs until foamy. Put 2 cups of flour in a large bowl. Add cooled butter mixture, yeast, and eggs and stir thoroughly. Add most of the remaining flour. While dough is still sticky, add 1 unbeaten egg. Continue to add flour until dough is very soft but no longer sticky. Knead dough about 10 minutes. Put in a lightly greased bowl, cover with a damp cloth, and let rise in a warm place for about 2 hours. When doubled, punch down the dough and divide into four balls. For each ball: form three ropes the length of a cookie sheet. Braid the three ropes on a greased cookie sheet. Squeeze the ends together so they do not separate. (For a round loaf, braid the bread and coil in a 9" round cake pan.) To decorate: Tuck at least one red egg in between the braids, and brush the dough with a wash of 1 whole egg beaten with 1 tablespoon of water. Sprinkle generously with sesame seeds or sliced blanched almonds. Cover with a damp cloth and let rise about a half hour. Bake at 350°F for 40-45 minutes or until bread browns. Reduce heat to 250°F and bake until bread sounds hollow when tapped. Makes four medium loaves.

Note: The spices, *machlépi* and *mastícha*, found in specialty stores or gourmet shops, give the bread its unique flavor. *Machlépi* is a ground seed from Syria. *Mastícha* comes from the sap of the *mastichódendro* bush grown primarily on the Greek island of Chios and used in the production of gum. The translucent, light yellow chunks of *mastícha* must be crushed to powder before use. Greeks generally use the word *"tsouréki"* for Easter bread. The word *"Lambrópsomo"* refers to the bright (*lambró*) light of the Resurrection, and *"psomí"* means "bread."

EASTER SOUP

(*MAYERÍTSA*)

16 cups broth (10 of lamb and 6 of chicken or 16 of chicken – 1 split lamb head for broth)

12 cups finely chopped boiled parts of two spring baby lambs (may include liver, heart, and lungs)

2 cups finely chopped green onions	8 cups water
½ pound butter	7 eggs, separated
2 cups fresh chopped dill	1½ cups fresh lemon juice
1 heaping cup of converted rice	Salt to taste

Optional lamb broth: Wash split lamb head and place in a large pot with water salted to taste. Add 12 cups water, salt to taste, and simmer covered for about 1½ hours. If necessary, add enough water to make 10 cups. Remove meat, chop fine, and contribute toward the 12 cups of meat. Skim the broth and strain. (Chicken broth may be substituted for lamb broth.)

Wash desired lamb parts and place in a large pot of boiling water for 15-30 minutes. Drain and rinse with cold water. Chop into small pieces. Lightly saute onions in butter in a large pot. Add chopped meat and saute for several minutes. Add fresh dill, 8 cups water, and 16 cups broth. Cover and bring to a boil. Reduce heat and simmer covered for 1 hour. Add rice. Cover and simmer for 20 minutes. Meanwhile, in the bowl of an electric mixer or large blender, beat 7 egg whites until thick and foamy. Add egg yolks, 1½ cups fresh lemon juice and ⅓ cup ice water. Continue beating until well blended. Slowly add 2 cups hot soup from pot. Gradually add egg mixture back to main pot and warm. DO NOT BOIL. Makes about 35 cups.

THE ASCENSION OF JESUS CHRIST
Forty Days after Easter

Christ ascended to heaven forty days after his Resurrection. During those forty days he appeared at various times to his disciples, exhorting them to spread the gospel. The Ascension is described in Luke 24:51: "While he blessed them, he parted from them, and was carried into heaven." The church commemorates the Ascension with a Divine Liturgy.

PENTECOST
Fifty Days after Easter

Pentecost celebrates the founding of the Christian church fifty days after the Resurrection of Christ. According to scripture, the Holy Spirit descended upon Christ's disciples to enable them to spread his message throughout the world.

> When the day of Pentecost had come, they were all together in one place. And suddenly a sound came from heaven like the rush of a mighty wind, and it filled all the house where they were sitting. And there appeared to them tongues as of fire, distributed and resting on each one of them. And they were all filled with the Holy Spirit and began to speak in other tongues, as the Spirit gave them utterance. Acts 2:1-4

This significant event is recognized with the service of kneeling. The congregation kneels three times with the priest as he prays for the repose of the dead and for the descent of the Holy Spirit to give spiritual strength to all.

⚜ *Summer*

HOLY APOSTLES LENT
Monday after All Saints Sunday until the evening of June 28

This fast commemorates all the apostles of the Orthodox church. It begins on the Monday after All Saints Sunday and ends the evening of June 28. Some parishioners take communion on June 29, the Feast Day of Saints Peter and Paul the Apostles, but the majority receive it on June 30, the Feast Day of the Holy Apostles. For those who observe this Lenten period, the fast is generally light, and fish, for example, is often eaten.

FEAST DAY OF SAINTS PETER AND PAUL THE APOSTLES
June 29

Saints Peter and Paul the Apostles, the great missionary pillars of the church in its early years, are honored together for their tremendous contributions to Christianity. St. Peter, the leader of Christ's apostles, conducted an extensive ministry for Jesus, founding the church in Rome and Antioch. St. Paul was the greatest missionary of the church. A fervent Jew, he was converted to Christianity during a blinding light on the road to Damascus, and proceeded to convert thousands to Christ. His extensive writings (almost half of the New Testament) have greatly influenced Christian thought. Parishioners attend church and take communion. In Greece an evening church service is held on the hill of the Areopagus in Athens from which St. Paul made a speech to the Athenians.

FEAST DAY OF THE HOLY APOSTLES
June 30

Although each of the apostles has his own feast day, the church honors all of them together on June 30. It reminds people of the great contributions they made and the positive role models they provide for generations of Christians. Most parishioners extend their fast to this day and take communion.

DORMITION OF THE MOTHER OF GOD LENT
August 1 — August 14

Preparation for one of the greatest feast days in the church, the Dormition of the Virgin Mary on August 15, begins on August 1. The faithful fast through the eve of August 14. Eating fish is permitted on August 6, The Transfiguration.

THE TRANSFIGURATION OF JESUS CHRIST
August 6

The Transfiguration celebrates the revelation of Christ's divine nature to three of his disciples shortly before his betrayal and crucifixion. To convince the apostles of his divinity before his death, Christ took Peter, James, and John to Mount Tabor where he was transformed in front of them. His face became bright as the sun, his clothing became white as light, and the voice of God said, "This is my beloved Son in whom I am well pleased, hear him." Moses and the Prophet Elias appeared beside Christ. For the first time the veil of his humanity was lifted. The event reminds all Christians of the brilliance of Christ and that his light brings hope and change to mankind. Transfiguration occurs during the Dormition Lent, but fish may be eaten on this feast day.

In Greece the harvest season traditionally began on the Transfiguration. Grapes, in particular, were not eaten before August 6. In some parishes, the first grapes would be brought to church for a blessing and distributed to parishioners.

THE DORMITION OF THE MOTHER OF GOD
August 15

The Orthodox revere the Mother of God (Theotokos) above any other saint in the church. She always stands on Christ's right-hand side in each church *iconostásion*, and an enormous icon of her with the Christ child dominates the space above the altar. Through her, the Virgin Mary, Christ proves his humanity. Four of the church's twelve great feast days are devoted to her, of which The Dormition is the most significant. Two weeks of fasting and special prayer services precede August 15 when the faithful crowd the church to honor her and remember her feast day. People commonly refer to the day as "Tis Panayias" ("Panayia's [feast day]").

The Dormition of the Mother of God

APOCRYPHA

Unlike most of the events related to Christ's death and Resurrection, The Dormition (Falling Asleep) of the Mother of God was not recorded by eye witnesses in the four Gospels. Writings and legends exist about her death, but they have not been historically verified. They are known as "apocrypha." Therefore the Orthodox church has not promulgated dogma concerning this important event. Yet some of these legends have become an inseparable part of the Orthodox belief. There is the popular view that when the Virgin Mary was about to give up her spirit, all the apostles, except for Thomas, miraculously appeared in Jerusalem from all parts of the world to pay their respects and receive her blessing. As they were preparing for her funeral and burial, angels came in the presence of the apostles and took her body to heaven. When the Apostle Thomas, who had not come earlier, went to her grave, he found it empty.

In the hymnology of the Orthodox church and especially in the beautiful poetry of St. John of Damascus, reference is made to this belief of the assumption of the body to heaven. St. Andrew of Crete also makes reference to it in his sermon on The Dormition of the Mother of God.

The Orthodox and the Roman Catholics differ on this belief. The Catholics have made the Assumption a part of dogma. As yet, Orthodox have not done so. In addition, the Orthodox believe that the Virgin Mary died in Jerusalem, whereas the Roman Catholics believe she died and was buried in Ephesus. The Orthodox visit the site of her tomb in Jerusalem at the Mt. of Olives.

PREPARATION

The Dormition of the Mother of God Lent (August 1 — August 14)

The devout prepare for this great feast day by fasting for two weeks, from August 1 to the evening of August 14. Fish is permitted on August 6, The Feast of the Transfiguration of the Lord. No weddings may be performed during these two weeks.

Great and Small Paraklisis (August 1 — 13)

A *paráklisis* is a service of supplication and prayer. The Orthodox church traditionally holds one every evening during the first two weeks of August, except Saturdays, the feast day of the Transfiguration (August 6), and on the eve of the Dormition when a vesper service is held instead. The Small Paraklisis, shorter than the Great Paraklisis, expresses the troubles of the soul surrounded by sin and asks for help in being restored both physically and spiritually to original health and beauty. The Great Paraklisis prays for society in general, including the captured city of Constantinople, calling on the Mother of God, the protector of the city, to free her from the enemy. Some parishioners give the priest a list of names of individuals for whom they want prayers to be said. The Small and Great Paraklisis alternate evenings. Check your church schedule, however, some churches do not hold a service each night. Your church may have copies of *The Service of the Small Paraklesis to the Most Holy Theotokos,*[17] or a copy may be purchased from Holy Cross Orthodox Book Store in Brookline, Massachusetts.

OBSERVANCES

Significance and Church Service

The feast day celebrates the death of the Virgin Mary, but the focus goes beyond her passing from the earth. Mary is the mother of all humanity and, through her, mankind also reaches heaven. Her special death in which her body did not become corrupted in a tomb but was carried to heaven glorifies her unique nature. This glorification of her soul and body is the true celebration of August 15.

The four services of the feast day (vespers, matins, litany, and Divine Liturgy) are outpourings of praise and supplication for the Theotokos in some of the church's most beautiful poetry.

> When the Translation of thy most pure tabernacle was being prepared, the apostles surrounded thy deathbed and looked upon thee with dread, and as they gazed at thy body, they were filled with awe. In tears Peter cried aloud to thee: 'O undefiled Virgin, I see thee who are the life of

all mankind lying here outstretched, and I am struck with
wonder: for He who is the delight of the future life made
His dwelling in thee. Pray, then fervently to thy Son and
God to save thy flock from harm.'

— Matins for the Dormition of Our Most Holy Lady from
   The Festal Menaion [18]

Families honoring the Virgin Mary come primarily to the Divine
Liturgy and often take communion. Some bake *prósforo* and/or
bring a single flower or small bouquet to decorate her icon. After
the service everyone greets each other with, *"Ke tou chrónou"*
(And to next year) and to those celebrating their name day, *"Chrónia
pollá."*

Name Day

August 15 may be the most popular name day of the year.   Many
names for both men and women come from the Virgin Mary or
Panayia such as Mary, Maria, Despina, Panayiota, Mario, and
Panayiotis.

Celebrations in Greece

In Greece August 15 is a national holiday with dances, fireworks,
and *paniyíria* (festivals). Some churches and monasteries hold all-
night vigils from the late evening of August 14 to the early morning of August 15.

You may want to make a pilgrimage during this time as a special
tribute to the Theotokos or to fulfill a *táma*. The most famous
pilgrimage site in Greece relating to the Virgin Mary is on the
island of Tinos. Thousands of pilgrims jam the docks and city
streets to visit the Church of the Evangelistria that safeguards a
miraculous healing icon of Mary. Revealed in a vision, it was
found buried in a field in 1823, and the church was built to house
it. Pilgrims bring items of precious metals and other gifts to leave
at the church. On August 15 and March 25 (The Annunciation)
the icon is carried through town in a grand procession.

1. "I Yennisis Sou" adapted from Nick and Connie Maragos, eds., *Sharing in Song,* 9.

2. Mother Mary and Kallistos Ware, trans. *The Festal Menaion,* 277.

3. George A. Megas, *Greek Calendar Customs,* (Athens: Press and Information Department, Prime Minister's Office, 1958), 50.

4. St. Basil, "Exhortation to Youths as to How they shall best Profit by the Writings of Pagan Authors," In *Patrology,* vol. 3, by Johannes Quasten (1960; reprint, Westminster, Md.: The Newman Press, 1963), 214.

5. Mother Mary and Kallistos Ware, trans. *The Lenten Triodion.*

6. A. C. Calivas, *Great Week and Pascha in the Greek Orthodox Church* (Brookline, Mass.: Holy Cross Orthodox Press, 1992). Alexander Schmemann, *Great Lent* (Crestwood, N.Y.: St. Vladimir's Seminary Press, 1969).

7. Mother Mary and Kallistos Ware, trans., *The Lenten Triodion.* Nomikos Michael Vaporis, *The Services for Holy Week and Easter* (Brookline, Mass.: Holy Cross Orthodox Press, 1993). Holy Transfiguration Monastery, trans., *Pentecostarion.*

8. Holy Cross Orthodox Bookstore, 50 Goddard Avenue, Brookline, MA 02146; and Light and Life Publishing Company, 4836 Park Glen Road, Minneapolis, MN 55416.

9. Alexander Schmemann, *Great Lent,* 46.

10. N. Michael Vaporis and Evie Zachariades-Holmberg, trans., *The Akathist Hymn and Small Compline* (Brookline, Mass.: Holy Cross Orthodox Press, 1992), 16.

11. "Ti Ipermacho" adapted from Nick and Connie Maragos, eds., *Sharing in Song,* 16.

12. From "Sunday of Orthodoxy Vespers" Service conducted by the Orthodox Christian Clergy Council of Metropolitan Washington, D.C.

13. "Ethnikos Imnos" adapted from Nick and Connie Maragos, eds., *Sharing in Song,* 39. English translation by Thanasis Maskaleris, "Hymn to Liberty" in *Hellenic Journal,* 11 March 1976.

14. N. Michael Vaporis and Evie Zachariades-Holmberg, trans. *The Akathist Hymn and Small Compline,* 7.

15. "Christos Anesti" adapted from Nick and Connie Maragos, *Sharing in Song,* 20.

16. Nomikos Michael Vaporis, *The Services for Holy Week and Easter,* 304.

17. Demetri Kangelaris and Nicholas Kasemeotes, *The Service of the Small Paraklesis to the Most Holy Theotokos* (Brookline, Mass.: Holy Cross Orthodox Press, 1984).

18. Mother Mary and Kallistos Ware, trans. *The Festal Menaion,* 514.

PART FOUR

The Global Community

Byzantine Eagle

The preceding Greek traditions and customs have been described above in the context of America. However, their observance is worldwide. People of Hellenic heritage live all over the globe, not just in Greece, and the Greek Orthodox Church is part of a broader family of Orthodox churches. With increased global communications, Greek Americans may read about a soccer team of Greek Australians in Melbourne, and listen to a Greek-Canadian radio station on the Internet. Likewise, the exposure to Orthodox Christians in other autocephalous (self-governing) churches has increased. Since the fall of communism at the end of the 1980s, the "Iron Curtain" that separated Orthodox in the East and West lifted. Now it is apparent that the majority of Orthodox in the world live on the other side of that dropped curtain. Who are they?

The following two chapters broaden the historical and geographical context of Greek Orthodoxy and Greek Americans. The chapter entitled "The Historic Orthodox Church" relates the history of Orthodoxy from the early Christian church to the autocephalous churches. Despite the jurisdictional and political differences, the religious traditions, teachings, and beliefs of Orthodoxy remain remarkably uniform throughout the world. The chapter entitled "The Greek Diaspora" gives a broad overview of Greeks living outside Greece and the challenges and opportunities they face.

⚜ *The Historic Orthodox Church*

Every Sunday morning around the world parishioners in Orthodox churches celebrate the Divine Liturgy in a manner that seems to transcend time and place with its mystical approach to worshipping God. Indeed, this service, written by St. John Chrysostom in the fourth century, originates from a place called Constantinople, one of the most important cities in the history of Christianity. The Divine Liturgy is only one of the historic traditions the Orthodox respectfully guard and practice. A previous chapter entitled, *The Church,* explained the dogma, the sacraments, architecture, icons, and their relevance for today's life but did not place them in their historic context. The following chapter puts them into context by briefly tracing the Orthodox church from the time of Christ through the Byzantine Empire, the expansion into Slavic countries, the suppression of the Ottoman Empire, and the stultifying effect of communism. A contemporary update gives a glimpse at the present-day situation in each autocephalous church.

THE AUTOCEPHALOUS CHURCHES OF EASTERN ORTHODOXY

The Orthodox church is a group of fourteen independent churches without a single administrative head, such as the Pope in the Roman Catholic church. Each Orthodox church is autocephalous, i.e., each governs itself with its own leadership. While each functions independently, the churches are all in agreement on doctrine and in communion with one another. (Differences do occur in rare instances, creating breaches in communion where they do not recognize one another's sacraments.) Given that the churches developed with diverse and often traumatic political histories, it speaks to the power of the Holy Spirit that Orthodox traditions remain so uniform throughout the world.

THE AUTOCEPHALOUS CHURCHES OF EASTERN ORTHODOXY

CHURCHES	JURISDICTION	MEMBERS
Ecumenical Patriarchate of Constantinople	Turkey, parts of Greece, Mt. Athos, Northern and Western Europe, North and South America, Australia and New Zealand, Southeast Asia, and the Diaspora	6 million
Patriarchate of Alexandria	All Africa	350,000
Patriarchate of Antioch	Syria, Lebanon, Iraq, Iran	750,000
Patriarchate of Jerusalem	Palestine (Israel) Jordan, Arabia, and Mt Sinai	60,000
Church of Russia	Former Soviet Union	100-150 millic
Church of Serbia	Former Yugoslavia [Serbia and Montenegro, Bosnia-Herzegovina, and Croatia]	8 million
Church of Romania	Romania	23 million
Church of Bulgaria	Bulgaria	8 million
Church of Georgia	Georgia (Iberia)	5 million
Church of Cyprus	Cyprus	450,000
Church of Greece	Greece	9 million
Church of Poland	Poland	750,000
Church of Albania	Albania	160,000
Church of the Czech Lands and Slovakia	Czech Republic and Slovakia	55,000

AUTONOMOUS ORTHODOX CHURCHES

Sinai	Sinai, Egypt	900
Finland	Finland	56,000
Japan	Japan	25,000
China	China	(?10-20,000)

About This Chart

"Churches" are listed in the traditional order of hierarchy. The Ecumenical Patriarchate of Constantinople is "first among equals" *(primus inter pares)* because of its historical role in the development of Christianity. (See "Christianity Recognized and Defined," below.) The geographic areas listed in **"Jurisdiction"** are from *Yearbook 2006* of the Greek Orthodox Archdiocese of America.[1] Jurisdiction often extends beyond present-day nation-state borders. For example, the Patriarchate of Serbia in Belgrade has jurisdiction over Serbian Orthodox parishes in the United States. **"Autonomous Orthodox Churches"** and **"Members"** (estimated) are for those baptized in the faith according to Timothy Ware in *The Orthodox Church*.[2]

Unlisted churches include the Orthodox Church in America and the Oriental Orthodox churches. The Orthodox Church in America is not recognized as autocephalous by the Ecumenical Patriarchate. However, the Church of Russia recognized it as such in 1970. The Oriental Orthodox churches "fall into two groups: the *Church of the East* (mainly in what are today Iraq and Iran; sometimes called the 'Assyrian', 'Nestorian', 'Chaldean,' or 'East Syrian' Church); and the five *Non-Chalcedonian Churches*: the Syrian Church of Antioch (the so-called 'Jacobite' Church), the Syrian Church in India [Malankara], the Coptic Church in Egypt, the Armenian Church, the Ethiopian Church; [and the Eritrean Orthodox Church]."[3] The Church of the East has different views from the Non-Chalcedonian Churches, and its classification within the Oriental Orthodox Church family is debatable. See "The First Schism: The Oriental Orthodox Churches" below.

THE FLEDGLING CHRISTIAN CHURCH

CHRIST AND HIS APOSTLES IN A PAGAN WORLD

Two thousand years ago, Jesus Christ lived, died, and was resurrected in the Holy Land. His teachings and life revealed divine truths that became the basis for Christianity. Fifty days after Christ's Resurrection, the Christian church began at Pentecost with the descent of the Holy Spirit to his twelve apostles, filling them with the grace, will, and ability to carry on his message. The apostles and their followers than began the enormous task of convincing others that Christ was the Son of God and that his message of love and eternal life was valid. The message competed with hundreds of other religious sects, including the worship of pagan gods by the Romans, who had borrowed extensively from the Greek pantheon. Roman leaders required their citizens to make offerings to the gods and the Roman Emperor. When the Christians refused to do this because they believed in one God, they were tortured and killed. This abuse lasted for three hundred years during a period commonly called the era of the martyrs.

EARLY MONOTHEISM

Although Christianity with its belief in one God, existed in a pagan world of many gods, monotheism was not unknown. Zoroastrianism, founded in the sixth century BC by a young man named Zarathustra, eventually became the religious system of the ancient Persians. Its major belief was in one God named Ahura Mazda. The Hebrews called their one God, Yahweh. In addition, Greek intellectuals were evolving to a belief in monotheism. As early as the sixth century BC, the Greek philosopher Heraclitus suggested that *logos* (divine reason) created the universe. By the fourth century BC the ancient philosopher Plato states in *Laws* 716c: "God rather than man should be the measure of all things for man." In *The Greeks, Their Heritage and Its Value Today,* Rev. Demetrios Constantelos explains, "Their faith in human intelligence, reason, and rigorous and rational action did not indicate lack of a belief in something beyond themselves."[4] Eventually "the Greeks arrived at the belief in an 'unknown God' who was ultimately identified with the Logos of the Gospel of John — Jesus Christ."[5] "In the beginning was the Logos and the Logos was with God, and the Logos was God." John 1:1

CHRISTIANITY AND HELLENISM

Although Christ did not speak Greek, it was the most respected language and thought of the time. "Long before the establishment of Roman rule, the Greeks had achieved the cultural unity of the Mediterranean world," peaking with the spread of Hellenism by Alexander the Great, according to Rev. Constantelos in *Understanding the Greek Orthodox Church*.[6] The New Testament and the church dogmas of the Ecumenical Councils were defined and articulated in the Greek language, along with most writings by the early church fathers. Abstract Hellenic concepts such as *philanthropía* (love of humans) and agape (divine love) were used by the early

Christian thinkers. Greek, therefore, is the historic language of Christianity in the way that Hebrew is of Judaism and Sanskrit of Hinduism. Speros Vryonis, Jr., a Byzantine scholar notes the symbiotic relationship of Hellenism and Orthodoxy: "Christianity had to survive, develop and spread in the great world of Hellenism and . . . Hellenism had to survive in a world that was fast becoming Christian. In effect, this fusion, at a secular level, was the result of historical necessity. . . ."[7]

CHRISTIANITY RECOGNIZED AND DEFINED

ST. CONSTANTINE THE GREAT: THE FIRST CHRISTIAN EMPEROR

Despite efforts to suppress Christianity, the faith grew in numbers and refinement of thought with writings by the apostles and other great missionaries such as St. Paul. One of the major turning points in Christianity was the conversion of the Roman Emperor Constantine. According to Timothy Ware in *The Orthodox Church,* "Constantine stands at a watershed in the history of the Church. With his conversion, the age of martyrs and the persecutions drew to an end, and the Church of the Catacombs [underground burial grounds where Christians worshiped in secret] became the Church of the Empire."[8] In 312, while with his army in France, Constantine in either a dream or a vision heard, "In this sign conquer." The sign was two Greek letters, *Hi (X)* and *Ro (P),* the first letters of the name, Christ. The first Roman Emperor to become a Christian, Constantine and his fellow Emperor Licinius in the East issued the Edict of Milan in 313, which officially tolerated Christianity.

Hi and *Ro*

CONSTANTINOPLE AND THE FIRST ECUMENICAL COUNCIL

Eleven years later, in 324, Emperor Constantine, after defeating Licinius, declared his intention to expand the Roman Empire to the East, moved the capital from Italy to the small Greek town of Byzantium in Asia Minor on the Bosphorus River, and renamed it after himself, Constantinople (modern-day Istanbul). Meanwhile, Christians struggled to define their faith, especially the nature of Christ and the structure of the church. In a bold move, Emperor Constantine called for and presided over the first of seven Ecumenical Councils that defined the Christian faith.

The First Ecumenical Council held in nearby Nicaea (Iznik, Turkey) in 325 dealt with the Arian controversy.   A priest from Alexandria, Arius, argued that Christ was less than fully God, not co-eternal with the Father. Arianism was a heresy that denied the consubstantiality (one in essence or substance) of the Father and the Son.   The council defeated Arius's position and declared that Christ was one in essence *(homooúsios)* with the Father, a central dogma of the church. The council also designated administrative centers in Rome, Alexandria, Antioch, and Jerusalem.[9] (Until the Great Schism in 1054, Rome was first in the church hierarchy.) Constantinople was added later and placed after Rome and was commonly called "New Rome." Together these first ancient centers are known as the Pentarchy, a system of five sees (headquarters).

In 326 Emperor Constantine went back to Rome for a visit and commanded that St. Peter's Basilica be built on Vatican Hill. (That basilica was replaced during the Renaissance with the current Basilica of St. Peters, at the Vatican, the center of the Roman Catholic church.) The Christian church was sinking deep roots in both the eastern and western Roman empires and was undivided. Building continued in Constantinople, and in 330 the city was dedicated to the Theotokos, officially beginning the Eastern Roman Empire (later called the Byzantine Empire), a guardian of Christianity and Greek learning that lasted over a thousand years, from 330 to 1453. (The symbol of the Byzantine Empire is a single eagle with two heads: one head looking east and one head looking west.)   Seven years, later in 337, Emperor Constantine died. The world had radically changed with his bold recognition of the Christian faith.

THE PATRISTIC ERA AND THE NICAEA/CONSTANTINOPLE CREED

The fourth century stands out as one of the most remarkable in the history of Christianity because that is when the faith was recognized and defined. Some of the greatest theologians of Christianity, such as Saints Athanasius (d. 373), Basil the Great (d. 379), Gregory the Theologian (d. 390), Gregory of Nyssa (d. ca 394), and John Chrysostom (d. 405), lived and wrote during this time of church maturation. According to tradition, Saints Basil the Great and John Chrysostom wrote Divine Liturgies still used in the Orthodox church today. At Constantinople in 381, the Second Ecumenical Council expanded the Nicene Creed to declare the

Holy Spirit divine, equal to the Father and the Son and proceeding from the Father. This Nicaea/Constantinople Creed adopted in 381 is the same one recited today in all Orthodox churches, and commonly known as the Nicene Creed, the symbol of the faith. (See *The Church* — "The Nicene Creed.") At that same council, Constantinople was assigned the second place in the church hierarchy after Rome.[10] Ten years later, in 391-392, Emperor Theodosius I issued two decrees banning all pagan cults, thus making the empire a Christian state.

THE FIRST SCHISM: THE ORIENTAL ORTHODOX CHURCHES

The triumphs of the fourth century contrast with the problems of the fifth century. The first major break in Christian unity occurred when the Church of the East (Assyrian) broke away from the church in 431 in reaction to the Council of Ephesus and its definition of the nature of Christ and His mother, Mary. The Non-Chalcedonian Oriental Orthodox Churches (see "Unlisted churches" above) separated in 451 in reaction to the Council at Chalcedon and how the dual nature of Christ should be defined. While the Non-Chalcedonians believed in dual nature, they defined it differently [miaphysite].[11] The break in 451 resulted in the two major groups in Orthodoxy: The Non-Chalcedonian who accept the declarations of the first three ecumenical councils and the Eastern Orthodox (see chart of "Autocephalous Churches of Eastern Orthodoxy" above) who accept the declarations of the seven ecumenical councils. This schism continues until today, although the churches are in dialogue over differences. This break was of such significance that it ranks as the first major break in Christianity, followed by the Great Schism in 1054 and the Protestant Reformation in the 1517.

In addition to religious problems in the Empire, the western half of the Roman Empire came under constant attack from tribes in the north, culminating with the sack of Rome in 410 by the Visigoths and the eventual fall of the Roman Empire. The weakened west entered into a period of decline.

JUSTINIAN THE GREAT EXPANDS THE BYZANTINE EMPIRE

In contrast, the eastern half, known as the Byzantine Empire, entered into its first golden era in the sixth century, during the reign of Emperor Justinian the Great (527-565), who extended the empire to its farthest points and codified laws into the Justinian Code, the basis for legal codes in many countries. At his direction ten thousand men built in Constantinople in five years (532-537) the Cathedral of St. Sophia (Holy Wisdom), the greatest work of Byzantine architecture, with the world's largest dome until the Basilica of St. Peter's in Rome was constructed one thousand years later. Throughout the history of Orthodoxy, St. Sophia has been the setting for some of the church's most dramatic moments, such as the sacking of Constantinople by the Crusaders in 1204 and the fall of the Byzantine Empire in 1453. (After the fall, Muslims eventually added the buttresses and minarets to St. Sophia present today.) Constantinople continued in its important role in Christendom by hosting both the Fifth and Sixth Ecumenical Councils in 553 and 681, during which the nature of Christ continued to be debated and defined.[12]

Cathedral of St. Sophia,
Constantinople

THE RISE OF ISLAM

Serious difficulties arose in the seventh century with the rise of Islam, the monotheistic Muslim religion with Allah as the supreme deity and Mohammed (570?-632) its chief prophet and founder. Shortly after his death in 632, armies of Islam exploded out of Arabia and within one hundred years captured Syria, Palestine, Egypt, the three Patriarchates of Alexandria, Antioch, Jerusalem, northern Africa, parts of Spain, and parts of France and threatened Constantinople. Although still intact, the Christian Byzantine Empire was badly shaken.

THE ICONOCLAST CONTROVERSY

Internally the church faced a new crisis with the iconoclast controversy that began in 726. Iconoclasts thought it improper for religious art to represent either human beings or Christ. If Christ was God, he should not be depicted and the veneration (honoring) of icons was idolatry. However the Seventh Ecumenical Council (and the last), in the year 787 at Nicaea, upheld the use of icons and their veneration. Worship was reserved for God in Trinity alone. Unsatisfied, the iconoclasts continued to fight, led by Leo V, destroying many precious icons. Finally, in 843, the Byzantine Empress Theodora settled the issue by reinstating the icons, an occasion still celebrated today on the Sunday of Orthodoxy, the first Sunday of Lent when a statement of the faith, "The Triumph of Orthodoxy," is read and icons are carried in procession throughout the church.[13]

TRADITION SOLIDIFIED: "THE CHURCH OF THE SEVEN COUNCILS"

With these last events and the cumulative work of the Seven Ecumenical Councils, the Tradition of Orthodoxy became fixed. The Orthodox call themselves "the Church of the Seven Councils" and, according to Timothy Ware, ". . . the great period of doctrinal controversies, the age of the seven councils, was at an end; the main outlines of the faith — the doctrines of the Trinity and the Incarnation — had already been worked out, and were delivered to the Slavs in their definitive form."[14] This Tradition (with a capital "T") includes "the books of the Bible; it means the Creed; it means the decrees of the Ecumenical Councils and the writings of the Fathers; it means the Canons, the Service Books, [and] the

Holy Icons — in fact, the whole system of doctrine, Church government, worship, spirituality and art which Orthodoxy has articulated over the ages."[15] (For a more details on Tradition, see "Part One: The Enduring Traditions of Orthodoxy" and "Part Three: Feast Days, Fasts, and Holidays" in this book.)

THE SEVEN ECUMENICAL COUNCILS

First	325 AD	Nicaea (Iznik, Turkey)
Second	381	Constantinople (Istanbul, Turkey)
Third	431	Ephesus, Turkey
Fourth	451	Chalcedon (Kadikoy, Turkey)
Fifth	553	Constantinople
Sixth	681	Constantinople
Seventh	787	Nicaea

Locations of the Ecumenical Councils

EXPANSION OF ORTHODOXY TO THE SLAVIC COUNTRIES

SAINTS CYRIL AND METHODIUS APOSTLES TO THE SLAVS

Patriarch Photius, one of the greatest patriarchs in the Orthodox church, began one of the church's biggest missionary efforts in the ninth century. (His work coincided in part with the second golden age of the Byzantine Empire from 867 to 1056 during the Macedonian Dynasty.) Patriarch Photius selected two brothers to pioneer this work, Cyril (d. 869) and Methodius (d. 884), who had learned a Slavonic dialect in their childhood city of Thessaloniki in northern Greece. The Slavonic language played a crucial role in the coming centuries. According to Timothy Ware, "Few events have been so important in the missionary history of the church."[16] In 863 a prince of Moravia (a region of former Czechoslovakia) requested that the brothers come to his country, but wanted the services and texts translated into the Slavonic language. Cyril and Methodius invented a Slavonic alphabet, the same Cyrillic alphabet used today in Russia, Bulgaria, and other Slavic countries. The translations in church Slavonic proved to be their most valuable contribution, since their missionary work in Moravia did not result in many Orthodox converts. However, their Slavonic texts, which were used by other missionaries, were crucial in transmitting the Christian faith to the people of Bulgaria, Serbia, and Russia. Eventually Orthodoxy became the major religion of each country, earning the brothers the title Apostle to the Slavs.

RUSSIA AND ST. VLADIMIR

Patriarch Photius also sent a bishop to Russia around 864, but Orthodoxy did not firmly establish itself until Prince Vladimir of Kiev converted to Christianity in 988. Sometime earlier the Prince had sent emissaries to various countries to find a religion for himself and his people. After observing services at St. Sophia Cathedral in Constantinople in 987, the envoys wrote in the *Russian Primary Chronicle:* " . . . we knew not whether we were in heaven or on earth. For on earth there is no such splendor or such beauty."[17] Prince Vladimir made Orthodoxy the official state religion of Russia, married the sister of the Byzantine Emperor, and proceeded to "Christianize his realm: priests, relics, sacred vessels, and icons were imported, mass baptisms were held in the

rivers."[18] He emphasized the social message of the Gospel, generously giving food to the poor and sick, setting a tone of spirituality
and social concern associated with the Russian church.

CHRISTIANITY DIVIDED: THE GREAT SCHISM

THE EAST AND WEST DRIFT APART

While Orthodoxy was spreading to the north and east, a gulf was
widening between the East and West, leading to one of the sad-
dest events in the history of Christianity — the formal break
between Rome and Constantinople, known as the Great Schism
(also Schism of the East), in 1054.   Up until that time, the church
had been united (except for the formal split in the fifth century
from the Oriental Orthodox churches).   In reality, however, the
East and West of the Roman Empire had been drifting apart for
centuries, culturally, politically, and theologically.   While initially
they shared a Greco-Roman culture, by the fifth century few in the
West spoke or read Greek and a hundred years later, few in the
East spoke or read Latin.   Politically, the East and West each had
their own emperors.   In addition, contact became more difficult
when barbarians captured large landmasses in the West starting in
the fifth century, and Islamic military forces took over land in the
Mediterranean in the seventh and eighth centuries.   Travel and
communication became extremely difficult with these hostile geographic barriers.   The coronation of Charlemagne by the Pope as
head of the Holy Roman Empire in 800 created further alienation.

RELIGIOUS DIFFERENCES

Theologically, differences had been accumulating for years: The
East did not agree with the requirement that clergy be unmarried,
the use of unleavened bread for Holy Communion, the centralized
decision-making power of the Pope, and the addition of the phrase,
"and from the Son" *(filioque)* to the Nicaea/Constantinople Creed.
That creed, adopted by the Second Ecumenical Council in 381 and
still used by the Orthodox today, states that the "Holy Spirit proceeds from the Father."   However, starting as early as 589 at the
Third Council of Toledo, the Spanish Church changed the creed
by saying the Holy Spirit proceeds from the Father <u>and from the</u>

Son *(filioque)*. The East viewed this addition as subordinating the Spirit to the Father and the Son. Simply stated by scholar Steven Runciman in *The Eastern Schism*, "The introduction of the *Filioque* upset the delicate balance of properties within the Trinity."[19] Use of the *filioque* spread throughout the Western church. But in 879-880 a council, and eventually Pope John VIII of Rome and Patriarch Photius of Constantinople, reaffirmed the Nicaea/Constantinople Creed of 381, declaring that no additions should be made to it. However, the Papacy officially first inserted the *filioque* in the creed at the coronation of the Emperor Henry II in 1014. In addition to the concept, the Byzantines believed such a change could be made only by vote of an Ecumenical Council (a conciliary approach) versus by the Pope (a monarchical approach).

MUTUAL ANATHEMAS

Eventually the Byzantines stopped commemorating the Pope in their services. Meanwhile in the West, Eastern Byzantine Rite churches were asked to conform to Latin practices, and the Latin churches in the East were asked to conform to Byzantine practices. When the Latin churches refused, the Patriarch closed them in 1052. In attempt at reconciliation, Patriarch Michael Cerularius invited a delegation from Rome to try to resolve the differences. After a series of diplomatic mishaps, the Patriarch refused to meet with the delegates, who then entered St. Sophia Cathedral in Constantinople and placed an anathema [bull (decree) of excommunication] of Patriarch Michael on the altar, specifying the omission of the *filioque* from the creed as one of the complaints. The Byzantines retaliated by anathematizing (excommunicating) the head delegate, Cardinal Humbert.[20] Few realized that a schism had occurred. (The *filioque* continues to be a major difference between Roman Catholics and Orthodox today along with issues of whether clergy may marry, the infallibility of the Pope, the Immaculate Conception of the Virgin Mary, and the use of unleavened bread for Holy Communion. However, in 1965, the mutual anathemas were finally lifted by the two churches.)

A FATAL WOUND: THE FOURTH CRUSADE

The final blow to the unity of the East and West occurred 160 years later in 1204, when Crusaders from the West sacked Constantinople. The Crusades were Western Christian military campaigns to regain the Holy Land captured by Islamic armies. The First Crusade successfully regained territory, setting up Latin Patriarchs in Antioch in 1098 and Jerusalem in 1099. (Jerusalem fell back to the Muslims in 1187.) The Third Crusade out of eight accomplished little, and the Fourth was an outright disaster. According to Steven Runciman in *A History of the Crusades,* the Fourth Crusaders had made a deal with a young Byzantine man named Alexius who wanted to get back his father's throne and become Byzantine emperor. In exchange for the Crusaders' military support, he promised to supply money and men to help the Crusaders conquer Egypt. In addition, he would convince the Church of Constantinople to submit to the Church of Rome, which wanted to unite the East and West. Through the Crusaders' military assistance, Alexius was installed as Emperor Alexius IV in 1203. However, new taxes to raise money for the Crusaders and pressure to submit to Rome proved highly unpopular, and Alexius was killed by his own people. Frustrated that their promises would not be met, the Crusaders sacked the city. The Italians took treasures for adornment of their cities back home, such as the famous four bronze horses now above the entrance of St. Mark's Cathedral in Venice. The Frenchmen and Flemings destroyed, murdered, and raped throughout the city. Drunken soldiers tore down the silver *ikonostásion* (icon screen) at St. Sophia Cathedral and drank from the altar vessels.[21]

The Latins then controlled Constantinople and the Byzantine Empire for fifty-seven years. Although the Byzantines regained control in 1261, they never recovered from the destruction. Runciman refers to the sack as a "great crime against humanity . . . that upset the whole defense of Christendom" because the Byzantines had protected Europe from the infidels in the East and the barbarians in the north."[22] The wounds never healed, making the Great Schism complete. (The resentment in the East toward the West lingers today, though it softened in 2001 when John Paul II, the first Pope to visit Athens, offered deep regret for the Crusaders' sacking of Constantinople.)

ATTEMPTS AT RECONCILIATION

Feeling vulnerable from the threats of Islam, the Byzantines turned to the West for support and a reuniting of Christendom. In 1274 and 1438-1439 Orthodox delegates to reunion councils in Lyons, France, and Florence, Italy, agreed to recognize Papal claims and recite the creed with the *filioque*, while respecting one another's various rites and traditions. However, the clergy and laity back home refused to accept these concessions, and the schism was never healed. Since 1966, however, theological dialogues between the Roman Catholic and Orthodox churches have taken place frequently to increase understanding between the two churches, including discussions about the *filioque*.

THE FALL OF CONSTANTINOPLE

In 1453, due to internal and external weaknesses, the Byzantine Empire of over one thousand years (330-1453) fell to the Ottoman Turks with the capture of Constantinople. Again, the Cathedral of St. Sophia became a dramatic venue for the finale. After his men sacked the cathedral and murdered worshippers, the leader of the Ottomans, Sultan Mehmet, stood at the pulpit and proclaimed the name of Allah, the All-Merciful and Compassionate: There is no God but Allah, and Mohammed is his Prophet. St. Sophia Cathedral became a Muslim mosque complete with buttresses and minarets. The Christian icons were covered with plaster until the cathedral became a tourist attraction in 1936 and some of the plaster was removed. No religious services of any kind are held there. Despite its sad ending, the glorious Byzantine Empire was a continuous link between ancient Greece and the Italian Renaissance while developing and preserving the Orthodox faith.

THE GROWTH OF ORTHODOXY IN RUSSIA

During this time of turmoil, the roots of Orthodoxy spread and deepened in Russia, particularly in Kiev, where Prince Vladimir declared Orthodoxy the state religion in 988. Early Russian saints exemplified the spirituality characteristic of Russian Orthodoxy. Prince Vladmir's sons, Boris and Gleb, who attained sainthood, so revered the Gospel that when their elder brother tried to take over their principalities, they chose to be murdered rather than fight. St. Theodosiu was so important in the strong monastic tradition, living humbly and in poverty, that he is revered as the Father of Russian monasticism.

A GOLDEN AGE OF SPIRITUALITY

Orthodoxy's beginning in Kiev came to an abrupt halt when the city was sacked by the Mongols in 1237. Despite being under the Mongols from 1237 to 1448, the church kept the Russian spirit alive, engaging in extensive missionary work carried out primarily from monasteries. Of special note is "Saint Sergius of Radonezh (1314-1392), the greatest national saint of Russia."[23] Through his encouragement, Moscow ascended politically, monasteries flourished, and his spiritual approach using mystical prayer "deepened the inner life of the Russian Church."[24] In fact, the period between 1350 and 1550 is considered the Golden Age in Russian spirituality, reflected in the outstanding icons produced through the hands of many followers of St. Sergius, including Andrei Rublev (1370-1430). One of Orthodoxy's most famous icons, "Holy Trinity" by Rublev was created for the *ikonostásion* at Holy Trinity Chapel at the St. Sergius Monastery in the town of Sergiev Posad outside Moscow. (Russians today consider St. Sergius Monastery the heart of Russian Orthodoxy.) Rublev, along with such other famous iconographers as Theophanes the Greek (1335-1405), took Russian icons to a new height. While Russian Orthodoxy was ascending, the Byzantine Empire fell in 1453. Russia took Byzantium's place, and Moscow popularly became the "Third Rome."

SURVIVING THE OTTOMANS

When the Ottomans conquered the Byzantine Empire in 1453, their understanding of the relationship between religion and state determined the political and religious destiny of the Christians. The Muslims viewed Christians and Jews as people of the Book *(dhimmis),* acknowledging the Bible as a holy work and incorporating some of its passages in their sacred book, the Koran. They recognized Jesus Christ as a prophet and Christianity as a religion, allowing it to exist as long as the Christians submitted to the power of Islam and paid taxes. Because the religion of Islam was a fundamental part of the governing state, Christianity existed as a state within a state, but of an inferior status. The Christian state/church, known as the *Rum Millet* (Roman nation), was governed by religious heads *(éthnarchs)* who were the patriarchs of Constantinople which had to be approved by the Sultan. This system led to corruption and bribery. Despite this unfortunate situation and the outlawing of missionary work and conversion of Muslims, the church and the laity managed to keep the faith and traditions alive. This Ottoman period lasted approximately four hundred years from the mid-fifteenth century until the nineteenth century, depending on when individual areas gained independence. Greece, for example, declared independence in 1821, but it took many years for the modern Greek state to be created. As the Ottoman Empire slowly crumbled, national churches were carved out of the Patriarchate, and recognized by the Ecumenical Patriarchate as autocephalous: the Church of Serbia (1879), Church of Greece (1850), and Church of Romania (1885).

IN THE WEST: THE REFORMATION

THE RENAISSANCE, A PRECURSOR TO THE REFORMATION

While the Byzantine Empire waned, the West began a "rebirth" known as the Renaissance starting in the fourteenth century and lasting through the sixteenth. Before the Renaissance, Roman Catholic clerics dominated intellectual life in the Middle Ages in the West. Starting in the fourteenth century in Italy, writers such as Dante and painters such as Giotto, broke with tradition, stressing more human dimensions in their works. This new Humanism emphasized the ability of human beings to question, accumulate knowledge, and master their world, resulting in scientific discoveries and inventions. Artists featured human beings more realistically in their works, in contrast to the strict conventions of icons depicting the spiritual world. Classical sources from ancient Greece and Rome inspired the greatest thinkers and artists of the Renaissance. The fall of Constantinople in 1453 provided a windfall of primary sources and expertise from the East to the West. Byzantine scholars escaped to Italy bringing materials relating to Greek scholarship. The greatest work of the artist Raphael, "The School of Athens," shows philosophers and artists in thoughtful discussion. Raphael finished this work, located in the Vatican at St. Peter's Cathedral in Rome, in 1511, one year before Michaelangelo completed the Vatican's Sistine Chapel in 1512.

THE REFORMATION

The intellectual stimulation of Humanism helped bring about the third major schism in Christianity, the Reformation, directed toward the Roman Catholic church and the Papacy. The Reformation began in 1517 when a Roman Catholic friar, Martin Luther,

posted his Ninety-five Theses about indulgences on the door of All
Saints Church, in Wittenberg, Germany. Luther believed the church
policy of indulgences (accepting money as penance for forgiveness of sins) was misused. (Indulgences had become a major
fund-raising method for the building of St. Peter's in Rome, but are
no longer in use today.) These objections came out of Luther's
broader underlying belief that salvation is by faith alone *(sola
fide)*, not good works. In addition, he believed that only scripture
is authoritative *(sola Scriptura)* and that saints have no foundation
in the Gospel. While Luther questioned, he did not intend to
break away from the church. However, he was excommunicated
in 1521. Other reformers quickly followed Luther, including Ulrich
Zwingli in Zurich and John Calvin in Geneva. The printing press,
a Renaissance invention, spurred the dissemination of information
and challenges. John Calvin published the *Institutes of the Christian Religion,* in 1536, the first extensive theological treatise of the
reform movement. In England, King Henry VIII broke from the
Roman Catholic church when the Pope refused to grant him a
divorce, and the king established the Anglican church in 1534.
Under the leadership of the Scottish Parliament, John Knox established a Reformed Presbyterian national church in 1560. Within a
short time, by the mid-sixteenth century, the Reformation dominated northern Europe. In time, many denominations under the
umbrella term, Protestantism, grew out of the Reformation. The
major Protestant faiths today are Baptist, Congregationalist, Friends
(Quaker), Lutheran, Methodist, Presbyterian and Reformed, and
Unitarian Universalist.

RUSSIA — "THE THIRD ROME"

RUSSIAN ORTHODOXY ASCENDS

Russian Cross

A few years before the fall of Constantinople, the Russian Orthodox asserted their independence in 1448 and elected their own
church head without approval from the Patriarchate in
Constantinople. A new emperor, Ivan III the Great (1462-1505),
declared himself the successor to the Roman Empire with Moscow
as the Third Rome, and took the title *tsar* (Russian for Caesar).
The Church of Russia continued to grow. However, in the sixteenth century a serious split occurred within Russian Orthodoxy
when many Orthodox turned their allegiance to the Pope due to
various conquests by Roman Catholic military/political entities.

Peace was established by the Brest-Litovsk of 1596, and the new adherents became known as Eastern Rite Catholics, Greek Catholics, or Uniates (a derogatory term) because they kept the Eastern rites of the Byzantine Liturgy and married clergy but were loyal to the Pope. This split continues today, creating one of the most serious issues between Orthodox and Roman Catholics due to seized church properties in the sixteenth and twentieth centuries. (See "Contemporary Updates — Church of Russia," below.)

VARYING INTERPRETATIONS OF TRADITION

The history of Russian Orthodoxy developed primarily around varying interpretations of how tradition should be kept. The monastic movement split over possessors and non-possessors. Possessors believed monasteries should own land to produce income to teach and care for the poor and that the state could be helpful to the church. They believed rituals associated with icons and church music, for example, should be continued. Non-possessors thought monks should live in poverty with no possessions, detached from worldly goods, so they could devote themselves to prayer as a way of helping others. The church should not be allied with the state.[25]

The Russian church's emphasis on spirituality was reflected in a reform movement started in 1619 for longer services and prayers, and more fast observances. In reaction the Patriarch Nikon (1605-1681) wanted to move back to the Greek practices of the ancient Patriarchates, including conforming Russian service books to Greek Orthodox texts and making the sign of the cross with three fingers. The reformers, known as Old Believers (Raskolniki) resisted, leading to a schism that still exists today in Russia and throughout the Russian Diaspora.[26] Patriarch Nikon's determined style was not appreciated by the existing Emperor, Peter the Great (1682-1725). A few years after Patriarch Nikon's death, the emperor abolished the Russian Patriarchate in 1700, establishing in its place a Holy Synod consisting of members nominated (and dismissed) by the emperor. This arrangement lasted from 1700 to 1917 when the Patriarchate was reestablished.

SPIRITUALITY, A RUSSIAN HALLMARK

Spirituality remained a strong theme in the ensuing years, including publication into Slavonic of the *Philokalia* (writings by the early Greek Fathers), and the practice of obedience to an elder *(starets),* such as St. Seraphim of Sarov (1759-1833). After with-drawing into seclusion for twenty years, St. Seraphim opened his monastery cell door at the age of sixty to advise and heal others. Another monastic tradition, repeated recitation of the one-sentence Jesus Prayer ("Lord Jesus Christ, Son of God, have mercy on me.") became popular with the people. *The Way of a Pilgrim,* a book by an anonymous author about a Russian peasant going from place to place saying the prayer remains an inspiration today. Missionary work increased, led by the "greatest of the nineteenth century missionaries, St. Innocent (1797-1879), Bishop of Alaska."[27] However, the Russian Orthodox world changed drastically with the Bolshevik Revolution in 1917 and with the formation of the Soviet Union, a communist government actively promoting athe-ism. The Church of Russia was damaged under tremendous politi-cal pressures. (See "Contemporary Updates — Church of Russia," below.)

CONTEMPORARY UPDATES

The preceding history gives an overview of the broad develop-ments in Orthodoxy since the beginning of the Christian church until roughly the beginning of twentieth century. The following short summaries of the fourteen autocephalous churches are con-temporary updates. For additional information, see Timothy Ware, *The Orthodox Church,* and its annotated list of "Further Reading."

The term "see" refers to the official seat, or center of authority, for each Church. "Jurisdiction" and "estimated members" are those baptized in the faith as presented in the above chart, "The Autocephalous Churches of Eastern Orthodoxy."

ECUMENICAL PATRIARCHATE OF CONSTANTINOPLE

See: **Constantinople (Istanbul), Turkey** *Estimated members:* **6 million**

Jurisdiction: **Turkey, Parts of Greece, Mt. Athos, Northern and Western Europe, North and South America, Australia and New Zealand, South-east Asia and the Diaspora**

The Ecumenical Patriarchate is first among equals because of the historic role of Constantinople in the founding of the Christian faith. Most of the members under the Patriarchate live outside Turkey around the world. The resident Greek Orthodox population in present-day Turkey has dwindled to several thousand from two million in the early twentieth century as the result of war casualties, ethnic cleansing, and population exchanges (removal of Greek people in Turkey to Greece and Turkish people in Greece to Turkey). This traumatic ten-year period — beginning in 1913, at the end of the Balkan War, and lasting through World War I, the fall of the Ottoman Empire in 1918, and a war between Greece and Turkey from 1919 to 1922 — largely removed the susbstantial Greek presence of over two thousand years in Asia Minor. The Treaty of Lausanne in 1923 put the Greeks in Constantinople under protected status to practice and maintain their faith. But in 1955 attacks against Christians and their churches caused many more Greeks to leave. Turkish authorities closed the nearby Orthodox School of Theology at Halki in 1972.

Nevertheless, the Patriarchate continues to lead the Orthodox church from its headquarters in a Greek neighborhood of Constantinople known as the Phanar. All Orthodox faithful are encouraged to worship at its St. George Cathedral, visit the great St. Sophia Cathedral (now a museum), and other Orthodox sites in the city. Update: www.patriarchate.org

PATRIARCHATE OF ALEXANDRIA

See: **Alexandria, Egypt**   *Estimated members:* **350,000**
Jurisdiction: **All Africa**

St. Mark the Apostle brought Christ's message to this area and is considered the founder of the Patriarchate of Alexandria. The Christians of the area were part of the first schism in the church in the fifth and sixth centuries, resulting in the Oriental Orthodox churches that make up the majority of the Christians in northeast Africa today. For example, in the country of Egypt in 1995 there were over eight million Coptic Orthodox and only ten thousand members affiliated with the Patriarchate of Alexandria (also referred to as the Greek Orthodox Patriarchate of Alexandria).[28] A large Greek Orthodox community existed in Egypt until the early twentieth century, when many left because of political persecution.

Today the majority of the 350,000 Orthodox members of the Patriarchate of Alexandria belong to parishes in the sub-Saharan countries of Benin, Cameroon, Ghana, Kenya, Madagascar, Mauritius, South Africa, Uganda, and Zimbabwe. Most of these churches began in the twentieth century as a result of a native African Orthodox movement. Update: www.greekorthodox-alexandria.org

PATRIARCHATE OF ANTIOCH

See: **Damascus, Syria**   *Estimated Members:* **750,000**
Jurisdiction: **Syria, Lebanon, Iraq, Iran**

St. Peter, the leader of the Twelve Apostles, founded the church in Antioch, where the term, "Christians" was first applied to the apostles. It was also the birthplace in the fourth century of one of the greatest Orthodox saints, St. John Chrysostom. The early church here was greatly affected by the divisions that occurred, primarily in the fifth century, over the nature of Christ. (See "The First Schism: The Oriental Orthodox Churches," above.) Consequently, today the majority of Orthodox in the Middle East belong to the Orthodox Oriental churches, and a smaller number come under the Patriarchate of Antioch. The majority of its faithful are ethnically Arab.

The Patriarchate also has jurisdiction over a large Diaspora population, primarily in North and South America, Australia, and Europe. In 2003, the Patriarchate granted self-rule status to the Antiochian Orthodox Christian Archdiocese of North America. Update: www.antiochpat.org

PATRIARCHATE OF JERUSALEM

See: **Jerusalem, Palestine**   *Estimated Members:* **60,000**
Jurisdiction: **Palestine (Israel), Jordan, Arabia and Mt. Sinai**

The primary responsibility of the Patriarchate of Jerusalem is maintaining and guarding sacred Christian Holy Land sites such as the Church of the Holy Sepulchre in Jerusalem and the Basilica of the Nativity in Bethlehem.

Jerusalem is also home to sites sacred to Islam and Judaism, creating tremendous tensions in the area for centuries. The formation of the country of Israel in the Palestinian area in 1948 by the Allied Powers has added to those tensions. The Palestinians (primarily Muslim and some Christian) did not accept the division, and currently have no state. Christians (including Orthodox, Roman Catholics, and Protestants), make up approximately two percent of the population in the Holy Land. Tension also exists between the Arab Orthodox and the Greek-dominated Patriarchate of Jerusalem. However, the region remains an important pilgrimage for all Christians. Update: www.jerusalem-patriarchate.org

CHURCH OF RUSSIA

See: **Moscow, Russia**   *Estimated members:* **100-150 million**
Jurisdiction: **Former Soviet Union**

The Church of Russia has the largest number of Orthodox members in the world, estimated between 100 and 150 million. Its contemporary history in the twentieth century is covered in detail here because communism affected it and the churches in surrounding countries so deeply. While each neighboring country has a unique history and experience, the communist repressions described below occurred throughout the region, although in varying degrees.

Under Communism

Just as the Eastern Orthodox church was traumatized after the fall of the Byzantine Empire in 1453 to the Ottomans, the Church of Russia experienced great difficulties under communism from the beginning of the Bolshevik Revolution in 1917 until the demise of the Soviet Union in 1989. As Timothy Ware points out, it was the first time Christianity existed in an atheist state. During the early Roman Empire, most of society believed in pantheism (existence of more than one God). Under the Ottoman Empire, the Muslims believed in one God. But the communists actively tried to curtail religious belief by taking church property and banning religious education and social work. At the same time, the communists permitted a few schools to train priests and allowed services in the limited number of churches left open. Sermons were monitored by the secret police, and many priests and faithful became martyrs for the faith or were exiled to prison camps. Many schoolteachers and groups such as the Youth League promoted atheism.[29] Despite these extreme conditions, many Orthodox kept the faith alive by meeting in secret underground churches.

A substantial number of Orthodox fled Russia, and the remaining clergy were in an extremely awkward situation. How could a church coexist with an atheist state? The Russian Patriarch Tikhon in 1917 tried unsuccessfully to keep the church neutral. Likewise Metropolitan Sergius tried to keep church and state separate, but after imprisonment persuaded the Russian clergy in 1927 to accept a Declaration of Loyalty to Russia, stating, "We wish to be Orthodox and at the same time to recognize the Soviet Union as our

civil fatherland . . . ."[30]   This stand (known as "Sergianism")
created tremendous tension in the Church of Russia and abroad.
(See "The Orthodox Diaspora in the United States — Complica-
tions from Mother-country Politics," below, regarding the Metropolia
and the Russian Orthodox Church Outside Russia.)

By 1939 only a few hundred churches remained open, but with
the advent of World War II, Soviet Premier Stalin needed the
support of the church for the war effort and loosened restrictions
somewhat. After the war Stalin allowed as many as twenty thousand Orthodox churches to open, along with sixty-seven monasteries, two theological schools, and eight seminaries.[31] At the same
time, he confiscated Eastern Rite Catholic churches, some dating as
far back as the split between the Orthodox and Roman Catholics
in 1596 at the Council of Brest-Litovsk, giving them to the Orthodox. (See "Russian Orthodoxy Ascends," above.)

After Stalin's death, Soviet Premier Nikita Khrushchev closed churches
again in the early 1960s, allowing only seven thousand to remain
open. When Khrushchev was removed in 1964, state-church relations were affected by dissidents.[32] One of the most outspoken
was Alexander Solzhenitsyn, a devout Orthodox and winner of the
Nobel Prize for Literature, who wrote extensively about Soviet
state abuse of its citizens in Gulag labor camps, including one of
the most famous camps set up at Solovetsky Monastery on the
Solovetsky Islands in the White Sea. A softening in hard-line
policies, *glasnost* (openness), and *perestroika* (restructuring) began
shortly after 1985 when Mikhail Gorbachev became Soviet premier. Within seven years, the Soviet Union collapsed, and the law
restricting religious association ended. The church now had the
right to own property and was separated from the state. The
Soviet Union voted to dissolve in 1991.

Post-Communism

The religious faith of the Soviet people frustrated for over seventy
years has made a remarkable recovery. As of 1996, seventeen
thousand churches and 337 monasteries were open.[33] Churches
are allowed to do missionary, educational, and philanthropic work.
Children in school may be given religious instruction. A stunning
example of the determination and faith of the Russian people may
be seen in the total rebuilding from 1995 to 2000 of one of its

most important churches, the Cathedral of Christ the Savior, in Moscow. In 1931 the communists completely demolished the magnificent cathedral that had taken forty years to build (1839-1879) to make way for the Palace of the Soviets. The palace was never built, and the site became a public swimming pool until the resurrection of the cathedral.

However, many challenges face the Church of Russia today: the poor physical condition of neglected churches and monasteries, a shortage of priests, few materials for religious education, inexperience in social outreach, distrust of the clergy for "cooperating" with the authorities, churches breaking away from the Church of Russia (especially in the Ukraine), and disputes with the Eastern Rite Catholics over church properties. In the sixteenth century the Eastern Rite Catholics took over Orthodox churches (Brest-Litovsk Council). In 1946 Stalin gave them back to the Orthodox, but few Eastern Rite Catholics converted. With the fall of communism, the Eastern Rite Catholics began reclaiming their churches, to the protests of the Orthodox. The tension has become a major issue in Roman Catholic-Orthodox relations today. Resentment about this issue and others marred the visit of the John Paul II to the Ukraine in 2001.

Another difficult question is status of churches in the fifteen constituent republics that formerly made up the Soviet Union. Will they remain under the Church of Russia? Already Orthodox churches are breaking away from it in the Ukraine, a large independent country with forty-nine million people. Three rival churches now exist in the Ukraine: The Church of Russia with nine thousand parishes, the Ukrainian Orthodox Church under the Kiev Patriarchate with three thousand parishes, and the Ukrainian Autocephalous Orthodox Church with one thousand parishes.[34] The latter two schismatic churches are currently considering joining together and asking for official recognition by the Ecumenical Patriarchate in Constantinople. Such recognition would create enormous tensions between the Church of Russia and the Ecumenical Patriarchate.

Churches in general present political challenges for the society, prompting a new law about religions in Russia. Orthodoxy remains one of the few unifying forces in a fractured region. Perhaps this is one of the reasons, along with the fear of missionary groups, that the Russian Parliament passed the Freedom of Conscience and Religious Associations bill in 1997 separating church and state but also putting restrictions on religious practices. An article in *Christian Century* explained that "Russian Orthodoxy received privileged status; Judaism, Islam, and Buddhism were recognized in various geographic regions, and the Roman Catholic and Protestant (mainline and evangelical) traditions that could show they had been legally recognized during the Soviet era had to apply for re-registration."[35] (This law provoked worldwide criticism.) Many challenges confront the Church of Russia in the twenty-first century. Update: www.mospat.ru

SERBIAN CHURCH (CHURCH OF SERBIA)

See: **Belgrade, Serbia and Montenegro**   *Estimated Members:* **8 million**

Jurisdiction: **Serbia and Montenegro, Bosnia-Herzegovina, and Croatia (former Yugoslavia)**

The Serbian Church oversees Orthodox churches primarily in the countries of Serbia and Montenegro, Bosnia-Herzegovina, and Croatia. Until recently, these countries, along with Slovenia and the former Yugoslavia Republic of Macedonia, were united in the Socialist Federal Republic of Yugoslavia. In 1945 the communists came to power, seizing church property. Both the clergy and the laity suffered martyrdom. With the decline of communism in 1990, Yugoslavia began to break apart. In 1991 and 1992 four republics declared independence: Boznia-Herzegovina, Croatia, the former Yugoslavia Republic of Macedonia, and Slovenia.   In 2003 the name "Yugoslavia" was eliminated when a new country called, "Serbia and Montenegro," was created. In 2006 the people of Montenegro voted to become independent from Serbia.

Tensions remain in Serbia and Montenegro, especially in the autonomous region of Kosovo. The Orthodox majority in the country is reluctant to lose Kosovo, the historic heart and soul of Serbian culture and religion. The Serbians lost the Battle of Kosovo (near Pristina) to the Muslim Turks in 1389. The defeated leader, Lazar of Kosovo, is immortalized as the defender of Christian ideals in Serbian national epic poetry.   Many medieval Orthodox churches and monasteries are located in Kosovo, including the famous monasteries of Decani and Gracanica.

Kosovo has a high percentage of Muslim Albanians. The Kosovo Liberation Army, made up of Muslim Albanians, demanded independence in 1998, resulting in civil war in Serbia, refugees fleeing to Albania, NATO bombardment in 1999, and the installation of a NATO peacekeeping force. Despite the peacekeeping presence, many Orthodox churches and monasteries in Kosovo continue to be destroyed or desecrated by rebels. Update: www.serbian-church.net

CHURCH OF ROMANIA

See: **Bucharest, Romania**   *Estimated members:* **23 million**
Jurisdiction: **Romania**

The Church of Romania is the second largest Orthodox church in the world. Although communists took control in 1948, Orthodox parishioners could still worship in some churches and the theological schools remained open. While Communists favored the Orthodox church, there were many persecutions of the people and clergy, closing of churches, and continual surveillances under the brutal dictatorship of Nicolae Ceausescu starting in 1967. In 1989 Romanians assassinated Ceausescu and his wife, bringing an end to communism. The country of Romania is eighty-five percent Orthodox and fourteen percent Catholic.[36] As in Russia in 1948, the Orthodox reclaimed Eastern Rite Catholic churches from centuries ago, creating tension after the fall of communism when the Eastern Rite Catholics wanted them back. Update: www.patriarhia.ro

CHURCH OF BULGARIA

See: **Sofia, Bulgaria**   *Estimated members:* **8 million**
Jurisdiction: **Bulgaria**

Before World War II eighty-five percent of the Bulgarian people were Orthodox. But religious life declined sharply when the communists came into power in 1944 and an invasion by the Soviet Union made Bulgaria a Soviet satellite. Enemies of the state were sent to prison or labor camps or were killed. In 1953, after pledging loyalty to the Communist party, church properties that had been seized were returned and one seminary and one university theological faculty allowed to function. However, a survey in 1953 found that only twenty-seven percent of the people identified themselves as Orthodox. Communism ended in 1991 with the adoption of a new constitution, but difficulties developed in the church creating a schism. The matter was resolved by the Ecumenical Patriarchate.[37] In 2001, eighty-six percent of Bulgaria's population of eight and a half million are Orthodox. Today two seminaries and four university theological faculties instruct in Orthodoxy.[38] Update: www.llbulch.tripod.com/bec/

CHURCH OF GEORGIA

See: **Tiflis, Georgia**   *Estimated members:* **5 million**
Jurisdiction: **Georgia**

Since the fourth century, the Georgian Orthodox church has been a main force in preserving Georgian identity and culture. In 1917 there were 2,455 parishes. In 1921 the Russian Communists invaded Georgia and made it part of the Soviet Union, subjecting the church and people to the same oppression, imprisonment and harassment as citizens of the other Soviet republics. By 1970 there were only eighty officially recognized parishes. However, a religious revival begun in the 1970s blossomed with the 1990 election of non-communist leaders and the declaration of independence in 1991. The Church of Georgia Patriarch Ilya II said, "The world needs to know that we are a Christian nation and that we are returning to our Christian roots."[39] As in other countries, tensions have surfaced with the Eastern Rite Catholics over church properties. Update: www.patriarchate.ge

CHURCH OF CYPRUS

See: **Nicosia, Cyprus**   *Estimated members:* **450,000**
Jurisdiction: **Cyprus**

The first bishop of Cyprus was Lazarus of the New Testament, who had been raised from the dead by Christ. This ancient church, granted autocephaly in 431, is decidedly Greek Orthodox in its 450 parishes. The Cypriots, while an independent country, speak the Greek language and continue the Hellenic culture. The island was tragically divided by a Turkish invasion in 1974 which drove most of the Orthodox to the southern two-thirds of the island,[40] while the occupied north is predominantly Muslim.[41] Update: www.churchofcyprus.org.cy

CHURCH OF GREECE

See: **Athens, Greece**   *Estimated members:* **9 million**
Jurisdiction: **Greece**

Greek Orthodoxy is the official state religion, and the government pays for theological schools, clergy salaries, the salaries of religion teachers in the schools, most of church maintenance, and philanthropic institutions such as orphanages. The Greek population of over ten million is ninety-three percent Orthodox .[42] Update: www.ecclesia.gr

CHURCH OF POLAND

See: **Warsaw, Poland**   *Estimated members:* **750,000**
Jurisdiction: **Poland**

Autocephalous since 1924, the Church of Poland had four million Orthodox members before 1939. With a boundary change that year, part of Poland was absorbed into the Soviet Union, and the Orthodox in those areas came into the Church of Russia.[43] Communism lasted in Poland from 1945 to 1989. Today, only three percent of the total population is Orthodox, and ninety-two percent is Roman Catholic.[44] Update: www.orthodox.pl

CHURCH OF ALBANIA

See: **Tirana, Albania**   *Estimated members:* **160,000**
Jurisdiction: **Albania**

Albania became a communist state in 1944, and in 1967 the government declared Albania the "first truly atheist state in the world," subjecting its citizens to severe religious persecution. All churches, synagogues, and mosques were closed. When communism fell in 1990, religious institutions underwent a revival. With the help of mission teams, the Orthodox Archbishop Anastasios reopened the seminary, and began rebuilding churches and monasteries and opening medical clinics. In 1995 Muslims made up thirty-nine percent of the population of the country, Roman Catholics seventeen percent, and Orthodox (living primarily in the South) sixteen percent.[45] www.orthodoxalbania.org

CHURCH OF THE CZECH LANDS AND SLOVAKIA

See: **Prague, Czech Republic**   *Estimated members:* **55,000**
Jurisdiction: **The Czech Republic and Slovakia**

Recently granted autocephalacy in 1998 by the Ecumenical Patriarchate, the church oversees parishes in two countries, the Czech Republic and Slovakia. The twentieth-century country of Czechoslovakia was created in 1918 after the collapse of the Austro-Hungarian Empire and became communist in 1946. Relative to its neighbors, religious practice was more tolerated with freedom of religion theoretically guaranteed. By 1987 strikes and protests began, eventually resulting in the end of communism in 1990 and the withdrawal of Soviet troops in 1991. This smooth transition has been called the "Velvet Revolution." However, a "Velvet Divorce" resulted in the division of Czechoslovakia into the two separate countries in 1993.

Today both the Czech Republic and Slovakia are predominantly Roman Catholic (forty percent in Czech and sixty-eight percent in Slovakia). Protestants are the second most predominant religion. The Orthodox rank third with fewer than one percent in each country.[46] The Orthodox, primarily Ruthenians, live in eastern Slovakia near Ukraine. Unlike the Orthodox and Eastern Rite Catholics in other former communist countries, the Orthodox gave back the Roman Catholic churches, and the governments have given money for the Orthodox to build new ones.
Update: www.pravoslav.gts.cz

THE ORTHODOX IN THE UNITED STATES

For many centuries, the Orthodox faithful lived primarily in the East in their mother church jurisdictions. Today many reside throughout the world as Diaspora, people of a common national origin or of common beliefs. The largest Orthodox Diaspora in the world is in North America. The Greek Orthodox comprise the largest group, followed by the Russians and the Antiochians. Regretfully, space does not permit discussion of Diaspora in other countries. For additional information, see Timothy Ware, *The Orthodox Church,* "Diaspora Mission."[47]

The United States welcomes people of diverse race and religious beliefs. The separation of church and state and the freedom to worship is ideal soil for new immigrants to transplant their religion from their home country. As a result, many Orthodox churches of different jurisdictions exist in the United States.

ORTHODOX CHURCHES IN THE UNITED STATES AND CANADA
(LISTED IN ORDER OF OFFICIAL RANK OF THE MOTHER CHURCH)

	ESTIMATED MEMBERS
THE ECUMENICAL PATRIARCHATE OF CONSTANTINOPLE	
The Greek Orthodox Archdiocese of America	2,000,000
The Ukrainian Orthodox Church of the U.S.A.	100,000
The Ukrainian Orthodox Church of Canada	129,000
The American Carpatho-Russian Orthodox Diocese	20,000
The Albanian Orthodox Diocese of America	1,100
The Belarusian Council of Orthodox Churches in North America	1,000
THE PATRIARCHATE OF ANTIOCH	
The Antiochian Orthodox Christian Archdiocese of North America	250,000
THE PATRIARCHATE OF MOSCOW AND ALL RUSSIA	
Parishes of the Russian Orthodox Church	9,780
THE PATRIARCHATE OF SERBIA	
The Serbian Orthodox Church in the USA and Canada	140,000
THE PATRIARCHATE OF ROMANIA	
The Romanian Orthodox Archdiocese in America and Canada	12,835
THE PATRIARCHATE OF BULGARIA	
The Bulgarian Eastern Orthodox Church	10,000
THE ORTHODOX CHURCH IN AMERICA	
The Orthodox Church in America (formerly the Russian Orthodox Greek Catholic Church of America or Metropolia)	845,000
The Romanian Orthodox Episcopate of America	65,000
The Bulgarian Orthodox Diocese	10,000
The Albanian Orthodox Archdiocese in America	30,000
UNRECOGNIZED STATUS	
The Russian Orthodox Church Outside Russia (ROCOR) or The Russian Orthodox Church Abroad (ROCA)	100,000
Old Calendar Greek Orthodox Churches	15,000

About This Chart

Chart reproduced from *Orthodox Christians in America* by John H. Erickson.[48]   The estimated number of Orthodox church members in America and Canada varies greatly. Erickson suggests 3.7 million members. Timothy Ware in *The Orthodox Church*[49] claims three million, and Thomas Fitzgerald in *The Orthodox Church* suggests three million in the United States alone.[50]   These figures do not include the Oriental Orthodox.

ORTHODOXY COMES TO THE AMERICAS

Russian missionaries were the first to bring Orthodoxy to America in an official capacity. Their work was part of a broader Russian effort to expand the Russian empire and start commercial ventures. In 1794 the devout missionaries established the first ecclesiastical mission at Kodiak Island, Alaska. One of the missionaries, Father Herman (1756?-1837), worked so diligently in spreading Orthodoxy and defending the natives against abuse that he was named America's first Orthodox saint by the Church of Russia in 1970. Likewise in 1978 the Church of Russia canonized another missionary, St. Innocent the Enlightener of the Aleuts and Apostle to America (1797-1879) for his many accomplishments. Unfortunately the commercial venture, the Russian-American Company, that supported much of the mission, closed in 1863. Four years later in 1867 the United States purchased Alaska from Russia. The Church of Russia moved their headquarters to San Francisco in 1872. Despite these changes, according to Thomas Fitzgerald in *The Orthodox Church,* "on the eve of the October 1917 revolution in Russia, it is estimated there were 10,000 Orthodox Christians in Alaska and nearly one hundred churches or chapels."[51] However, John Erickson in *Orthodox Christians in America* notes that United States' federal assimilationist policies of the Alaska natives driven by Protestant missionaries resulted in a declining Orthodox population. Despite this, Orthodoxy still has a presence in Alaska today.[52]

ETHNIC CHURCHES OF THE IMMIGRANTS

By the late 1800s, ethnic groups immigrated to the United States mainland in large numbers and established Orthodox churches. In 1864 Greek merchants, under the direction of the local Greek consul, formed a multi-ethnic parish named the Eastern Orthodox Church of the Holy Trinity in New Orleans. The first Serbian parish soon followed in 1894, Arabian in 1895, Bulgarian in 1907, and Albanian in 1908.[53] By 1914 approximately 250,000 Eastern Rite Roman Catholics (including many Carpatho-Russians) emigrated from various parts of Eastern Europe. However, when the Latin Rite Catholics in the United States would not recognize them, the Church of Russia accepted them and moved its headquarters from San Francisco to New York to assist with the new church entrants.[54]

CHALLENGES

The new Orthodox churches became centers for both religious and social purposes for the new immigrants. While these provided safe havens in the short run, in the long term they have led to continuing challenges for Orthodoxy in America: Each church becomes entangled in the political situation of its mother country, overlapping jurisdictions preclude a unified Orthodox church in the United States, and parishes dependent on their members' ethnic identification face uncertainty about the loyalty of the younger generations with limited ethnic identification and poor mother-country language skills.

Complications from Mother-country Politics

Difficulties within American parishes have often mirrored politics of the home country. The most devastating example occurred in the Russian and Slavic parishes. By 1917 the Russians had numerous parishes that included not only Russian but also other Slavic churches. Russian Bishop Tikhon who served in the United States from 1898 to 1907, envisioned one Orthodox church of all ethnic groups in America. However, the Bolshevik Revolution fractured not only that dream but also the Church of Russia itself. In America three Russian church jurisdictions resulted from the fractures caused by the advent of communism.

Just before the communist revolution, Bishop Tikhon, now back in Russia, became Patriarch of Moscow. While resisting the demands of the government, he was persecuted and died under house arrest in 1925. (After the fall of communism in 1989, he was made a saint). Meanwhile the Russian Church in America fell into disarray. Because of bickering over leadership and church property, it received no financial help from the Mother Church (Church of Russia). The first splinter church and the largest, the Russian Orthodox Greek Catholic Church of America (also called "Metropolia") broke away from the Moscow Patriarchate in 1924. In 1926 an ardent anti-communist group known as the Karlovtsky Synod broke from the Metropolia to form the Russian Orthodox Church Outside Russia (ROCOR), or the Russian Orthodox Church Abroad (ROCA) in 1927.[53] A third church was formed in 1933 when the Mother Church established its own jurisdiction in America to embrace those parishes loyal to Moscow. This situation remained until 1970, when the Church of Russia granted autocephaly to the Metropolia and its name was changed to the present-day Orthodox Church in America (OCA). In 2006 ROCOR and the Moscow Patriarchate began discussing restoration of canonical communion with self-governing status for ROCOR.

The other Slavic parishes were affected primarily after World War II, when they fell under the orbit of communism. Between 1945 and 1947 communist governments took over Poland, Romania, Bulgaria, Yugoslavia, Czechoslovakia, and Albania. Parishes in America became torn over the issue of whether to remain with their mother churches in Eastern Europe or break away completely. Each jurisdiction resolved the issue somewhat differently. For example, the American clergy in the Bulgarian parishes formally broke with Bulgaria in 1947. But in 1962, the Church of Bulgaria in Sofia recognized the American bishop heading the breakaway church. This recognition precipitated another breach within the American Bulgarian community, resulting in a new breakaway bishop being consecrated by ROCOR (Russian Orthodox Church Outside Russia).[54] Each church has its own story, and each was disturbed by divisions and issues of correct canonical procedure.

With the fall of communism, some churches in America reconciled with their mother churches, such as the Serbians in 1992 and some of the Romanian parishes in 1993.[57] However, as shown in the above list, "Orthodox Churches in the United States and Canada," duplicate Romanian and Bulgarian churches come under the jurisdiction of their mother churches and the Orthodox Church of America.

Mother-country politics also affected the American Greek Orthodox Diaspora community. Parishes became divided over those loyal to elected Greek Prime Minister Eleftherios Venizelos and those loyal to Greece's King Constantine, whom Venizelos had exiled in 1917 (Venizelists vs. Royalists). Archbishop Meletios of Athens, a Venizelist, came to America to organize the parishes under the Church of Greece. When Venizelos was defeated in the election of 1920, Archbishop Meletios was deposed. Shortly thereafter he became the Patriarch of Constantinople and issued a charter in 1922 putting the American parishes under the jurisdiction of Constantinople. But political feuding in the American parishes continued until 1930, when the Patriarchate of Constantinople and the Church of Greece recalled all the feuding bishops and appointed Archbishop Athenagoras, who helped heal the community.[58]

Overlapping Jurisdictions — a Fractured Situation

While the mother-country politics have been distracting, national loyalties remain, resulting in many overlapping jurisdictions in America. The hierarchy of the Orthodox church see this as an uncanonical situation. Orthodox canons specify that the church be organized by geographic diocese, each headed by one bishop only. Theoretically, a mature Orthodox church in the United States would be united, without overlapping jurisdictions. Whether and when this might happen is one of the biggest challenges facing the Diaspora churches in America. The subject is discussed in various arenas, such as the Standing Conference of Canonical Orthodox Bishops in the Americas (SCOBA) and at meetings of lay groups such as the Orthodox Christian Laity, which wants a unified autocephalous American Church. The bishops face many political hurdles in making this a reality. Timothy Ware predicts change will come at the grass roots: "Unity in the west . . . will probably come not so much from above . . . as from below, through the mutual love and the holy impatience of the people of God."[59]

Ethnic Identity and Future Growth

Another major challenge is how to sustain and increase membership in the parishes if the upcoming generations do not feel a strong ethnic attachment or speak the language used in services. The older generations worry about losing the cultural and spiritual heritage that has been instrumental in keeping the church together. But is keeping the ethnic tie viable if the younger generation does not seem interested? In addition, how will new people without ethnic ties become interested in Orthodoxy? How will the church grow? Most parishes recognize the importance of using English and having clergy educated in the West. They understand the delicate balance required and continue to listen and accommodate.

PRELUDE TO UNITY?

Many believe Orthodoxy will become mainstream in the United States only by eliminating the overlapping ethnic jurisdictions and uniting into one church. Church theologians point out that Orthodox canon law specifies there should be only one bishop per diocese, the bishops should form a synod (church council), and one among them be chosen as head. Recognizing the existing situation as uncanonical, the American hierarchy made preliminary efforts to come together with such initiatives as the Proposed Conference of Orthodox Bishops in 1937 and the Federated Orthodox Greek Catholic Primary Jurisdictions in America in 1943. Finally, in 1960, under the leadership of the Greek Orthodox Archbishop Iakovos, the Standing Conference of Canonical Orthodox Bishops in the Americas (SCOBA) was created and continues to meet and function today.[60]

SCOBA members include nine churches: Albanian Orthodox Diocese of America, American Carpatho-Russian Orthodox Diocese, Antiochian Orthodox Christian Archdiocese of North America, Bulgarian Eastern Orthodox Church (Diocese of the USA, Canada, and Australia), Greek Orthodox Archdiocese of America, Orthodox Church in America, Romanian Orthodox Archdiocese in America and Canada, Serbian Orthodox Church in the USA and Canada, and Ukrainian Orthodox Church of the USA.

SCOBA, a consultative, voluntary body, has no actual authority and cannot adjudicate differences or claim to speak for all of the Orthodox in America. But on the subject of unity, at a meeting in 1994, twenty-nine bishops at Ligonier, Pennsylvania, "forcefully restated the need for a greater sense of mission and reaffirmed their commitment to the goal of visible Orthodox unity in America."[61] SCOBA meets twice a year for discussions and to implement programs under its jurisdiction such as the Military Chaplaincy Commission, International Orthodox Christian Charities (IOCC), the

Orthodox Christian Mission Center (OCMC), Orthodox Christian Education Commission (OCEC), and Ecumenical Dialogues. These dynamic programs, like confidence-building measures, show the churches can work together.

CHALLENGES FOR ORTHODOX CHURCHES WORLDWIDE

While SCOBA addresses concerns on Orthodoxy in America, a worldwide effort to address the challenges facing Orthodoxy worldwide is also underway. One of the major issues is the aforementioned situation of multiple jurisdictions that exists in America and all the Orthodox Diaspora.

The Secretariat for the Preparations of the Holy and Great Synod of the Orthodox Church at the Orthodox Center of the Ecumenical Patriarchate in Chambesy (a suburb of Geneva) is preparing an agenda of major challenges. In the conciliar manner of the seven Ecumenical Councils held from 325 to 787, the Orthodox church will someday convene a Holy and Great Synod (council) to discuss and resolve these issues. Planning began at four pan-Orthodox conferences held in 1961 (Mt. Athos), 1963 (Rhodes), 1964 (Rhodes), and 1968 (Geneva). Since 1976 church officials have attended regular meetings at the Orthodox Center in Chambesy of a Pre-Conciliar Commission to review background papers on ten proposed issues on the agenda.

PROPOSED ISSUES FOR THE HOLY AND GREAT SYNOD[62]

1) The Orthodox Diaspora

2) Autocephaly and how it is proclaimed

3) Autonomy and how it is proclaimed

4) Diptychs (the official ranking of churches)

5) The question of a common calendar

6) Impediments to marriage

7) Adjustments of the rules of fasting to the conditions of the present day

8) Relation of the Orthodox churches to the rest of the Christian world

9) Orthodoxy and the ecumenical movement

10) Contribution of the local Orthodox churches to the promotion of the ideals of peace, freedom, and brotherhood among peoples, and to the eradication of racial discrimination

Of top importance is the situation of overlapping jurisdictions in the Diaspora and the process of how a church becomes autocephalous. The granting of autocephaly to the Orthodox Church in America in 1970 by Moscow precipitated a significant exchange of letters between the Patriarchate of Constantinople and Moscow in which both agreed only one unified Orthodox church can properly exist in any country and that the Holy and Great Synod will finally confirm the development of a united church in America. However, they agreed to disagree about processes until the Holy and Great Synod is held. Constantinople believes only Constantinople has the right to declare autocephaly. Moscow believes the mother church of the Diaspora has the right.[63] These letters are part of the background being prepared on each topic for the Holy and Great Synod meeting. No date has been set.

Ecumenicism is the goal of increased understanding and reconciliation among all Christian churches. The Orthodox formally became involved in this issue when some of its churches became founding members of the World Council of Churches in Geneva in 1948 and the National Council of Churches of Christ in the USA (NCCC). In the 1960s bilateral dialogues began between the Orthodox and individual churches (Episcopal, Roman Catholic, Lutheran, Reformed and the Orthodox Oriental) to facilitate understanding about doctrinal points of agreement and differences.[64]

In 1964 Pope Paul VI and Patriarch Athenagoras of Constantinople met in Jerusalem, leading in 1965 to the mutual lifting of anathemas pronounced in 1054 during the Great Schism,[65] and dialogues between the Roman Catholic and Orthodox began. Major differences between the two churches include the long-standing issues of married clergy, Papal Infallibility, the Immaculate Conception of the Virgin Mary, and the *filioque* (issue concerning the derivation of the Holy Spirit). Severe tensions regarding church property ownership resurfaced after the fall of communism. Despite their differences, the two churches co-celebrate the feast days of their Apostle founders; and every year an Orthodox delegation goes to Rome on June 29 (Feast Day of Ss. Peter and Paul), and a Roman Catholic delegation to Constantinople on November 30 (Feast Day of St. Andrew). The Roman Catholics have recognized the Orthodox sacraments. In the United States the North American Orthodox-Catholic Theological Consultation and the Joint Committee of Orthodox and Catholic Bishops hold frequent meetings. For statements of agreement see www.scoba.us/resources/index.asp.

SUMMARY

The history of the Orthodox church is a marvel of continuity, difficulty, and triumph. The continuous connection back to Jesus Christ and the Pentecost inspires awe and respect for a church so instrumental in developing Christian theology in Greek thought and language. Once that Tradition was established, the church endured the triumphs of growth, the pain of schisms, disappoint-ments, jurisdictional splits, and oppressions, especially under the Ottoman Empire and communism.

Yet the church survives as a testimony to the truth of God's love, Christ's teachings, the work of the Holy Spirit, and millions who find a place to meet God and renew the Body of Christ at a Divine Liturgy. As difficult as the church history has been, there is enormous hope and joy in seeing Orthodox around the world in the past and the present who have shared this common Tradition. There is optimism that the people and institutions will continue to triumph, especially with an increased awareness of how each Orthodox church has expressed the precious Tradition that binds all together.

ORTHODOX SITES TO VISIT

The following sites are of major significance in the Orthodox world. Each expresses Orthodoxy according to tradition within its national context. For example, the cave monasteries in Cappadocia in Turkey are made from natural stone formations. Onion-shaped domes characteristically adorn Russian Orthodox churches. Some have become museums, and many are on the World Heritage Committee List of the United Nations Educational, Scientific and Cultural Organization (UNESCO). For the significance of the site and further details, go to www.unesco.org/whc, use a search en-gine on the Internet, or check travel books.

Bulgaria
Boyana Church (Sofia) (UNESCO)
Rila Monastery (near Rila) (UNESCO)
Rock-hewn Churches of Ivanovo (Ivanovo) (UNESCO)

Cyprus
Nine painted churches in the Troodos Region (UNESCO)

Egypt
Monastery of St. Catherine (Mt. Sinai Peninsula)

Former Yugoslav Republic of Macedonia (FYROM)
St. Pantelemon Monastery (near Skopje/Nerezi)

Georgia
Bagrati Cathedral and Gelati Monastery (Kutaisi) (UNESCO)

Greece
Daphne Monastery (Athens) (UNESCO)
Meteora Monasteries (Kalambaka)
Mt. Athos Monasteries (Chalkidiki Peninsula) — men only
Mystras (near Sparta) (UNESCO)
Nea Moni Monastery (Chios) (UNESCO)
Ossios Loukas Monastery (Steiri) (UNESCO)
St. John Monastery (Patmos) (UNESCO)
St. Demetrios Cathedral and Church of the Holy Apostles
    (Thessaloniki) (UNESCO)

Holy Land
Church of the Holy Sepulchre (Jerusalem) (UNESCO)
Basilica of the Nativity (Bethlehem)
Church and Tomb of the Panagia (Gethsemane)

Italy
Early Christian Monuments (Ravenna) (UNESCO)
St. Mark's Cathedral (Venice) (UNESCO)

Romania
The Hurezi Monastery in Walachia (UNESCO)
Painted Monastery Churches of Humor, Moldavia, Sucevita and Voronet
    (near Suceava in Bucovina area) (Moldavia designated by UNESCO)
The Wooden Churches of Maramures (region of Maramures) (UNESCO)

Russian Federation
Church of the Transfiguration (Kizi/Lake Onego)
Ferapontov Monastery (Vologda region) (UNESCO)
Holy Transfiguration of our Holy Savior on Ilyina Street
    (Novgorod)(UNESCO)
St. Sophia Cathedral (Novgorod)
Solovetsky Monastery (Solovetsky Islands in White Sea) (UNESCO)
> *In or near Moscow*
> Ascension Church (Kolomenskoye) (UNESCO)
> Christ the Savior Cathedral (Moscow)
> St. Basil Basilica (Moscow) (UNESCO)
> Tretiakov Gallery — icon section (Moscow)
> St. Sergius Monastery and Holy Trinity Church (Sergiev Posad)
>   (UNESCO)
> Churches of Vladimir and Suzdal (Vladimir and Suzdal) (UNESCO)

In or near St. Petersburg
Holy Transfiguration (Valaam Island in Lake Ladoga)
Our Lady of Kazan Cathedral (St. Petersburg) (UNESCO)
Russian Museum — icon display (St. Petersburg)
St. Isaacs Cathedral (St. Petersburg) (UNESCO)
Ss. Peter and Paul Cathedral (St. Petersburg) (UNESCO)

Serbia and Montenegro (Former Yugoslavia)
Church of Christ the Pantocrator at Decani Monastery (near Pec in
    Kosovo)
Sopocani Monastery (near Novi Pazar in Serbia) (UNESCO)
Studenica Monastery (near Rasca in Serbia) (UNESCO)

Turkey
Cappadocia cave sanctuaries (valley near Goreme) (UNESCO)
Church of the Holy Savior (now Kariye Museum) (Constantinople/Chora)
St. George Cathedral (Constantinople/Istanbul in the Phanar
    neighborhood)
St. Sophia Cathedral (museum) (Constantinople/Istanbul) (UNESCO)

Ukraine
St. Sophia Cathedral and Monastic Building (Kiev) (UNESCO)

THEOLOGICAL SCHOOLS, SEMINARIES, AND INSTITUTES

In the forefront of keeping the Orthodox Tradition are the theological schools, seminaries, and institutes that train priests, theologians, and laity to continue the faith. The following list by country
from the Greek Orthodox Archdiocese of America website
www.goarch.org is only a sampling of the many fine institutions
around the world. It is neither comprehensive nor ranked by
importance.

Australia
St. Andrew's Greek Orthodox Theological College (Sydney, New South Wales)

Bulgaria
St. Kliment Ohridski Faculty of Theology, University of Sofia (Sofia)

Canada
Greek Orthodox Theological Academy of Toronto (East York, Ontario)
St. Andrew's College in Winnepeg, Ukrainian Orthodox Church,
    University of Manitoba (Winnepeg, Manitoba)

England
Institute for Orthodox Christian Studies, University of Cambridge
    (Cambridge)

Greece
Aristotle University of Thessaloniki, Department of Theology (Thessaloniki)
University of Athens, Department of Theology (Athens)

Kenya
The Orthodox Patriarchal School (Nairobi)

Lebanon
St. John of Damascus, Faculty of Theology, University of Balamand
(Balamand)

Romania
Faculty of Orthodox Theology, Babes-Bolyai University (Cluj-Napoca)

Russia
Pimen Orthodox Institute (St. Petersburg)
St. Philaret Orthodox Christian Institute for Advanced Studies (Moscow)
St. Tikhon Orthodox Theological Institute (Moscow)

Slovakia
Orthodox Theological Faculty of Safarik University (Presov)

United States of America
Holy Cross Greek Orthodox School of Theology (Boston, Massachusetts)
Patriarch Athenagoras Orthodox Institute of the Graduate Theological
Union (Berkeley, California)
St. Athanasius Academy of Orthodox Theology (Elk Grove, California)
St. Herman's Theological Seminary (Kodiak, Alaska)
St. Tikhon's Orthodox Theological Seminary (South Canaan,
Pennsylvania)
St. Vladimir's Orthodox Theological Seminary (Crestwood, New York)

ORTHODOX ACADEMIC JOURNALS

Listing not comprehensive.

Greek Orthodox Theological Review (Brookline, Massachusetts)
St. Vladimir's Theological Quarterly (Crestwood, New York)

RESOURCES — UNITED STATES

PUBLISHING

Listing not comprehensive.

Conciliar Press (Ben Lomond, California)
Greek Orthodox Archdiocese of America — Department of Religious
    Education (Brookline, Massachusetts)
Holy Cross Press (Brookline, Massachusetts)
Light and Life Publishing (Minneapolis, Minnesota)
St. Vladimir's Seminary Press (Crestwood, New York)

CHURCH NEWSPAPERS

The following official church newspapers and newsletters are
distributed nationally:

Albanian Orthodox Archdiocese in America, South Boston: *Archdiocesan
    Council Update*
American Carpatho-Russian Orthodox Diocese, Perth Amboy, New Jersey:
    The Church Messenger
Antiochian Orthodox Christian Archdiocese of North America,
    Englewood, New Jersey: *The Word*
Greek Orthodox Archdiocese of America, New York: *Orthodox Observer*
Orthodox Church in America, Syosset, New York: *The Orthodox Church
    in America*
Romanian Orthodox Archdiocese in America and Canada, Chicago:
    Credinta/The Faith
Romanian Orthodox Episcopate of America (OCA), Grass Lake,
    Michigan: *Solia/The Herald*
Russian Orthodox Church Outside Russia, New York:
    Orthodox Russia
Serbian Orthodox Church in the USA and Canada, Bridgeport, West
    Virginia: *The Path of Orthodoxy*
Ukrainian Orthodox Church of the U.S.A, South Bound Brook, New
    Jersey: *Ukrainian Orthodox World*

RADIO

Ask your church about local radio shows featuring Orthodox programming or see radio listings in the *Yearbook 2006* published by
the Greek Orthodox Archdiocese of America. The following show
is available via webcasting on the Internet:

"Come Receive the Light," Orthodox Christian Network (Fort Lauderdale,
    Florida) www.receive.org

ORTHODOX INTERNET WEBSITES

The Internet greatly broadens information relating to Orthodoxy. For example, in a few minutes you can learn about the Serbian Orthodox church or take a class about Orthodoxy via webcasting. You can also see the famous painted churches of Moldavia in Romania or buy icons from a Russian dealer. Even prayerful worship at the computer is possible with Bible readings, a live Divine Liturgy via webcasting, and a candle lighting at a monastery at Mt. Athos. Information on a local monastery may encourage you to go on a weekend retreat. Or you may want to attend an international Orthodox conference for young adults. The following sites will get you started on Internet exploration of the many facets of Orthodoxy.

Caveat: Internet websites are unpredictable. Some stay current with frequent updates, others are accessible but have outdated information, and a few vanish. If a website does not appear after entering its address, go to a search engine, and enter the name.

Disclaimer: This listing is not an endorsement of a website's content, products, or vendors.

AUTOCEPHALOUS ORTHODOX CHURCHES

The following websites, listed in the traditional order of hierarchy, provide information on Orthodox theology, individual church history and administration, parishes, current events, and links to other websites. Some of the websites are official (check the website itself), others are not designated as such, and some are in a foreign language. Websites under construction or unavailable are noted with the words, "search engine." These sites may be accessible in the future via a search engine.

www.patriarchate.org
　　Ecumenical Patriarchate of Constantinople
www.greekorthodox-alexandria.org
　　Patriarchate of Alexandria
www.antiochpat.org
　　Patriarchate of Antioch
www.jerusalem-patriarchate.org
　　Patriarchate of Jerusalem

www.mospat.ru
    Church of Russia
www.serbian-church.net
    Church of Serbia
www.patriarhia.ro/
    Church of Romania
http://bulch.tripod.com/boc/
    Church of Bulgaria
www.patriarchate.ge
    Church of Georgia
www.churchofcyprus.org.cy
    Church of Cyprus (in Greek only)
www.ecclesia.gr
    Church of Greece
www.orthodox.pl
    Church of Poland (in Polish only)
www.orthodoxalbania.org
    Church of Albania
www.pravoslav.gts.cz
    Church of the Czech Lands and Slovakia (in Czech only)

AUTONOMOUS ORTHODOX CHURCHES

search engine
    The Orthodox Church of Sinai
www.ort.fi
    The Finnish Orthodox Church
www2.gol.com/users/ocj/
    The Orthodox Church in Japan
www.chinese.orthodoxy.ru/
    The Orthodox Church in China

ORTHODOX CHURCHES IN THE UNITED STATES AND CANADA

The following websites, listed in the traditional order of hierarchy, provide information on Orthodox theology, individual church history and administration, parishes, current events, and links to other websites. Some of the websites are official (check the website itself), others are not designated as such. Websites under construction or unavailable are noted with the words "search engine." These sites may be accessible in the future via a search engine.

The Ecumenical Patriarchate of Constantinople
www.goarch.org
    The Greek Orthodox Archdiocese of America
www.gocanada.org
    The Greek Orthodox Metropolis of Toronto (Canada)

www.uocofusa.org
  The Ukrainian Orthodox Church of the United States of America
www.uocc.ca
  The Ukrainian Orthodox Church of Canada
www.acrod.org
  The American Carpatho-Russian Orthodox Diocese
search engine
  The Albanian Orthodox Diocese of America
search engine
  The Belarusian Council of Orthodox Churches in North America

The Patriarchate of Antioch
www.antiochian.org
  The Antiochian Orthodox Christian Archdiocese of North America

The Patriarchate of Moscow and All Russia
www.mospat.ru/
  Parishes of the Russian Orthodox Church

The Patriarchate of Serbia
www.serborth.org
  The Serbian Orthodox Church in the USA and Canada

The Patriarchate of Romania
www.romarch.org/eng
  The Romanian Orthodox Archdiocese in America and Canada

The Patriarchate of Bulgaria
www.bulgariandiocese.org
  Bulgarian Eastern Orthodox Diocese of the USA, Canada, and
  Australia

The Orthodox Church in America
www.oca.org
  The Orthodox Church in America [and Canada]
www.roea.org
  The Romanian Orthodox Episcopate of America
www.oca.org
  The Bulgarian Orthodox Diocese
www.oca.org
  The Albanian Orthodox Archdiocese in America

Unrecognized Status
www.rocor.org
  The Russian Orthodox Church Outside Russia (ROCOR) or
  The Russian Orthodox Church Abroad (ROCA)
www.thegreekorthodoxchurch.com
  Old Calendar Greek Orthodox Churches

GENERAL DIRECTORY

www.theologic.com
> TheoLogic Systems. Go to "Orthodox Worldlinks" for links to sites on all aspects of Orthodoxy. Bethel Park, Pennsylvania.

BOOKS, ICONS, DEVOTIONAL ITEMS, AND OTHER PRODUCTS

www.conciliarpress.com
> Conciliar Press. Books, icons, multimedia, and other devotional items. Ben Lomond, California.

www.goarch.org
> Greek Orthodox Archdiocese of America. Books, icons and devotional items available at "Orthodox Marketplace." Free "Iconograms" for name days and other special occasions. New York.

www.holycrossbookstore.com
> Holy Cross Bookstore. Books, icons, multimedia, and other devotional items. Brookline, Massachusetts.

www.light-n-life.com
> Light and Life Publishing.   Books, icons, multimedia, and other devotional items. Minneapolis, Minnesota.

www.skete.com
> St. Isaac of Syria Skete. Icons and other devotional items. Boscobel, Wisconsin.

www.svspress.com
> St. Vladimir's Seminary Bookstore. Books, icons, and multimedia. Crestwood, New York.

www.thehtm.org
> Holy Transfiguration Monastery. Icons, multimedia, and other devotional items. Brookline, Massachusetts.

www.theologic.com
> Theologic Systems. For links to worldwide suppliers of all Orthodox items, go to "Orthodox Worldlinks" and then "The Orthodox Marketplace." Bethel Park, Pennsylvania.

HISTORIC SITES TO VISIT

Check the list of "Orthodox Sites to Visit" in the text above. If the site has not been designated by United Nations Educational, Scientific and Cultural Organization (UNESCO), try to find it using a search engine. For the sites selected by UNESCO, go to:

www.unesco.org/whc
> United Nations Educational, Scientific and Cultural Organization, World Heritage Committee.   Listing of all designated properties for preservation around the world. Paris.

MONASTERIES

www.balamandmonastery.org.lb
> Our Lady of Balamand Patriarchal Monastery. Go to "Monasteries" for links to monasteries around the world. Patriarchate of Antioch. University of Balamand, Lebanon.

www.inathos.gr
> Welcome to Mt. Athos. General information on the Holy Mountain and histories and pictures of the interiors of many of its monasteries; light a candle online.

www.theologic.com
> TheoLogic Systems. Go to "Churches/Monasteries" for website listings. Bethel, Pennsylvania.

NEWS ABOUT ORTHODOXY

Check also the above websites of the "Autocephalous Orthodox Churches" and the "Orthodox Churches in the United States and Canada" for updates, press releases, and current events.

www.orthodoxnews.com
> Orthodox News. Selected digest of Orthodox news from around the world compiled by Orthodox Christian News Service of Orthodox Christian Laity. Chicago.

www.receive.org
> Come Receive the Light. National radio show with news, music, and discussion of contemporary issues. Fort Lauderdale, Florida.

www.theologic.com
> TheoLogic Systems. Go to "Orthodox WorldLinks" and then "News" for links to Orthodox news sources. Bethel, Pennsylvania.

ORGANIZATIONS (GENERAL)

www.syndesmos.org
> Syndesmos. The World Fellowship of Orthodox Youth. Brings together youth from Orthodox churches around the world at special events, camp, and seminars. Hoargos, Greece.

www.iocc.org
> International Orthodox Christian Charities. Cooperative effort of Orthodox churches to assist with disaster and emergency relief under the auspices of the Standing Conference of Canonical Orthodox Bishops in the Americas (SCOBA). Baltimore, Maryland.

www.ocf.net
> Orthodox Christian Fellowship. Official campus ministry under the auspices of SCOBA. Starts campus chapters, organizes spring-break mission trips and conferences, and provides readings for worship on the Internet. Berkeley, California.

www.ocmc.org
> The Orthodox Christian Mission Center.   Official mission and evangelism agency of SCOBA.   Supports missionary priests and missionary teams abroad and in America.   St. Augustine, Florida.

www.yalchicago.org
> Greek Orthodox Diocese of Chicago Young Adult League.   Local events, religious information, links to other Greek Orthodox Archdiocese Young Adult Leagues across America.   Chicago.

SEMINARIES IN THE UNITED STATES AND LINKS ABROAD

www.hchc.edu.
> Hellenic College/Holy Cross Greek Orthodox School of Theology. Brookline, Massachusetts.

www.dioceseofalaska.org
> Russian Orthodox Diocese of Alaska. Go to "Seminary"
>
> St. Herman's Theological Seminary.   Kodiak Alaska.

www.svots.edu
> St. Vladimir's Orthodox Theological Seminary.   Crestwood, NY

www.stots.edu
> St. Tikhon's Orthodox Theological Seminary.   For links to seminaries abroad go to "Electronic Resources," then "Orthodox Seminaries and Schools of Theology."   South Canaan, Pennsylvania.

WORSHIP AND STUDY ONLINE

www.abbamoses.org.
> God is Wonderful in His Saints. Lives of the saints, prayers and readings.

www.goarch.org.
> Greek Orthodox Archdiocese of America.   "Online Chapel" for services and daily Bible readings; "Our Faith" for theology, saints, patristics and history; "Ministry Resources" for prayers, hymns, saints, icons and music; "Multimedia Programs" for live broadcasts, audio, video, and Internet School of Orthodox Studies. New York.

www.myriobiblos.gr
> Myriobiblios.   E-text library of the Church of Greece.   Selection of writings by Church Fathers, articles by well-known theologians, texts of "The Divine Liturgy of St. John Chrysostom," and "Akathist Hymn." Mix of Greek and English language. Athens.

www.theologic.com
> TheoLogic Systems.   Go to: "Art," "Music," "Multimedia," "Music," "Reading Room," and "Worship."   Bethel Park, Pennsylvania.

1. *Yearbook 2006* (New York: Greek Orthodox Archdiocese of America, 2006), 68.

2. Timothy Ware, *The Orthodox Church*. 1963. New Edition (London: Penguin Books, 1997), 6.

3. Ibid., 4.

4. Demetrios J. Constantelos, *The Greeks, Their Heritage and Its Value Today* (Brookline, Mass.: Hellenic College Press, 1996), 42.

5. Ibid., 30.

6. Demetrios J. Constantelos, *Understanding the Greek Orthodox Church: Its Faith, History and Practice* (Brookline, Mass.: Hellenic College Press, 1990), 21.

7. Speros Vryonis, Jr., "The Relationship of Hellenism and Orthodoxy in the Greek-American Communities" (unpublished manuscript, undated), 13.

8. Timothy Ware, *The Orthodox Church,* 18.

9. Ibid., 22.

10. Ibid., 22-23.

11. Ibid., 24-5; 28-29.

12. Ibid., 29-30.

13. Ibid., 31-34.

14. Ibid., 77.

15. Ibid., 196.

16. Ibid., 74.

17. Deno John Geanakoplos, *Byzantium: Church, Society and Civilization Seen Through Contemporary Eyes* (Chicago: University of Chicago Press, 1984), 190.

18. Timothy Ware, *The Orthodox Church,* 78.

19. Steven Runciman, *The Eastern Schism* (Oxford: Oxford University Press, 1955), 31.

20. Timothy Ware, *The Orthodox Church,* 58-59.

21. Steven Runciman, *A History of the Crusades,* vol. 3. Reprint (London: Cambridge University Press, 1955),112-123.

22. Ibid., 130.

23. Timothy Ware, *The Orthodox Church,* 84.

24. Ibid., 86.

25. Ibid., 105-6.

26. Ibid., 110-12.

27. Ibid., 123.

28. *World Christian Encyclopedia,* vol. 1, 2d ed., s.v. "Egypt."

29. Timothy Ware, *The Orthodox Church,* 145-7.

30. Ibid., 152.

31. Ibid., 154-6.

32. Ibid., 157-8.

33. Ibid., 162.

34. Susan B. Glasser, "Legacy of Religious Struggle to Confront Pope in Ukraine," *The Washington Post,* 20 June 2001).

35. Walter Sawatsky, review of *Proselytism and Orthodoxy in Russia: The New War for Souls,* John Witte, Jr., and Michael Bourdeaux, eds., *Christian Century,* 21-18 March 2001, 32.

36. *The World Christian Encyclopedia,* s.v. "Romania."

37. Ibid., s.v. "Bulgaria."

38. Interview with Bulgarian Eastern Orthodox Church Diocese of the USA, Canada, and Australia, November 2001.

39. *The World Christian Encyclopedia,* s.v. "Georgia."

40. Ibid., s.v. "Cyprus."

41. Ibid., s.v. "Northern Cyprus."

42. Ibid., s.v. "Greece."

43. Timothy Ware, *The Orthodox Church,* 170.

44. *The World Christian Encyclopedia,* s.v. "Poland."

45. Ibid., s.v. "Albania."

46. Ibid., s.v. "Czech Republic" and s.v. "Slovakia."

47. Timothy Ware, *The Orthodox Church,* 172-191.

48. John H. Erickson, *Orthodox Christians in America* (New York: Oxford University Press, 1999), 129-131.

49. Timothy Ware, *The Orthodox Church,* 181.

50. Thomas E. Fitzgerald, *The Orthodox Church,* (Westport, Conn: Praeger, 1998), 120.

51. Thomas E. Fitzgerald, *The Orthodox Church,* 13.

52. John H. Erickson, *Orthodox Christians in America,* 46-47.

53. Thomas E. Fitzgerald, *The Orthodox Church,* 33.

54. Ibid., 30.

55. John H. Erickson, *Orthodox Christians in America,* 80-82.

56. Thomas E. Fitzgerald, *The Orthodox Church,* 70-71.

57. Ibid., 119.

58. John H. Erickson, *Orthodox Christians in America,* 87-9.

59. Timothy Ware, *The Orthodox Church,* 185.

60. Thomas E. Fitzgerald, *The Orthodox Church,* 57-62.

61. John H. Erickson, *Orthodox Christians in America,* 126.

62. Thomas E. Fitzgerald, *The Orthodox Church,* 114-115.

63. Ibid., 105-106.

64. Ibid., 90-92.

65. Ibid., 91.

❖ *The Greek Diaspora*

For generations, seagoing Greeks told stories to their families of faraway places where their ships had docked. These stories invariably included meeting *patriótes* (fellow countrymen) in restaurants and at card tables in exotic places. Years ago these chance encounters seemed wondrous. A Greek could travel halfway around the world and find a fellow Greek speaking the mother tongue and sharing common friends and relatives from a village or town in Greece. These transplanted Greeks comprised the Greek Diaspora still thriving throughout the world. According to a Greek government ministry, "[M]ore than five million Greeks (or more than half of Greece's domestic population) live outside of Greece's borders."[1]

The word, Diaspora, is one of various Greek terms commonly used when referring to Greeks living outside Greece. Diaspora comes from the Greek word, *diaspora,* which means "scattering." Another word, *omogenia,* translates as "same birth." (The English word, "homogeneous" comes from this root.) The Greek government uses the term Apodimos Ellinismos (Greeks Abroad) for the General Secretariat for Greeks Abroad, a department of the Foreign Affairs Ministry created to interface with Hellenes in other parts of the world. In this text the term Diaspora is used according to the *Oxford English Dictionary* definition: "a dispersion, as of people of a common national origin or of common beliefs."

However, this seemingly simple term, "Diaspora," creates controversy among the Greeks. Some of the controversies are semantic or academic, relating to the circumstances of settlement and migration. On a personal level, some individuals take exception to the term as not describing their own condition or attitudes. For instance, some Greek Americans say they are Americans of Greek ancestry, not Diaspora Greeks. For simplicity's sake, the *Oxford English Dictionary* definition is used here.

DEMOGRAPHICS

Accurate statistics about the various Diaspora populations and the definition of who belongs in them are difficult to obtain, but the

Greek national government published the following numbers in 1997:

America (US, Canada, and South America)	3,402,220
Oceania (Pacific islands, Australia, and New Zealand)	710,000
Asia	69,200
Europe	1,286,740
Africa	139,790
Total	5,607,950[2]

According to Richard Clogg in *The Greek Diaspora in the Twentieth Century,* the countries with the largest Greek Diaspora populations, in descending order, are the United States, Australia, the republics of the former Soviet Union, Canada, South Africa, Germany, Argentina, and Brazil.[3] Greek communities exist in other parts of the world also, including Egypt, England, Morocco, the countries surrounding the Persian Gulf, and Zaire.

A LONG HISTORY OF GREEKS ABROAD

Distant settlements date back to the times of the ancient Greeks who were not organized into a single nation but by city-states, leagues, and colonies throughout the Mediterranean, Asia Minor, and beyond. Herodotus, the Father of History, writes in the fifth century BC in *The Histories* about Greek colonies stretching from Olbia (near Odessa) on the Black Sea in the East to Thuria, Italy, in the West.[4] The Greek language and culture were not confined to the present-day boundaries of the Greek state, and were expanded further when Alexander the Great established Hellenistic communities from the great city of Alexandria, Egypt, to India, in the fourth century BC. Greeks, along with their language and thought, were prominent in the vast Byzantine Empire, which lasted one thousand years from 324 to 1453 A.D.

Throughout the centuries, countless small migrations occurred from the motherland and surrounding communities. A Greek presence was recorded in such distant places as the state of Florida in 1768; in Russia, in part due to the invitation of Catherine the Great, in 1779; and in Calcutta with the completion of a Greek Orthodox church in 1780. During the 1800s, migration from Greece accelerated primarily to the nearby areas of Russia, Romania, Turkey, and Egypt. However, migrations to further locations also occurred, such as the exodus to England of people from the island of Chios after the massacre during the Greek war of independence in 1822. In the late 1800s Greece, still recovering from the transition from the Ottoman Empire to a republic, was hit with an economic crisis in the 1890s. This economic crisis, plus the unequal distribution of land and the demands of the dowry system, propelled the mass migrations of the early 1900s worldwide.[5]

Richard Clogg in *The Greek Diaspora in the Twentieth Century* states that the largest migrations "occurred during the fifteen years or so before the Balkan Wars of 1912-13; in the aftermath of the Asia Minor 'catastrophe' of 1922; and during the 1950s and 1960s [as a result of devastation from World War II, the Civil War and an opening of immigration quotas abroad]. Together these great migrations laid the foundations of the present Greek communities in America, Canada, Australia, Germany and elsewhere."[6] Unavailable as yet are accurate numbers reflecting the effect of the collapse of communism in 1989 in the former Soviet Union and other Eastern bloc countries.

THE FOUR LARGEST DIASPORA

Unfortunately, space does not allow for the stories of all the countries with Greek Diaspora. Briefly described below are short histories of the four largest Diaspora today, in descending order of population.

UNITED STATES OF AMERICA

America is the home of the largest Greek Diaspora in the world, with a conservative estimate of one million persons of Greek ancestry.[7] The first three parts of this book discuss the Greek-American Diaspora and how they keep their heritage. See "Part One: The Enduring Traditions of Orthodoxy"; "Part Two: Customs of Everyday Life"; and Part Three: Feast Days, Fasts, 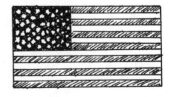 and Holidays." For specific details of their immigration, ethos, dilemmas, and institutions, see the chapters entitled "Introduction: Greek Americans Past and Present," "Greek American Values," and "Community Life."

For further reading see Charles Moskos' chapter entitled, "The Greeks in the United States" in *The Greek Diaspora in the Twentieth Century* edited by Richard Clogg.[8]

AUSTRALIA

While Australia is home to the second largest Greek Diaspora, with a conservative estimate of 450,000 Greek Australians,[9] the large influx of immigrants is relatively recent compared with the

immigration pattern of America. The first Greeks to arrive were seven seamen in 1827 from the island of Hydra. The rest of the 1800s saw sporadic immigration, such as two hundred Greeks seeking their fortune in the gold rush of the 1850s. By 1900, one thousand had immigrated, many opening shops selling fish and chips, milk shakes, and groceries.[10] Before World War II, there were fewer than ten thousand Greek Australians.[11]

In 1898 the foundations were laid for the first Greek Orthodox church, Holy Trinity, in Sydney, and in 1924 the Ecumenical Patriarchate of Constantinople assumed jurisdiction, creating the Archdiocese of Australia. New Zealand was made a separate diocese in 1970 with its own archbishop.[12]

Despite independence from Great Britain in 1901, a British way of life dominated Australia. Greeks, along with other immigrants, suffered discrimination and intolerance. This spurred their determination to stick together and continue the Greek culture. The immigrants formed communities called *koinótites*, patterned after local governments back in Greece, each with its own constitution, presidency, and council. The *koinótites* ran community affairs, including churches, and represented local Greek interests to the Australian government. On occasion this created tensions between the laity and the clergy.[13] Additional tensions sometimes surfaced among groups' loyalties based on controversial politics in Greece, such as the division over the Greek military dictatorship and the Greek leftists in 1967.

The major explosion in immigration to Australia occurred after World War II. It was spurred by both the devastation from war in Greece and a major new strategy of the Australian Department of Immigration in 1945 to open up the country to increase its popula-

tion and build its economy and defense. From 1947 to the early
1980s, close to 225,000 Greeks migrated to Australia. These immigrants came from many parts of Greece, boosting the total population of Greek Australians by 1988 to 350,000.[14] Approximately 657
institutions were started between 1897 and 1973, including
regional societies, independent chapters of American Hellenic Educational Progressive Association (AHEPA), church and philanthropic
organizations and sporting clubs.[15] Twenty-one soccer clubs formed
between 1951 and 1973, the most prominent being the nationally
dominant South Melbourne [Hellas] Soccer Club.[16] Other diverse
organizations include the Hellenic Australian Chamber of Commerce and Industry and the National Union of Greek Australia
Students (NUGAS).

In 1972 an Australian government policy relating to multiculturalism
positively impacted the Diaspora community. The government,
backing away from its former White Australia Policy, not only
lifted all forms of racial discrimination, but also recognized ethnic
diversity. In 1975 this official policy included spending public
money to sustain ethnic cultures, and helping the recent influx of
Greek immigrants to retain a strong Greek identity.[17] Typical was
the public grant resulting in a book, *Greek Pioneers of Western
Australia,* by R. A. Appleyard and John Yiannakis.[18] For a broad
history, read the definitive trilogy by Hugh Gilchrist: *Australians
and Greeks Volumes I, II and III.*

Thanks partially to help from both the Australian and Greek governments, the biggest Greek event in Australia has become the
Antipodes Festival (Glendi), held in Melbourne. Melbourne, with
a Greek-Australian population of 250,000 has the third largest
Greek population of any city in the world, after Athens and
Thessaloniki. The Festival includes a glendi on Lonsdale Street
celebrating Greek food, music arts, culture and tradition. Two
universities in Melbourne now have Hellenic centers: Australian-
Greek Resource and Learning Centre at the Royal Melbourne Institute of Technology and the National Centre for Hellenic Studies
and Research at La Trobe University. The neighborhood with the
highest concentration of Greeks is the southeastern suburb of
Oakleigh.

Given the recent influx of immigrants and the positive political
climate, many Greek Australians retain a strong Greek identity,
including speaking the language. They have built an impressive
number of Greek day and afternoon schools. Social services,

which are supported in part by the Australian government, include welfare centers, St. Basil's homes for the aged, retirement villages, and Provicare for drug and alcohol rehabilitation. Most church services at the 122 churches continue to be conducted in Greek, necessitated by a lack of Australian-born priests. In general, however, the hierarchy encourages bilingual church services wherever possible. More English-speaking priests will be entering the community soon with the opening of the Greek Orthodox Theological College of St. Andrew in Sydney in 1986. Change has already come to radio, television, and newspapers that now report in both Greek and English. The Greek Orthodox Archdiocese now owns *VEMA,* the largest newspaper (established in Sydney in 1913), and distributes it throughout Australia. Two 24-hour Greek-Australian radio stations broadcast from Melbourne and one 24-hour station from Sydney. Other shorter programs are also available along with access to television broadcasts directly from Greece. As of 1991, the highest concentrations of Greek Australians were in Melbourne (forty-eight percent), Sydney (thirty percent) and Adelaide (nine percent),[19] but communities are also active in Perth, Brisbane, and Tasmania.

Changes are occurring in the Greek-Australian community, including more education, upward mobility, moves to the suburbs, more interfaith marriages, and dynamic professional and academic communities. How this traditional Greek-Australian community will balance change and its role in a new global community remains to be seen.

Learn more about the Greek Diaspora in Australia on the Internet at:

www.ahepa.org.au
Australasian Hellenic Educational Progressive Association.
www.antipodesfestival.com.au
Antipodes Festival for Melbourne.
www.greekcity.com.au
Greek City. General website, primarily in Melbourne.
www.greekembassy.org.au
Embassy of Greece. Sydney, Australia.
www.hacci.com.au
Hellenic Australian Chamber of Commerce and Industry
Western Australia, Inc., Perth.
www.latrobe.edu.au/nhc
La Trobe University. National Centre for Hellenic Studies and
Research, Melbourne.
www.rmit.edu.au
Royal Melbourne Institute of Technology. Australian Greek Resource
and Learning Centre. Melbourne.
www.thegreekshop.com.au
The Greek Shop. Books and DVDs related to Greece. Newtown NSW.
Search engine
Greek Orthodox Archdiocese of Australia.

REPUBLICS OF THE FORMER SOVIET UNION

It is extremely difficult to obtain accurate numbers about the size
of the Greek Diaspora in the republics of the former Soviet Union.
According to the census taken at the time of the breakup of the
Soviet Union in 1989, the number was 356,000.[20]   Another source
estimates 500,000, divided as follows: 120,000 in Ukraine, 120,000
in Russia, 110,000 in Georgia, 57,000 in Kazakhstan, 15,000 in
Uzbekistan, 7,500 in Armenia, 3,000 in Kyrgyzstan, as well as
smaller numbers in Turkmenistan, Azerbaijan, Belarus, Lithuania,
Moldova, and other areas.[21]   One major difficulty in obtaining
accurate numbers was the reluctance of people under communism
to declare their ethnic background for fear of persecution.   This
was not the case before the advent of communism in 1917, when
it is thought there may have been 750,000 Greek people in the
Russian Empire.[22]

Of the four largest Diaspora today, most of the Greeks have lived
in this region far longer than those in the New World. Apostolos
Karpozilos, in a chapter entitled "The Greeks in Russia" in *The
Greek Diaspora in the Twentieth Century,* notes that ancient Greek
colonies populated the edges of the Black and Azov seas in today's
modern states of Georgia, Ukraine, and Russia. Some present-day

populations might be directly descended from such ancient Greek settlements in the Crimean Peninsula in the seventh century BC. As late as 1779, Catherine the Great, the Empress of Russia, at the request of the Greek population living in the Crimean Peninsula, helped organize and support the immigration of the region's Christian population to the north, resulting in the founding of the modern-day city of Mariupol, Ukraine, and numerous surrounding villages.[23]

While a small portion of the Greek population here dates back to the time of classical historian Herodotus, the contemporary Diaspora is the result of large migrations primarily from Asia Minor (present-day Turkey) because of wars and dislocation. Greeks lived for thousands of years in Asia Minor, especially in Constantinople, along the western coast known as Ionia, and the Pontos area of the northeast. With the fall of the Byzantine Empire in the fifteenth century, many fled to nearby Russia. Greeks from the Pontos area in the nineteenth and twentieth centuries gravitated toward Georgia and Russia. During the Crimean War (1856-1866) an estimated sixty thousand immigrants moved from Pontos to the Kuban and Stavropol areas. During the Russian Turkish War (1878-1884) an estimated 100,000 left Pontos for Russia. The largest and most dramatic migration of perhaps 200,000 Pontic Greeks occurred in 1918 when Russian troops withdrew from Pontos. They migrated to such cities as Bat'umi, Sokhumi, and Novorossiysk.[24] (The horrific removal and slaughter from 1913 to 1923 of the significant Greek, Armenian, and Assyrian communities in Asia Minor is beyond the scope of this section, but its importance is noted.)

Another dramatic chapter began for the Diaspora when the Russian Revolution of 1917 ended Tsarist Russia and inaugurated the Soviet Era and communism. The Greek Diaspora communities were divided about supporting the revolutionaries. Most remained neutral, but some Greeks became involved by organizing unions, publishing newspapers in Greek, and sponsoring ethnic clubs. As explained by Apostolos Karpozilos, the Soviet government policy initially was that "each ethnic group should develop its own language, literature and culture but within the socialist system." This created some controversy since the Pontic population spoke primarily Pontic, and the Mariupol Greeks had their own dialect. In 1926 demotic Greek (everyday language currently used in Greece) became the official language in the Greek communities of the

Soviet Union, necessitating Greek-language schools, teacher training, and textbooks. However, this tolerance ended with the devastating purges ordered by the Soviet leader, Stalin, and by 1938
Greek schools, publications, and organizations were completely
suppressed.[25] Again a traumatic shift occurred during this time,
with many Greeks exiled to Siberia and Central Asia. The communities suffered through World War II and again there were
massive exiles at end of the war. After the death of Stalin, the
new premier, Nikita Khrushchev, loosened restrictions in the 1950s
and 1960s, allowing some Greeks to go back to their homes in
such republics as Georgia, Russia, and Ukraine. Later, during the
liberalization of *perestroika* and *glasnost,* the Greek language was
reintroduced in the curriculum in Georgia and in some parts of the
Ukraine.[26]

Remarkably, when communism collapsed in 1989, a "submerged
ethnic Greek population" reemerged.[27] By 1998, the 150,000 Greeks
in Mariupol celebrated the 220th anniversary of the Greek founders
of the city with song and dance. They established a Greek Folk-
lore Museum. Today, Greek organizations include: the Confederation of Ukrainian Greek Associations, Confederation of Crimean
Greek Associations, and Greek-Ukranian Chamber of Commerce
listing one hundred Greek companies doing business in the Ukraine.[28]
The "Hellenes of Mariupol" website describes "The Azov region
[as] home to the largest concentration of Greeks in the Ukraine."[29]

But the political, economic, and social uncertainty resulting from
the dissolution of the Soviet Union has created tremendous strains.
Millions of people displaced during the Soviet era are relocating,
some of Greek descent desiring to go to Greece. Between 1980
and 1990 almost ten thousand migrated to Greece, which has now
set a quota of fifteen thousand Pontic Greek immigrants per year.[30]
(About 120,000 were expected to be repatriated to Greece by
2000.)[31] Meanwhile, the Greek government is helping start Greek
language programs, training teachers, opening cultural centers and
churches, and encouraging investments. In 1998 the Greek government sponsored a Greek Cultural Month in seven cities of the
Ukraine with concerts, theater, and lectures. The World Council of
Hellenes Abroad, a Diaspora organization, is setting up health
clinics in Armenia, Georgia, Kazakhstan, Southern Russia, Ukraine,
and Uzbekistan to assist the Greek Diaspora during yet another
traumatic transition.[32]

**Learn more about the Greek Diaspora in the republics of the former
Soviet Union on the Internet at:**

www.saeworld.org
> World Council of Hellenes Abroad. Go to "Medical Relief Program"
> for Armenia, Georgia, Kazakhstan, Southern Russia, Ukraine and
> Uzbekistan"

http://azov.nostos.gr/en
> "Hellenes of Mariupol"   History and activities of Greeks in Mariupol,
> Ukraine

search engine
> Greeks in individual countries listed above

CANADA

Greek Canadians make up the fourth largest Diaspora with approximately 200,000 people, over half of whom arrived from Greece after 1950.[33] Movement into Canada progressed slowly

for the first one hundred years. The first recorded Greek Canadian was George Kapiotis, a sailor in the British navy, who immigrated in 1851 and settled in Victoria, British Columbia.[34] A handful of Greeks followed, settling primarily in Vancouver, Toronto, and Montreal. But only two hundred Greek immigrants were recorded living in Canada in 1900, and the first Greek Orthodox church was established in 1906 in Montreal.[35]

From 1900 to 1945 Canadian government policy encouraged immigration for cheap labor to boost economic development. Greek men immigrated to make money but with the intention of returning to Greece. Many decided to stay, however. Women immigrants eventually followed and roots were established, resulting in organizations such as the Greek Orthodox church, AHEPA founded in 1928, and Anagennesis (Regeneration). As in America and Australia, these early immigrants endured prejudice from their status as "nonpreferred," and these organizations helped the newcomers deal with their difficulties.[36]

Matters radically changed after 1945 and World War II. Looking for a new life after the turmoil and ensuing Greek civil war from 1946 to 1949, immigration to Canada increased steadily. Canada's federal policy encouraged immigration as a way of developing its economy. From 1950 to 1980 over 131,000 Greeks arrived in Canada,[37] more than half of the Greek-Canadian population of 200,000 today. The liberalization of Canadian government policy, recession in Western Europe, and the military dictatorship begun in Greece in 1967 encouraged Greeks to immigrate to Canada. However, few had professional skills, financial resources, or much education. Consequently, they had low-status jobs and low income. Most of the time their jobs did not require them to learn English, and they continued to use the Greek language in their everyday lives.

With this large influx of immigrants, more churches and organizations were established. Power struggles developed between the clergy and laity over administration of the churches, and community divisions mirrored political controversies in Greece such as the military dictatorship in Greece in 1967. However, in 1971 a new Canadian federal policy of multiculturalism offered an opportunity for improvement in this growing community. Its purpose was to help all ethnic groups retain their language and culture, assist with integration of new immigrants, and assure equal opportunity.[38] Thus, full-time Greek daily and afternoon schools flourished. This encouraged Greek Canadians to celebrate and retain their Hellenic heritage. Today, the federal multiculturalism policy still exists, but it emphasizes helping groups with mainstream issues such as health care and discrimination. Fortunately, the roots of Greek Orthodox and Hellenic institutions were already thriving and the Greek communities remain strong.

The Greek Orthodox church, the largest organization, with 75 parishes, became the Greek Orthodox Metropolis of Toronto (Canada) in 1996 when the Ecumenical Patriarchate in Constantinople divided the Archdiocese of North and South America into three jurisdictions: America, Canada, and South America. Canada's Archbishop Metropolitan reports directly to the Ecumenical Patriarch. *The Orthodox Way,* published by the church, is the primary national newspaper. New priests may be trained at the recently opened Greek Orthodox Theological Academy of Toronto.

Today, most Greek Canadians live in the large urban centers of Toronto, Montreal, and Vancouver. According to *Statistics Canada* in 1991 metropolitan Toronto had about seventy-six thousand, the largest Greek community in Canada. Montreal was second with about fifty-five thousand,[39] and Vancouver with between seven thousand and fifteen thousand.[40] (All are conservative estimates.) Most of the remaining Greek Diaspora population lives in smaller cities throughout the provinces.

Toronto boasts the largest Greektown in the Americas. Anchored by Danforth Avenue between the Chester and Pape subway stops, the nearby area has churches, travel agencies, markets, and outdoor cafes, and many Toronto Greeks still live in the neighborhood. The largest Greek celebration, the second weekend of every August, is a giant street festival called the Taste of Danforth, which lasts for three days and attracts 400,000 people. Four Greek radio stations, three Greek TV stations and eight Greek newspapers keep the community informed. The Greek Community of Metropolitan Toronto, Inc. (GCMT), a nonprofit organization that owns four Greek Orthodox churches, provides social services and community outreach and facilitates many activities in the community that help preserve Hellenism. Each of the sixteen Greek Orthodox churches throughout Toronto and vicinity has its own Greek school programs, and the area has one full-time Greek Orthodox parochial day school.

The Greek community of Montreal exists within a predominantly French culture. In 1971 Quebec voted to make French the language of instruction in the schools. Over time, for the new Greek immigrants who did not speak French, everyday life became more difficult, and they were concerned that their children were not learning English. Many decided to leave, going to other parts of Canada, the United States, or back to Greece. Unlike the federal government, which stopped assisting with ethnic programs, the province of Quebec continues to help subsidize Greek-language schools. Many of the fifty-five thousand Greek Canadians living in Montreal today have moved into the middle class and into the suburbs, particularly the Chomedey district north of Montreal and the Brossard District south of the city. They attend the five Greek Orthodox churches in Montreal proper and six in the suburbs. Despite the cold winter, an annual March 25 Greek Independence Day parade is held.

Vancouver has three Greek Orthodox churches, one full-time webcasting station, two Greek radio shows, and one local bi-weekly newspaper, *Opinion*. As in other parishes across Canada, each of the three churches holds an annual Greek festival, and celebrates such holidays as Greek Independence Day and Oxi Day (commemoration of Greece's resistance to the Italian forces during World War II). Regional societies such as Alexander the Great Society, Cretan Association, and Laconian Community, provide opportunities for people from the same area of Greece to socialize and honor their shared roots.

According to sociology professor Peter Chimbos, the communities
are facing a number of changes: a drop in the number of new
immigrants, an increase in interfaith marriages, a decline in ethnic
group membership, and generational differences. However, he
predicts the rise of a middle class and more secular organizations
to meet the cultural and political needs, such as the Hellenic-
Canadian Congress, an umbrella organization formed in 1982 to
unite Canadians of Hellenic heritage and promote Hellenism.[41]
Efie Gavaki, an associate professor of sociology, observes that
during the 1990s "a new middle class has been emerging where
the majority of the Greeks are Canadian-born, educated, skilled
and trilingual and which is gradually changing the socio-cultural
profile of the group."[42]

Learn more about the Greek Diaspora in Canada on the Internet at:

www.ahepacanada.org
    American Hellenic Educational Progressive Association — AHEPA
    Canada. Links to chapters, its organizations, events, and programs.
www.greekvillage.com
    Greek Village.com. General portal for links to Greek Canadian and
    Diaspora organizations, all aspects of Greek community in Toronto,
    radio, news, resources in Greece. Toronto.
www.gocanada.org
    Greek Orthodox Metropolis of Toronto (Canada). Information
    relating to the Canadian Greek Orthodox community. East York,
    Ontario
www.greekradio.net
    Greek Radio Network/Canadian Hellenic Worldwide Broadcasting.
    Programming from Canada and Greece. Video clips. Montreal.
www.tasteofthedanforth.com
    Taste of the Danforth. Street festival in Toronto each August.
search engine
    Greeks in Canada

EXPECTATIONS AND CHALLENGES OF THE DIASPORA

The growing knowledge about fellow Greeks around the world
raises many expectations along with questions and challenges.
With the ability to travel to Greece by airplane in a few hours, call
or e-mail fellow Hellenes anywhere in the world, access daily
news on the Internet, invest in the Athens stock market, and form
international business alliances, a feeling of kinship raises expectations about celebrating Hellenism worldwide and the possible for-

mation of alliances for political, economic, and cultural purposes. Yet this new awareness also raises questions and challenges. Who is Greek? Who makes up the Diaspora? Are Greeks with ancestors going back several thousand years in Asia Minor in the Diaspora?[43] Do the people of the Diaspora and people in Greece know and understand each other? How are they alike, and how are they different? What is the Diaspora's role in its home country in extending Hellenism and Greek Orthodoxy? What is the responsibility of the Diaspora toward the Greek state in foreign and economic affairs? Can the Diaspora be organized, and for what purpose? What opportunities are presented and who benefits? How important is the Greek language in continuing Hellenism?

In the leading popular magazine of the Diaspora, *Odyssey: The World of the Greeks,* founder Gregory Maniatis maintains in an article entitled, "Hellenism: A Way Forward," that a true global community of Greeks does not yet exist. "We must build a bridge: first between Greece and Hellenes and Philhellenes everywhere; then between Hellenism and the world."[44] He envisions a definite role for the Diaspora in the preservation of Hellenism. "A Greek . . . lives in Greece; a Hellene can live anywhere. . . . A Hellene is anyone who takes any bit of our heritage — from Mycenae to Aristophanes, Byzantium, Daniel Webster, Byron, Mercouri, Elytis, Callas, Hadjidakis — and vows to the death to pass it on, in better shape than he found it, to the next generation."[45] However, a community of Hellenes is built on institutions, and the current ones are not yet adequate for the task.[46]

MEETING THE CHALLENGES

Individuals and organizations are trying to build the necessary bridges to answer the questions and challenges of the Diaspora. Whether scholars at conferences, writers of poetry, translators of contemporary Greek articles, individuals browsing the Internet and e-mailing distant relatives in another part of the world, each brings a unique perspective to the community. The following listing gives an idea of some of the activities and entities concerned with this endeavor.

PUBLICATIONS AND CONFERENCES

Heightened interest in the Diaspora has spawned various books,

journals, conferences, and popular magazines. In 1999 Richard
Clogg edited *The Greek Diaspora in the Twentieth Century,* a collection of essays by leading scholars about Greeks in Egypt, Australia, Canada, the United States, South Africa, and Russia. Putting
the Diaspora in historical context, he brings together academic
studies of seven countries.[47] A semiannual review, *Journal of the
Hellenic Diaspora* "views the modern Greek experience in a global
context in terms of its Balkan, Mediterranean and Diaspora dimensions."[48] The Greek Ministry of Foreign Affairs, General Secretariat
for Hellenes Abroad also publishes related articles on its website.[49]
Odyssey: The World of Greece, a popular magazine, features wide-
ranging articles on contemporary Greece and the Diaspora.[50]

Examples of conferences include "The Greek Diaspora in the Twenty-
first Century" held in October, 2000, at Hellenic College in Brookline,
Massachusetts; and a 1994 conference held at the Speros Vryonis
Center in Sacramento, California, with presentations published in a
book, *Greeks in English-Speaking Countries: Culture, Identity Politics.* [51]

GENERAL SECRETARIAT FOR GREEKS ABROAD
GENIKI GRAMMATIA APODIMOU ELLINISMOU (GGAE)

The Greek Ministry of Foreign Affairs established the General
Secretariat for Greeks Abroad (GGAE) in 1983 to plan, coordinate,
and implement policy regarding Diaspora Hellenes. From Greece's
perspective, "Greeks [are] an ideal bridge of friendship and cooperation between Greece and a host of foreign nations. A prosperous and active Hellenism abroad can lead to a prosperous Greece
in the international community, as well as to the multicultural
enrichment of the host countries. . . ."[52] Foreign Affairs Ministry
resources that help further that aim include:

- The Foundation for Hellenic Culture with branches in New
  York, Berlin, London, Paris, Odessa (Ukraine), and Alexandria
  (Egypt) sponsors art exhibits, lectures, and concerts in the
  Diaspora countries.

- Greek-language instructional materials for use in Greek schools
  abroad advance knowledge of the mother tongue.

- Filoxenia Program brings children of Greek origin living abroad
  to camps in Greece for three weeks in July and August. Age
  categories: 8-12 years old, 18-25 years old, and seniors over

65. Contact local Greek consulate and embassy.

- The GGAE website lists Greek organizations and individuals abroad, home pages from the Diaspora countries; a Manual for Greeks Living Abroad with information on Greek insurance, education, investment, repatriation, military service, laws in host countries regarding Greeks, and other laws; and a Manual on Returning to Greece. (Manuals in Greek language only.) General Secretariat for Greeks Abroad at www.mfa.gr/ggae

WORLD COUNCIL OF HELLENES ABROAD
SYMVOUILO APOTHIMOU ELLENISMOU (SAE)

World Council of Hellenes Abroad (SAE) was created in 1995 as a nonprofit, nongovernmental organization by a Greek government presidential decree to advise Greece on the interests of the Diaspora and to act as a formal entity for dialogue between the Hellenes abroad and Greece. SAE, with the financial assistance of the Greek government, hosts a meeting of Diaspora delegates every two years in Thessaloniki, location of the headquarters of World SAE. Under SAE are four regional SAEs, each with its own agenda and vice-president: North and South America, Asia-Africa, Europe, and Oceania, as well as a vice-president for Cyprus.

Goals include strengthening the ties among the Diaspora and Greece, promoting Hellenic heritage, and strengthening Greece's political position in world affairs. At the Fourth World SAE Convention in Thessaloniki in 2001, 850 delegates adopted resolutions relating to such matters as the political division of Cyprus, Greece's role in the Balkans, protection of the Aegean, promotion of the Olympic Games 2004 in Athens (and volunteer recruitment), and promotion of Hellenic education and culture abroad. A primary project continues to be the medical relief program for the former republics of the Soviet Union. World Council of Hellenes Abroad (SAE), headquarters Thessaloniki at www.saeamerica.org

AMERICAN HELLENIC EDUCATIONAL PROGRESSIVE ASSOCIATION (AHEPA)

American Hellenic Educational Progressive Association has chapters throughout the United States, Canada, Greece, and Cyprus and a close association with AHEPA Australasia (Australia and New

Zealand). Its international projects include erecting at the American Embassy in Athens a statue of George Marshall, author of the Marshall Plan that resulted in aid to Greece after World War II. In 1999 it created AHEPA International, a committee of leaders from AHEPA from the aforementioned countries to "implement common worldwide goals and objectives benefiting Hellenism." Two of its major goals are the return of the Parthenon marbles to Athens from the British Museum in London, and the organization of volunteers throughout the Diaspora to help with the 2004 Olympic Games in Athens. www.ahepa.org

FOUNDATIONS

Foundations funded by wealthy estates from Greece and Cyprus have begun advancing Hellenism in the United States: The Alexander S. Onassis Public Benefit Foundation at the Onassis Cultural Center in New York, sponsors lectures, cultural events, visiting professors from Greece, and scholarships. The Stavros S. Niarchos Foundation sponsors a Hellenic Studies lecture series at Queens College, City University of New York, Queens, New York, and contributes to various Greek-American institutions. In honor of the late Greek President Constantinos Karamanlis, his family foundation established the Karamanlis Chair in Hellenic and Southeastern European Studies at Tufts University School of Law and Diplomacy in Medford, Massachusetts. A. G. Leventis Foundation of Cyprus sponsored one of the Cypriot galleries in the Cesnola Collection at the Metropolitan Museum of Art in New York.

MEDIA

Diverse communication links connect the Diaspora and Greece. In the United States newspapers such as *Ethnikos Kiryx (National Herald), The Greek Star,* and the *Hellenic Journal* carry regional, national, and foreign news. The magazine *Odyssey: The World of Greece,* features stories about Hellenes around the globe. Local radio and television shows feature news, discussions, and music.

New technologies are rapidly changing the media scene. Greek and Canadian radio stations on the Internet are replacing the crackling shortwave radio. Viewers around the world receive directly from Greece popular television shows such as Antenna, ERT, Mega, Star, and Alpha via cable and satellite dishes. Via the

Internet, information relating to Greece — from the sculptures on the Parthenon to a Greek festival in Toronto to ancient Olympic games — are instantly accessible. You can organize a cause, meet Hellenes in a chat room, or write an e-mail to a Greek cousin in South Africa. The promise of the Internet in linking the Diaspora tantalizes, but it remains to be seen how effective this medium will be. Economically, shipping costs for small items outside one's country remain prohibitive. Politically, it is as difficult on the Internet as in real life to unify people for a cause such as the preservation of the beach at Marathon. Dedication, hard work, and economic viability are required to maximize this enormous potential.

GREEK DIASPORA INTERNET WEBSITES

The Internet websites listed below offer examples of ways to explore the world of Greece. It is not comprehensive, but many of these sites provide links to other websites. Websites are in English unless Greek language noted. Software is available to convert (not translate) unintelligible characters into the Greek language at www.hri.org/fonts.

Caveat: Internet websites are unpredictable. Some stay current with frequent updates, others are accessible but with outdated information, and a few vanish. If a website does not appear after entering its address, go to a search engine and enter the name.

Disclaimer: This listing is not an endorsement of a website's content, products, or vendors.

GENERAL DIRECTORIES AND SEARCH ENGINES

www.gogreece.com
> GoGreece.com. General portal for access to information regarding culture, business, travel, government, sports, classified, and shopping. Santa Monica, California.

www.in.gr

In.gr. Largest Greek portal with Greek text. Links to most major
Greek newspapers and magazines. Large index of Greek websites.
Lambrakis Press, Athens.

www.robby.gr

Robby, the Hellenic Search Engine. Information and links relating to
past and present Greece and Hellenes, art and culture, education,
sports, health and medicine, stocks, travel, business, and
government. Athens.

COMMERCIAL

www.amcham.gr

American-Hellenic Chamber of Commerce. Non-profit organization of
American companies doing business in Greece. Sponsors conferences
and exhibitions, and facilitating investment opportunities. Member of
US Chamber of Commerce. Athens and Thessaloniki.

www.caratzas.com

Caratzas Books/Melissa International Publications, Ltd. Primarily
scholarly books relating to Hellenism, Byzantium, the Ottomans, and
modern Greece. New Rochelle, New York/Athens.

www.filetron.com/grkmanual

Greek Folk Dance Resource Manual. Listing of resources relating to
Greek folkdancing, music, costumes, videos, and events and links to
other information and organizations. San Francisco.

www.greekbooks.gr

Greekbooks.gr. Large selection of books in Greek. Athens.

www.greeceinprint.com

Greece in Print. Selection of Greek-content books, books by Greek
authors, CD-ROMs, audio and video materials. Cosmos Publishing,
River Vale, New Jersey.

www.greekmusic.com

Greekmusic.com. Selection of modern and traditional Greek music,
videos and CD-Roms. Sample some selections online before
purchase. Greek Music and Video. Astoria, New York.

www.greekshops.com

GreekShops.com. Selection of Greek-related items, including food,
ceramics, books, maps, calendars, apparel, accessories, floral
arrangements in Greece, ancient Greek replicas, folk art, jewelry,
music, and software. Santa Monica, California.

www.hermesexpo.com

Hermes Expo International. Tradeshows in Chicago, New York, and
Atlantic City showcasing Greek products and services. Havertown,
Pennsylvania.

GOVERNMENTS

www.greekembassy.org
   Embassy of Greece, Washington, DC. Official Greek government website features press statements, news, politics, biographies of current office holders in Greece, visa applications, links to consulates, and Greek government ministries. Washington, D.C.
www.mfa.gr
   Hellenic Republic Ministry of Foreign Affairs/General Secretariat for Greeks Abroad. Official site explains the policies of the Greek government toward Diaspora Greeks and provides links to "Greek Home Pages of the Diaspora." English and Greek. Athens.
www.usembassy.gr
   United States Embassy, Athens, Greece. Official website contains information on current issues/news, U.S. policies, consular services, and regional security offices. Athens

HELLENIC CULTURE

www.ancientgreece.com
   Ancient Greece. General information from art and architecture to history. Links to other resources. New York.
www.culture.gr
   Odysseus, the WWW Server of the Hellenic Ministry of Culture. Links to Greek museums, monuments, and archaeological sites, as well as contemporary culture, events, and organizations. Athens.
www.geocities.com/rebetology
   The Institute of Rebetology. An archive of articles about *rebétika* (a special Greek music) and links to other sources. London.
www.filetron.com/grkmanual
   Greek Folk Dance Resource Manual. Links to articles on Greek dancing, music, costumes, pertinent events, and groups, such as the Greek Orthodox Folk Dance Festival in the Greek Orthodox Diocese of San Francisco. San Francisco.
www.umass.edu/aesop
   Aesop's Fables. Fables retold with illustrations by art students at the University of Massachusetts. Amherst, Massachusetts.
www.museum.upenn.edu
   University of Pennsylvania Museum. "Search" for "The Ancient Greek World." Information on the land, time periods, pottery, daily life, economy, religion, and mythical characters. Philadelphia.
www.grdance.org
   Theatre Dora Stratou: The Living Museum of Greek Dance. Information about the Dora Stratou dance company, shows, classes, costume collection. Nonprofit organization supported by Greek Ministry of Culture and the Greek

www.perseus.tufts.edu
>   The Perseus Digital Library. Digital library relating to the ancient
>   Greek classics. Go to "Classics," then "Greek Historical Overview,"
>   then "Contents" for general summaries and links to visual arts at
>   universities around the world, archaeological sites, and primary texts
>   and documents. Tufts University. Medford, Massachusetts.

www.tlg.uci.edu
>   The Thesaurus Linguae Graecae (TLG)/A Digital Library of Greek
>   Literature. Explains the TLG project at the University of California,
>   Irvine, to digitize all ancient texts from Homer to the present era.
>   Partially completed text available only on CD-ROM and to institutions
>   with a website license. Irvine, California.

MEDIA

News Sources

www.ana-mpa.gr
>   Athens News Agency-Macedonia Press Agency. National news
>   agency of Greece provides stories from Greece and other
>   international agencies. Athens.

www.athensnews.gr
>   *Athens News.* Weekly edition of Athens newspaper in English.
>   Athens.

www.athenspost.com
>   Athenspost.com. Articles relating to Greece and Greeks abroad from
>   newspapers around the world. Links to other sites. Compiled by
>   Worldnews.com. Athens.

www.ekathimerini.com
>   *Kathimerini.* Daily English edition of Athens newspaper. Athens.

www.helleniccomserve.com
>   Hellenic Communication Service. Online-only articles and news
>   relating to Greece and the Greek-American community (emphasis on
>   New England). Portsmouth, New Hampshire.

www.thenationalherald.com
>   *The National Herald* Online. Daily Greek-American newspaper.
>   Weekend edition in English. Long Island City, New York.

Magazines

www.greece.gr
>   Greece Now. Articles on contemporary Greek politics, finance,
>   lifestyles, restaurant and hotel recommendations, travel, and festival
>   events. Compiled by the Greek government. Athens.

www.odyssey.gr
>   *Odyssey: The World of Greece.* Articles with a contemporary angle on
>   Greece and Greeks abroad. Washington, DC.

<u>Webcasting/Radio</u>

www.gaepis.org.
> GAEPIS (Greek American Educational Public Information System, Inc.). A nonprofit radio station dedicated to the preservation and promotion of Hellenic heritage in the United States. Brooklyn, New York.

www.voanews.com/greek
> Voice of America Greek Services. Daily webcasts in Greek with general news and occasional features on the Greek-American community. Washington, DC.

ORGANIZATIONS

The following two sites give lists and links to many of the Hellenic organizations in the Diaspora. To find additional organizations, such as those listed in the "Community Life" chapter, use a search engine, entering the name of the organization.

www.omogenia.com
> Omogenia.com. List of sample organizations inside and outside of Greece. Go to "Organizations," then "Organizations and Societies." Go to letter of alphabet for listings in alphabetical order.

www.ggae.gr
> General Secretariat for Greeks Abroad. Hellenic Republic Ministry of Foreign Affairs. Listing of some organizations
> throughout the Diaspora. Go to "Greeks of the Diaspora," then "Greek Home Pages of the Diaspora." Athens.

STUDY AND ENRICHMENT PROGRAMS IN GREECE

The following are a few of the educational institutions in Greece accessible to English-speaking students. Most schools conduct classes in English unless learning the Greek language is the purpose of the class. Some institutions give academic credit; others specialize in not-for-credit offerings simply for enjoyment and enrichment. Use the search engines mentioned below for additional schools and programs.

www.acg.edu
> American College of Greece. Also known as Deree/Pierce College. Athens.

www.ahepa.org and www.uindy.gr
> AHEPA and the University of Indianapolis. One-month summer program in Greece for students 17-20 years of age. Study modern

and ancient Greece for transferable college credit. Based in Athens
with excursions.

www.anatolia.edu.gr/act

American College of Thessaloniki. Thessaloniki.

www.arcadia.edu/cea

Arcadia University Center Education Abroad. Affiliated with
Arcadia University (formerly Beaver College) (Glenside,
Pennsylvania), Athens.

www.ascsa.edu.gr

American School of Classical Studies at Athens. ASCSA is the official
link between American archaeologists/classicists and the
Archaeological Service of the Greek Ministry of Culture. Affiliated
with Princeton University (Princeton),   Athens.

www.athenscentre.gr

The Athens Centre. Classes for cultural enrichment and learning the
Greek language. Athens.

www.cyathens.org

College Year in Athens. One-year undergraduate program.
(Cambridge, Massachusetts), Athens.

www.ggae.gr

General Secretariat for Greeks Abroad. Hellenic Republic Ministry of
Foreign Affairs. Greek government-sponsored summer camps and
enrichment programs in Greece for children ages 8-12 with at least
one parent of Greek descent. *Camp and program site in Greek only.*

www.grdance.org

Theatre Dora Stratou: The Living Museum of Greek Dance. One-
week workshops on Greek folk dance and folk culture in English
during August. Supported by the Greek Ministry of Culture and the
Greek National Tourism Organization.   Athens.

www.greekingreece.gr

Ikarian Centre. Summer School Greek Language Program. Greek
language courses for non-native speakers. Classes conducted in a
village on the island of Ikaria from Easter to October.

www.greeksummer.org and www.afs.edu.gr

American Farm School. Five-week service program in small Greek
villages for U.S. and international teenagers for community service
credit. Includes travel in Greece. Based in Thessaloniki.

www.hau.gr

Hellenic American Union. Classes teaching Greek and English
languages, teacher education and computers. Geared to Greek
students. Learn Greek online. Athens.

www.ionianvillage.org

Ionian Village. Summer camp for ages 12-19. Affiliated with the
Greek Orthodox Archdiocese of America, New York.   Located forty-
five miles south of Patras.

www.Lmu.edu.

Loyola Marymount University and the Basil P. Caloyeras Center for
Modern Greek Studies. Study Abroad: The Odyssey Program. Five-
week summer program in Greece for college students for
transferable credit. Based on the island of Spetses with excursions.

www.nyu.edu/fas/summer/athens/index.html
New York University. Summer Study Abroad for college students includes language, history and Greek for transferable credit. Based in Athens with excursions.

www.paideiaonline.org
Center for Hellenic Studies Paideia, University of Connecticut, U of Athens, Aristotle U, U of Macedonia and U of Aegean. Study modern and transferable university credits. Based in Thessaloniki with excursions.

www.robby.gr
Robby, The Hellenic Search Engine. Go to "Education" for academic and enrichment opportunities. Athens.

www.ulv.edu/athens
University of La Verne. Affiliated with University of La Verne (La Verne, California)   Athens.

www.usembassy.gr
United States Embassy — Athens, Greece. For information on the Fulbright Program and links to American schools in Greece, go to "About Greece/General Information," "American Educational Institutions in Greece."

TRAVEL TO GREECE

To date, the best overview of cultural attractions, recreation, accommodations, and dining remains a printed guidebook. While the following websites are helpful, none are totally comprehensive and may contain commercial bias.

www.gogreece.com
Gogreece.com. "Travel & Leisure" for sights, hotels, maps and tips.

www.greektourism.com
Greek National Tourism Organization. Official Greek government website. Athens headquarters with branches worldwide.

www.greektravel.com
A Travel Guide to Greece. Matt Barrett's view of how to travel in Greece. Reviews of accommodations and restaurants. Tips and warnings. Athens.

www.robby.gr
Robby, The Hellenic Search Engine. Listing of sights, hotels, agents, transportation.   Go to "Travel and Tourism."   Athens

www.travelinfo.gr
Travelinfo.gr. Listing of sights, hotels, maps, and travel tips.

1. Stavros Lambrinidis, "The Greeks in the World: The Hellenic Diaspora," *Thesis: A Journal of Foreign Policy,* vol. 1, issue 1 (Spring 1997) www.greekembassy.org/wgreece/greece/diaspora.html.

2. Ibid.

3. Richard Clogg, "The Greek Diaspora: the Historical Context," in *The Greek Diaspora in the Twentieth Century,* Richard Clogg, ed., (New York: St. Martin's Press, Inc., 1999), 14.

4. Aubrey de Selincourt, trans., *Herodotus the Histories.* Reprint (Middlesex, England: Penguin Books, 1987), 8, 11.

5. Efie Gavaki, "Greek Immigration to Quebec: The Process and the Settlement," *Journal of the Hellenic Diaspora,* vol. 17.1 (New York: Pella Publishing Co., Inc., 1991), 71-2.

6   Richard Clogg, "The Greek Diaspora: the Historical Context," in *The Greek Diaspora in the Twentieth Century,* 11.

7. U.S. Bureau of the Census, QT-02 "Profile of Selected Social Characteristics: 2000."

8. Charles Moskos, "The Greeks in the United States," in *The Greek Diaspora in the Twentieth Century,* Richard Clogg, ed., (New York: St. Martin's Press, Inc., 1999), 103-119.

9. Rev. Miltiades Chryssavgis, "The Greek Orthodox Church," in *The Australian People, an Encyclopedia of the Nation, Its People and Their Origins,* James Jupp, ed., (Melbourne, Cambridge University Press, 2001).

10. Nicholas Doumanis, "The Greeks in Australia," in *The Greek Diaspora in the Twentieth Century,* Richard Clogg, ed., (New York: St. Martin's Press, Inc., 1999), 59-60.

11. Miltiades Chryssavgis, "The Greek Orthodox Church," 409.

12. *Handbook 2001* of the Greek Orthodox Archdiocese of Australia (Melbourne: Venus Press, 2000), 38-39.

13. Nicholas Doumanis, "The Greeks in Australia," 61-62.

14. Ibid., 64-65.

15. Ibid., 71.

16. Victoria Kyriakopoulos, "You'll Never Walk Alone," in *Odyssey: The World of Greece,* January/February, 1999), 60.

17. Nicholas Doumanis, "The Greeks in Australia," 74-75.

18. R. A. Appleyard and John Yiannakis, *Greek Pioneers of Western Australia* (Nedlands, Western Australia: University of Western Australia Press, 2002).

19. Nicholas Doumanis, "The Greeks in Australia," 66.

20. Richard Clogg, "The Greek Diaspora: The Historical Context," 12.

21. Dionyssis Kalamvrezos, "The Greeks of the Former USSR," *The National Herald,* 10-11 March 2001).

22. Ibid.

23. Apostolos Karpozilos, "The Greeks in Russia," in *The Greek Diaspora in the Twentieth Century* (New York: St. Martin's Press, Inc., 1999), 137.

24. Ibid., 138-9.

25. Ibid., 148-153.

26. Ibid., 152-4.

27. Richard Clogg, "The Greek Diaspora: The Historical Context," in *The Greek Diaspora in the Twentieth Century,* 12.

28. Rachel Howard, "Dancing at the End of History: The Greeks of the Ukraine," *Odyssey: The World of Greece,* November/December 1998, 47-8.

29. "Hellenes of Mariupol" at http://azov.nostos.gr/en, 2001.

30. Apostolos Karpozilos, "The Greeks in Russia," 154.

31. Dionyssis Kalamvrezos, "The Greeks of the Former USSR."

32. The World Council of Hellenes Abroad (SAE) at www.saeworld.org. 2001.

33. Efie Gavaki, "The Greeks in Canada: Where Are We Today: A Socio-economic Profile," in *Hellenism in the Twenty-first Century: International Relations, Economy, Society, Politics, Culture, and Education,* St. Constantinides and Theo. Pelagides, eds., (Athens: Papazisis Press, 2000), 343. See also www.statcan.ca/english/census96/feb17/eo1can.htm

34. Efie Gavaki, "Greek Immigration to Quebec: The Process and the Settlement," 74.

35. Peter D. Chimbos, "The Greeks in Canada: An Historical and Sociological Perspective in *The Greek Diaspora in the Twentieth Century,* Richard Clogg, ed., (New York: St. Martin's Press Inc., 1999), 88-90

36. Ibid., 88-90.

37. Gavaki, "The Greeks in Canada," 343.

38. Chimbos, "The Greeks in Canada," 97.

39. Gavaki, "The Greeks in Canada," 344-5.

40. Correspondence Rev. Panagiotis Pavlakos, Sts. Nicholas & Dimitrios Greek Orthodox Church, Vancouver, British Columbia, 8 June 2001.

41. Chimbos, "The Greeks in Canada," 97-100.

42. Gavaki, "The Greeks in Canada," 355.

43. Renee Hirschon, "Identity and the Greek State: Some Conceptual Issues and Paradoxes" in *The Greek Diaspora in the Twentieth Century,* Richard Clogg, ed., (New York: St. Martin's Press, Inc., 1999), 158-180.

44. Gregory Maniatis, "Hellenism: A Way Forward," *Odyssey: The World of Greece,* September/October, 1998), 33.

45. Ibid., 37.

46. Ibid., 33.

47. Richard Clogg, ed. *The Greek Diaspora in the Twentieth Century* (New York: St. Martin's Press, Inc., 1999).

48. *Journal of the Hellenic Diaspora* (New York: Pella Publishing Co., Inc.)

49. General Secretariat for Greeks Abroad, Greek Ministry of Foreign Affairs, at www.mfa.gr/ggae.

50. *Odyssey: The World of Greece* (Athens: Zephyr Publications).

51. Christos P. Ioannides, ed. *Greeks in English-speaking Countries: Culture, Identity, Politics* (New Rochelle, New York/Athens: Aristides D. Caratzas), 1994.

52. Stavros Lambrinidis, "The Greeks in the World: The Hellenic Diaspora," *Thesis: A Journal of Foreign Policy,* vol. 1, issue 1 (Spring 1997) www.greekembassy.org/wgreece/greece/diaspora.html.

EPILOGUE

I have respectfully tried to increase the reader's understanding of Hellenism and Orthodoxy as observed by Greek Americans and others around the world. Ultimately, one realizes the challenge of treating these topics in a single book. I hope, however, to have heightened your interest in these two great heritages, making clear the universal, timeless qualities that make them relevant and accessible to all.

Hellenism, developed by the ancient Greeks, emphasized human scale and spirit with its belief that people could use reason to solve problems, articulate dilemmas, create beautiful objects, question, observe, and compromise. A classical drama such as *Orestes* by Euripides poses the problem of how to stop the cycle of revenge killings, a dilemma still plaguing humans all over the world today. The idea of democracy — that political power resides in a collective body, not in one individual — came from ancient Athens and is now the leading form of government around the world. Classical Greek sculpture depicting the majesty of the human form continues to be admired and copied. These ideas and many more from Hellenism are the basis of Western civilization, because admirers of the Greeks (Philhellenes) such as the Romans, intellectuals of the Renaissance, and the founders of America recognized their universal value.

Orthodoxy, one of the oldest religions in the world, proclaims the timeless Christian message of love, forgiveness, kindness, and eternal life. Christianity's broad appeal has made it the religion with the most adherents today. Of special interest is the historic connection between Hellenism and Christianity. Christianity was formulated in the Greek language and Greek thought. Greek therefore is the historic language of Christianity in the way that Hebrew is the historic language of Judaism and Sanskrit of Hinduism. Thus, Hellenism and Christianity were historically joined.

For those born into this heritage, may this book increase your understanding and appreciation. Perhaps it will inspire you to deepen your commitment to your legacy. Your conviction and hard work will perpetuate the treasure handed down through the centuries.

For individuals who were not born into this heritage, but who have become interested through other pathways, I say, *welcome!* This book was also written for you, to explain that the Orthodox Christian message embraces you with love and warmth. The Hellenic tradition invites everyone to share its universal heritage. Isocrates, a Greek orator in the fourth and fifth centuries BC, stated in *Panegyrikos (Encomium of Athens):* "The name 'Hellenes' suggests no longer a race, but a way of thinking, and . . . the title 'Hellenes' is applied rather to those who share our culture than those who share our blood."

In this spirit, everyone is invited to celebrate these remarkable customs and traditions.

— Marilyn Rouvelas

APPENDIX
REVISIONS TO FIRST EDITION

The Second Edition of *A Guide to Greek Traditions and Customs in America* contains the following updates, additions, and corrections for the first edition.

UPDATES

"The Preface," "Acknowledgments," and "Introduction: Greek Americans Past and Present," and "Community Life" have been rewritten entirely. Minor secular updates appear throughout the book

UNCHANGED

"Parts One, Two, and Three" remain essentially the same as a memorial to the book's late religious editor, His Grace Bishop George of Komanon (formerly Rev. Fr. George Papaioannou). This loving individual always emphasized the compassion of the Greek Orthodox faith and the value of the Greek secular heritage. That spirit is preserved. While many new religious books have been published since 1993, they have not been added. That would have required integration into the text without Bishop George's guidance. I suggest readers refer to "Further Reading" in *The Orthodox Church* (New Edition) by Timothy Ware.[1] Consult with your priest if you have additional questions.

ADDITIONS

A few traditions from the island of Cyprus have been added throughout the book. Although Cyprus is not politically Greek, its language, religion, and secular culture are.

"The Historic Orthodox Church" chapter puts the Greek Orthodox Church in America into its context as part of historic worldwide Orthodoxy practiced in different countries for many centuries. A listing of Orthodox Internet websites is included.

"The Greek Diaspora" chapter briefly explains that Greek Americans are part of a contemporary Greek Diaspora around the world where Greek immigrants and their children perpetuate Hellenism and Orthodoxy. A listing of Greek Internet websites is included.

CORRECTIONS

The following substantive errors appeared in earlier printings and have been corrected.

p. 33   Since it is possible for a baby to receive its name in a religious service on the eighth day, modify references to first time use of the name at the baptism. (Correct text on pp. 37, 38, 165, and 171.)

p. 35   Delete the quote from Matt. 5:16.

p. 61   Item number 2. Delete the phrase, "The couple must commit" and substitute "the couple should be willing."

p. 72   Delete reference to taking Holy Oil home from Holy Unction. Only a priest can administer Holy Unction. (Correct text p. 113.)

p. 75   Minor orders are ordained by a bishop outside the framework of a Divine Liturgy and outside the sanctuary (altar area).

p. 95   Change the name day of St. Theodore to the first Saturday of Lent.

p. 100   In the first paragraph, change November 9 to December 12 for the St. Spyridon celebration in Corfu.

p. 124   Change "C" to "XC" on the illustration of the *sfrayitha*.

p. 143   Fourth paragraph: Add: "The Greek Orthodox Church does not believe that a deceased person's soul stays on earth for forty days." (Correct text pp. 133, 146, and 147, and 293.)

p. 261   Delete "baptism" from prohibited activities in paragraph on "Demeanor."

p. 274   Delete reference to "Deaf Week."

p. 294   Holy Apostles Lent begins the Monday following All Saints Sunday.

p. 309   The Assyrian Church of the East broke away in 431 over the definition of the nature of Christ and His mother, Mary. The Non-Chalcedonian Oriental Orthodox broke away in 451 over the definition of the dual nature of Christ. The classification of the Church of the East in the Oriental Orthodox church is debatable.

p. 334   The correct dates for St. Innocent are 1797-1879.

---

1.   Timothy Ware, *The Orthodox Church*. New Edition (London: Penguin Books, 1997), 329-344.

BIBLIOGRAPHY – WORKS CITED

Appleyard, R. A., and John Yiannakis. *Greek Pioneers of Western Australia.* Nedlands, Western Australia: University of Western Australia Press, 2002.

Athenagoras. "Encyclical on the Greek Language Schools." August 7, 1937. In *The Odyssey of Hellenism in America,* by George Papaioannou. Thessaloniki, Greece: Patriarchal Institute for Patristic Studies, 1985.

———. "An Encyclical on Marriages and Family." September 27, 1948. In *The Odyssey of Hellenism in America* by George Papaioannou.

Calivas, A. C. *Great Week and Pascha in the Greek Orthodox Church.* Brookline, Mass.: Holy Cross Orthodox Press, 1992.

Callinicos, Constance. *American Aphrodite: Becoming Female in Greek America.* New York: Pella Publishing Company, Inc., 1990.

Chimbos, Peter D. "The Greeks in Canada: An Historical and Sociological Perspective." In *The Greek Diaspora in the Twentieth Century,* edited by Richard Clogg. New York: St. Martin's Press, Inc., 1999.

Chryssavgis, Miltiades. "The Greek Orthodox Church." In *The Australian People, an Encyclopedia of the Nation, Its People and Their Origins,* edited by James Jupp. Melbourne: Cambridge University Press, 2001.

Clogg, Richard, ed. *The Greek Diaspora in the Twentieth Century.* New York: St. Martin's Press, Inc., 1999.

Constantelos, Demetrios J. *The Greeks, Their Heritage and Its Value Today.* Brookline, Mass.: Hellenic College Press, 1996.

———. *Understanding the Greek Orthodox Church: Its Faith, History and Practice.* Brookline, Mass.: Hellenic College Press, 1990.

Cummings, D. *The Rudder.* Chicago: The Orthodox Christian Educational Society, 1957.

d'Aulaire, Ingri, and Edgar Parin. *Book of Greek Myths.* Garden City, N.Y.: Doubleday and Company, 1962.

Davidson, Catherine Temma. *The Priest Fainted.* New York: Henry Holt and Company, 1998.

de Selincourt, Aubrey, trans. *Herodotus the Histories.* 1954. Reprint. Middlesex, England: Penguin Books, 1987.

Doumanis, Nicholas. "The Greeks in Australia." In *The Greek Diaspora in the Twentieth Century,* edited by Richard Clogg.

Economou, Steven G. *Greek Proverbs*. N.p. 1976.

Erickson, John H. *Orthodox Christians in America*. New York: Oxford University Press, 1999.

FitzGerald, Kyriaki Karidoyanes. *Women Deasons in the Orthodox Church: Called to Holiness and Ministry*. Brookline, Massachusetts: Holy Cross Orthodox Press, 1998.

Fitzgerald, Thomas E. *The Orthodox Church*. Westport, Conn.: Praeger, 1998.

Frangos, Steve. "Grassroots Efforts to Preserve Hellenism." 17-18 January 2004. *The National Herald*.

"Future Theological Agenda of the Archdiocese — Conclusion." *Orthodox Observer*, March, 1991.

Gage, Eleni N. *North of Ithaka*. New York: St. Martin's Press, 2004.

Gage, Nicholas, *Eleni*. New York: Random House, 1983.

———. *Hellas: A Portrait of Greece*. American Heritage Press, 1971. 2d. ed. New York: Villard Books, 1986. 3d ed. Greece: Efstathiadis Group, 1987.

———. *A Place for Us*. Boston: Houghton Mifflin Company, 1989.

Gavaki, Efie. "Greek Immigration to Quebec: The Process and the Settlement." *Journal of the Hellenic Diaspora,* vol. 17.1. New York: Pella Publishing Company, 1991.

———, Efie. "The Greeks in Canada: Where Are We Today: A Socio-Economic Profile." In *Hellenism in the Twenty-first Century: International Relations, Economy, Society, Politics, Culture, and Education.* edited by St. Constantinides and Theo. Pelagides. Athens: Papazisis Press, 2000.

Geanakoplos, Deno John. *Byzantium: Church, Society, and Civilization: Seen Through Contemporary Eyes*. Chicago: University of Chicago Press, 1984.

Georgakas, Dan and Charles Moskos. *New Directions in Greek-American Studies*. New York: Pella Publishing Company, Inc., 1991.

Gilchrist, Hugh. *Australians and Greeks Volume I: The Early Years, Volume II: The Middle Years, Volume III: The Later Years*. Rushcutters Bay, NSW Australia: Halstead Press, 1992, 1997, 2005.

Gvosdev, Matushka Ellen. *The Female Diaconate: An Historical Perspective*. Minneapolis: Light and Life Publishing Company, 1991.

Halo, Thea. *Not Even My Name*. New York: St. Martin's Press, Inc., 2000.

Handbook 2001 Greek Orthodox Archdiocese of Australia. Melbourne: Venus Press, 2000.

Hirschon, Renee. "Identity and the Greek State: Some Conceptual Issues and Paradoxes." In *The Greek Diaspora in the Twentieth Century,* edited by Richard Clogg.

Holy Transfiguration Monastery, trans. *Pentecostarion*. Brookline, Mass.: Holy Transfiguration Monastery, 1990.

Holst, Gail. *Road to Rembetika: Music from a Greek Sub-culture*. Athens: Anglo Hellenic Publishing, 1975.

Holst-Warhaft, Gail. *Theodorakis: Myth and Politics in Modern Greek Music*. Amsterdam: Adolf Hakkert, 1980.

Howard, Rachel. "Dancing at the End of History: The Greeks of the Ukraine." *Odyssey: The World of Greece,* November/December, 1998.

Ioannides, Christos P., ed. *Greeks in English-speaking Countries: Culture, Identity, Politics*. New Rochelle, New York/Athens: Aristides D. Caratzas, 1994.

Journal of the Hellenic Diaspora. New York: Pella Publishing Company, Inc.

Kangelaris, Demetri, and Nicholas Kasemeotes, *The Service of the Small Paraklesis to the Most Holy Theotokos*. Brookline, Mass.: Holy Cross Orthodox Press, 1984.

Karageorge, Penelope. *Red Lipstick and the Wine-dark Sea*. New York: Pella Publishing Company, Inc. 1997.

Karpozilos, Apostolos. "The Greeks in Russia." In *The Greek Diaspora in the Twentieth Century,* edited by Richard Clogg.

Kazan, Elia. *America, America*. New York: Stein and Day, 1962.

Kazantzakis, Nikos. *Report to Greco*. Translated by P. A. Bien. New York: Simon and Schuster, 1965. Reprint. New York: Bantam Books, 1966.

Kopan, Andrew. *Education and Greek Immigrants in Chicago, 1892-1973*. New York: Garland Publishing, 1990.

Kourvetaris, George A. *Studies on Greek Americans*. Boulder, Colo.: University of Colorado, 1997.

Kyriakopoulos, Victoria. "You'll Never Walk Alone." *Odyssey: The World of Greece,* January/February, 1999.

Lambrinidis, Stavros. "The Greeks in the World, the Hellenic Diaspora." *Thesis: A Journal of Foreign Policy,* vol. 1, issue 1 (Spring, 1997).

Maniatis, Gregory. "Hellenism: A Way Forward." *Odyssey: The World of Greece,* September/October, 1998.

Maragos, Nick and Connie Maragos, eds. *Sharing in Song: A Songbook for Greek Orthodox Gatherings*. Sherman Oaks, Calif.: The National Forum of Greek Orthodox Church Musicians, 1988.

Margaris, Theano Papazoglou. *The Chronicle of Halsted Street*. Athens: Fexis, 1962.

Maskaleris, Thanasis. "Hymn to Liberty" in *Hellenic Journal,* 11 March 1976.

Mastrantonis, George. "Holy Communion, The Bread of Life." St. Louis, Mo.: Ologos, n.d.

Matsakis, Aphrodite. *Growing up Greek in St. Louis.* Chicago: Arcadia Publishing, 2002.

Megas, George A. *Greek Calendar Customs.* Athens: Prime Minister's Office, Press and Information Department, 1958.

Members of the Faculty of Hellenic College/Holy Cross Greek Orthodox School of Theology, trans. *The Divine Liturgy of Saint John Chrysostom.* Brookline, Mass.: Holy Cross Orthodox Press, 1985.

Moskos, Charles C. *Greek Americans: Struggle and Success.* Englewood Cliffs, N.J.: Prentice-Hall, 1980. 2d ed. New Brunswick, N.J.: Transaction Publishers, 1989.

_____. "The Greeks in the United States." In *The Greek Diaspora in the Twentieth Century,* edited by Richard Clogg.

Mother Mary, trans. *The Parakletike (Octoechos).* Bossy-en-Othe, France: Orthodox Monastery of the Veil of Our Lady, nd.

Mother Mary and Kallistos Ware, trans. *The Festal Menaion.* London: Faber and Faber, 1969. Reprint. South Cannan, Pa.: St. Tikhon's Seminary Press, 1990.

_____, trans. *The Lenten Triodion.* London: Faber and Faber, 1978.

Odyssey: The World of Greece. Athens: Zephyr Publications.

Orthodox Christian Clergy Council of Metropolitan Washington, D.C. "The Synodikon Of Holy Orthodoxy." N.d.

Ouspensky, Leonid. *Theology of the Icon.* Translated by E. Meyendorff. Crestwood, N.Y.: St. Vladimir's Seminary Press, 1978.

Ouspensky, Leonid and Vladimir Lossky. *The Meaning of Icons.* Rev. ed. Crestwood, N.Y.: St. Vladimir's Seminary Press, 1982.

Papaioannou, George. *The Odyssey of Hellenism in America.* Thessaloniki, Greece: Patriarchal Institute for Patristic Studies, 1985.

_____. "Tell Me, Father." *Orthodox Observer.* 11 February 1987.

Papanikolas, Helen. *Emily-George.* Salt Lake City.: University of Utah Press, 1987.

_____. *Small Bird, Tell Me.* Athens, Ohio: Swallow Press/Ohio University Press, 1993.

_____. *The Time of the Little Black Bird.* Athens, Ohio: Swallow Press/ Ohio University Press, 1999.

Petrakis, Harry Mark. *A Dream of Kings.* New York: David McKay Company, 1966.

_____. *Pericles on 31st Street.* Chicago: Quadrangle Books, 1965.

_____. *Stelmark: A Family Recollection.* New York: David McKay Company, 1970.

Poulos, George. *Orthodox Saints: Spiritual Profiles for Modern Man.* 4 vols. Brookline, Mass.: Holy Cross Orthodox Press, 1976-1982.

_____. *Lives of the Saints and Major Feast Days.* 1981. Reprint. Brookline, Mass.: Department of Religious Education, Greek Orthodox Archdiocese of North and South America, 1989.

Runciman, Steven. *The Eastern Schism.* Oxford: Oxford University Press, 1955.

_____. *A History of the Crusades,* vol. 3. Reprint. London: Cambridge University Press, 1955.

St. Basil. "Exhortation to Youths as to How They Shall Best Profit by the Writings of Pagan Authors." In *Patrology* by Johannes Quasten. Vol. 3. 1960. Reprint. Westminster, Md.: The Newman Press, 1963.

Saloutos, Theodore. *The Greeks in the United States.* Cambridge: Harvard University Press, 1964.

_____. "Growing Up in the Greek Community of Milwaukee," *Historical Messenger of the Milwaukee County Historical Society* 29, no. 2. Summer 1973. In *The Greek Americans* by Alice Scourby. Boston: Twayne Publishers, 1984.

Samaras, Nicholas. *Hands of the Saddlemaker.* New Haven: Yale University Press, 1992.

Sawatsky, Walter. Review of *Proselytism and Orthodoxy in Russia: The New War for Souls.* John Witte, Jr., and Michael Bourdeaux, eds. *Christian Century,* 21-28 March 2001.

Schmemann, Alexander. *Great Lent.* Crestwood, N.Y.: St. Vladimir's Seminary Press, 1969.

Scourby, Alice. *The Greek Americans.* Boston: Twayne Publishers, 1984.

Thomopoulos, Elaine, ed. *Greek-American Pioneer Women of Illinois.* Chicago: Arcadia Publishing, 2000.

Topping, *Holy Mothers of Orthodoxy: Women and the Church.* Minneapolis: Light and Life Publishing Company, 1990.

_____. *Saints and Sisterhood: The Lives of Forty-eight Holy Women.* Minneapolis: Light and Life Publishing Company, 1990.

Tsemberis, Sam, Harry Psomiades, and Anna Karpathakis. *Greek American Families: Traditions and Transformations.* New York: Pella Publishing Company, Inc., 1999.

U.S. Bureau of the Census. *1990 Census of Population and Housing, Population Ancestry.* Summary Tape File 3A (CD-ROM).

_____. *1990 Detailed Ancestry Groups for States.* CP-S-1-2.

_____. *1990 Foreign-born Population in the United States*. CPH-L-98.

Vaporis, N[omikos] M[ichael], ed. *An Orthodox Prayer Book*. Brookline, Mass.: Holy Cross Orthodox Press, 1977.

_____, trans. *The Services for Holy Week and Easter*. Brookline, Mass.: Holy Cross Orthodox Press, 1993.

Vaporis, N. M., and Evie Zachariades-Holmberg, trans. *The Akathist Hymn and Small Compline*. Brookline, Mass.: Holy Cross Orthodox Press, 1992.

Vardoulakis, Mary. *Gold in the Streets*. New York: Dodd, Mead, 1945.

Vryonis, Jr., Speros. "The Relation of Hellenism and Orthodoxy in the Greek-American Communities." Unpublished manuscript, n.d.

Ware, Timothy. *The Orthodox Church*. 1963. New Edition. London: Penguin Books, 1997.

Ware, Kallistos [Timothy]. *The Orthodox Way*. Oxford: A. R. Mowbray and Company, 1979. Reprint. Crestwood, N.Y.: St. Vladimir's Seminary Press, 1986.

World Christian Encyclopedia, vol. 1. 2nd ed. Oxford: Oxford University Press, 2001.

World Council of Churches. "Report on the Consultation of Orthodox Women, 11-17 September 1976, Agapia, Roumania." Geneva, Switzerland: World Council of Churches, 1977.

_____. "The Place of Women in the Orthodox Church and the Question of the Ordination of Women, Rhodes, Greece," 30 October-7 November 1988. Istanbul: The Ecumenical Patriarchate, 1988.

_____. "Church and Culture: Second International Orthodox Women's Consultation," 16-24 January 1990, Orthodox Academy of Crete. Geneva, Switzerland: World Council of Churches.

Yearbook 2006. New York: Greek Orthodox Archdiocese of America, 2006.

Yiannias, John. "Orthodox Art and Architecture." In *A Companion to the Greek Orthodox Church,* edited by Fotios K. Litsas. New York: Department Communications, Greek Orthodox Archdiocese of North and South America, 1984.

For additional publications, see "Further Reading" in The Orthodox Church *by Timothy Ware, 1997, and the extensive catalogues of Holy Cross Bookstore (Brookline, Massachusetts), Light and Life Publishing Company (Minneapolis), and St. Vladimir's Seminary Press (Crestwood, New York).*

INDEX

NOTES